Palgrave Studies in the History of Social Movements

Series Editors
Stefan Berger
Institute for Social Movements
Ruhr University Bochum
Bochum, Germany

Holger Nehring
Contemporary European History
University of Stirling
Stirling, UK

Around the world, social movements have become legitimate, yet contested, actors in local, national and global politics and civil society, yet we still know relatively little about their longer histories and the trajectories of their development. This series seeks to promote innovative historical research on the history of social movements in the modern period since around 1750. We bring together conceptually-informed studies that analyse labour movements, new social movements and other forms of protest from early modernity to the present. We conceive of 'social movements' in the broadest possible sense, encompassing social formations that lie between formal organisations and mere protest events. We also offer a home for studies that systematically explore the political, social, economic and cultural conditions in which social movements can emerge. We are especially interested in transnational and global perspectives on the history of social movements, and in studies that engage critically and creatively with political, social and sociological theories in order to make historically grounded arguments about social movements. This new series seeks to offer innovative historical work on social movements, while also helping to historicise the concept of 'social movement'. It hopes to revitalise the conversation between historians and historical sociologists in analysing what Charles Tilly has called the 'dynamics of contention'.

More information about this series at
http://www.palgrave.com/gp/series/14580

Ettore Costa

The Labour Party, Denis Healey and the International Socialist Movement

Rebuilding the Socialist International during the Cold War, 1945–1951

Ettore Costa
Independent Scholar
Rome, Italy

Palgrave Studies in the History of Social Movements
ISBN 978-3-319-77346-9   ISBN 978-3-319-77347-6 (eBook)
https://doi.org/10.1007/978-3-319-77347-6

Library of Congress Control Number: 2018936357

© The Editor(s) (if applicable) and The Author(s) 2018
This work is subject to copyright. All rights are solely and exclusively licensed by the Publisher, whether the whole or part of the material is concerned, specifically the rights of translation, reprinting, reuse of illustrations, recitation, broadcasting, reproduction on microfilms or in any other physical way, and transmission or information storage and retrieval, electronic adaptation, computer software, or by similar or dissimilar methodology now known or hereafter developed.
The use of general descriptive names, registered names, trademarks, service marks, etc. in this publication does not imply, even in the absence of a specific statement, that such names are exempt from the relevant protective laws and regulations and therefore free for general use.
The publisher, the authors and the editors are safe to assume that the advice and information in this book are believed to be true and accurate at the date of publication. Neither the publisher nor the authors or the editors give a warranty, express or implied, with respect to the material contained herein or for any errors or omissions that may have been made. The publisher remains neutral with regard to jurisdictional claims in published maps and institutional affiliations.

Cover illustration: © Keystone / Stringer / Getty Images

Printed on acid-free paper

This Palgrave Macmillan imprint is published by the registered company Springer International Publishing AG part of Springer Nature.
The registered company address is: Gewerbestrasse 11, 6330 Cham, Switzerland

Series Editors' Preface

Around the world, social movements have become legitimate, yet contested, actors in local, national and global politics and civil society, yet we still know relatively little about their longer histories and the trajectories of their development. Our series reacts to what can be described as a recent boom in the history of social movements. We can observe a development from the crisis of labour history in the 1980s to the boom in research on social movements in the 2000s. The rise of historical interests in the development of civil society and the role of strong civil societies as well as non-governmental organisations in stabilising democratically constituted polities has strengthened the interest in social movements as a constituent element of civil societies.

In different parts of the world, social movements continue to have a strong influence on contemporary politics. In Latin America, trade unions, labour parties and various left-of-centre civil society organisations have succeeded in supporting left-of-centre governments. In Europe, peace movements, ecological movements and alliances intent on campaigning against poverty and racial discrimination and discrimination on the basis of gender and sexual orientation have been able to set important political agendas for decades. In other parts of the world, including Africa, India and South East Asia, social movements have played a significant role in various forms of community building and community politics. The contemporary political relevance of social movements has undoubtedly contributed to a growing historical interest in the topic.

Contemporary historians are not only beginning to historicise these relatively recent political developments; they are also trying to relate them to a longer history of social movements, including traditional labour organisations, such as working-class parties and trade unions. In the longue durée, we recognise that social movements are by no means a recent phenomenon and are not even an exclusively modern phenomenon, although we realise that the onset of modernity emanating from Europe and North America across the wider world from the eighteenth century onwards marks an important departure point for the development of civil societies and social movements.

In the nineteenth and twentieth centuries the dominance of national history over all other forms of history writing led to a thorough nationalisation of the historical sciences. Hence social movements have been examined traditionally within the framework of the nation state. Only during the last two decades have historians begun to question the validity of such methodological nationalism and to explore the development of social movements in comparative, connective and transnational perspective taking into account processes of transfer, reception and adaptation. Whilst our book series does not preclude work that is still being carried out within national frameworks (for, clearly, there is a place for such studies, given the historical importance of the nation state in history), it hopes to encourage comparative and transnational histories on social movements.

At the same time as historians have begun to research the history of those movements, a range of social theorists, from Jürgen Habermas to Pierre Bourdieu and from Slavoj Žižek to Alain Badiou as well as Ernesto Laclau and Chantal Mouffe to Miguel Abensour, to name but a few, have attempted to provide philosophical-cum-theoretical frameworks in which to place and contextualise the development of social movements. History has arguably been the most empirical of all the social and human sciences, but it will be necessary for historians to explore further to what extent these social theories can be helpful in guiding and framing the empirical work of the historian in making sense of the historical development of social movements. Hence the current series is also hoping to make a contribution to the ongoing dialogue between social theory and the history of social movements.

This series seeks to promote innovative historical research on the history of social movements in the modern period since around 1750. We bring together conceptually informed studies that analyse labour movements, new social movements and other forms of protest from early modernity to the present. With this series, we seek to revive, within the context of historiographical developments since the 1970s, a conversation between historians on the one hand and sociologists, anthropologists and political scientists on the other.

Unlike most of the concepts and theories developed by social scientists, we do not see social movements as directly linked, a priori, to processes of social and cultural change and therefore do not adhere to a view that distinguishes between old (labour) and new (middle-class) social movements. Instead, we want to establish the concept of 'social movement' as a heuristic device that allows historians of the nineteenth and twentieth centuries to investigate social and political protests in novel settings. Our aim is to historicise notions of social and political activism in order to highlight different notions of political and social protest on both the left and the right.

Hence, we conceive of 'social movements' in the broadest possible sense, encompassing social formations that lie between formal organisations and mere protest events. But we also include processes of social and cultural change more generally in our understanding of social movements: this goes back to nineteenth-century understandings of 'social movement' as processes of social and cultural change more generally. We also offer a home for studies that systematically explore the political, social, economic and cultural conditions in which social movements can emerge. We are especially interested in transnational and global perspectives on the history of social movements, and in studies that engage critically and creatively with political, social and sociological theories in order to make historically grounded arguments about social movements. In short, this series seeks to offer innovative historical work on social movements, while also helping to historicise the concept of 'social movement'. It also hopes to revitalise the conversation between historians and historical sociologists in analysing what Charles Tilly has called the 'dynamics of contention'.

Ettore Costa's *The Labour Party, Denis Healey and the International Socialist Movement* discusses the important period of the post-Second-World-War attempts to rebuild the Second International. The Labour Party, and in particular its international secretary, Denis Healey, were central to these attempts, but they operated within a network of international socialists, many of whom had sought refuge in London during the Second World War. As the old Labour and Socialist International slipped into crisis in the interwar years, it was the most unlikely contender for leadership inside international socialism, namely the British Labour Party, who rose to prominence. In 1908, many socialists did not want to admit the party to the International on account of its rejection of Marxism.

Labour travelled a long way from being an outsider in the International to becoming the key motor for renovation after 1945.

The Labour Party took the leadership in efforts to rebuild the International with the first post-war conference in Clacton in 1946 and remained in the driving seat of socialist internationalism up until the refoundational congress in Frankfurt am Main in 1951. Its version of democratic reformist socialism became the model on which the Socialist International was rebuilt. Especially after 1945 a major concern was how to deal with and strengthen independent social democratic parties behind the Iron Curtain who were threatened by subordination by Communist Parties in alliance with the Soviet Union whose army was occupying much of East Central and Eastern Europe. Ultimately the British Labour Party and the Socialist International had to realise that there was little that could be done to help their comrades behind the Iron Curtain. Even before the Prague coup of February 1948, it was clear to many socialists in the West that the uneasy cohabitation between socialists and communists in Eastern Europe could only last as long as the socialists did not oppose the communists. After Prague, the battle-lines were drawn and the nascent socialist international became more firmly anti-Communist.

Costa not only traces the international debates and discussions but also has a keen eye for how internationalism and internationalist networks were put to good effect in domestic political struggles inside socialist parties, especially with regard to the question over which direction the party should take after the war. Internationalist fraternalism also helped at times to pave the way for the generational handover to a new generation of socialist leaders in the diverse parties of Western Europe. The milieu of international post-war socialism is really brought to life in this volume. Costa is also particularly interested in tracing the many differences of opinion between the internationalists in the Labour Party and the post-war Labour government and analysing the tensions that resulted from those different attitudes to international socialism.

By distinguishing three groups of European socialists, namely planners, leftists and federalists, Costa highlights the internal divisions among the group of international socialists in the post-war period. He also emphasises that contention and factional strife were as important as agreement to produce the convergence that allowed the Socialist International to emerge in 1951.

Costa pays special attention to the British Labour Party's relationship with Italian socialism in the post-war years, when it was the main motor behind attempts to reconcile the Italian social democrats and the Italian socialists. However, this in turn produced major rifts within the Labour Party, where different factions were supporting the different wings in Italy. Furthermore, as Costa can show, existing stereotypes of Italians and Mediterranean culture in general prevented the Labour Party from fully understanding the situation within the socialist parties in Italy. This chapter is a timely reminder how lack of intercultural competence often marred internationalist socialism—in the past and, one may add, in the present.

Overall, Costa makes a very important contribution to explaining why socialist internationalism was rebuilt in the way it was after the end of the Second World War. He analyses the practice of socialist internationalism and hence writes a transnational history that is impressive in its geographical scope and in closely analysing the multiple networks of international socialists in the post-war period. This book adds substantially to a rich literature on socialist internationalism that is already in existence and on which Costa can build.

Bochum, Germany Stefan Berger
Stirling, UK Holger Nehring

ACKNOWLEDGEMENTS

I want to thank professor Vittorio Vidotto and professor Giovanni Sabbatucci for having supervised the early research from which this entire project started. The bulk of this research was carried out during my PhD, so I am thankful to professor Giorgio Caredda and professor Umberto Gentiloni Silveri for their scrupulous supervision. Special thanks go to professor Andrew Thorpe, of the University of Exeter, for having counselled and guided me during the period spent at his institution. I want to thank professor Stefan Berger for his assistance during the last stage of this research and for having guided me throughout the editorial process.

The University of Rome, La Sapienza deserves special thanks for granting me the privilege of spending years in intense and passionate research as a doctoral student and post-doc researcher and for having financed the intensive archival and bibliographical research around Europe. I want to thank the University of Exeter for hosting me as a Visiting Scholar during the writing of the doctoral dissertation. I am grateful for the period spent at the Institut für soziale Bewegungen of the Ruhr Universität Bochum, which allowed me to come into contact with a very stimulating intellectual environment.

The research has involved archives across Europe. I am grateful to the people at the Labour History Archive and Study Centre of the People's History Museum, especially Darren Treadwell. Documents from this archive are reproduced by kind permission of the Labour Party. I wish to thank the archivists of the National Archives, Kew and the International Institute of Social History, Amsterdam. Documents from the Archivio Centrale dello Stato are reproduced 'Su concessione del Ministero per i

Beni e le attività culturali' and documents from the Archivio Storico Diplomatico del Ministero degli Affari Esteri, Rome are reproduced 'Su concessione del Ministero degli Affari Esteri e della Coooperazione Internazionale'. I also wish to thank the archivists of the Fondazione Pietro Nenni, Rome and l'Office Universitaire de Recherche socialiste, Paris.

I am grateful to the Fondazione Spadolini Nuova Antologia for granting an award to my master dissertation and my doctoral dissertation and to the Fondazione La Sapienza for granting an award to my doctoral dissertation. The recognition of my work and their material support has encouraged me to go forward with my research

I want to thank my colleagues Matthew Broad, Cristian Cercel, Michele Di Donato, Margherita Martelli, Tommaso Milani, Phil Child, James Parker, Martina Piperno and Federico Carlo Simonelli. Their observations and criticism have been a continuous stimulus for my research.

Finally, I am most grateful to my parents, Alda and Enrico, for the material, moral and emotional support they have provided me throughout every stage of the research and, even before, for having been an example of passion and discipline in their field of research and a model for me in mine. I dedicate this book to them.

Contents

1 **Introduction**   1
   Bibliography   16

2 **From the Old International to the New Internationalism (1940–45)**   21
   1 Innovative Internationalism   21
   2 The Crisis of the Labour and Socialist International   23
   3 The Wartime Provisional Organisations   27
   4 Unity and Dissent   32
   5 The International Preparatory Committee   36
   Bibliography   46

3 **Parties and People, the Labour Party and the International Socialist Network**   49
   1 Labour Party's Centrality   49
   2 The Labour Model and Reformist Factions   56
   3 Labour Party and Labour Government, 'A Mere Tool of Imperialist Policy'?   59
   4 Discipline and Dissent in the Labour Party   65
   5 The International Network of Leaders and Secretaries   71
   Bibliography   91

4 The Labour Party and Eastern Europe, Social Democracy Behind the Iron Curtain 95
1. *The New Social Democrats from Eastern Europe* 95
2. *The Choice Between London and Lublin* 99
3. *National Character and Socialism* 103
4. *'The Disloyal MPs'* 108
5. *'A Mark of Special Favour to the Polish Socialist Party'* 111
6. *The Beginning of the Cold War* 117
Bibliography 133

5 The Institutional Development, from the International Socialist Conference to Comisco (1946–48) 137
1. *Formal and Informal Socialist Internationalism* 137
2. *'Co-operation, or at Least Mutual Tolerance'* 139
3. *John Price's Blueprints for the Socialist International* 145
4. *The Three Blocs of European Socialism: Planners, Leftists and Federalists* 148
5. *The Creation of New Institutions* 151
6. *Breach and Restructuring* 158
Bibliography 172

6 The Labour Party and Italy, Social Democracy Below the Olive Line 175
1. *The Mediterranean Character* 175
2. *Italian Social Democracy in the Era of Cohabitation* 179
3. *Italian Social Democracy in the Era of Anti-communism* 185
4. *The Debate Inside Comisco* 192
5. *The Results and Limits of Intervention* 195
6. *Tactical Stereotypes* 201
Bibliography 218

7 'The Little Foreign Office of Transport House', British Foreign Policy and Socialist Internationalism 221
1. *South Tyrol: A Case of Triangular Socialist Diplomacy* 221
2. *Admitting the Germans* 228
3. *The Emotional Greeks* 233
4. *The Comisco Mission to Greece* 238
Bibliography 261

8 The Rebirth of the Socialist International (1948–51) 265
1 *Comisco's Two Roads* 265
2 *The Martyrology of Eastern European Socialists* 272
3 *Ideology Designed by Committee* 275
4 *From Frankfurt to Bad Godesberg* 283
5 *The Frankfurt Congress and the New Foundation* 288
Bibliography 303

9 Conclusion 309
Bibliography 318

Index 321

Abbreviations

ACS	Archivio Centrale dello Stato, Rome
b.	box or *busta*
BIS	Bureau International Socialiste
BLP	British Labour Party
CGIL	Italian General Confederation of Labour
CGT	French General Confederation of Labour
Cominform	Communist Information Bureau
Comintern	Communist International
Comisco	Committee of the International Socialist Conference
ČSSD	Czechoslovak Social Democratic Party
DNA	Labour Party (Norway)
EAM	National Liberation Front (Greece)
f.	folder or *fascicolo*
IISH	International Institute of Social History, Amsterdam
ISK	*Internationaler Sozialisticher Kampfbund*
KKE	Greek Communist Party
LHASC	Labour History Archive and Study Centre, People's History Museum, Manchester
LP	Labour Party
LPACR	Labour Party Annual Conference Report
LSI	Labour and Socialist International
MAE	Ministero degli Affari Esteri, Roma
NEC	National Executive Committee, British Labour Party
n.d.	no date
OEEC	Organisation for European Economic Cooperation
OURS	L'Office Universitaire de Recherche Socialiste, Paris
PCI	Italian Communist Party

PPS	Polish Socialist Party
PPR	Polish Workers' Party, communist
PSB	Belgian Socialist Party
PSDI	Italian Democratic Socialist Party
PSI	Italian Socialist Party
PSIUP	Italian Socialist Party of Proletarian Unity
PSL	Polish Popular Party
PSLI	Italian Workers' Socialist Party
PSU	Unified Socialist Party, Italy
PvdA	Labour Party (the Netherlands)
SAP	Swedish Social Democratic Labour Party
SED	Socialist Unity Party of the Soviet Occupation Zone, later German Democratic Republic.
SFIO	French Socialist Party
s.f.	sottofascicolo
SI	Socialist International
SILO	Socialist Information and Liaison Office
SK-ELD	Greek Socialist Party
SPD	German Social Democratic Party
SPÖ	Austrian Socialist Party
SUCEE	Socialist Union of Central-Eastern Europe
SVG	Socialist Vanguard Group
TGWU	Transport and General Workers' Union
TNA	The National Archive (Kew)
TUC	Trades Union Congress
UCL	University College London
USI	Union of Italian Socialists
WFTU	World Federation of Trade Unions
WRN	Freedom, Equality, Independence, the Polish Socialist Resistance Organisation

CHAPTER 1

Introduction

Socialist internationalism must surely be a true faith if it has survived so long despite the faults of its practitioners. Among the infamous failures are its impotence in preventing the First World War, the paralysing divisions thwarting any action against Fascism, the prioritising of national interests over international concerns—leading Ignazio Silone and André Philip to argue that no nationalisation has been so successful as the 'nationalisation of socialism'.[1] When talking about the Socialist International, communists, disappointed internationalist socialists and social democrats seeking nationalist respectability insisted on the chasm between internationalist aspirations and national reality. Henri De Man complained about this 'overblown fiction',[2] while Turati melancholically concluded that what was left of the International was the song of that name.[3] As is often the case, political historians borrowed the concepts and framework of contemporary politicians as heuristic tools, as it is evident in the older histories of the Socialist International by Braunthal—first secretary of the Socialist International.[4] Sassoon argued that the Socialist International 'did little else besides formulate compromise resolutions which never had the slightest importance'.[5] However, Furet claims, historical players have a false consciousness of their role, and thus historians must be critical of their self-representation.[6] New knowledge of the Socialist International does not simply require more data from archives and publications, but a theoretically rich framework to analyse this data, pose new questions and test new hypotheses.

This is what Guillaume Devin did in the most important history of the Socialist International, describing how the institution actually worked and how the 'weak links' of the organisation influenced the national parties.[7] Talbot C. Imlay also concentrates on internationalism as practice that influenced national policies.[8] In their approach to studying internationalism, the question was not 'why did internationalism fail?' but rather 'why did it exist?', as its advantages are not self-evident. This book adopts a similar approach to explain the actual functioning of socialist internationalism, why it survived so long, which benefits and dangers it bore and how it influenced the life of the national parties. It describes how the British Labour Party assumed the leadership of the European socialist movement and rebuilt the Socialist International from scratch, from the first post-war conference in Clacton in 1946 to its formal rebirth in 1951 in the Frankfurt Congress. It investigates how an era of radical transformation for Europe and the world shaped the form the social democratic parties assumed for decades.

This new approach is made possible by wider developments in historiography, which have made new conceptual tools available and rendered new questions relevant. The growth of global and transnational history challenged the nation state as the exclusive framework; it underscored international connections and non-state actors.[9] Especially significant was the contribution of Wolfram Kaiser, Brigitte Leucht and Michael Gehler. Correcting Milward's idea of European integration as the product of bargaining between national governments, they highlighted the role of 'governance', defined as a non-hierarchical and decentralised form of decision making, and coordination by state and non-state actors alike.[10] European governance took place at a local, regional, national and transnational level, as formal and informal networks of politicians, experts and interest groups competed to advance their goals and interests.[11] Transnational political networks play a prominent role; according to Kaiser's definition, they link political actors across national borders and coordinate their activities. The integration of national actors into transnational networks influenced their national policies, not by imposing binding decisions, but by communicating interests and concerns, exchanging information, socialising the elites and testing out proposals.

While Kaiser extensively studied the Christian democratic network, others applied the transnational network approach to international socialist cooperation. In addition to the already-mentioned Imlay, Oliver Rathkolb analysed the Brandt–Kreisky–Palme network,[12] Matthew Broad and Kristian Steinnes the role of the socialist transnational network in the Labour Party's attitude towards the European Free Trade Association (EFTA) and the European Economic Community (EEC),[13] Michael Gehler the role of the socialist network in the Austrian entry to the European Union (EU),[14] Peter Van Kemseke the role of the Socialist International for development policies in the 1950s,[15] Michele Di Donato the relations between the Italian Communist Party and the European Social Democrats,[16] Christian Salm the role of the transnational socialist network in defining the European Community's policy to southern enlargement and its development policies.[17] There are other studies on the bilateral or multilateral relations between socialists, for example, Misgeld's extensive research on the international activities of the Swedish Social Democratic Labour Party (SAP),[18] Insall's book on relations between the British Labour Party[19] and the Norwegian Labour Party (DNA),[20] Drögemöller's book on relations between German Social Democracy (SPD) and the Dutch Labour Party (PvdA),[21] and the troubled relationship between the British Labour Party and Italian socialism, studied at different times by Sebastiani, Varsori, Favretto and Nuti.[22]

This book owes a debt to previous studies for their conceptual innovation and extensive empirical research. However, some of these instances of research come with the warning that they are special cases, made possible by extraordinary circumstances. This reflects history's preference for empirical research of individual cases, but if one takes all these studies and treats each warning seriously, one finds multiple examples of the same phenomenon each claiming to be unique. Imlay correctly states that 'international socialist cooperation resembled a fever more than a forward march', varying in intensity,[23] but for him the high noon of international socialist cooperation was from 1945 to 1960, for Steinnes it was from 1958 to 1973, for Salm it covered the entire 1970s. Before defining special cases, we have to define normality. There is another problem as well. While certain factors made international socialist cooperation more likely for some parties and in certain periods, it is not enough to discover the initial conditions to describe how the phenomenon evolved. Once begun, international contacts followed their own internal logic. The aim of this book is to describe the logic of 'normal' international interactions between socialists. Therefore, it concentrates on the rebirth of the Socialist International—the focus of most international socialist cooperation—from the death of the old International to the formal rebirth of the new. It was an age of experimentation, as socialists discarded old conventions and experimented new forms of international cooperation, establishing the formal and informal rules of socialist internationalism. Throughout this period, the leadership belonged to the British Labour Party: most often it took the initiative to experiment with new ways and always resisted the initiative of others to return to the old ways. The history of socialist internationalism in this period in many ways runs through the Labour Party. As the main agent of the events described, it needs to be the main subject of the book.

What follows are a number of concepts and hypotheses to gain a better understanding of socialist internationalism in practice. These are going to be tested in the empirical research.

While Kaiser's model is useful, we should question whether international socialist interaction should be treated as a transnational network like others or whether it had greater ideological weight. Rhodes and Marsh distinguish between an issue network—which is a loose and temporary alliance of actors striving for a limited goal—and a policy community—whose members share values and views.[24] While the Socialist International was closer to a policy community, it would be better said that its members had an ideological commitment to finding ideological unity, even when their views differed. The cohesion of the community was provided by a sense of brotherhood, meaning that each party recognised the other as an equal member of the same family or a branch of the same church. Rather than 'international contacts', we should speak of 'international fraternal relations'.

Another issue is how to define the borders between the national and international spheres of socialism. Contemporaries and historians called the Cold War era a period of 'nationalisation of socialism', with socialists concerned only about national elections and domestic policies. However, this same period corresponded to the convergence of socialist parties in Western Europe to one model: reformist socialism committed to democracy and anti-communism that would achieve its goals mainly through the power of the nation state. Popular fronts, counter-society organisations and direct action were no longer viable options. The traditional way to narrate this phenomenon, the parallel histories of the national parties reacting in similar ways to similar opportunities and limitations, is inadequate.

We should assume mutual influence or 'connectedness', meaning that the actions of power-holders in one region of the network affected the population in another region.[25] The transfer of influences between the national and international spheres is never one-way or static but rather takes the form of a circular motion: the national sphere influences and transforms the international sphere, which in turn can transform the national. It is potentially a momentum building up a spiral, although it can easily be interrupted. What follows is a list of hypothetical ways in which international fraternal relations influenced the development of the national parties and their convergence.

First, by joining the Socialist International, socialist parties expressed their affiliation to the international movement. Agreement could often be found only through studied ambiguity and lack of commitment, but Devin argues that affiliation was an important feature of the public identity of the socialist parties.[26] The Labour and Socialist International (LSI)—the International in the inter-war period—sought to coordinate the policies of the largest number of socialists, so it did not define its principles.[27] At its birth, the Socialist International adopted a charter of principles, 'Aims and Tasks of Democratic Socialism', also known as the Frankfurt Declaration, which defined socialism as the fulfilment of democracy in every field. Exclusivity was the main innovation of the Socialist International, as Sassoon recognises: 'as is the case in many clubs, its only purpose was to provide its members with the respectability it denied others. Those parties of the Left too close to the communist position, such as the Italian socialists, were excluded until they repented.'[28] This research will show how gatekeeping influenced the national parties.

This form of coercion could be important, but, according to Imlay and Dietrich Orlow, voluntary coordination was more important; it took place through regular exchanges of opinion. Socialist politicians were forced to consider the concerns and interests of their foreign counterparts, presenting their policies in an acceptable way.[29] The Socialist International was not the centre of global revolution, but a permanent negotiating table—which suited its reformist members. Devin argues that these 'weak ties' were more effective in changing national policies. However, it is not enough to assess the existence of a transnational network; it is necessary to find cases where national policies actually changed through cooperation. Indeed, the existence of the network is not enough to deduce the existence of trust and familiarity among its members, as friction and mistrust were also possible.

The British Labour Party might also have played a major part in this convergence. After the First World War, radical socialists who rejected the reformist leadership, compromised with the war, found inspiration in the Soviet Union.[30] Social democrats refusing the Russian way had problems finding another example of actually existing socialism. After Labour's landslide victory in 1945, the Labour leadership presented Labour Britain as 'a living proof that Democratic Socialism is both morally right and practically efficient'.[31] Did the European social democrats accept this model? What features did it come to represent? What role did it play in factional struggles? Did it also have negative connotations?

A key hypothesis for this book is that conflict was as important as cooperation for the convergence. Factional struggle was an accelerant factor for transnational exchanges. Following Panebianco's model, we treat political parties not as cohesive entities, but networks of individuals and factions vying for power. Power inside the organisation derives from the ability to distribute assets (*atouts* or 'trump cards') of a symbolic or material nature.[32] According to this hypothesis, international fraternal relations are considered a source of assets, such as exemplary policies, symbols, publicity, respectability, information and expertise.[33] A faction wanting to define its identity could seek association with a faction or party pursuing a similar strategy. For example, until 1948 the British Labour Party backed socialists resisting communist absorption in the Eastern European socialist parties, while the Eastern European socialists backed and were backed by the left-wing factions in Western Europe.[34]

This phenomenon is here defined 'internationalisation of domestic quarrels',[35] a term coined by William Gillies. This means that a dispute over strategy between two factions from the same national party could become an international issue, as socialists from other nations would take sides. Weak divided parties were prone to invite the intervention of stronger parties or the Socialist International. The original division could create a similar division in another party, as the factions of the second party squabbled over which faction of the first party to support. In this case, the 'internationalisation of domestic quarrels' produced a 'nationalisation of international quarrels'. For example, when in 1957 the Labour Party was trying to reconcile Italian socialists and social democrats, Gaitskell and the Bevanite group had a quarrel over which group to support. Richard Crossman noted 'it would be very funny if we managed to split the Labour Party on the issue of how to unify the Italian!'[36]

The problem of the internationalisation of domestic quarrels, already clear at the time of the First International,[37] became evident in the Second International, under the leadership of the SPD. From 1897 to 1903, the clash between the revisionism of Bernstein and the orthodox Marxism of Kautsky dominated its ideological debate. The issue was, apparently, settled by a condemnation of opportunism by the 1903 SPD congress. Having repudiated revisionism at national level, the SPD's leadership enshrined this condemnation at international level: in 1904 Bebel had the Amsterdam Congress of the Second International condemn bourgeois reforms and revisionism. The international resolution influenced French socialism, helping the Marxist Guesde prevail over Jaurès. The German national quarrel became an international and then a French quarrel. 'The SPD's support therefore acts as an authoritative argument. Given its prestige, real or supposed, to make reference to German Social Democracy and to benefit from its support makes it possible to prevail over competitors'.[38] In the late 1920s, the left-wing of the Labour Party and the SPD cooperated to fight their respective party leaderships, which in turn supported each other.[39] When the Belgian government took a neutral line in the Spanish Civil War, Vandervelde encouraged the LSI to take sides, leading Spaak and De Man to protest.[40] In 1939 the secretary of the LSI, the left-wing socialist Adler, published in the newsletter of the LSI a statement by Stafford Cripps about his expulsion from the Labour Party. This episode provoked Gillies to invent the phrase mentioned earlier.

International fraternal relations were an elitist field of party activities. Party activists and electors could express their interest in some issues, but they were not involved in regular meetings.[41] International contacts involved a 'tight network of international secretaries and secretaries-general',[42] in addition to experts and party leaders. Not only was the group small, but it was consistent: for years, sometimes decades, the same people held international responsibilities. It was a group of old acquaintances and new people who became acquainted with its customs and habits. Taking inspiration from the 'high politics' school, we can draw a 'collective biography' of the group involved in international fraternal relations.[43] This approach has the advantage of highlighting how decisions concerning international fraternal relations fell to a small group of leaders and bureaucrats. The question is whether this transnational network of leaders and secretaries developed a common attitude towards the important issues and what role familiarity or mistrust played.

Another way to approach this group of people is through the generational lens. Kramer has already used this approach to study socialists as a transnational group.[44] According to Mannheim's definition, a generation is a set of people who, due to their shared location in time, come to have the same experience.[45] The impression left by first experiences in youth coalesce into a natural view, through which future experiences are interpreted. A generational unit is a subset of people whose response to the experiences of their generation is similar. Just after the war, international secretaries and young leaders were people born just before or during the First World War and experienced the Depression, war and reconstruction. How did their early experiences and the experience of increased transnational cooperation in wartime and post-war Europe shape the attitude of this group? More importantly, how did this generation of socialist militants influence post-war European social democracy?

A hypothesis worth testing is whether international fraternal relations helped the generational turnover in the socialist parties. Veteran socialists thought so: at the Zurich Conference (June 1947) Louis de Brouckère handed over the baton to the new leader of the Belgian Socialist Party (PSB), Max Buset, saying that as the practice of internationalism had nurtured the old generation of socialists, it would do the same for the new.[46] If the people involved in the international socialist network acquired assets within the party, they could use it to obtain even better positions. The book will identify the people responsible for international fraternal relations, assess their position in the party and illustrate how it helped their careers.

A methodological note is necessary. This book is a piece of research of political history, which holds that the traditional subject of party politics is still relevant, but it also requires a new methodology. The 'high politics' approach studies politics as a competitive system with its own rules, where individuals and groups select policies and rhetoric to conquer power.[47] While this approach is usually criticised for not considering ideas or politics from below, it can yield results even in the era of mass political parties.[48] 'New political history' integrates a 'high politics' analysis with a greater interest for ideas and rhetoric, thanks to the concern on how culture and language shape world-views stimulated by the 'linguistic turn'. Competition is central, but it takes place in a context of ideas and perceptions that defines the terms of what it is possible to say and think.[49]

It is not enough to describe the culture of politicians; culture must be used to explain political choices. According to Formisano, 'The logic of political culture is always comparative',[50] it must be used to explain why a group of people behaved differently from others. However, there is the risk of essentialism, explaining away different choices by appealing to different cultures. The question of whether the agency of the individual can overcome the constraint of culture is largely theoretical, but it can be solved in individual instances.

Following Gareth Stedman Jones, 'New political history' asserts the centrality of language in politics. Politicians employ a language their followers identify with and they adapt the old language to new ends.[51] Political mobilisation is successful when the followers adopt the political language as their code for interpreting their grievances and aspirations in the real world. Following the 'linguistic turn', language is treated as self-referential and independent from social facts.[52] Linguistic analysis is the tool to analyse the culture of political actors: 'the ideology of Chartism cannot be constructed in abstraction from its linguistic form'.[53] Political entrepreneurs offer a political community that people wish they were a part of. Socialists found unity in a common discourse expressing their shared values, but they also had different, opposing discourses reflecting their divergences.

The struggle over meaning was a struggle over strategy: the different parties competed to acquire the centre of the Socialist International and impose their language, whether Marxist, gradualist or religious. This can be understood thanks to the 'performative turn', inspired by the anthropologist C. Geertz and the linguist J.L. Austin.[54] Rituals, performances and speech acts did not just express meanings, they created social realities. The International Socialist Conference, later the Socialist International, was a creative force: it did not describe democratic socialism, it created the common definition of democratic socialism. The goal is to reconstruct the relationship between the shift in languages of the socialists and their strategic choices, whether language reflected a shift in strategy or created it. A further question is the 'felicity' of speech acts, whether they were accepted or rejected. Communists did not accept the claim of the Socialist International to speak for socialism, but neither did many socialists or workers.

The challenge to methodological nationalism opened up the way for transnational analysis and a new kind of comparative history. Labour history traditionally explained developments from an internalist perspective and used comparison to reinforce the exceptionalism of the national labour movements.[55] However, the role of comparison is to test models and causal explanations, challenging the idea of uniqueness. For example, the socialists often contrasted the success of social democracy in Northern Europe with Continental Europe,[56] invoking different factors, especially national character. Comparison should reveal how national outcomes were not preordained, but the result of contingency.[57] This book concentrates on one aspect of party organisation: the management of fraternal international relations. This limited comparison allows a comprehensive analysis of multiple parties, and the drawing-up of a typology. While the scope is limited, it should allow a better understanding of other features of party organisation and culture.

Others challenging methodological nationalism contest comparison for reinforcing the idea of homogeneity and separation of national cultures. The supporters of cultural transfers (Michel Espagne), entangled history and *histoire croisée* (Michael Werner and Bénédicte Zimmermann) argue that the border between national units was porous, not rigid. Encounters and migration resulted in practices, goods and ideas passing from one culture to another through local adaptation.[58] The transnational approach is particularly appropriate to analyse international relations between socialist parties, as it reveals complexity, interdependence and hybridity. An internalist history of the national parties is insufficient without considering how transnational exchanges influenced their development.

Binary opposition is wrong, as comparison can be integrated with the study of transnational transfers. In their interactions, the socialist parties exposed similarities and differences, which are often not immediately evident. Similarities and convergences could be the result of transfer and successful adaptation, but equally important was rejection.

Having introduced some methodological questions in Chap. 1, Chap. 2 covers the 'prehistory' of the Socialist International: how the old Labour and Socialist International went into a crisis and how the British Labour Party came into dominance; how socialists in war-time London preserved a socialist community and experimented new rules and practices, which set precedents for the Socialist International after the war. Chapter 3 describes the institutions and people involved in inter-party relations and the central role of the Labour Party in the international socialist movement. It describes the people who carried out the international contacts of the Labour Party and their strategies, how the Labour Party was the model for the other socialist parties and similarities and divergences with those parties. Also, it deals with the ambiguity and tension between the Labour Party and the Labour Government, how this interacted with British foreign policy and how it influenced discipline and dissent. Chapter 4 shows how the Labour Party and other Western parties dealt with the socialist parties from Eastern Europe, which involved issues of foreign policy, culture and internal discipline. Co-habitation with pro-communist socialists went on until the Prague Coup of February 1948 made it impossible. Chapter 5 discusses how the Labour Party led the institutional development of the International Socialist Conference, the provisional Socialist International, at first a weak and informal organisation. The developing Cold War and anti-communism promoted greater institutional development of the International Socialist Conference, which, however, never overcame its organisational limitations. Chapter 6 deals with the intervention of the provisional Socialist International in the Italian socialist movement, which stood as the mirror opposite of the Labour Party. Divisions called for external intervention, but in turn it generated dissent over strategy and resistance of the locals. The issue of how British culture represented Mediterranean peoples and how those people reacted was a stumbling block for the Labour Party. Chapter 7 discusses the involvement of the Labour Party in British foreign policy. The Labour Party served both as an instrument of informal intervention and a channel for the locals to speak their concerns to the British government. Cooperation of party and government towards a common goal was possible, but disagreement was just as likely. The cases of Austrian, German and Greek socialism are discussed as exemplary. Chapter 8 describes the rebirth of the Socialist International. Despite disagreement over the task of Socialist International, whether to develop techniques for national planning or to promote European unity, European socialists successfully defined their common identity based on democracy and anti-communism. They emphasised the martyrdom of the Eastern European socialists and defined the principles of democratic socialism in the Frankfurt Declaration. In turn, the Frankfurt Declaration encouraged the ideological renovation of socialism in the 1950s, particularly the Bad Godesberg programme of the SPD.

Notes

1. I. Silone (2002) 'Missione europea del Socialismo', in N. Novelli (ed.), *Per Ignazio Silone* (Firenze: Polistampa), 91–92 (originally published in 1947). A. Philip (1950) *Le socialisme et l'unité européenne: réponse a l'exécutif de Labour Party* (Paris: Mouvement socialiste pour les états-unis d'Europe), 15. In every chapter, translations from a non-English document or publication are by the author of the book and responsibility thereof.

2. J. Polasky (1995) *The Democratic Socialism of Emile Vandervelde: Between Reform and Revolution* (Oxford: Berg), 235.
3. Quoted in S. Fedele (2001) 'Il laburismo nell'emigrazione antifascista', A. Landuyt and G.B. Furiozzi (eds), *Il modello laburista nell'Italia del Novecento* (Milano: Franco Angeli), 105.
4. R. Steininger (1979) *Deutschland und die Sozialistische Internationale nach dem Zweiten Weltkrieg, Darstellung und Dokumentation* (Bonn: Neue Gesellschaft). J. Braunthal (1980) *History of the International*, Vol. 3, *World Socialism 1943–1968* (London: Gollancz). E.H. Carr (1982) *The Twilight of Comintern, 1930–1935* (London: Macmillan), 94f; 424–427.
5. D. Sassoon (2010) *One Hundred Years of Socialism: The West European Left in the Twentieth Century* (London: Tauris), 210.
6. F. Furet (1981) *Interpreting the French Revolution* (Cambridge: Cambridge University Press), 190–193.
7. G. Devin (1993) *L'Internationale Socialiste: histoire et sociologie du socialisme internationale: 1945–1990* (Paris: Presses de la Fondation national des sciences politiques), 202. G. Devin (1996) 'L'internationalisme des socialistes', in M. Lazar (ed.) *La gauche en Europe depuis 1945: invariants et mutations du socialisme européen* (Paris: Presses de la Fondation national des sciences politiques), 413–414.
8. T.C. Imlay (2014) '"The Policy of Social Democracy is Self-Consciously Internationalist": The German Social Democratic Party's Internationalism after 1945', *The Journal of Modern History*, 86, 1, 81–86. T.C. Imlay (2016). 'The Practice of Socialist Internationalism during the Twentieth Century'. *Moving the Social*, 55, 17–18.
9. A. Iriye (2013) *Global and Transnational History: The Past, Present, and Future* (Basingstoke: Palgrave Macmillan), 10–17.
10. W. Kaiser, B. Leucht, M. Gehler (2010) 'Transnational Networks in Regional Integration: Historical Perspectives on an Elusive Phenomenon', in W. Kaiser, B. Leucht, M. Gehler (eds), *Transnational Networks in Regional Integration: Governing Europe 1945–83* (London: Palgrave Macmillan), 1–2; 10–11.
11. W. Kaiser (2009) 'Transnational Networks in European Governance. The Informal Politics of Integration', in W. Kaiser, B. Leucht, M. Rasmussen (eds), *The History of the European Union: Origins of a Trans- and Supranational Polity 1950–72* (New York: Routledge), 14–15.
12. O. Rathkolb (2010) 'Brandt, Kreisky and Palme as Policy Entrepreneurs: Social Democratic Networks in Europe's Policy Towards the Middle East', in Kaiser, Leucht, Gehler, *Transnational Networks in Regional Integration*, 152–175.
13. K. Steinnes (2014) *The British Labour Party, Transnational Influences and European Community Membership, 1960–1973* (Stuttgart: Franz Steiner).

INTRODUCTION   13

M. Broad (2017) *Harold Wilson, Denmark and the Making of Labour European Policy* (Liverpool: Liverpool University Press).
14. M. Gehler (2010) 'Geschichte vergleichender Parteien–Außenpolitik und Mitgliedschaft in der Europäischen Union: SPÖ und ÖVP in internationalen Organisationen und transnationalen Netzwerken 1945-2005,' *Moving the Social*, 43, 7–46.
15. P. Van Kemseke (2006) *Towards an Era of Development, The Globalization of Socialism and Christian Democracy: 1945-1965* (Leuven: Leuven University Press).
16. M. Di Donato (2015) *I comunisti italiani e la sinistra europea: il PCI e i rapporti con le socialdemocrazie (1964-1984)* (Roma: Carocci). M. Di Donato (2015). 'The Cold War and Socialist Identity: The Socialist International and the Italian "Communist Question" in the 1970s', *Contemporary European History*, 24, 2, 193–211.
17. C. Salm (2016) *Transnational Socialist Networks in the 1970s: European Community Development Aid and Southern Enlargement* (London: Palgrave Macmillan).
18. K. Misgeld (1984) *Sozialdemokratie und Aussenpolitik in Schweden: Sozialistische Internationale, Europapolitik und die Deutschlandfrage 1945–1955* (Frankfurt: Campus Verlag).
19. Throughout the book, 'Labour Party' without any other adjective refers to the British Labour Party; the Dutch Labour Party and the Norwegian Labour Party are referred as PvdA and DNA.
20. T. Insall (2010) *Haakon Lie, Denis Healey and the Making of an Anglo-Norwegian Special Relationship 1945-1951* (Oslo: Oslo Academic Press).
21. M. Drögemöller (2008) *Zwei Schwestern in Europa. Deutsche und niederländische Sozialdemokratie 1945-1990* (Berlin: Vorwärts Buch).
22. P. Sebastiani (1983) *Laburisti inglesi e socialisti italiani: dalla ricostituzione del Psi(up) alla scissione di Palazzo Barberini* (Roma: Elengraf). A. Varsori (1988) 'Il Labour Party e la crisi del socialismo italiano (1947–1948)', *Socialismo Storia. Annali della Fondazione Giacomo Brodolini e della Fondazione di Studi Storici Filippo Turati*, 2, 159–211. I. Favretto (1996) 'La nascita del centrosinistra e la Gran Bretagna, Partito socialista, laburisti, Foreign Office', *Italia Contemporanea*, 2, 5–44. I. Favretto (2006) 'The Wilson Government and the Italian Centre-Left Coalition: Between "Socialist Diplomacy" and Realpolitik, 1964–1970', *European History Quaterly*, 36, 3, 421–444. L. Nuti (1999) *Gli Stati Uniti e l'apertura a sinistra, Importanza e limiti della presenza americana in Italia* (Roma-Bari: Laterza).
23. Imlay, 'The Practice of Socialist Internationalism during the Twentieth Century', 20.
24. Kaiser, 'Transnational Networks in European Governance', 15.

25. C. Tilly (1984) *Big Structures, Large Processes, Huge Comparisons* (New York: Russell Sage Foundation), 62.
26. Devin, 'L'internationalisme des socialistes', 430.
27. L. Rapone (1999) *La socialdemocrazia europea tra le due guerre: dall'organizzazione della pace alla Resistenza al fascismo, 1923–1936* (Roma: Carocci), 22.
28. Sassoon, *One Hundred Years of Socialism*, 210. Also, L. Hamon (1983) 'L'Internationale Socialiste depuis 1945 et la tradition des internationales ouvrières', in H. Portelli (ed.), *L'Internationale socialiste* (Paris: Les Éditions Ouvrières), 19.
29. Imlay, '"The Policy of Social Democracy is Self-Consciously Internationalist"', 120. D. Orlow (2000) *Common Destiny: A Comparative History of the Dutch, French, and German Social Democratic Parties, 1945–1969* (New York: Berghahn Books), 145.
30. S. Pons (2014) *The Global Revolution: A History of International Communism, 1917–1991* (Oxford: Oxford University Press), 29–30.
31. 'Mr Denis Healey's speech at the Italian Unification Congress,' The National Archives, Kew, FO 371/79301-Z8223.
32. A. Panebianco (1988) *Political Parties: Organization and Power* (Cambridge: Cambridge University Press), 33–46.
33. Devin, *L'Internationale socialiste*, 347–348
34. P. Heumos (2004) 'Einleitung', in P. Heumos (ed.), *Europäischer Sozialismus im Kalten Krieg: Briefe und Berichte 1944–1948* (Frankfurt: Campus), 37.
35. C. Collette (1998) *The International Faith: Labour's Attitude to European Socialism, 1918–39* (Aldershot: Ashgate), 89.
36. Entry, 23 May 1957, R. Crossman (1981) *The Backbench Diaries of Richard Crossman* (London: Cape), 597.
37. G. Stedman Jones (2016) *Karl Marx: Greatness and Illusion* (London: Allen Lane), 475.
38. E. Jousse (2007) *Réviser le marxisme? d'Edouard Bernstein à Albert Thomas: 1896–1914* (Paris: L'Harmattan),119; also 164–167.
39. S. Berger (1994) *The British Labour Party and the German Social Democrats, 1900–1931* (Oxford: Clarendon), 245.
40. Polasky, *The Democratic Socialism of Emile Vandervelde*, 243.
41. However, the opinion of electors and rank and file was always the first concern of socialist leaders, as their power in the party and in national politics depended on them.
42. Salm, *Transnational Socialist Networks in the 1970s*, 16.
43. J. Lawrence (2003) 'Political history' in S. Berger, H. Feldner, K. Passmore (eds), *Writing History: Theory and Practice* (London: Hodder Arnold), 184.

44. S.P. Kramer (1984) *Socialism in Western Europe: The Experience of a Generation* (Boulder-London: Westview Press).
45. K. Mannheim (1970) 'The Problem of Generations', *Psychoanalytic Review*, 57,3, 378–400.
46. Stenogramme, 8 June 1947, International Institute of Social History, Amsterdam, Socialist International, 235.
47. Lawrence, 'Political history', 185–187; 192–195. D. Craig (2010) '"High Politics" and the "New Political History"', *Historical Journal*, 53, 2, 453–475.
48. R. Crowcroft (2008) 'The "High Politics" of Labour Party Factionalism, 1950-5', *Historical Research*, 81, 214, 679–709.
49. S. Pedersen (2002) 'What is Political History now?', in D. Cannadine (ed.) *What is History Now?* (Basingstoke: Palgrave), 45.
50. R.P. Formisano (2001) 'The Concept of Political Culture' *Journal of Interdisciplinary History*, 31, 3, 424.
51. G. Stedman Jones (1983) *Languages of Class: Studies in English Working-Class History 1832-1982* (Cambridge: Cambridge University Press), 19–24. L. Black (2001) 'Popular Politics in Modern British History', *Journal of British Studies*, 40, 3, 431–445.
52. L. Black (2003) '"What Kind of People are you?" Labour, the People and the "New Political History"', in J. Callaghan, S. Fielding, S. Ludlam (eds) *Interpreting the Labour Party: Approaches to Labour politics and History* (Manchester University Press), 23–26.
53. Stedman Jones, *Languages of Class*, 94.
54. D. Bachmann-Medick (2016) *Cultural Turns: New Orientations in the Study of Culture* (Berlin: De Gruyter), 86. J.C. Alexander and J.L. Mast (2006) 'Introduction: Symbolic Action in Theory and Practice: The Cultural Pragmatics of Symbolic Action', in J.C. Alexander and J.L. Mast (eds) *Social Performance: Symbolic Action, Cultural Pragmatics, and Ritual* (Cambridge: Cambridge University press), 3.
55. S. Berger (1995) 'European Labour Movements and the European Working Class in Comparative Perspective', in S. Berger, D. Broughton (eds), *The Force of Labour: The Western European Labour Movement and the Working Class in the Twentieth Century* (Oxford: Berg), 245–248. S. Berger, H. Nehring (2017), 'Series Editors' Preface', in Salm, *Transnational socialist networks in the 1970s*, xii.
56. In British culture, 'Continent' and 'Continental' usually refer to Western Europe excluding Britain and Scandinavia. Though vague, the term is used throughout the book with this meaning.
57. S. Berger (2003) 'Comparative History', in Berger, Feldner, Passmore, *Writing History*, 161–165. H.-G. Haupt, J. Kock (2009) 'Comparison and Beyond: Traditions, Scope, and Perspectives of Comparative History', in

H.-G. Haupt, J. Kock (eds), *Comparative and Transnational history: Central European Approaches and New Perspectives* (New York: Berghahn Books), 1–5.
58. H. Kaelble (2009) 'Between Comparison and Transfers – and What Now? A French-German Debate', in Haupt, Kock, *Comparative and transnational history*, 33–38. Berger, 'Comparative History', 169–171. M. Juneja, M. Pernau (2009) 'Lost in Translation? Transcending Boundaries in Comparative History', Haupt, Kock, *Comparative and transnational history*, 109.

Bibliography

Alexander, J.C. & Mast, J.L. (2006). Introduction: symbolic action in theory and practice: the cultural pragmatics of symbolic action. In J.C. Alexander & J.L. Mast (Eds.). *Social performance: symbolic action, cultural pragmatics, and ritual* (pp. 1–28). Cambridge: Cambridge University press.

Bachmann-Medick, D. (2016). *Cultural turns: new orientations in the study of culture*. Berlin: De Gruyter.

Berger, S. (1994). *The British Labour Party and the German Social Democrats, 1900–1931*. Oxford: Clarendon.

Berger, S. (1995). European Labour Movements and the European Working Class in Comparative Perspective. In S. Berger & D. Broughton (Eds.). *The Force of Labour: The Western European Labour Movement and the working class in the Twentieth Century* (pp. 245–261). Oxford: Berg.

Berger, S. (2003). Comparative history. In S. Berger, H. Feldner & K. Passmore (Eds.). *Writing History: Theory and practice* (pp. 161–179). London: Hodder Arnold.

Black, L. (2001). Popular Politics in Modern British History. *Journal of British Studies*, 40 (3) 431–445.

Black, L. (2003). "What kind of people are you?" Labour, the people and the "new political history". In J. Callaghan, S. Fielding & S. Ludlam (Eds.). *Interpreting the Labour Party: Approaches to Labour politics and History* (pp. 23–38). Manchester University Press.

Braunthal, J. (1980). *History of the International*, Vol. 3, *World socialism 1943–1968*. London: Gollancz.

Broad, M. (2017). *Harold Wilson, Denmark and the making of Labour European policy*. Liverpool: Liverpool University Press.

Carr, E.H. (1982). *The twilight of Comintern, 1930–1935*. London: Macmillan.

Collette, C. (1998). *The international faith: Labour's attitude to European socialism, 1918–39*. Aldershot: Ashgate.

Craig, D. (2010). High politics and the "new political history". *Historical Journal*, 53 (2), 453–475.

Crossman, R. (1981). *The backbench diaries of Richard Crossman*. London: Cape.
Crowcroft, R. (2008). The "high politics" of Labour party factionalism, 1950–5. *Historical Research*, 81 (214), 679–709.
Devin, G. (1993). *L'Internationale socialiste: histoire et sociologie du socialisme internationale: 1945–1990*. Paris: Presses de la Fondation national des sciences politiques.
Devin, G. (1996). L'internationalisme des socialistes. In M. Lazar (Ed.). *La gauche en Europe depuis 1945: invariants et mutations du socialisme européen* (pp. 413–431). Paris: Presses de la Fondation national des sciences politiques.
Di Donato, M. (2015a). *I comunisti italiani e la sinistra europea: il PCI e i rapporti con le socialdemocrazie (1964–1984)*. Roma: Carocci.
Di Donato, M. (2015b). The Cold War and Socialist Identity: The Socialist International and the Italian "Communist Question"' in the 1970s. *Contemporary European History*, 24 (2), 193–211.
Drögemöller, M. (2008). *Zwei Schwestern in Europa. Deutsche und niederländische Sozialdemokratie 1945–1990*. Berlin: Vorwärts Buch.
Favretto, I. (1996). La nascita del centrosinistra e la Gran Bretagna, Partito socialista, laburisti, Foreign Office. *Italia Contemporanea*, 2, 5–44.
Favretto, I. (2006). The Wilson government and the Italian centre-left coalition: Between "Socialist diplomacy" and Realpolitik, 1964–1970. *European History Quaterly*, 36 (3), 421–444.
Fedele, S. (2001). Il laburismo nell'emigrazione antifascista. In A. Landuyt & G.B. Furiozzi (Eds.). *Il modello laburista nell'Italia del Novecento*. Milano: Franco Angeli.
Formisano, R.P. (2001). The concept of political culture. *The Journal of Interdisciplinary History*, 31 (3), 393–426.
Furet, F. (1981). *Interpreting the French Revolution*. Cambridge: Cambridge University Press.
Gehler, M. (2010). Geschichte vergleichender Parteien–Außenpolitik und Mitgliedschaft in der Europäischen Union: SPÖ und ÖVP in internationalen Organisationen und transnationalen Netzwerken 1945–2005. *Moving the Social*, 43, 7–46.
Hamon, L. (1983). L'International Socialiste depuis 1945 et la tradition des internationales ouvrières. In H. Portelli (Ed.). *L'Internationale socialiste* (pp. 9–22). Paris: Les Éditions Ouvrières.
Haupt, H.-G. & Kock, J. (2009). Comparison and beyond: traditions, scope, and perspectives of comparative history. In H.-G. Haupt& J. Kock (Eds.). *Comparative and transnational history: central European approaches and new perspectivesI* (pp. 1–30). New York: Berghahn Books.
Heumos, P. (Ed.). (2004). *Europäischer Sozialismus im Kalten Krieg: Briefe und Berichte 1944–1948*. Frankfurt: Campus.

Imlay, T.C. (2014). "The policy of social democracy is self-consciously internationalist": The German Social Democratic Party's Internationalism after 1945. *The Journal of Modern History*, 86 (1), 81–123.
Imlay, T.C. (2016). 'The Practice of Socialist Internationalism during the Twentieth Century'. *Moving the Social*, 55, 17–38.
Insall, T. (2010). *Haakon Lie, Denis Healey and the making of an Anglo-Norwegian special relationship 1945–1951*. Oslo: Oslo Academic Press.
Iriye, A. (2013). *Global and transnational history: the past, present, and future*. Basingstoke: Palgrave Macmillan.
Jousse, E. (2007). *Réviser le marxisme? d'Edouard Bernstein à Albert Thomas: 1896–1914*. Paris: L'Harmattan.
Juneja, M. & Pernau, M. (2009). Lost in Translation? Transcending Boundaries in Comparative History. In H.-G. Haupt & J. Kock (Eds.). *Comparative and transnational history: central European approaches and new perspectives* (pp. 105–129). New York: Berghahn Books.
Kaelble, H. (2009). Between Comparison and Transfers—and What Now? A French-German Debate. In H.-G. Haupt & J. Kock (Eds.). *Comparative and transnational history: central European approaches and new perspectives* (pp. 33–38). New York: Berghahn Books.
Kaiser, W. (2009). Transnational networks in European governance. The informal politics of integration. In W. Kaiser, B. Leucht & M. Rasmussen (Eds.). *The history of the European Union: origins of a trans- and supranational polity 1950–72* (pp. 12–33). New York: Routledge.
Kaiser, W., Leucht, B. & Gehler, M. (2010). Transnational Networks in Regional Integration: Historical Perspectives on an Elusive Phenomenon. In W. Kaiser, B. Leucht & M. Gehler (Eds.). *Transnational Networks in Regional Integration: governing Europe 1945–83* (pp. 1–17). London: Palgrave Macmillan.
Kramer, S.P. (1984). *Socialism in Western Europe: the experience of a generation*. Boulder and London: Westview Press.
Lawrence, J. (2003). Political history. In S. Berger, H. Feldner & K. Passmore (Eds.). *Writing History: Theory and practice* (pp. 183–202). London: Hodder Arnold.
Mannheim, K. (1970). The Problem of Generations. *Psychoanalytic Review*, 57 (3), 378–400.
Misgeld, K. (1984). *Sozialdemokratie und Aussenpolitik in Schweden: Sozialistische Internationale, Europapolitik und die Deutschlandfrage 1945–1955*. Frankfurt: Campus Verlag.
Nuti, L. (1999). *Gli Stati Uniti e l'apertura a sinistra, Importanza e limiti della presenza americana in Italia*. Roma-Bari: Laterza.
Orlow, D. (2000). *Common destiny: a comparative history of the Dutch, French, and German Social Democratic parties, 1945–1969*. New York: Berghahn Books.

Panebianco, A. (1988). *Political parties: organization and power*. Cambridge: Cambridge University Press.
Pedersen, S. (2002). What is Political History now?. In D. Cannadine (Ed.). *What is history now?* (pp. 36–56). Basingstoke: Palgrave.
Philip, A. (1950). *Le socialisme et l'unité européenne: réponse a l'exécutif de Labour Party*. Paris: Mouvement socialiste pour les états-unis d'Europe.
Polasky, J. (1995). *The democratic socialism of Emile Vandervelde: between reform and revolution*. Oxford: Berg.
Pons, S. (2014). *The global revolution: a history of international communism, 1917–1991*. Oxford: Oxford University Press.
Rapone, L. (1999). *La socialdemocrazia europea tra le due guerre: dall'organizzazione della pace alla Resistenza al fascismo, 1923–1936*. Roma: Carocci.
Rathkolb, O. (2010). Brandt, Kreisky and Palme as Policy Entrepreneurs: social democratic networks in Europe's policy towards the Middle East. In W. Kaiser, B. Leucht & M. Gehler (Eds.). *Transnational Networks in Regional Integration: governing Europe 1945–83* (pp. 152–175). London: Palgrave Macmillan.
Salm, C. (2016). *Transnational socialist networks in the 1970s: European Community development aid and southern enlargement*. London: Palgrave Macmillan.
Sassoon, D. (2010). *One hundred years of socialism: the West European Left in the twentieth century*. London: Tauris.
Sebastiani, P. (1983). *Laburisti inglesi e socialisti italiani : dalla ricostituzione del Psi(up) alla scissione di Palazzo Barberini*. Roma: Elengraf.
Silone, I. (2002). Missione europea del Socialismo. In N. Novelli (Ed.). *Per Ignazio Silone* (pp. 87–95). Firenze: Polistampa.
Stedman Jones, G. (1983). *Languages of Class: Studies in English Working-Class History 1832–1982*. Cambridge: Cambridge University Press.
Stedman Jones, G. (2016). *Karl Marx: greatness and illusion*. London: Allen Lane.
Steininger, R. (1979). *Deutschland und die Sozialistische Internationale nach dem Zweiten Weltkrieg, Darstellung und Dokumentation*. Bonn: Neue Gesellschaft.
Steinnes, K. (2014). *The British Labour Party, transnational influences and European Community membership, 1960–1973*. Stuttgart: Franz Steiner.
Tilly, C. (1984). *Big structures, large processes, huge comparisons*. New York: Russell Sage Foundation.
Van Kemseke, P. (2006). *Towards an Era of Development, The Globalization of Socialism and Christian Democracy: 1945–1965*. Leuven: Leuven University Press.
Varsori, A. (1988). Il Labour Party e la crisi del socialismo italiano (1947–1948). *Socialismo Storia. Annali della Fondazione Giacomo Brodolini e della Fondazione di Studi Storici Filippo Turati*, 2, 159–211.

CHAPTER 2

From the Old International to the New Internationalism (1940–45)

1 Innovative Internationalism

As Marx said, all great world-historic facts appear twice. The breakup of the Second International in the First World War was a tragedy, a trauma that reshaped the worldview of socialists. Conversely, the demise of the Labour and Socialist International (LSI) was a farce. The organisation, long paralysed by dissent, could not even take a stand against Hitler, due to divisions between appeasers, neutralists and supporters of confrontation—themselves divided over possible cooperation with the communists.

Rapone argues that it was a symptom of the death of internationalism of socialists and communists.[1] However, equally remarkable is how the internationalist spirit survived the dissolution of the internationalist organisation. Even without formal rules and institutions, international socialism survived as a network of contacts, a set of practices, an identity of views and values. In this era of transition, the absence of bureaucratic rules allowed the dropping of old practices that had failed to solve old problems and to experiment with innovative practices to deal with both old and new problems. Between 1940 and 1951, the genetic model of the new Socialist International was established: as these new practices set a pattern, they became precedents and were finally codified in the constitution of 1951.[2]

Some defining features of international socialism appeared or became prominent in this period.

The ascendancy of the British Labour Party was the most prominent feature of the war and post-war period. Its centrality in the international socialist movement lasted for two decades. As a secretary of the Socialist International Janitscheck said: 'The Socialist International is like a bird, with a right wing and a left wing; but the British were always the head and body'.[3] Their failure to fight Nazism discredited French and German socialists—who had been the dominant parties in the past—while Labour's opposition to appeasement and its contribution to the war gave it great prestige. In addition, its organisation was not destroyed by military occupation, but it grew and it was overhauled. It could also employ the services of a powerful state machinery with international influence.

The second feature, the most relevant in the long term, was the adoption of restrictive criteria for the admission in the Socialist International. The LSI was intended to be an instrument of cooperation for all socialists outside the Comintern, while the British and their allies wanted stringent conditions and a stricter definition of socialism. As Camille Huysmans told the Labour Conference:

> But the attribute 'Socialist' is not enough. We accepted this as being sufficient at one time, but we have now learned our lesson. There must be Socialism, Democracy, Security, Freedom, and Peace in the heart, and not only upon the lips.[4]

In wartime a socialist party could recognise as 'brother' only another party with an uncompromising militancy against the enemy. The 'enemy' assumed a central role in defining the identity of social democracy, even when the 'enemy' passed from Nazism to communism. By 1951 the international organisation had a charter of values and a constitution that served to make it explicit that only one form of socialism would be allowed. A clear distinction was set between the parties inside and the parties outside, turning the Socialist International into what Sassoon called the 'club'.

The third feature was the integration of the Socialist International within the state. Already begun during the first total war, the integration of the socialists in the bourgeois state provoked little resistance or backpedalling this time, thanks to anti-fascism. The Labour Party was fully committed to the British war effort and socialists from occupied nations identified with their governments in exile and the underground state, even in cases like Poland, where they had been harassed and marginalised before. After the war socialism became identified with the state that had managed to defeat Fascism and to plan the economy, in war and peace. In turn, the state recognised the potential of socialist parties and trade unions, especially against communism, and encouraged their development.

The fourth feature, also a result of wartime militancy, was the priority given to avoiding embarrassments in international fraternal relations. The more a party was powerful, the more international interaction was a source of risk. The Labour Party and other social democratic parties that backed the Allied governments fighting Nazism could not afford to be suspected of connivance with and leniency towards Germany because of their association with German socialists, whose commitment to fight was suspicious and who rejected the collective guilt of the German people.

Finally, the fifth feature was the development of a new elite inside the Socialist International and the national parties. The rise of fascism and the destruction of almost all the socialist parties completed the delegitimisation of the social democratic leadership and opened the doors to a new generation of leaders, whose formative experience was the war. In this environment, the career of prominent socialist leaders, such as Denis Healey, began.

2 The Crisis of the Labour and Socialist International

In the 1930s the unity of the European socialist movement floundered as it failed to reach a joint position on communism, fascism and rearmament. Two blocs emerged, equally committed to peace but with a different interpretation.[5] The right-wing bloc (*Rechtssozialismus*)—influenced by liberal internationalism—argued that the cause of war was the system of international anarchy, to which the solution was the implementation of a system of laws guaranteed by the League of Nations. This was in line with the attitude of reformism and Hilferding's theories: the workers should not have smashed the organisations of the capitalist system but placed them under democratic control. They had to rely on institutions and technocrats to defend their interests. The left-wing bloc (*Linkssozialismus*) identified capitalism as the only cause of war and the transition to socialism as the only solution, therefore the socialist movement had to rely on direct action (strikes, boycotts, insurrection) to prevent war.

Immediately after the First World War, there were two socialist Internationals, roughly corresponding to the two blocs: the Second International, reborn in Berne in 1919,[6] and the Vienna Union.[7] While the Labour Party had a major role in rebuilding the Berne International, the Austrian socialists led the Vienna Union, which included the socialist parties openly rejecting social patriotism and striving for a unitary International of socialists and communists. Once the attempt to mediate between the Second and Third International—hence the name Two and Half International—failed, left-wing socialists accepted a compromise with right-wing socialists, worked out by the secretary of the Vienna Union, Friedrich Adler, and Ramsay MacDonald, the leader of the Labour Party. The LSI was born in 1923, with Adler secretary. He represented the commitment to peace, internationalism and separation from bourgeois politics of left-wing socialism. The LSI was empowered to produce binding resolutions in case of war, which was the desire of left-wing socialists.[8]

After 1925 and even more after 1933, the issue of fascism came to the forefront, but instead of becoming the focus for common action, the diagnosis revealed underlying disagreement over the nature of capitalism and democracy.[9] The reformist wing, including British Labour, believed in the natural development of socialism from the progressive elements of the capitalist economy and bourgeois state, through a process of reform and democratisation. Fascism was a backward element going against the current of progressive development; rather than a general problem, it was limited to underdeveloped nations. For left-wing socialists, fascism was the general trend of capitalism, as the bourgeoisie abandoned democracy and resorted to violence to resist the working-class. Gradual evolution would not suffice for the transition to socialism, there would be a revolutionary rupture with emergency legislation to educate the masses and destroy the economic power of capital.[10]

In the 1920s, with economic growth and relative stability, the first, optimistic explanation was more common. The British delegation at the LSI Congress of 1928 argued that communism and fascism were internal problems of Russia and Italy,[11] while Vandervelde, the veteran Belgian leader, lent his authority to a 'geographical' interpretation of Fascism:

> A great captain of industry [. . .] recently said to us: 'If without taking into account political frontiers you trace an imaginary line from Kovno to Bilbao, passing through Cracow and Florence, you will find before you two

Europes—the one in which horse-power dominates, the other where it is the living horse, the one where there are parliaments, the other where there are dictators.' It is in reality exclusively in the latter economically and politically backward Europe that dictatorships more or less brutal, more or less hypocritical, abound, whether veiled or no by a sham national representation.[12]

Nenni, the leader of Italian socialism, resented the division of Europe and the argument that 'Fascism is the regime typical of the countries that are poor, illiterate, devoid of hygiene and comfort':

> Expedient theories that allowed a rosy forecast. But then came the day when Hitler sent 107 deputies to the Reichstag, the day Fascism settled in the Ministry of Interior in Austria, the day Finland felt under fascist domination.
> Farewell Cambo's statistics and—Vandervelde dearest—farewell to your geography. Every easy explanation collapses and one explanation—tragic but true—stands: *Fascism is the modern form of the struggle of the bourgeoisie against socialism and the proletariat.*[13]

In a 1934 conference, the two opposite strategies became evident: Austrians and Italians wanted an active LSI and global negotiation with the Comintern, since they wanted an alliance with the communists but feared their disruptive tactics. Hugh Dalton—a Labour leader who considered the conference 'rather a sad and ineffectual affair'[14]—said that Fascism did not threaten democracy, but it only affected countries without true democracy. The national parties needed the autonomy to decide their own strategy; indeed, it was necessary to limit the role of the parties in exile. At the time the Labour leadership was resisting pressure from left-wingers asking for a Popular Front in Great Britain, so they did not want to give them external legitimisation. British, Scandinavian and Dutch parties refused global negotiation, while French, Spanish and Italians agreed to popular fronts, outside the framework of the LSI.[15]

Even as a forum for exchanging views and information, the International did not work, compounding incomprehension. While the British, Scandinavian and Dutch parties did not understand the other parties and were often naïve about Fascism, Adler and the left-wing parties considered them the rump of defeated and deluded reformism. Instead, the 1930s were a period of intense transformation for the British Labour Party and the Dutch Social Democratic Party, not to mention the government experience of the SAP. The new critique of capitalism—owing more to

Keynes than to Marx—recognised the faults of free-market and classical liberalism. New thinkers (Sturmthal, De Man, Dalton, Myrdal) prescribed a new mixed economy with planning, demand management at the national level and the extension of social welfare.[16] The goal was controlling and correcting capitalism, not substituting it. Thus, they built the foundation for post-war social democracy.

With the Spanish Civil War, right-wing socialists finally recognised the danger of fascism, but they identified the problem with aggressive nations instead of capitalism and the fascist movement. The Labour Party leadership moved towards rearmament, irritating both left-wing pacifists and the parties from the small nations, which embraced neutrality to escape the German threat.[17] The French Socialist Party (SFIO) effectively split between appeasers and anti-appeasers over the Munich agreement.

As international tension grew and the LSI became more divided, the Swedish and Danish parties asked in 1938 for a reform, arguing that the great nations were ready to abandon the small ones, as the French had done with Czechoslovakia—the Czechoslovak Social Democratic Party left the LSI in protest against Munich. The resignation of Louis de Brouckère and Adler as chairman and secretary of the LSI in May 1939 ratified its unsolvable crisis.[18] Despite differences on foreign policy, the International Secretary of the Labour Party, William Gillies, came to an agreement with the Scandinavian, Dutch and Belgian parties to approve far-reaching reforms that would reconstruct the International 'in accordance with the realities of the political situation in the different countries' and ensure the control of the 'living and active Parties'.[19]

According to new president Albarda, the reformed LSI would not give orders to or embarrass the national parties, which were in a better position to evaluate the situation, but it would become a forum to exchange opinions and technical information.[20] The plan of Gillies and De Man would reduce the expensive bureaucracy—especially the Austrian staff—exclude some exile parties entirely (Mensheviks and Italians) and reduce the role of the others. Important decisions would be taken in a restricted bureau where the most important parties had permanent representation.

In a memorandum, Adler focused his attacks on the Labour Party, accusing it of chauvinism and returning to the nationalism of 1914. Gillies informed Adler that the Labour Party did not consider the constitution of LSI binding any longer—'the International could only be consultative, not authoritative'[21]—and he asked for his resignation on this occasion. Camille Huysmans, who was secretary of the Second International during the First World War, was elected chairman in place of Albarda, who had become a minister. Unsurmountable dissent made it impossible to elect a new secretary or even produce a Mayday Manifesto mentioning Hitler or Stalin. When Germany invaded Belgium and took over the Brussels headquarters, the LSI was already completely impotent.

3 THE WARTIME PROVISIONAL ORGANISATIONS

After the Second World War, most proposals for reforming the LSI were implemented. However, the new constitution also adopted the new practices that emerged during the war and Cold War, despite these practices often defeating the initial intentions of the parties involved, especially the British Labour Party. Immediately before the war, the Labour leadership had approved a retrenchment from the LSI and embarrassing entanglements with unreliable foreigners. With the war, the Labour Party became the most prestigious socialist party and the leadership enjoyed the advantages for party cohesion and diplomacy. Above all, the leadership and the rank and file had a vague but undeniable commitment to internationalism. The expansion of the bureaucratic machinery dealing with international fraternal relations followed two imperatives: carrying out more activities and containing the risks that came with these activities.

In the reform of the LSI, Gillies had tried to limit the role of the socialist parties in exile, but by July 1940 the British Labour Party was the only extant socialist party committed to fight Hitler, the other parties being in exile, underground or in an ambiguous position, like the Swedish, Swiss and Finnish parties. The leaders in exile testified to the refusal to yield and the support of the whole socialist movement to Britain, but they were still a source of trouble to be managed in order to extract the maximum advantage. Gillies organised informal and confidential meetings at the St. Ermin's Hotel, inviting only socialist representatives from the allied countries[22]—provoking the protests of the excluded nationalities. The International Department made it clear that it considered the LSI dead— Adler, in exile in New York, would soon confirm this interpretation—and that it was just a meeting of independent parties with a view to forming a consultative committee to advise the Labour Party and co-ordinate activities against Fascism.

Camille Huysmans professed his willingness to keep the International alive, at least in his person, as during the First World War—'Believe me, it must not be said later that we quietly strangled the Second International'.[23]

The LSI would have had greater authority for propaganda on the Continent and in the USA. Gillies argued that Huysmans did not have any authority and the other parties were ready to devolve all responsibility to the International Department of the Labour Party. As on many other occasions thereafter, the Belgians were the only ones supporting a greater internationalist commitment, met with reluctance by the British.[24]

In November 1940, Gillies informed the socialists in exile of the creation of the International Consultative Committee (meeting every month), commonly known as the Dallas Committee from the name of its chairman, George Dallas, also chairman of the International Sub-Committee. Dallas, using the typical language of a Labour Party leader, informed the participants that this committee was of little importance and to keep expectations low:

> These meeting are certainly not conferences, important or unimportant. Nor are they meetings of a Committee. There is no agenda, no minutes are taken or circulated. There is no voting, and no publicity. The meetings are described in the invitations as being those of the group of International friends who meet at St. Ermins. They are neither more nor less than informal and friendly meetings of British comrades with well-known Socialists from the conquered territories who, for the most part, do not even claim to attend by virtue of mandates from their Parties which as a matter of fact, no longer exist or have only a fragmentary existence in a state of illegality.
>
> It is clear to us that the presence or absence of any particular person at such meetings does not raise questions of a constitutional character, and certainly does not constitute a precedent for the Credentials Committee of the Labour and Socialist International, when it may be re-constituted after the war by Labour and Socialist parties on the Continent of Europe who have renewed their political activity on their native soil in the fullness of freedom and publicity.
>
> In the meantime the representatives of the British Labour Party are at liberty to confer with any Socialists whom they wish to consult.
>
> I trust therefore that you and your Committee will not read into this invitation a significance which it does not possess.[25]

A second committee, the Huysmans Committee, was created in November 1941.[26] It included socialists from enemy and neutral nations as well, but it was still secret, without agenda or minutes, although Gillies conceded that 'this Committee should be regarded as a Preparatory Committee for the reconstruction of the International'.[27]

The two committees corresponded to different phases of the war. Despite its anti-communism, the Labour Party included many who considered the Soviet Union necessary to make collective security and deterrence credible. The Molotov-Ribbentrop Pact led to some soul-searching: some envisaged a socialist federal union that could take the place of the Soviet Union,[28] others like Bevin were already imagining a greater role for the United States or the Western Union he proposed after the war.[29] The Dallas Committee was created when Churchill and Dalton believed they could 'set Europe ablaze', with resistance and revolutionary upheavals defeating Nazi Europe.[30]

In 1941, it became clear that the Soviet Union would provide the manpower to defeat the Wehrmacht, so the revolution of the German people—of which there were no signs anyway—was no longer necessary. Indeed, leniency went against the commitment to 'unconditional surrender'. In 1940, the Labour Party still made a distinction between the German Government and the German people,[31] but in 1943 the Annual Conference officially accepted the thesis that military expansion was intrinsic to the German people, presenting complete disarmament and prolonged military occupation as the only solution.[32] This stance was in line with the mainstream theory of a naturally aggressive Germany developed by diplomat Robert Vansittart.[33]

While the Dallas Committee was born to carry out propaganda and encourage resistance, the Huysmans committee served to represent the entire socialist movements and allow negotiations with the Soviet Union, which was the plan of Harold Laski. Laski—together with Cole and Tawney, one of the 'Red professors'—was the spokesperson of the Labour left during the war. After Germany invaded the Soviet Union, Laski sponsored the cause of a general agreement between Soviets and socialists to fight fascism.[34] He believed in cooperation with the communists, but local agreements would leave the social democrats vulnerable to communist infiltration. The International—or the Labour Party in its stead—had the responsibility to negotiate with the Soviet Union a general, global agreement to allow cohabitation.[35]

Laski's proposed negotiations with the Comintern and his support for the nationalities excluded from the Dallas Committee put pressure on the National Executive Committee of the Labour Party (NEC), which wanted to preserve party unity. Gillies repeated that the LSI could not meet officially, but Huysmans's precedent during the First World War allowed the joint action of the President of the LSI and the Labour Party to establish a consultative committee, which became the Huysmans Committee. However, the Dallas Committee was not disbanded.[36]

The 'two-chamber system' provoked protests from the Austrians and Spanish, who felt demoted to 'second-class Socialists' or 'Socialists of lesser breed'[37] by their exclusion from the Dallas Committee. This was particularly humiliating for the Austrian Socialists—in Britain represented by Oscar and Marianne Pollak, Karl Czernetz, Julius Braunthal—who had dominated the LSI under Adler. Gillies and Huysmans, who shared a strong hatred of the Germans, put them in their place, repeating that the British Labour Party, as the only extant party, was alone responsible for international socialism. The Austrians were generals without troops, worse their troops were now in the Wehrmacht.[38]

The German social democrats suffered the most. Gillies helped them come to Britain and mediated the union of mainstream SPD with the dissenter groups—*Sozialistische Arbeiterpartei Deutschlands, Neue Beginnen, Internationaler Sozialisticher Kampfbund* (ISK)—in the 'Union of German Socialist Organisations in Great Britain',[39] with Hans Vogel as chairman. Once hopes of a revolution in Germany disappeared, the German social democrats were marginalised, which Gillies justified by presenting the history of the SPD as characterised by nationalism and accommodation with Nazism.[40]

The hierarchy was clearly defined: the Labour Party on top, with the power to impose conditions; then the socialists from Allied countries, who could offer their symbolic contribution to the war; socialists from the enemy countries at the bottom, entirely dependent on others.

Once again, the social democratic community divided into two factions. The majority bloc, which included Gillies and all the parties backing him, wanted to keep contacts informal, accept the collective guilt of the German people and concentrate on winning the war. The minority included left-wing Labourites (Laski, Philip Noel-Baker) and the German-speaking socialists. They condemned the collective guilt of the German people as a betrayal of internationalism, they proposed to rebuild the International rapidly in order to negotiate with the communists and they wanted to agitate for a socialist plan for reconstruction.

In addition to the Dallas and Huysmans committees, there were marginal groups organising Labour leftists and Continental internationalist socialists rejecting the collective guilt of the Germans.[41] Personal connections, which would influence the socialist parties and the Socialist International after the war, were developed.

The Socialist Clarity Group, close to the dissident German social democratic group *Neue Beginnen*, included people who became deeply involved in international contacts in the post-war era: Austen Albu, Patrick Gordon Walker and William Warbey.[42] The Socialist Vanguard Group (SVG) was organised by Mary Saran in 1934 as the British section of the ISK, the political group-cum-socialist community founded by the philosopher Leonard Nelson on strong ethical principles—Kantian ethics, vegetarianism, teetotalism and communal living. The SVG included German and British members and had close contacts with all the socialist parties. The SVG would later become the Socialist Union, which published the journal *Socialist Commentary* and influenced British revisionism in the 1950s. Mary Saran would continue to keep contacts with socialists all around Europe, playing a minor role in the rebuilding of the International.[43] Willi Eichler, Nelson's secretary, would influence the SPD after the Second World War, especially the Bad Godesberg programme.

Another important venue for building connections was the International Bureau organised by the Fabian Society in May 1941, with Philip Noel-Baker as chairman and the participation of important Labour personalities, like John Hynd, Rita Hinden, Laski, Leonard Woolf, Zilliacus, Ernest Davies and Evan Durbin.[44] Margaret Cole concedes its limited importance, beyond keeping contacts with the exiles.[45] Their task to present the conflict as a war of ideologies not nations and to prepare the active role of German socialists and trade unionists in the democratisation of Germany was hindered by the refusal of Transport House—the headquarters of the Labour Party—to circulate their material among militants and speakers.[46]

The most significant experience for the future of the Socialist International was the *International Socialist Forum*, organised by the Austrian socialist Julius Braunthal with the backing of the publisher Victor Gollancz—champion of many left-wing causes in the 1930s and an opponent of Vansittart during the war.

Braunthal was born in Austria in 1891 in a Jewish family. A worker from young age, he received his education in the party school, with the encouragement of Otto Bauer.[47] He worked for Austrian socialist newspapers and journals until the coup in 1934 forced him into exile. He lived for two years as a guest in the home of Hugh Gaitskell,[48] future leader of the Labour Party, working for the *Tribune* and as deputy secretary of the LSI. However, in exile Braunthal became the 'problem child'[49] of the Austrian group, because of his unrealistic political plans and his close relationship with Friedrich Adler, who had become completely alienated from the Austrian socialists. After the war, Braunthal did not return to Austria and separated from the Austrian movement.[50] Braunthal kept close links with the circles of the Labour left, the *Tribune*, Laski and Gollancz. This would help him become the secretary of Comisco in 1949.

The *International Socialist Forum* was an appendix to *Left News*, the monthly journal of the Left Book Club. The group around the publication included the main internationalist figures in London: Laski, De Brouckère, Louis Levy (French Socialist Party–SFIO), Vogel, Oscar Pollak, Paolo Treves (Italian socialist) and Richard Löwenthal (*Neue Beginnen*). Braunthal set ambitious goals for the *International Socialist Forum*, which he called 'the first Tribune of International Socialism': defining the 'peace aims of International Socialism' and studying the Socialist International.

> [How] the International Socialist movement may be revived, and on what conditions it may become 'a living reality'. This will itself involve an analysis of why the Socialist International has not, during recent years, been a living reality, and why it has been paralysed in the decisive hours of history.[51]

International Socialist Forum was the most important publication in which the German socialists could publish their contribution, as the Labour Party gave space in its publications only to socialists from the Allied countries.

4 UNITY AND DISSENT

What it meant for the Socialist International to be a 'living reality' was hard to define, but international action was successful in its 'performative' function. This was effective in expressing unity and legitimising dissent.

In periods of crisis a community could restore its unity by rhetoric, as different opinions and interests were subsumed under a single voce.[52] Huysmans understood that by speaking on the radio he was fulfilling this responsibility. The ritualistic repetition of the appeals served as a performance of the unity and vitality of socialism, but the same repetition could be read as sign of impotence. As Gillies lamented, what was the point of appeals when force was the rule of war?[53]

The Dallas Committee coordinated the broadcasting of socialist propaganda via radio.[54] The Labour Party also used the committee to vet the content of the broadcast—for example Gillies cut a reference to the creation of a Jewish state in Palestine, as he did not want to commit the Labour leadership. It also helped foreign socialists to negotiate more time on the airwaves with the state bureaucracy, as many feared that the Tories would favour their conservative and liberal compatriots.

The Dallas committee coordinated a major radio offensive at the end of 1940, with the participation of many socialists.[55] The radio propaganda offensive of the German social democrats was directed personally by Richard Crossman.[56] With speeches on Mayday from 1941 to 1943, Huysmans and the Labour Party spoke to the continent in the name of the movement.[57] How effective these appeals were in occupied Europe is difficult to say,[58] but they were effective in keeping the Labour Party united. At the 1941 conference, George Dallas rejected the charge that the leadership had not done enough to coordinate the European socialists, presenting the Mayday message as 'one of the greatest successes in the whole period of the War'.[59] It was not simply a cynical ploy, Dalton reported how he had become emotional at a meeting organised by Polish socialists.[60]

Internationalism was also expressed in public receptions where European and British socialist leaders made joint appeals.[61] In the critical phase of the war, all public events suffered poor attendance. In July 1942, the NEC suggested that the Constituency Labour Parties organised events with the participation of socialist speakers from the Allied countries.[62] In some cases, as with a Polish speaker, the attendance was terrible, while the French speakers had greater success. These meetings were meant to show to the rank and file that the Red Army was not alone in fighting Nazi Germany, but the party members wanted Soviet speakers. From July 1943 to December 1944, 300 public events took place around Britain with the presence of a socialist leader from an Allied country.[63]

The main public event was the Annual Conference of the Labour Party, where the socialist leaders and Huysmans addressed the floor in a mutually beneficial exchange: the exiled socialists were recognised as legitimate; in return they praised the Labour leaders and asked them to lead the world socialist movement. Huysmans's speech requested a greater involvement of Great Britain in the continent, even infantilising the Continentals:

> But if I am permitted to make a timid remark: Do not leave us alone when Peace is concluded [...]. To my mind, little countries resemble sometimes young children. You cannot leave them ... alone in a room where an open fire is burning.[64]

There were still risks for embarrassment, as when some Labour members joined the condemnation of the assassination of the Jewish Bund leaders Viktor Alter and Henryk Ehrlich by the Soviet Union. To avoid irritating the Soviet embassy, the Labour Party disavowed these statements.[65]

Language was not only an instrument of unity but also of division. As mentioned, two languages were employed to explain fascism: one emphasising cultural and national differences, the other economic and social factors. Vansittart rejected the Marxist explanation of Nazism in favour of a cultural one, which found acceptance in the ranks of the Labour Party thanks to its consonance with Dalton's theory about fascism. Gillies presented the SPD as a nationalist party that was too close to Nazism. This critique was backed by dissenting German social democrats who broke with the mainstream SPD in exile, such as Carl Herz, Walter Loeb and Curt Geyer. The paradox noted by Später[66] was that the left-wing socialists supporting a radical moral reform of Germany proved to be the best allies of Vansittart. The publishing house Fight For Freedom played a central part in the anti-German propaganda; it had strong links to James Walker, Camille Huysmans and the Czech social democrats opposing the Sudeten social democrats.[67] Gillies wrote the prefaces to some of their books and defended them from the attacks of the Socialist Clarity Group, threatening legal action. In 1942, the Labour leadership approved the sale of literature from Fight For Freedom at the party conference.

An important performative role was played by 'performative utterances'. J.L. Austin argued that 'performative utterances' do not describe things, but they produce a social act. A parent can give a name to a child, a person can make a commitment by simply saying 'I promise' and a marriage can be created by saying 'I do'. These acts require nothing more than uttering words.[68] The Socialist International had a similar power: it could assign the label 'socialist' to a party and deny it to another. It did not describe a party as socialist, it declared that party as the official socialist party. When different factions or parties made exclusive claims to represent socialism in their country, the recognition of the Socialist International was an asset, especially when small parties had few other elements to back their claim.[69] However, this utterance was 'felicitous', that is, accepted as valid, only if the person recognised the Socialist International's authority to do so.[70]

The involvement of the Socialist International in factional struggles and splits came from its ability to grant recognition. The Socialist International 'was probably one of the most powerful symbols that supported the claim and identity of the socialist party as authentic workers' party'[71] and it 'was the authority which could issue the "socialist" or "social democratic" label. It was a label of quality that in moments of needs could be displayed to the rank and file'.[72]

This power became prominent during the war, as it emerged with the party for German workers of Sudetenland. After the Munich agreement, its leader Wenzel Jaksch reformed the organisation in exile as the *Treuegemeinschaft Sudetendeutscher Sozialdemokraten*, with a programme for the federal reform of Czechoslovakia and refusing transfers of population. This made an agreement with the other Czechoslovak parties impossible.[73] In Autumn 1940, the dissenters Zinner and Lenk formed their own splinter group—known as the *Zinnergruppe*—which accepted cooperation with Beneš. The Dallas Committee became involved when Jaksch asked to circulate some documents condemning the *Zinnergruppe* and Zinner asked for admission.[74] Following the advice of the Czech social democratic party, Gillies decided to admit both groups. Jaksch threatened to remove the *Treuegemeinschaft* from the Dallas Committee, as there was no precedent in the LSI to invite a splinter group; the Labour Party was 'claim[ing] for themselves the authority to alter or extend the mandates of oppressed Labour Movements'.

> We have refrained from any interference in this matter considering that one of the unwritten laws in international Socialist intercourse enjoins upon all parties to act with utmost impartiality and reserve in any conflicts that may arise within a sister Party, unless mediation is desired by all persons concerned [...]
> By the recognition of secessionist groups, without previous verification of their mandates by a legally instituted commission and proper proceedings, every exiled Party can be broken up. It is obvious that every ambitious outsider may avail himself of this opportunity to form a group of his own. And the fact of an official recognition, however easily gained, will enable him to exploit the prestige of the Labour Party for his disruptive activities.[75]

Events after the war would prove Jaksch's description very accurate. The Labour Party and Huysmans repeated their prerogative to invite whomever they chose.[76] In this occasion Gillies wanted to help Beneš' policy and the argument about the need of representing all shades of opinion was instrumental. For example, when Prager, a member of *Vitlagossag*, the organisation of Hungarian socialists in exile, asked to represent the Hungarians in Czechoslovakia, Huysmans asked permission from the Czechs, who refused. On other occasions Gillies did not have sufficient information and the decision to choose who was representative went according to his political sympathies and inclinations, for example when he refused any recognition to the *Comité d'action socialiste*, the main socialist force of French resistance.

The Labour Party had a more active role in the divisions of the German social democrats: when the quarrel between Vogel and Geyer was brought to the attention of the International Sub-Committee, Gillies backed Geyer.[77] The Polish socialist leader Adam Ciolkosz—who had an interest in weakening German social democracy—pressured Huysmans to include Geyer in his Committee.[78] Ollenhauer, Vogel's number two and future leader, lost his support from the Relief Fund.[79] The Austrian socialists denounced these moves to Huysmans:

> To justify [this entirely arbitrary decision] you have invoked the principle that every shade of organised Socialist opinion should be represented on your Committee. We do not agree unreservedly with this principle as it seems to us to encourage dissidents in exiled Socialist movements (which already suffer from too many divergencies [sic]), whereas we think it should be the privilege of your high office to do everything possible to prevent further splits.[80]

The Labour Party and Huysmans had effectively claimed the power to define the limits of the social democratic community, to say who was in and who was out. The principles behind the individual decisions were completely arbitrary, since it was impossible to say which was a 'living party'. The principles of representing all shades of opinion was sometimes employed, other times the condition was that the party from the same nation agreed. Wartime created the precedent for an asymmetry of power, where legitimacy was not mutually exchanged, but was a gift given by a stronger party, the Labour Party, to the weaker ones.

5 THE INTERNATIONAL PREPARATORY COMMITTEE

The commitment of the Labour Party was necessary for any move to rebuild the International, but its leaders were concerned above all with winning the war and engaged in the debate only when victory seemed certain. Laski pleaded to build a unitary International in order to achieve a general agreement between the Labour Party and the Communist Party of the Soviet Union.[81] The International Department considered sending a delegation to negotiate, with the condition that each socialist party should have been democratic and free from interference.

The proposal came at a time of lively internal debate. During the war, the organisation of the Labour Party was being weakened, while the communists grew stronger thanks to the success of the Soviet Union. Pressure mounted, even from centrist figures, to cooperate with the communists or even to allow their affiliation to the party.[82] The 1943 Annual Conference would decide the matter, so the Labour leadership launched a campaign against affiliation, denouncing the disruptive tactics of the communists, their language, their past ambiguity, and, in the case of Herbert Morrison—future Home Secretary—employing racist tones condemning the communists as 'dirty' and carriers of contamination. At the same time, the leadership committed to radical social policies—embracing the Beveridge Plan and nationalisations—in order to highlight discontinuity with conservatives.

At the same conference, the Labour leadership committed to rebuild the International after the war, in a completely new form.[83] Konni Zilliacus (a future critic of Bevin and supporter of friendship with the Soviet Union) and John Hynd (a friend of the German and Austrian socialists, later minister responsible for the occupation of these countries) proposed to send a delegation to the Soviet Union to resolve outstanding problems and prepare a unitary International.[84]

During 1944, pressure to revive the Socialist International grew from within the Labour Party and without. Requests came from the Swiss Party,[85] the International Group of Democratic Socialists—another international union of socialist exiles, in Stockholm[86]—and the Italian socialists from the Resistance and liberated Italy.[87] The Norwegian, Polish, Dutch and Austrian socialist exiles in the Huysmans Committee demanded the creation of a study group (the 'International Preparatory Committee') with a greater authority.[88] Gillies stuck to his line: the International had failed and its centralist constitution was unfit for parties with government responsibilities.[89] 'In short, the International would be reconstructed from the bottom on the basis of living parties', there would be no place for the exiles.[90] The debate would restart only after the national parties had been rebuilt, until then the International Department of the Labour Party would manage the international socialist relations on a bilateral basis.[91] 'London has been the recognised centre of Democratic Socialism during the war, and the British Labour Party has been the undisputed leader'.[92] However, Huysmans returned to his previous positions that international socialism needed an independent rallying point.[93] Huysmans and *Tribune*, a journal of the Labour left, convinced the International Sub-Committee to create an International Labour and Socialist Preparatory Committee, with the goal 'to collect information, keep in touch with the Parties and to undertake studies of the problem of an exploratory nature'.[94] However this committee was formed with members of the Dallas Committee.

The Labour Party Conference of December 1944 was the occasion to show off international socialist solidarity. It approved the Post-War International Settlement, the plan drafted by Dalton and circulated in the Dallas Committee—although there seems to be little evidence that suggestions from foreign socialists modified his original draft. The programme committed to German collective guilt, but also collective security through the United Nations and a bigger role of the International Labour Organisation.[95] There was an explicit commitment to 'the close association in the future of the Socialist Parties in all countries'.[96] The NEC approved the enlargement of the Preparatory Committee—the Italians were admitted under the condition that they would not ask for the revision of the Armistice terms—but it asked to reject Zilliacus' motion to create a unitary International.[97] For the first time non-allied socialists (Italians, Swedes and Swiss) attended the conference as observers, but Huysmans sent a violent speech against the Germans, requesting that their socialist credentials be re-examined before being readmitted to the socialist community.[98] The secretary of the SFIO, Daniel Mayer, affirmed his commitment to rebuild the International.[99] On 10 and 14 December, the Preparatory Committee convened and decided to meet again at the time of the World Trade Union Conference.

From 3 to 5 March 1945, Dalton chaired a socialist conference in London. After a debate, the conference approved a 14-point declaration calling for a new world order based on disarmament, collective security and arbitration, and the extension of democracy and economic rights to underdeveloped areas. The conference also approved the collective guilt of the Germans, complete disarmament and extraction of reparations from Germany. The first serious disagreement was on the territorial integrity of Germany, which pitted the Italians and French against the others, particularly the Poles. The motion on Germany was approved; the French agreed not to make their dissent public.[100] The conference renewed its commitment to study how to revive the Socialist International:

The Socialist Groups represented at this Conference are resolved to give new life to the Socialist International. To this end, they hereby resolve to nominate a Committee to prepare a plan for consideration at a further meeting in the early future.[101]

However, after the conference nothing happened. All the parties were involved in national problems, the Labour Party had to fight an election and had fired Gillies. Until the Labour electoral victory was announced on 22 July 1945, the new General Secretary, Morgan Phillips, could not deal with the matter. By then, the situation was vastly different from what could have been expected during the war. Labour was in government and the new Foreign Secretary, Ernest Bevin, wanted to avoid embarrassments. In Eastern Europe, new socialist parties emerged with a pro-communist and anti-Western line. Even in Western Europe, the socialist parties were transformed.

As everyone waited for the dust to settle, socialist internationalism entered a period of pause, which signified the passage from the war era to the post-war era. Wartime was an important period: new patterns emerged, which would become dominant after the war. Old illusions were shredded and new ideas took hold. However, no one in exile had predicted the shape of post-war Europe. Before this precarious asset was to be recast once again by the Cold War, the socialists of Eastern and Western Europe had to navigate in the new political, social and economic system that was not of their own making.

NOTES

1. L. Rapone (1989) 'La crisi finale dell'Internazionale operaia e socialista', *Socialismo Storia. Annali della Fondazione Giacomo Brodolini e della Fondazione di Studi Storici Filippo Turati*, 2, 37–43. A. Bergounioux (1983) 'L'Internationale ouvrière socialiste entre les deux guerres', in H. Portelli (ed.), *L'Internationale socialiste* (Paris: Les Éditions Ouvrières).
2. A. Panebianco (1988) *Political Parties: Organization and Power* (Cambridge: Cambridge University Press), 50–53.
3. Quoted in D. Hanely (1983) 'Un socialisme aux couleurs de l'Angleterre: le parti travailliste et l'Internationale Socialiste depuis 1945', in H. Portelli (ed.), *L'Internationale socialiste* (Paris: Les Éditions Ouvrières), 57.
4. Labour Party Annual Conference Report (LPACR) 1943, 170.
5. L. Rapone (1999) *La socialdemocrazia europea tra le due guerre: dall'organizzazione della pace alla Resistenza al fascismo, 1923–1936* (Roma: Carocci), 33–40; 61–76.

6. See R. Sigel (1986) *Die Geschichte der Zweiten Internationale: 1918–1923*, (Frankfurt-New York: Campus).
7. H. Steiner (1985) *Die Internationale Arbeitsgemeinschaft Sozialisticher Parteien (2 ½ Internationale) 1921–1923*, in E. Collotti (ed.), *L'Internazionale Operaia e Socialista tra le due guerre* (Milano: Feltrinelli), 45–61.
8. R. Steininger (1979) *Deutschland und die Sozialistische Internationale nach dem Zweiten Weltkrieg, Darstellung und Dokumentation* (Bonn: Neue Gesellschaft), 5–10.
9. For socialist interpretations of Fascism see M. Hájek (1985) 'Il fascismo nell'analisi dell'Internazionale operaia e socialista', in Colotti, *L'Internazionale Operaia e Socialista tra le due guerre*, 389–430.
10. Rapone, *La socialdemocrazia europea tra le due guerre*, 248–265.
11. P. Nenni, La lotta fascista e l'unità socialista, *Avanti!*, 10 June 1928, in P. Nenni (1977) *La battaglia socialista contro il fascismo, 1922–1944* (Milano: Mursia), 229. Gordon argues that the majority of the Labour Party shared the idea that Fascism was the acute form of capitalism (M.R. Gordon (1969) *Conflict and Consensus in Labour's Foreign Policy, 1914–1965*, (Stanford: Stanford University Press), 19).
12. Quoted in R. Palme Dutt (1935) *Fascism and Social Revolution: A Study of the Economics and Politics of the Extreme Stages of Capitalism in Decay* (New York: New York International publishers), 252. Also J. Polasky (1995) *The Democratic Socialism of Emile Vandervelde: Between Reform and Revolution* (Oxford: Berg), 207–213.
13. Noi [Pietro Nenni], L'attacco fascista contro Vienna rossa, *L'Avanti!*, 11 October 1930, in Nenni, *La battaglia socialista contro il fascismo*, 258.
14. Entry, 18 August 1933, B. Pimlott (1986) *The Political Diary of Hugh Dalton: 1918–40, 1945–60* (London: Cape), 178.
15. Rapone, *La socialdemocrazia europea tra le due guerre*, 247–276.
16. D. Sassoon (2010) *One Hundred Years of Socialism: The West European Left in the Twentieth Century* (London: Tauris), 60–73.
17. Steininger, *Deutschland und die Sozialistische Internationale nach dem Zweiten Weltkrieg*, 13–18. Rapone, 'La crisi finale dell'Internazionale', 43–79.
18. H. Balthazar (1972) 'L'Internationale Socialiste, Les debats de Londres en 1940–1941', *Cahiers d'histoire de la seconde guerre mondiale*, 2, 193.
19. Minutes of the International Sub-Committee, 23 January 1939, Labour History Archive and Study Centre, People's History Museum, Manchester (LHASC), Labour Party (LP), International Department (ID), Minutes and Documents, 1939.
20. LPACR 1939, 265.
21. Minutes of the International Sub-Committee, 13 July 1939, LHASC, LP, International Sub-Committees, Minutes and Documents, 1939.

22. Minutes of the International Sub-Committee, 25 June 1940, LHASC, LP, Labour and Socialist International (LSI), 25, 1. W. Gillies to W. Jaksch, 9 July 1940 25/1/15; J. Belina to Gillies, 4 July 1940 25/1/19; P. Tofahrn to Gillies, 3 July 1940 25/1/4; J. Deutsch to Gillies, 10 August 1940 25/1/52; Minutes of the International Sub-Committee, 22 July 1940 25/1/5, LHASC, LP, Labour and Socialist International (LSI).
23. C. Huysmans to Gillies, 30 July 1940 25/1/40, LHASC, LP, LSI.
24. Huysmans to Gillies, 23 July 1940 25/1/26; Gillies to Huysmans, 26 July 1940 25/1/32; Gillies to Huysmans, 1 August 1940 25/1/42; J. Necas to Gillies, 31 July 1940 25/1/38; T. Wold to Gillies, 9 August 1940; M. Buset to Gillies, 31 July 1940 25/1/37; Gillies to A. Philip, 30 July 1942 25/1/108; Gillies to various parties, 8 November 1940 25/1/64, LHASC, LP, LSI.
25. G. Dallas to Jaksch, 21 August 1941 25/1/142, LHASC, LP, LSI.
26. Minutes of the International Sub-Committee, 12 December 1941 26/1/28, LHASC, LP, LSI.
27. Gillies to M. Phillips, 17 January 1942 26/2/5, LHASC, LP, LSI.
28. J. Braunthal to G.D.H. Cole, 30 June 1941, International Institute of Social History (IISH), Julius Braunthal Papers, 44.
29. P. Corthorn (2008) 'The Labour Party in the Era of the Nazi-Soviet Pact, 1939–41', P. Corthorn, J. Davis (eds), *The British Labour Party and the Wider World* (London: Tauris 2008), 88–93.
30. B. Pimlott (1985) *Hugh Dalton* (London: Cape), 299–301. L. Eiber (1998) *Die Sozialdemokratie in der Emigration: die Union deutscher sozialistischer Organisationen in Grossbritannien 1941–1946 und ihre Mitglieder: Protokolle, Erklärungen, Materialien* (Bonn: Dietz), xxii–xxiii.
31. LPACR 1940, 7.
32. LPACR 1943, 38–42.
33. J. Später (2003) *Vansittart: britische Debatten über Deutsche und Nazis 1902–1945* (Göttingen: Wallstein). I. Tombs (1996) 'The Victory of Socialist "Vansittartism": Labour and the German Question, 1941–5', *Twentieth Century British History*, 7, 287–309. For example, 'On the other hand, when I [Gillies] pointed out to Levy that our friends in Poland had reported that six to seven million people had been killed in Poland by the Germans, and remarked that the Germans had earned the curse of extermination, he agreed' (Gillies to Dallas, 11 March 1944, LHASC, LP, LSI, 25, 1).
34. H. J. Laski, Toward Friendship with the Soviet Union, *New Statesman and Nation*, 5 July 1941.
35. Minutes of the joint meeting of the Policy and International Sub-Committee, 31 March 1942, LHASC, LP, International Sub-Committee, Minutes and Documents, 1942.

36. LPACR 1941, 152–153. Huysmans to Gillies, 29 April 1941 26/6/1; Minutes of the International Sub-Committee, 4 July 1941 26/1/12; [W.Gillies], 'The International'; Circular letter from William Gillies, 8 August 1941 26/1/22; [Camille Huysmans, William Gillies], 'Labour and Socialist International' 26/1/11/, LHASC, LP, LSI.
37. K. Czernetz, O. Pollak to C. Huysmans, 19 April 1942 26/6/4, LHASC, LP, LSI.
38. Huysmans to Gillies, 31 March 1942 26/2/9; Gillies to Huysman, 1 April 1942 26/2/11; Huysmans to Gillies, 7 January 1943 26/2/20, LHASC, LP, LSI.
39. Minutes of the International Sub-Committee, 1 April 1941, LHASC, LP, International Sub-Committee, Minutes and Documents, 1941. Später, *Vansittart*, 315–324. Eiber, *Die Sozialdemokratie in der Emigration*, xxv–lxxiii.
40. Minutes of the International Sub-Committee, 14 November 1941 and 21 November 1941; 'German Social Democracy – Notes on its Foreign Policy in World War', October 1941; 'On the Eve of the Third Reich – The Trade Unions'; 'On the Eve of the Third Reich – The German Social Democratic Party', LHASC, LP, International Sub-Committee, Minutes and Documents, 1941.
41. I. Tombs (1991) 'The Fight for Freedom Publishing Company: A Case Study of Conflicting Ideas in Wartime' in J.R. Ritchie (ed.) *German-speaking Exiles in Great Britain*, Vol. 3 (Amsterdam: Rodopi), 59–72.
42. Eiber, *Die Sozialdemokratie in der Emigration*, cxxxvii–cxlvi.
43. M. Saran to Braunthal, 15 June 1944, IISH, Julius Braunthal Papers, 84.
44. *Fabian International Bureau*, attached to Minutes of the International Sub-Committee, 2 September 1942, LHASC, LP, International Sub-Committee, Minutes and Documents, 1942. Also Eiber, *Die Sozialdemokratie in der Emigration*, xlv–xlvi.
45. M. Cole (1963) *The Story of Fabian Socialism* (Stanford: Stanford University Press), 288–293.
46. Minutes of the International Sub-Committee, 2 September 1942, LHASC, LP, International Sub-Committee, Minutes and Documents, 1942.
47. M. Ackermann (1972) *Julius Braunthal. Ein Leben, dem Sozialismus geweiht* ([Wien]: Bund sozialistischer Freiheitskämpfer und Opfer des Faschismus).
48. J. Braunthal to H. Dalton, 3 December 1940, IISH, Julius Braunthal Papers, 46.
49. M. Pollak to Schackerl [Jacques Hannak], 11 November 1941, IISH, Friedrich Adler Papers, 83.

50. W. Wodak to K. Renner, 17 December 1945, W. Wodak (1976) *Diplomatie zwischen Ost und West* (Graz: Styria), 194–200.
51. J. Brauthal, International Socialist Forum, *The Left News*, May 1941. See also Braunthal to Gillies, 23 May 1941, LHASC, LP, International Sub-Committee, Minutes and Documents, 1941. Victor Gollancz, International Socialist Forum, *The Left News*, May 1941.
52. V. Pisanty (2007) 'Churchill, Martin Luther King e Berlusconi: tre discorsi incomparabili' in G.Cosenza (ed.), *Semiotica della comunicazione politica* (Roma: Carocci), 169–203.
53. Huysmans to Gillies, 1 December 1941, 26/2/1; Gillies to Huysmans, 12 March 1942 26/6/23, LHASC, LP, LSI.
54. Minutes of the International Sub-Committee, 22 July 1940; Minutes of the International Sub-Committee, 25 November 1940, LHASC, LP, International Sub-Committee, Minutes and Documents, 1940.
55. Britain is to launch Radio Offensive, *News Chronicle*, 5 December, 1940. Letters and plans in LHASC, LP, LSI, 25, 2.
56. Eiber, *Die Sozialdemokratie in der Emigration*, lviii–lxi.
57. LPACR 1941, 31. Gillies to N.F. Newsome, BBC European Service, 28 April 1943 26/7/18; 'May Day Message for 1943, of Camille Huysmans, Chairman of the Executive of the Labour and Socialist International', 26/7/19, LHASC, LP, LSI.
58. Gillies to Huysmans, 5 December 1941 26/2/2, LHASC, LP, LSI.
59. LPACR 1941, 153.
60. Entry, 9 November 1943, Ben Pimlott (ed.) (1986) *The Second World War Diary of Hugh Dalton 1940–45* (London: Jonathan Cape), 666.
61. LPACR 1941, 31. LPACR 1942, 21–22. LPRA 1943, 38–42.
62. A. Thorpe (2009) *Parties at War: Political Organization in Second World War Britain*, (Oxford: Oxford University Press), 203–204.
63. LPACR 1944, 22.
64. LPACR 1941, 147.
65. Minutes of the International Sub-Committee, 15 March 1943, LHASC, LP, International Sub-Committee, Minutes and Documents, 1943.
66. Später, *Vansittart*, 291–313.
67. 'The "Fight for Freedom" publishing society', *Labour Discussion Notes*, March 1942; Gillies to Socialist Clarity Group, 23 March 1942 and 8 April 1942; Minutes of the International Sub-Committee, 17 April 1942; Minutes of the International Sub-Committee, 21 May 1942, LHASC, LP, International Sub-Committee, Minutes and Documents, 1942.
68. J.L. Austin (1976) *How to do Things with Words: The William James Lectures delivered at Harvard University in 1955* (London: Oxford University Press), 6–7.

69. I. Campbell, W. E. Paterson (1974) *Social Democracy in Post-War Europe* (London: Macmillan), viii. L. Hamon (1983) 'L'International Socialiste depuis 1945 et la tradition des internationales ouvrières', in H. Portelli (ed.), *L'Internationale socialiste* (Paris: Les Éditions Ouvrières), 18.
70. J. Medina (2005) *Language: Key Concepts in Philosophy* (London: Continuum), 160–161.
71. P. Van Kemseke (2006) *Towards an Era of Development, The Globalization of Socialism and Christian Democracy: 1945–1965* (Leuven: Leuven University Press), 19.
72. Van Kemseke, *Towards an Era of Development*, 24.
73. F.D. Raška (2004) 'The Treuegemeinschaft Sudetendeutscher Sozialdemokraten and its Struggle against Czechoslovak Plans for German Transfer', *Kakanien Revisited*, http://www.kakanien.ac.at/beitr/fallstudie/FRaska1.pdf (accessed 28 December 2017).
74. Minutes of the International sub-committee, 4 July 1941 25/1/136; Gillies to J. Lenk 8 July 1941 25/1/137; Gillies to Wenzel Jaksch, 8 July 1941 25/1/138, LHASC, LP, LSI.
75. Jaksch to Dallas, 22 July 1941, 25/1/140, LHASC, LP, LSI.
76. Huysmans to Gillies, 5 January 1942 25/1/149; Huysmans to Gillies, 25 January 1943 25/2/24; Belina to Gillies, 7 February 1943 26/2/25; Gillies to Huysmans, 4 August 1942 26/6/26, LHASC, LP, LSI.
77. Eiber, *Die Sozialdemokratie in der Emigration*, lxxxiv; cii–cvii.
78. Huysmans to H. Vogel, 15 June 1942 26/6/30, LHASC, LP, LSI.
79. Minutes of the International Sub-Committee, 26 January 1943, LHASC, LP, International Sub-Committee, Minutes and Documents, 1943.
80. Karl Czernetz, Oscar Pollak to Huysmans, 15 September 1942 26/6/13, LHASC, LP, LSI.
81. 'The Labour Party Delegation to the USSR – Suggestions by H.J. Laski for the Consideration of the International Sub-Committee', August 1943; Minutes of the International Sub-Committee, 14 December 1943. LHASC, LP, International Sub-Committee, Minutes and Documents, 1942.
82. A. Thorpe (2014) 'Locking out the Communists: The Labour Party and the Communist Party, 1939–46', *Twentieth Century British History*, 25, 2, 226–250.
83. 'The International will be re-established after the war, though it may be necessary to reorganise it completely'. LPACR 1943, 118.
84. LPACR 1943, 149; 209.
85. Minutes of the International Sub-Committee, 17 August 1943, LHASC, LP, International Sub-Committee, Minutes and Documents, 1943. 'Swedish Call for "International"', 12 June 1944 27/1/5, LHASC, LP, LSI.

86. K. Misgeld (1976) *Die Internationale Gruppe demokratischer Sozialisten in Stockholm 1942–1945: zur sozialistischen Friedensdiskussion während des Zweiten Weltkrieges* (Bonn: Neue Gesselschaft).
87. 'An open letter to the Labour Party from Pietro Nenni', LHASC, LP, International Sub-Committee, Minutes and Documents, 1944. P. Sebastiani (1983) *Laburisti inglesi e socialisti italiani: dalla ricostituzione del Psi(up) alla scissione di Palazzo Barberini* (Roma: Elengraf). Riccardo Luzzatto repeated the Italian arguments in person (R. Luzzatto to P. Nenni, 12 October 1944, Fondazione Pietro Nenni (FPN), Fondo Pietro Nenni, b.31, f.1535).
88. 'The Socialist International more needed than ever', *London Information*, 1 August 1944, LHASC, LP, International Sub-Committee, Minutes and Documents, 1944.
89. W. Gillies, 'The International – Points for Consideration', 20 July 1944, LHASC, LP, International Sub-Committee, Minutes and Documents, 1944.
90. W. Gillies, 'The International', 31 August 1944, 27/1/33, LHASC, LP, LSI.
91. Gillies to Dallas, 3 August 1944, 27/1/3, LHASC, LP, LSI.
92. W. Gillies, 'The International', 31 August 1944, 27/1/33, LHASC, LP, LSI.
93. Huysmans to Gillies, 24 August 1944, 27/1/22, LHASC, LP, LSI. A Labour International, *Tribune*, 11 August 1944. Luzzatto to Nenni, 12 October 1944, FPN, Fondo Pietro Nenni, b.31, f.1535.
94. Minutes of the International Sub-Committee, 1 September 1944, 27/1/42; Issued by the Labour Party Press and publicity Department, 13 September 1944, 27/1/46, LHASC, LP, LSI.
95. Minutes of the International Sub-Committee, 18 April 1944; Labour Party, 'The International Post-War Settlement', LHASC, LP, International Sub-Committee, Minutes and Documents, 1944.
96. LPACR 1944, 132.
97. LPACR 1944, 135.
98. 'Message of Camille Huysmans to the Labour Party Conference, September 1944', 7 December 1944, 26/8/2, LHASC, LP, LSI.
99. Circular letter by Gillies, 19 December 1944, 27/3/21, LHASC, LP, LSI. LPACR 1944, 12–13.
100. Steininger, *Deutschland und die Sozialistische Internationale nach dem Zweiten Weltkrieg*, 40–42.
101. 'Declaration issued by the conference of European socialist parties held in London, 3rd, 4th, 5th March, 1945', 27/3/2, LHASC, LP, LSI.

Bibliography

Ackermann, M. (1972). *Julius Braunthal. Ein Leben, dem Sozialismus geweiht.* Wien: Bund sozialistischer Freiheitskämpfer und Opfer des Faschismus.
Austin, J.L. (1976). *How to do things with words: the William James lectures delivered at Harvard University in 1955.* London: Oxford University Press.
Balthazar, H. (1972). L'Internationale Socialiste, Les debats de Londres en 1940–1941. *Cahiers d'histoire de la seconde guerre mondiale,* 2, 191–210.
Bergounioux, A. (1983). L'Internationale ouvrière socialiste entre les deux guerres. In H. Portelli (Ed.). *L'Internationale socialiste.* Paris: Les Éditions Ouvrières.
Campbell, I. & Paterson, W.E. (1974). *Social democracy in post-war Europe.* London: Macmillan.
Cole, M. (1963). *The story of Fabian socialism.* Stanford: Stanford University Press.
Corthorn, P. (2008). The Labour Party in the Era of the Nazi-Soviet Pact, 1939–41. In P. Corthorn, J. Davis (Eds.). *The British Labour Party and the Wider World* (pp. 86–109). London: Tauris.
Eiber, L. (1998). *Die Sozialdemokratie in der Emigration: die Union deutscher sozialistischer Organisationen in Grossbritannien 1941–1946 und ihre Mitglieder: Protokolle, Erklärungen, Materialien.* Bonn: Dietz.
Gordon, M.R. (1969). *Conflict and consensus in Labour's foreign policy, 1914–1965.* Stanford: Stanford University Press.
Hájek, M. (1985). Il fascismo nell'analisi dell'Internazionale operaia e socialista. In E. Collotti (Ed.). *L'Internazionale Operaia e Socialista tra le due guerre* (pp. 45–61). Milano: Feltrinelli.
Hamon, L. (1983). L'International Socialiste depuis 1945 et la tradition des internationales ouvrières. In H. Portelli (Ed.). *L'Internationale socialiste* (pp. 9–22). Paris: Les Éditions Ouvrières.
Hanely, D. (1983). Un socialisme aux couleurs de l'Angleterre: le parti travailliste et l'Internationale Socialiste depuis 1945. In H. Portelli (Ed.). *L'Internationale socialiste* (pp. 57–66). Paris: Les Éditions Ouvrières.
Medina, J. (2005). *Language: key concepts in philosophy.* London: Continuum.
Misgeld, K. (1976). *Die Internationale Gruppe demokratischer Sozialisten in Stockholm 1942–1945: zur sozialistischen Friedensdiskussion während des Zweiten Weltkrieges.* Bonn: Neue Gesselschaft.
Nenni, P. (1977). *La battaglia socialista contro il fascismo, 1922–1944.* Milano: Mursia.
Palme Dutt, R. (1935). *Fascism and Social Revolution: a study of the economics and politics of the extreme stages of capitalism in decay.* New York: New York International publishers.
Panebianco, A. (1988). *Political parties: organization and power.* Cambridge: Cambridge University Press.

Pimlott, B. (1985). *Hugh Dalton*. London: Cape.
Pimlott, B. (Ed.). (1986a). *The political diary of Hugh Dalton: 1918–40, 1945–60*. London: Cape.
Pimlott, B. (Ed.). (1986b). *The Second World war diary of Hugh Dalton 1940–45*. London: Jonathan Cape.
Pisanty, V. (2007). Churchill, Martin Luther King e Berlusconi: tre discorsi incomparabili. In G. Cosenza (Ed.). *Semiotica della comunicazione politica* (pp. 169–203). Roma: Carocci.
Polasky, J. (1995). *The democratic socialism of Emile Vandervelde: between reform and revolution*. Oxford: Berg.
Rapone, L. (1989). La crisi finale dell'Internazionale operaia e socialista. *Socialismo Storia. Annali della Fondazione Giacomo Brodolini e della Fondazione di Studi Storici Filippo Turati*, 2, 37–93.
Rapone, L. (1999). *La socialdemocrazia europea tra le due guerre: dall'organizzazione della pace alla Resistenza al fascismo, 1923–1936*. Roma: Carocci.
Raška, F.D. (2004). The Treuegemeinschaft Sudetendeutscher Sozialdemokraten and its Struggle against Czechoslovak Plans for German Transfer. *Kakanien Revisited*, http://www.kakanien.ac.at/beitr/fallstudie/FRaska1.pdf
Sassoon, D. (2010). *One hundred years of socialism: the West European Left in the twentieth century*. London: Tauris.
Sebastiani, P. (1983). *Laburisti inglesi e socialisti italiani : dalla ricostituzione del Psi(up) alla scissione di Palazzo Barberini*. Roma: Elengraf.
Sigel, R. (1986). *Die Geschichte der Zweiten Internationale: 1918–1923*. Frankfurt and New York: Campus.
Später, J. (2003). *Vansittart: britische Debatten über Deutsche und Nazis 1902–1945*. Göttingen: Wallstein.
Steiner, H. (1985). *Die Internationale Arbeitsgemeinschaft Sozialisticher Parteien (2 ½ Internationale) 1921–1923*. In E. Collotti (Ed.). *L'Internazionale Operaia e Socialista tra le due guerre* (pp. 45–61). Milano: Feltrinelli.
Steininger, R. (1979). *Deutschland und die Sozialistische Internationale nach dem Zweiten Weltkrieg, Darstellung und Dokumentation*. Bonn: Neue Gesellschaft.
Thorpe, A. (2009). *Parties at war: political organization in Second World War Britain*. Oxford: Oxford University Press.
Thorpe, A. (2014). Locking out the Communists: The Labour party and the Communist party, 1939–46. *Twentieth Century British History*, 25 (2), 226–250.
Tombs, I. (1991). The Fight for Freedom Publishing Company: A Case Study of Conflicting Ideas in Wartime. In J.R. Ritchie (Ed.). *German-speaking Exiles in Great Britain*, Vol. 3 (pp. 59–72). Amsterdam: Rodopi.
Tombs, I. (1996). The Victory of Socialist 'Vansittartism': Labour and the German Question, 1941–5. *Twentieth Century British History*, 7, 287–309.

Van Kemseke, P. (2006). *Towards an Era of Development, The Globalization of Socialism and Christian Democracy: 1945–1965.* Leuven: Leuven University Press.

Wodak, W. (1976). *Diplomatie zwischen Ost und West.* Graz: Styria.

CHAPTER 3

Parties and People, the Labour Party and the International Socialist Network

1 Labour Party's Centrality

The international socialist movement was made up of a network of parties and leaders who kept in regular communication. This chapter discusses the institutions and people involved in international fraternal relations. John Price encouraged the adoption of a full-time International Secretary,[1] but often a member of the leadership, whether a sub-leader or the chief leader was responsible. The workload was heavy: studying international questions, keeping correspondence, attending conferences and meetings abroad, maintaining direct contact with the party leadership. Conversely, the office had many assets: prestige, international contacts, privileged access to the party leadership, influence on political decisions and international experience. Assuming the responsibility could be the beginning of a brilliant career, as it was for Denis Healey, who said it was 'the best job I've ever had'.[2]

Analysing the transnational network of leaders and secretaries is a prerequisite for a history of Socialist International, but it also reveals the inner workings of the socialist parties in the post-war era: their organisation, distribution of power, decision-making process and underlying cultural assumptions. The chapter employs an asymmetrical comparison: the Labour Party is analysed in depth and the other parties are described

© The Author(s) 2018
E. Costa, *The Labour Party, Denis Healey and the International Socialist Movement*, Palgrave Studies in the History of Social Movements, https://doi.org/10.1007/978-3-319-77347-6_3

through their similarities and divergences with the Labour Party. This approach reflects the fact that the Labour Party was the leader of the community, so the inner workings of its International Department had most influence on the development of the Socialist International.

The Clacton Conference (17–19 May 1946) formed the International Socialist Conference, the nucleus of the future Socialist International, reborn in 1951, but during this period, the Labour Party acted as a surrogate for the Socialist International: it maintained contacts between the socialist parties, exchanged information and granted legitimacy to the weaker parties. As Walter Wodak, the representative in London of the Austrian Socialist Party (SPÖ), wrote in December 1945, the International Department of the Labour Party, with Healey as International Secretary, would expand 'into a kind of International in miniature'.[3] The Labour Party was opposed to rebuilding the Second International immediately, but it wished to build its own network of international socialist contacts. Italian labour attaché Francesco Malfatti said that the International Department was 'the only liaison organism to maintain contacts with the foreign socialist parties'.[4]

There were two main differences from a proper International: first, the contacts were bilateral and centred on a hegemonic party not on an institution where all members were on an equal footing; second, the International Department was closely interwoven with the British Labour Government. The chapter explores these two themes.

The other reason for the Labour-centred approach is to highlight the features this investigation wants to uncover. Healey was the most prominent case of a party official acquiring power inside the party organisation thanks to international fraternal relations, becoming entangled with informal socialist diplomacy and being employed to manage dissent and to impose discipline. His case was different in scale but not in kind.

The history of the Labour Party influenced the people and institutions responsible for its international fraternal relations. The era of the Second International was marked by the strong personal friendship of the leaders and intense debates over principles and common action, as the Belgian socialist veteran Vandervelde lamented late in life.[5] The era of the LSI was marked by greater bureaucratic control, for the Labour Party as well. After the First World War, the two leaders of the Labour Party, Ramsey MacDonald and Arthur Henderson, strove to rekindle the ties broken by the war and rebuild the International. Henderson sought help from William Gillies, an official in the Research Department.[6] The NEC and the

Trade Union parliamentary committee established a joint international sub-committee—later Citrine, the chairman of the Trades Union Congress (TUC), opted out to concentrate on the trade unions International.[7] Thanks to MacDonald's return to parliament in 1922 and Henderson's willingness to delegate, Gillies gained great autonomy.[8] He also won the favour of Ernest Bevin—secretary of the biggest trade union federation and future Foreign Secretary—and Hugh Dalton. Dalton was one of the young intellectuals sponsored by Henderson and he had a key role in shifting the attitude of the Labour Party towards planning and Keynesian economy in internal policy and collective security, support for the Versailles system and rearmament in foreign policy.[9] Gillies became the spokesperson of the party abroad, had direct access to the party leaders and controlled the information they received. Gillies cooperated with the LSI and the other parties to collect information on the communists and their front organisations, starting the involvement of the International Department with disciplinary activities. Gillies created the precedent for the international secretary to become a position of power.

Gillies played a decisive influence on socialist internationalism. Austrian socialism was the dominant influence on the LSI, thanks to its secretary Friedrich Adler and his devoted clique—Adolf Sturmthal, Braunthal and Oscar and Marianne Pollak. When the Austrian party was banned in 1934, the group was attacked as cosmopolitan intellectuals without attachment to the nation, especially—as Gillies and De Man were eager to note—because they were Jews.[10] During the crisis of the LSI, Gillies was the main adversary of Adler and the strongest supporter of limiting the influence of exile parties, which could hurt those parties with government ambitions. During the war Gillies was responsible for the organisation of the socialist exiles in London and his fingerprints could be seen everywhere: the suspension of LSI and any debate about it and the marginalisation of German-speaking socialists.

However, with Gillies' expansion of power came questions about his constitutional legitimacy, as he often took political decisions without the approval of the NEC, the Policy Sub-Committee or the Annual Conference. This ambiguity resulted from the peculiar origin of the International Sub-Committee and there was no attempt at rationalisation after the Second World War. As mentioned, Gillies circulated documents charging the SPD with nationalism and being compromised with Nazism. This irritated the pro-German left of Noel-Baker and Laski, who questioned how a party bureaucrat could settle this issue.[11] Gillies asked for a vote of confidence, which the International Sub-Committee gave him with 4 votes against 2.[12] It was a bureaucrat's manoeuvre, reminding the organisation that they needed him and threatening not to offer his services any longer, but it also exposed him to factional scheming.[13]

The dominant coalition (the coalition of leaders controlling the party) balanced the imposition of its policy with the need to appease the minority and the rank and file. Towards the end of the war, Dalton acquired a decisive influence in the NEC and its sub-committees, thanks to the temporary absence of Morrison, due to his failed bid to be party treasurer. Dalton promoted the co-opting of young talented people like Douglas Jay and Hugh Gaitskell and actively encouraged them to develop the policies that were to become the foundation of the Attlee Government.[14]

The two main issues the International Sub-Committee debated in 1943 were the collective guilt of the Germans and Laski's proposal to send a delegation to the Soviet Union to discuss the creation of an all-inclusive, unitary International. In 1944, Dalton prepared the document *The International Post-War Settlement*, defining the policy over international affairs and he forged an alliance to have it approved. Dalton added weight to his anti-German line by exploiting the approval of the Dallas Committee, but he also made many concessions to the left and the constituency parties: he made the commitment to international socialist cooperation more explicit; he secured the approval in principle of the delegation to Moscow; he included a pledge to create a Jewish state—side-lining Gillies, who was opposed.[15] Laski and Noel-Baker opposed collective guilt in the name of socialist internationalism,[16] but while Noel-Baker remained intransigent, Laski came to an agreement with Dalton.[17] Laski's position as Party chairman would be prolonged; one month later Laski proposed Dalton as new Chairman of the International Sub-Committee, due to Dallas' retirement, despite opposition from Shinwell, one of the leaders of the Labour left. At the international conference in March 1945, Laski showed solidarity with the leadership in defending the Yalta Agreement against protests from the Poles.[18] As a reward Laski became chairman of the Dallas Committee. When Laski asked for Gillies' head, Dalton decided Gillies was no longer indispensable, so he sacrificed him for party unity.[19] This confirmed Labour's practice of having the party machinery completely subordinate to the parliamentary leadership—and served as a reminder to the bureaucrats of the fact.

With Attlee's surprising decision to make Bevin Foreign Secretary, Dalton lost control over foreign policy. In the 1945 electoral campaign,

Laski became the favourite target of the conservative press, which exploited anti-Semitic insinuations to denounce socialism as a Continental and dangerous idea.[20] Laski's public disagreements with Attlee were employed to show the former as the *éminence grise* of the Labour Party, even though Laski's public utterances embarrassed the Labour leadership only because they kept him out of the loop. The US Congress was reluctant to approve a loan to Britain because of Laski's notoriety. Attlee wrote to Laski: 'the constant flow of speeches from and interviews with you is embarrassing'.[21]

Without Gillies, the International Department was left unattended. Laski took over the responsibility of representing the Labour Party abroad during a period of great interest because of the surprising electoral victory. Sometimes he was the only person with enough free time to travel, because people like Morgan Phillips and Shinwell had more pressing engagements.[22] Abroad, Laski received the respect and admiration he was denied at home. A newsreel for the Congress of the Italian Socialist Party in 1946 referred to him as 'the great attraction of the congress'.[23]

> He was virtually lionized in European socialist circles, where his kind of secular socialist intellectual was a much more typical presence on the left and where his book and pamphlets were widely reprinted and his articles and speeches widely quoted.[24]

After experimenting with having a famous intellectual instead of a subservient bureaucrat as international spokesperson, the Labour leadership took care not to repeat it. Even as Laski was travelling abroad, his importance was in decline and Healey warned the Poles to give no consideration to what he said, because he was irresponsible and a producer of bad propaganda.[25]

The new General Secretary, Morgan Phillips, made many visits abroad and represented the party at the conferences where the rebuilding of the Socialist International and other important issues were debated. He later became the first president of the Socialist International. There is agreement that while a good organiser, Phillips left the political work to the more energetic Denis Healey.[26] Healey was responsible not just for running the office and writing memoranda, but also defining the political line—indeed, it was Bevin and Dalton who approved Healey's proposals, not Phillips. Van der Goes van Naters' autobiography often references Healey, but only once mentions 'the often half-drunk Morgan Phillips'.[27]

The nomination of Healey as International Secretary, a position he held between 1946 and 1952, was a result of the pact between Dalton and Laski. Before the war, Healey was a communist, but he broke with the party to join the war against Nazi-fascism, the formative experience of his generation. He had come into contact with the misery of Greece and Italy, making him a radical at first. After the war, he became a protégé of Dalton and started his brilliant career.

Under Healey, the International Department expanded from an old secretary to two assistants and two administrative secretaries.[28] The trend for party machinery was to enlarge to cover new responsibilities and to become more complex, centralised and bureaucratic in order to extend the control of the leadership over the movement.[29] In the last 18 months of the war, the party co-opted talented people, like Morgan Phillips and Michael Young, to substitute the old guard. After the electoral victory, Phillips prepared to expand the party machinery,[30] being confident that new funds would come after the abolition of the 1926 Trades and Dispute Act.[31] With the creation of the International Socialist Conference, the International Department received more resources[32] and a new assistant was hired in November 1947.[33] After the Prague Coup (21–25 February 1948), the International Department was restructured into a fighting machine for the confrontation with communists.

The party took an interest in winning over politically uncertain groups like French miners and railroad workers or colonial students. With encouragement from Jennie Lee,[34] the International Department fostered international contacts between local parties, youths, students and female branches.[35] Summer schools and camps for foreign socialists had been organised since 1946.[36] In September 1948, Jennie Lee and the women of the London Party arranged the visit of 80 Austrian socialists, hosted by socialist families in London and Glasgow.[37] They repaid the courtesy in 1949.[38] Other exchanges involved holidays for German children in Britain and the invitation of the children of British Labourites with tuberculosis or asthma to Swiss sanatoriums. *Labour Organiser*, the journal for party officials, publicised opportunities to exchange party officials with Germany, to visit the Netherlands as guests of local socialists or to go to summer camps in Stockholm.[39]

In October 1948, Healey was given responsibility over colonial questions, a new administrative assistant (Eric L. Randall) and a new colonial assistant (Edward G. Farmer).[40] By 1949, fifty people per month—

journalists, party officials, and students—visited the International Department to receive information.[41]

The growing political authority of the International Secretary showed the importance of international fraternal relations. The power of bureaucrats is a direct function of how irreplaceable they are believed to be: if only one person can do the job, he has bargaining power. In 1943, Gillies could not be replaced, but, in 1945, the dominant coalition considered his sacrifice acceptable to appease the minority, despite 22 years of service. On the contrary, Denis Healey was so successful that no substitute could match him. Towards the end of his tenure, Bevan thought Healey was getting 'too cocky' for a mere functionary at Transport House.[42] Dalton chose not to sacrifice him, indeed, he thought finding a substitute was difficult.[43] Foreign socialists shared his opinion:

> We missed Denis Healey because—at least in our impression—his successor has not quite the ability that Denis has. But then perhaps Denis really is an outstanding person and there would not be so many in any case.[44]

Bevan's irritation returned when Healey left the office of International Secretary in 1952 and was rewarded with a safe constituency and a salary paid to the end of the year. According to Bevan, leaving such power to a party official and a middle-class intellectual was a clear signal of the Labour Party falling to the level of the SFIO.[45]

How could the leadership control an independent and irreplaceable, official? The International Sub-Committee did not exercise any control.[46] Its members—Cabinet ministers and trade unionists with more important concerns and not enough experience—rubber-stamped the proposals.[47] The exception was Sam Watson, Chairman of the National Union of Mineworkers, but even he used briefs and notes prepared by Healey.[48] The publication of the pamphlet *European Unity*[49] was a revealing episode. Healey wrote the first draft while keeping in touch with the Foreign Office, then Dalton rewrote it in better language, Bevin gave his approval and it was finally approved by an NEC meeting attended by the party grandees. Still, after a poor reception by journalists and foreign governments, Attlee said he had not read it well.

The relationship between the leadership and the International Secretary—who received a low salary—was based on personal trust and expectations.[50] Indeed, not only was Healey rewarded with a safe seat,[51] but he was introduced into the inner circle of party leaders, where Dalton, then Gaitskell and, reluctantly, Wilson used his talent for foreign affairs and defence. Dalton was Healey's first patron, as he had been for many other talented young people,[52] and he was confident that Healey would become Foreign Secretary by 1972.[53] Starting his activities as International Secretary, Healey answered to Dalton.[54] Healey was taken by Dalton in the Labour delegation to the Consultative Assembly of the Council of Europe and he took control—without even being a MP—by writing speeches, framing policies, providing information and exploiting his contacts with the European socialist leaders. He was essential in setting the anti-European attitude of the Labour Party, while minimising the damage for the international fraternal relations. In 1949 and 1950, Dalton had high praise for his work in Strasbourg[55]; in 1951 Harold Macmillan identified Healey as the true leader of the Labour delegation.[56]

The person Healey had to actually answer to was Bevin, who became involved from the very beginning in the activities of the International Department.[57] In 1945, he vetoed Labour delegations abroad that could threaten his foreign policy.[58] Bevin was good at finding talent to train; he demanded loyalty and gave full support in public, while criticising in private. He did not trust unpredictable intellectuals except his own intellectuals.[59] When Healey publicly criticised the Italian Deputy Prime Minister, Saragat, provoking the ire of the Italian Government and the officials of the Foreign Office, Bevin refused to humiliate Healey in front of them.[60] When Dalton deserted Healey on the pamphlet *European Unity*, Bevin supported him. Healey said that he gave information to Bevin and helped him to draft his speeches for the Annual Conference.[61] It was thanks to Bevin's decision that the International Department started cooperating with the Foreign Office—through Hector McNeil, Minister of State for Foreign Affairs, and Christopher Mayhew, Under-Secretary of State – a cooperation that was to become one of the distinguishing features of international fraternal relations in this period.

2 The Labour Model and Reformist Factions

Throughout the period covered by this research, the Labour Party was in power with a Labour Government led by Clement Attlee. Labour's undisputed hegemony over the international socialist movement would not have been possible without the outstanding electoral victory of 1945 and the great achievements, such as nationalisation, welfare state, the National Health Service and the decolonisation of India. As Denis Healey said, the other parties could find the Labour Party 'a living proof that Democratic Socialism is both morally right and practically efficient'.[62]

Crosland would later criticise the 'cultural imperialism' of European socialist leaders, treating their version of social democracy as an ideological export,[63] but admiration of the Labour Party was voluntary, not imposed. Indeed, the adoption of the British model was the mark of social democrats, as a party and as a faction. It served as empirical evidence that the parliamentary way to socialism existed. European socialists embraced this Whig interpretation of Labour history, presenting socialism as the culmination of organised freedom. This variation argued that the British did not have the exclusivity but they had blazed the trail for others to follow. This association took advantage of a long tradition of associating Anglophilia with progressive—but not revolutionary—policies.[64]

Italian and Austrian socialism were exemplary cases for the influence of the British model on factional struggle. For their reformists, Labour Britain was the model to follow, whose pre-eminence they recognised.[65] Britain was 'a huge social experiment'[66] and 'the best "experimental lab" to test the validity of the methods for building socialism'.[67] At the Zurich Conference (6–9 June 1947) Max Buset reassured the British that the other parties would not embarrass the Labour government, as their success depended on its success:

> We all perfectly understand that the Labour government is engaged in an experience that could be of decisive importance for the future of socialism. If our Labour comrades, having come to power by playing the game of normal democratic institutions, succeeded in socializing the key economic sectors of Great Britain, if they succeeded in making these socialised enterprises live, they would render us an unparalleled service and they would have given the world the proof that it is possible to reach socialism through the democratic road. But if they failed, then it would be fair game for our conservatives and reactionaries and all our political adversaries to evoke the example of the British failure to counter our propaganda and to create a tide of opinion strongly hostile to the socialist idea.[68]

For Schumacher it was of huge significance that the 'great attempt to realise democratic socialism' be successful,[69] for Richard Löwenthal the Labour government was 'a decisive testament to the chances of democratic socialism'.[70] The Dutch social democrats took the name Labour Party because of their enthusiasm about its victory in 1945. Its posters for the May 1946 elections said 'Do as Tommy did: he chose the Labour Party'.[71] Leon Blum stated that British Labour demonstrated that 'to a certain degree it is possible to improve in terms of justice, equality and freedom not only the condition of the workers but also the lot of mankind before the legal system of capitalist ownership is due for a revolutionary transformation'.[72]

However, there was also an element of radicalism and working-class pride. The Labour Party was made up of workers like no other socialist party—Morgan Phillips made a great impression on the Soviet communists because he was a miner.[73] Briefly, even the communists said they would follow the slower road to socialism, shown by the British—and no less a figure than Stalin confirmed this interpretation.[74] Excessive enthusiasm could embarrass British diplomats: after Morgan Phillips attended its congress, the Czech Social Democratic Party (ČSSD) plastered Prague with posters with a picture of London covered by a huge red flag, with the slogan 'Our flag flies over thrones'.[75] This emphasis on building a socialist alternative and being the workers' party made the Labour Party—the party with less Marxist tradition than any other—most attractive to Marxists, like Angelica Balabanoff, a veteran revolutionary and former secretary of the Comintern:

> But where, I ask, is the contradiction between Labour Britain and the Marxist method? At the Milan Conference of our Party, a British Comrade [Healey] said that in Britain a fundamental change had taken place and it could be explained in very simple terms: The poor eat more and the rich eat less. He understood the Marxist method.[76]

In spite of its intentions to retrench from international fraternal relations, the party leadership made a commitment in 1944 to develop 'close association in the future of the Socialist Parties in all countries and likewise of the Trade Union Movement throughout the world'.[77] 'We are conscious of our special obligations of leadership'.[78] The Labour Party headquarters was flooded with pleas for help from the European socialist parties.[79] This satisfied all members of the party:

> One thing on which all were agreed was the world leadership role of Britain and the British Labour Party in particular. The self-styled 'greatest social democratic party in the world' was repeatedly told that it had to give moral and practical leadership to the world; depending on one's viewpoint the

party was enjoined to lead the world for peace, standing up to Communism, disarmament, solving world hunger, or developing the Commonwealth as a free multiracial union founded upon equality.[80]

It was the start of a mutually beneficial exchange: Continental socialists took British Labour as a model to offer against communism, while the Labour leadership used this prestige to convince its rank and file that there was no reason to change course.[81] Imitation and transmission confirmed the validity of the standing policies of the Labour Party and thus the leadership supporting them. It is hardly surprising that it was Bevan who said not to treat the Labour Party as ideal: 'So do not let us be so smug and self-righteous'.[82] At the 1952 conference, Guy Mollet was invited to speak, boosting his prestige, and he celebrated the Labour leadership, providing help against the Bevanite dissenters.[83]

3 Labour Party and Labour Government, 'A Mere Tool of Imperialist Policy'?

While the Labour Party and the British Government with Labour ministers were technically independent organisations, the border between the two was blurred and porous. In addition, the Labour Party was linked to other parts of the labour movement, including the Trades Union Congress (TUC), the Co-operative Alliance, individual MPs and local associations. Ambiguity and tension between the two poles, the movement and the state, had important consequences.

Perception mattered. The Poles were dismayed that General Secretary Morgan Phillips could not influence Government policies.[84] The Italian Government appealed to Attlee to stop interferences from the Labour Party.[85] Italians and Poles mistook *Tribune*, the journal of Labour left-wing, as the official voice of the movement,[86] but the issue is even more complex, since more than once the International Department and the Foreign Office 'inspired' articles for the journal. The BBC was mistaken as the voice of the Government or the Labour Party.[87] The diplomats could be frustrated with this confusion—'I fear we cannot for long continue to speak in this country with two voices'[88]—but they also exploited it to send signals and subtly influence local players.

Identification of the party and the government could be positive, because it showed what the national government could do for socialism. At the same time, it raised the suspicion that British Labour would betray its socialist ideals to advance the goals of the British state, particularly regarding the Cold War. It could either enhance or reduce the attraction of the British model.

The involvement of the international socialist network with the containment policies of the Western powers is a controversial matter, thanks to communist propaganda. A common accusation was that foreign social democrats were agents—or useful idiots—of British imperialism:

> Apparently the [Polish] CP is not a little suspicious about the visits of Polish socialists to Great Britain and hinted—if no more—that the British Labour Party is 'cock of the Socialist roost' and that other Socialist parties go to Great Britain for instructions.[89]

This was the official line of the Cominform, presented by Togliatti, leader of Italian communism, in 1949: right-wing social democrats exploited references to Western bourgeois democracy and party chauvinism to break unity of action with the communists. They 'again linked themselves with the forces of local and international reaction, entered the service of the British Labourites and the American imperialists'[90]:

> 'COMISCO', which began as a mere office for organising international socialist conferences, spent its time in a series of attempts to engineer and widen splits in the Labour movement internationally and nationally. Having created 'COMISCO' as a mere tool of their imperialist policy, the British Labourites attempted to use it to get the Socialist Parties in the people's democracies away from co-operation with the Communist Parties and to disrupt unity of action between Communists and Socialists in Italy.[91]

The international 'linkage' of social democrats with the British Labour Party was a central feature of the factional struggle, but the linkage with actors of state diplomacy (embassies, foreign ministries and organisations of various degrees of secrecy) was more complex. Van Kemseke confirms the communist charge: 'The Socialist International was predestined even from before its official birth, in 1951, to serve as an extension of the British Labour Party's foreign policy'.[92]

However, we ought to argue that it was cooperation rather than subordination, as explained through the model of State–private network. The methodological challenge to a state-centred and centralised perspective in international relations allows an appreciation of the role of informal contacts and 'non-state actors' in shaping political choices.[93] 'State–private network' describes the alliance between state institutions and private organisations to realise common goals.[94] The State delegates certain tasks to a private organisation while providing the necessary resources. This division of labour is fruitful as private organisations were motivated and competent, they could intervene where the State could not do so openly and acted with more flexibility.[95] There are debates over the subordination of the private organisation to State power.[96]

We can also classify this 'informal socialist diplomacy' as a form of 'Track Two Diplomacy', that is, 'unofficial policy dialogue, focused on problem solving, in which the participants have some form of access to official policymaking circles'. [97] Informal socialist diplomacy was not an alternative to official diplomacy, but a practice of employing socialist identity and contacts to achieve results in foreign politics. Before and during the war the British Government reacted to declining economic and military power by employing propaganda to project its influence abroad.[98]

> The difficulty was that the British had neither the money nor the manpower to put these policies into practice. What they had to rely on as a substitute was what they called influence or prestige, intangible and fragile assets left over from an imperial past and victory in war.[99]

Labour's victory increased the attraction of Britain and Bevin believed in countering Soviet power by showing off the achievements of British social democracy. The anti-communism of the Foreign Office was a good match for the anti-communism of the trade union leader who had fought communist infiltration for 20 years. Also, Bevin believed that leading by example was better than the aggressive projects of the military.[100] On becoming Foreign Secretary, he immediately investigated the impact of Labour's victory abroad, especially among the lower classes.[101] Indeed, Soviet communists worried about the progressive forces of Europe finding a new referent[102] and Britain creeping into their sphere of influence.[103]

Usually the Labour Party had little influence on the Labour Government, but Healey kept in contact with Bevin and gained access to Government officials and diplomats. For Bevin, the struggle against communism and the advancement of social democracy was the mission of both the British state and the Labour movement, therefore he expected full support from his comrades. In April 1946, Laski denounced the Italian Communist Party as being run from abroad, which delighted the diplomats, as it was more effective than the propaganda produced by the embassy.[104] In November 1946, Bevin instructed officials at the Foreign Office to keep Healey informed about all non-confidential matters; in exchange Healey offered information and helped diplomats to socialise with local socialists.[105] Healey sent regular reports to the Foreign Office about his travels, kept in touch with British authorities abroad and had regular discussions with officials, even trying to influence the policies of the Foreign Office in Poland, Greece and Italy.

By January 1947, the full involvement of the Labour Party in British policy in Eastern Europe had become official policy, in order to encourage anti-communism in the Eastern European socialist parties:

> Labour Party contacts with these [socialist] parties will be used to the full for this purpose and His Majesty's Representatives should devote special attention to promoting and reporting on opportunities for such contacts, for the information of Transport House. Visits of carefully selected and briefed British MP's are of great value, but much harm is done by the ignorant and those who criticise His Majesty's Government's policy.[106]

When the propaganda offensive against communism started in January 1948, the Labour Party was considered a major channel for delivering publicity,[107] particularly in Italy.[108] So influential and autonomous was Healey that in 1950 civil servants called him a 'little Foreign Secretary'[109] and in 1951 the *Economist* in 1951 spoke of 'the little Foreign Office of Transport House'.[110]

While anti-communism was a feature of the Labour movement and the Foreign Office, there were variants. Healey, Mayhew and Bevin said that communism was a result of social malaise, thus only social democracy could stop it by advancing a radical social programme. The anti-communism of the conservative-minded diplomats was purely defensive and negative. Cooperation was usually smooth, as foreign policy was dressed in socialist language or the realisation of social democracy was considered the second stage of the process. The ambassadors maintained contacts with very different politicians and they had a propensity for intrigue. While the British Council resisted the politicisation of its activities—or even mingling with members of the working-class—the diplomats welcomed the involvement of the Labour Party.

Healey asserted the independence of the party, but bowed to Bevin's authority. Bevin left Healey a great degree of freedom, but he ultimately trusted Healey to act responsibly. The British diplomats held a contradictory attitude: they wanted distance from the Labour Party so as not to compromise the Foreign Office, but they also wished to control Healey. Eventually, the diplomats, such as the British ambassador to Poland, had to recognise that Healey worked in a different world, with different priorities:

> In other respects, I found him [Healey] a curious person with a contradictory mind, at one moment strongly social-democratic, at another distinctly left of social democracy; critical of Mr Bevin's policy and more than critical of the Foreign Service both at home and abroad but his criticism does not, I think, tend to self-criticism. I found him very pleased with himself and unwilling to believe he might be mistaken while very sure that I was (and he may be right).[111]

A common criticism of Bevin was that he relied exclusively on career diplomats, who socialised in reactionary circles.[112] Bevin tried to correct this by expanding the role of the labour attachés.[113] They reported on the opinion of the working-class, extended the contacts of the embassy and influenced local trade unions and parties. In Poland, the labour attaché Kirby gave the embassy access to social circles it had been excluded from before.[114] According to Healey, the labour attaché in Italy, Braine, did a better job than the perpetually drunk ambassador.[115] The Italian Ambassador in London said that the labour attachés could even influence the ambassadors.[116] Labour attachés also maintained regular contacts between local socialists and the Labour Party.

The biggest contribution of the International Department to resistance against communism was disseminating information and propaganda:

> Denis Healey always stoutly and rightly insisted that since Soviet communism treated social democracy as its main enemy, it was part of his duty, as Labour's international secretary, to do his best to disseminate the truth about Stalinism.[117]

While claims of altruism can be doubted, what mattered was that the Labour Party was answering requests from the European socialists, particularly social democratic factions: demand generated supply. Requests to receive pamphlets, articles and books came from Italy, South America, Germany and Austria, and Czechoslovakia.[118] The craving of the citizens of Prague for British cultural products—newspapers, books, films and magazines—impressed the Labour delegate to the ČSSD Congress and other sources confirm this.[119] The demand for information material was not politically neutral, it was intended to fight communism and left-wing socialism. In May 1946, the International Sub-Committee decided to publicise abroad the results of the Labour Government[120] and the Annual Conference too demanded greater efforts in distributing propaganda.[121]

These limited party activities matched Bevin's desire to encourage social democratic propaganda to contain Soviet expansion. At the end of 1945, Bevin instructed the foreign legations to spread information about socialist achievements in Britain.[122] In January 1948, the Foreign Office founded a specialised branch, the Information Research Department (IRD),[123] with the task of distributing 'grey propaganda'—not direct lies, but selective truth according to the political goals—and cultivating intellectuals and opinion-makers of the non-communist left. Bevin's original intention was to present London as the Mecca of social democracy in alternative to Moscow. The IRD did not spread its material directly but supplied it to journalists and opinion-makers who published it under their own names and financed the publication of anti-communist literature—for example Orwell and Bertrand Russell. The Labour Party was directly involved, as Healey provided a list of reliable socialist leaders who might publish this material.[124] Paolo Treves, who in 1945 tried to have the Labour Party provide a regular supply of socialist articles for the reformist journal *Critica Sociale*, was one of the first two Italian socialists on the distribution list for IRD material.

The Socialist International also had a close relationship with the IRD. The IRD distributed material from its publications and the socialist parties employed material from the IRD, a relationship that lasted throughout the 1950s and 1960s—and probably even longer. The relationship between the IRD and the Socialist International shows the intermingling of state and non-state agencies, of propaganda and socialist organisations. For example, Frank J.C. Mennel, Denis Healey's deputy,[125] later joined the IRD and cooperated with Albert Carthy, who was secretary of the Socialist International from 1957 to 1969. Before, he was international secretary of the TUC and helped rebuild the German trade unions.[126] As they came from the same background, in the 1960s they had a mutually beneficial relationship and exchanged propaganda material.[127]

Other instruments of informal socialist diplomacy were delegations from Britain or invitations to Britain, which increased the prestige of the people involved. Tony Benn accurately describes this phenomenon:

> Petrilli [president of IRI] was a bright, dynamic managerial type, on a visit to build up his reputation, because he was engaged on a major project in the *Mezzogiorno*—the Alfa Romeo plant he was trying to get agreed in the south—and he wanted to be seen as a major international figure with full press coverage. This is a characteristic of Ministers visiting another country. Everybody falls into the spirit of the game: that is to say, you recognise that you won't make much progress in the talks, but you understand the Minister's need to build himself up at home and therefore all press facilities are laid on.[128]

Influence is a two-way street: the British Government believed it could use socialist contacts to project influence abroad and local socialists believed they would get a fair hearing and sympathy from the British Government thanks to their contacts. 'As International Secretary of the Labour Party I appeared to socialists abroad, both in Government and opposition, as an obvious channel for influencing the Labour Government in Britain'.[129] The SFIO and the French trade union federation had an office in London[130] and, despite the high costs, the SPD had its own London office headed by Wilhelm Sander and Hertha Gotthelf, a friend of James Middleton, secretary of the Labour Party in the 1930s.[131] Insall has shown how relations between the British Labour Party and the DNA improved understanding and cooperation between the two countries.[132] A member of the Polish embassy, Szapiro, maintained contacts with the Labour Party, and Healey encouraged the Polish socialists to open an office in London.[133]

4 DISCIPLINE AND DISSENT IN THE LABOUR PARTY

The identification with the Labour Government created the issue on how the Labour Party should treat opinions that were critical of its policies and ministers. A distinctive feature of the International Department under Healey was its involvement in what Eric Shaw calls 'party management'— the management by leaders of threats to internal cohesion. In the 1920s, the communist threat stimulated the expansion of party machinery to collect information and control the cadres through education.[134] Party organisation was defined by managerial control, enforced in three ways: defining ideological frontiers, preserving organisational integrity and controlling constituent parts.[135] The internationalisation of domestic quarrels defined how international relations were managed. In 1945, the International Department had little disciplinary power, but fighting communist disruptive tactics became a major task after 1948. In 1953, it was at the peak of its power: the International Secretary bypassed the National Agent and delivered a list of eighteen organisations (friendship societies with communist nations and peace groups) to be added to the Proscribed List—the penalty for associating with an organisation on this list was expulsion.[136] It was known that this information came from the Foreign Office. These disciplinary measures had a dubious legitimacy in the party constitution, as they punished not just being affiliated to these organisations, but also establishing contacts and attending their events, such as the Vienna Peace Conference.

The original power of the International Department was exclusive representation of the movement abroad. In a multipolar party, every faction tries to develop international contacts to increase its prestige, define its identity and establish supremacy. In a party with strict discipline, the dominant coalition is the single voice for the party abroad and any contact the minority has with a non-recognised organisation is treated as a disciplinary matter. A more pluralist party develops international relations not exclusively with the parties ideologically similar to the dominant coalition but also others, as a concession to the minority. So dissent is resolved through political compromise not disciplinary actions.

The problem of who had the authority to speak for British Labour was always central. In the 1920s, Citrine complained that Gillies worked without supervision from the TUC. Later, Laski and Noel-Baker accused Gillies of stretching his political authority about German collective guilt. Gillies' dismissal in 1945 was a response to a perceived abuse of power. Then, the Labour leadership contested Laski's authority to represent them. As mentioned, there was confusion about for whom Laski, *Tribune* or Morgan Phillips spoke. The urgent need to end individual initiatives encouraged the nomination of an International Secretary as official representative.[137]

For example, the issue of the fusion between communists and social democrats in occupied Germany was a divisive issue for Labour. Christopher Mayhew represented the Labour Party at the congress of the German social democrats in Bavaria, where this issue was debated. As the Germans waited for Labour's lead, Mayhew discouraged fusion, as per Morgan Phillips's suggestion.[138] Labour's leftists and centrists criticised Mayhew, arguing he lacked the authority to make the choice, but Bevin rewarded him and made him his Parliamentary Under-Secretary. Zilliacus, the voice of the pro-Soviet British left critical of Bevin, collected the signatures of 27 MPs to send a message of goodwill to the Congress of the German social democrats in the Soviet Occupation Zone, who had been forced to accept the fusion with the communists into the Socialist Unity Party (SED). Zilliacus said he wanted to show that the Labour Party was not opposed to working-class unity on the Continent. The British occupation forces in Germany warned that that these MPs did not represent the whole party. Even Jennie Lee condemned the message sent to the Berlin Congress, arguing that the communists could not be trusted, but it was a matter of political consideration, as nothing could be done to prevent Zilliacus from 'collecting and publishing the signatures of colleagues who share his views'.[139]

In March 1946, the International Sub-Committee refused to rule over Labour MPs visiting Poland,[140] but the visit proved very damaging for the reputation of the British Government.[141] Labour MPs who attacked the Government during their visits abroad had become a serious problem, so much so that in October 1946 Healey spoke of 'deliberate sabotage abroad by Labour MPs of Government or Party policy'.[142] Open dissent against majority decisions was framed as indiscipline. In April 1947, the Foreign Office produced a list of more than ten occasions when a Labour MP visiting either Eastern Europe or Greece had embarrassed the government.[143] Some of these politicians would be expelled later, such as Platts-Mills, Zilliacus, Leslie Solley. The British ambassador in Prague complained that the visits by British MPs made his work harder.[144] Zilliacus constantly contested Government policy on Poland. Other 'disloyal MPs'—the Foreign Office's label for them—were people like John David Mack, who had recurrent but not systematic bouts of dissent. Mack rebelled on Greece in December 1944 and signed the 'Nenni telegram' in March 1948. He travelled to Bulgaria and Romania in 1946 to support the British recognition of their Governments.[145] Mack purposefully avoided informing Bevin, 'who would make me take blooming Michael Foot and I refuse to have any reactionaries [sic!] of that sort about'.[146] However, there was also sabotage through ignorance by individuals—for example, James Callaghan in the Soviet Union[147]—who made comments that contradicted the Government line or gave the impression that the countries they visited were free democracies. Some of these MPs took part in public meetings organised by front organisations, like the Friends of Democratic Poland.

McNeil proposed to increase the role of the International Department of the Labour Party in selecting and briefing the delegates to send abroad.[148] An official in the Foreign Office proposed to use the Labour Party machinery to undermine the 'sinner' MPs:

> My own opinion is that Transport House should stir up criticism among Labour supporters in the constituencies of these people. I don't know if it can be done, but that would be effective. So would a shoal of shocked letters to the Daily Herald, etc.[149]

Delegates who were more loyal were selected and Healey briefed them in coordination with the Foreign Office. For example, when Harry Earnshaw visited Italy in April 1946, he received a long list of 'Questions on which NO opinion should be offered', which included most questions of internal politics and the Peace Treaty.[150] Healey also actively worked to discredit fellow traveller MPs and Laski among the Continental socialists.

Healey and Morgan Phillips had to travel extensively around Europe. Monopolising representation was the precondition to punishing rebellion—which British diplomats insistently demanded—as it became easier to isolate obstinate dissenters. Just before the Prague Coup, Attlee and Bevin concluded that it was impossible to legally bar British subjects abroad from criticising the Government, but the party could impose its own discipline.[151] The diplomatic missions would send information about the 'disloyal MPs' to Morgan Phillips, who created dossiers with which to expel some and intimidate the rest.

In the new disciplinary regime, the International Department was made responsible for spotting front organisations like friendship societies and peace societies[152] and Healey informing members and constituency parties.[153] Although the Foreign Office considered reforming them with 'two or three top-notchers' of the Labour Party, McNeil concluded the only way was for respectable people to desert them and warn responsible but ill-informed people.[154] From one episode, we know that MI5 and the Foreign Office provided the information.[155] The control was not just about communist activities, the International Department was also responsible for warning members not to join the European Movement because of Churchill's role.[156]

The increased authority of the International Department influenced the most important and famous insubordination during the Attlee government, the 'Nenni telegram'. In March 1948 Morgan Phillips and Denis Healey tried unsuccessfully to convince Nenni not to ally with the communists.[157] They then offered recognition to the splinter anti-communist socialists; Healey also directly appealed to the Italians through the BBC overseas service. Thirty-seven Labour MPs, led by Zilliacus and Platts-Mills, signed a telegram to Nenni wishing him victory. The party immediately denounced the episode as a disciplinary breach, 16 MPs recanted their support and some were expelled.[158] The episode was similar with what happened with German socialists in 1946—many signatories were the same—but what had changed was not just the international context but also the party organisation. The International Department had acquired the authority to determine which international organisations party members were allowed to interact with and going against its judgement had become a punishable offence.

The power of the International Department was limited and its constitutional position ambiguous. With the Nenni Telegram, disciplinary action was possible because the Labour left agreed with the leadership on anti-communism. In 1946, Michael Foot saw the Soviet subversive techniques first-hand in Iran and many European social democrats worked as foreign correspondents for *Tribune*, including the co-editor German socialist Evelyn Anderson, who had witnessed the annihilation of the German social democrats in the Soviet occupation zone. In 1948 and 1949, *Tribune* supported Government policies in Italy, Berlin and the Atlantic Treaty, leading to the resignation of Mikardo, a leading leftist.[159] Generally speaking, the *Tribune* left was in agreement with the Labour left over which organisations were respectable for party members to associate with.

This changed in the early 1950s, when the Bevanites developed their own international network of left-wing socialists outside the Socialist International, starting conversations with Yugoslav communists, Japanese socialists and Nenni. Crossman used Nenni's opinions on foreign affairs—which he misattributed to Stalin—as a basis for a new foreign policy.[160] Once again cultivating relations with parties outside the circle of respectability served as a mark of distinction for dissenters. Imposing harsh disciplinary measures on national politicians over issues of limited practical importance was politically unwise, thus managing dissent took the road of conciliation. Gaitskell opened to left-wing socialists like Nenni and started talking with the communists about the possibility of détente. The Gaitskell-Healey Plan for the neutralisation of Eastern Europe and the 1959 journey to Moscow were meant to heal the divisions of Europe but above all the divisions of the party. This was a return to the practice of 1945 and 1946, when the International Department had increased its involvement in the areas the minority was interested in for the sake of party unity, for example inviting Nenni to London in 1945 on the request of Laski.[161] The summoning of the first International Socialist Conference in Clacton was meant to satisfy the requests of the left:

> This position of the Labour Party is influence by fundamental considerations of internal politics. They believed that the tension between communists and socialists in Europe put the unity of the Labour Party in jeopardy and make a split possible. The right-wing would seek a new form of cooperation with the Conservatives, forcing the left-wing to join the communists in opposition. There are signs of this anxiety in some of the recent press.[162]

The International Department was also involved in ideological regulation. Denis Healey produced a number of pamphlets on controversial issues, like *Cards on the Table*, a defence of Bevin's policy answering *Keep Left*. Healey also wrote *Feet on the Ground* and *European Unity*, setting the policy on European integration. They were not normative documents, but they suggested which policy the leadership preferred. The ambiguity allowed a retreat from controversies, which Dalton did for *Cards on the Table*—as Zilliacus and Crossman attacked it because it had not been approved by the NEC or the Policy Sub-Committee.[163] Attlee did the same for *Feet on the Ground* and *European Unity*, because they used language that was offensive to Continental Europeans.

Leaving the International Secretary as the only representative had drawbacks: there were fewer occasions for embarrassment but they were more dangerous. In December 1949, Healey attacked the Italian Deputy Prime Minister, in a public congress and through the BBC. It was impossible to present Healey as a non-representative, since a year before he had addressed the Italians against Nenni.[164]

On another occasion the embarrassment was not of a political nature. In 1947, the Foreign Office and Bevin pressured the British Council to sponsor a series of lectures by one C. Duley, president of the Beckenham Labour Party, who had lived for a long time in South America.[165] His visit to Uruguay was a success, but his visit to Argentina was a disaster,[166] as the

PARTIES AND PEOPLE, THE LABOUR PARTY AND THE INTERNATIONAL... 71

local cultural associations protested over his political attitude and his contacts with local labour groups that were close to the Peronista government. However, similar cases in Finland and Italy suggest that there was an element of class prejudice: Anglophile societies were often social clubs for the well-to-do with a conservative bias.[167] Duley was very much unlike the lecturers the British Council used to send to South America.

The close link between international fraternal relations and party discipline is essential to understand the evolution of the International Socialist Conference. First, affiliation to the Socialist International granted great legitimacy to the main socialist party against the splinter groups. Second, after the Prague coup (21–25 February 1948) the International Socialist Conference no longer admitted pro-communist parties and it became an exclusive club which in 1951 adopted an anti-communist charter that prospective members had to accept. The Socialist International was the instrument with which the parties with greater Government responsibility—the British, the Dutch, the Scandinavian—could exercise a form of ideological control over the less reliable parties. They chose to interact only with the respectable parties that had accepted their conditions.

International fraternal relations were opportunities and risks. Party leaders could not control the external environment, even more so with foreign entanglements. The management of international fraternal relations, through the creation of rules and institutions, aimed not just to facilitate the circular exchange of influences, but also to control it.

5 THE INTERNATIONAL NETWORK OF LEADERS AND SECRETARIES

Despite taking the Labour Party as a model, each socialist party had a unique culture, policies, organisation and internal power relations, which made it similar or distinct from the British in some way. A comparison with the Labour Party in the management of international fraternal relations will reveal these differences. This is an 'encompassing comparison', which according to Tilly would 'select locations within the structure or process and explain similarities or differences among those locations as consequences of their relationship to the whole'.[168] Every party had someone responsible for international contacts, but their authority varied according to party organisation and tradition. It is possible to create a typology of the official in charge of international fraternal relations. The topology here proposed uses the political authority and the age of the people responsible for international fraternal relations as the two parameters. The people responsible could be a party bureaucrat, a sub-leader or a party leader; they could be young and upcoming, mature or veteran. All intersections were possible.

The party bureaucrat was responsible for the international representation in parties with a large organisation and specialised bureaucracy. While many parties had an International Department, the International Secretary usually left major political decisions to the person truly in charge, a sub-leader or the party leader. Only in the Labour Party and the SAP, an ordinary functionary—respectively Healey and Kaj Björk—had taken over control without having a source of political authority other than his position in the bureaucracy.

Representation by a sub-leader was the most common model. The sub-leader was a member of the leadership who was ultimately subordinate to the chief party leader. The authority and power of the sub-leader did not come exclusively from their responsibility for international fraternal relations. The sub-leader could be the party secretary—like Haakon Lie in Norway – the deputy leader and presumed successor—like Erich Ollenhauer in Germany – the editor of the party newspaper—like Victor Larock in Belgium—or an important intellectual. Choosing a sub-leader had many advantages: he—rarely she—knew the attitude of the leadership and had the authority to make important decisions in international meetings. Keeping the position in the inner circle of the leadership meant that the assets deriving from the position went to a member of the dominant coalition. This could serve to legitimise a future leader or it could be offered as a compensation to appease a potential adversary.

The party leader representing the national movement was common for the Second International and it would come back in 1960s, with jet diplomacy. In the 1940s, however, this was the exception. The presence of the party leader showed the dedication of the party, avoided minor functionaries undertaking important commitments, was a source of prestige in the party and for public opinion and, above all, prevented a potential adversary from taking the job and reaping the benefits. The obvious downside was the time required: a party leader had other more pressing responsibilities, especially in government. Tage Erlander attended only the Copenhagen Conference, which was carefully choreographed and covered by the press; Attlee did not attend any international socialist event while Prime Minister, becoming active as Opposition Leader. Apart from small parties which had few people available, the party leader took this responsibility only in the French and Austrian cases.

In addition, it has to be noted that many parties had 'socialist ambassadors' in London—usually a minor figure in their country's embassy or a foreign correspondent—who kept regular contact but did not have much political authority.

The age of the person in charge and the stage of their political career also revealed the mode of representation. A veteran was chosen to emphasise continuity, which was important after the war had exterminated entire sections of the socialist family and trust was required to speak frankly. Veterans could lend their authority to the delegation or the entire conference. Some veterans were no longer in the inner circle, so giving them a mission abroad could be an inoffensive consolation prize—although the Labour Party found out with Laski that it was not so inoffensive. Conversely, young people might have found the task a way to jumpstart their career and they often spoke English, the new lingua franca, unlike the older generation, either manual workers without a formal education or speakers of French and German. In addition, it is physiological that when a dominant coalition has been in charge of the party for a long time, a new, ambitious generation either takes over the party or is co-opted into the leadership.

The choice between young and old, between bureaucrat, sub-leader or party leader ultimately came down to the internal power distribution. Obviously, different kind of people managed international fraternal relations at the same time; what mattered was the predominant pattern, which evolved according to the transformations of the party.

French socialism was the other major pole of the international socialist movement, a necessary partner for cooperation but representative of different ideas and practices. Unlike the Labour Party, the post-war era of the SFIO was marked by crisis and the beginning of decline. French socialism was shaken by the failure of the Popular Front and deep divisions over the Munich Agreement and the Vichy Government. While the prestige acquired in the Resistance and by Leon Blum personally allowed the rebuilding of the SFIO, the French Communist Party became the strongest force of the left, dislodged the socialists from the working-class and the trade unions and continuously delegitimised them. Blum and the new resistance leadership tried a cautious ideological revision to adapt to the new situation.[169] As the French state became more democratic, created a mixed economy and assumed social responsibilities, the SFIO had to abandon its ideology of intransigence towards capitalist society and the bourgeois state, to become a natural party of government. This revised socialism would emphasise humanism and democracy and downplay Marxism and class struggle.

However, the *blumiste* secretary Daniel Mayer fell at the August 1946 Congress, substituted by the leftist Guy Mollet. The leadership of French socialism gained legitimacy from preserving ideological purity and Marxism. By challenging the original identity, Blum angered the federations and rank and file, which wanted a party of militants for socialist transformation instead of a party representing society, controlled by electors. The actual interpretation and practical policies varied considerably, but, since all factions proclaimed loyalty to Marxism, it guaranteed party unity. Mollet won the leadership and kept it for more than 20 years as a guardian of orthodoxy, even when he made compromises and concessions. The result was a contradiction between rhetorical radicalism and extreme moderation in the practice of coalition governments, which for the Labour Party was merely a sign of the dogmatism and opportunism of the intellectuals controlling the party.[170] To satisfy the rank and file, Mollet regularly had to reassert his commitment to socialism, which included intense involvement in international activities.

This complex situation was reflected in representation abroad. The SFIO's socialist ambassador in London was Louis Levy, a correspondent for *Le Populaire* and representative of French socialism in exile.[171] After Liberation, the French were represented by veterans emphasising continuity: Bracke, Levy, Grumbach and Vincent Auriol.[172] Leon Blum had moral prestige and prominence like no other socialist in France and Europe, as recognised by the invitation to address the Labour Annual Conference in 1946, as the spokesperson for the entire Continent.[173] Internal upheavals and two elections in 1946 prevented the SFIO from taking an active part in international fraternal relations. When in 1947 the new leadership tried to take back control, Levy was reluctant to renounce his autonomy.[174] However, the Labour Party was not satisfied with Levy, as he was not aware of the line of the SFIO leadership and he lacked authority.[175]

When Mollet became the new secretary, Salomon Grumbach and Brutelle were the members the *blumiste* centre that accepted the new direction for the sake of party unity.[176] They were both involved in international fraternal relations, especially Grumbach, who was an expert in international questions and a veteran of many international conferences.[177] Making Grumbach responsible was Mollet's concession to a member of his coalition, in addition to a recognition of his expertise and prestige. Another concession was changing party policy from the anti-German position of Mayer to Grumbach's pro-German stance.[178]

While preparing for the Zurich International Socialist Conference (6–9 June 1947), Levy complained that Mollet had not yet met his international comrades.[179] At the Zurich conference, Mollet stood on the sidelines, leaving the task of leading the French delegation to Grumbach. However, Grumbach backed his friend Nenni against the Italian social democrats. Mollet looked with favour at the Italian left-wing social democrats and hoped to build a leftist bloc of Western parties, so he stripped Grumbach of his responsibilities and gave them to Leon Boutbien, a left-wing socialist who was friendly to Italian left-wing social democrats.[180] While the old Grumbach embodied optimism and hope, the young Boutbien expressed pessimism. However, Grumbach would still play a part, especially when Mollet did not want direct exposure—as with the reconciliation with the SPD or in the drafting of the Frankfurt Declaration, when Mollet failed to have his proposals approved.[181]

In 1947, the SFIO suffered many setbacks. In the post-war euphoria, recruitment was chaotic, but when the regional federations—the real seat of power—took back control over membership, they discovered that numbers had been inflated—according to Devin, also to increase the standing of the party in the international movement.[182] The organisation was weak and finances were precarious. Mayer's right-wing was still an organised threat, while the left-wing abandoned Mollet, because of his anti-communism. With Blum ill, Mollet consciously chose to substitute him in international representation—despite the recent lack of interest[183]—paying attention to European integration and to rebuilding the Socialist International.[184] This meant delegating relations with the regional federations to his deputy secretaries, Pierre Commin and Brutelle. For example, in June 1948, Mollet gave up visiting the Bordeaux federation to attend the International Socialist Conference in Vienna. As Devin notes, Mollet defined the image of the SFIO with foreign socialists, often to the worse. His interest in ideological debates and safeguarding orthodoxy often led to the isolation of the French.[185] While there was an international secretary, Robert Pontillon, from the 1950s to 1979, he was an ineffective low-level official, as real control fell to Mollet and later Mitterand.

The 1930s saw the generational struggle in the Belgian Socialist Party (PSB) between the reformist old guard of Vandervelde, Huysmans and De Brouckère and a new generation in favour of Neo-socialism or '*socialisme nationale*'.[186] The most important figure, Henri De Man, proposed the radical restructuring of the party: he rejected Marxism and class struggle, emphasised the nature of socialism as a moral imperative, encouraged the alliance with Catholics and middle classes to form a national community. Socialism was not the final goal but something to be realised within the confines of the nation-state through 'structural reforms' and the *Plan du Travail*: nationalisation of monopolies, mixed economy, expansion of internal markets, full employment and a more efficient state.

De Man's ideas foreshadowed many features of the post-war social democratic compromise but he was irredeemably tainted by his collaboration with Nazism. The post-De Man leadership—Max Buset, Van Acker, Paul-Henri Spaak—allied with the pre-De Man leadership, keeping centralised control over the organisation and leaving little room for debate. There was no repetition of the violent generational struggle of the 1930s or even much ideological debate—as Victor Larock said, Buset and Van Acker had better things to do than explore theory. Attempts to radically open up the party by diluting its working-class and socialist identity—as in the Netherlands—came to nothing: the basic programme of 1894, Marxist and anti-clerical, was maintained. In a strongly segmented society, the party leadership had to guard its community while compromising in government. Rejecting *socialisme nationale* led to a return to traditional socialist internationalism. More than any other parties, the PSB struggled for internationalism in the socialist community. Buset was personally involved in the proposal to rebuild the Socialist International in 1947. In addition to De Brouckère, the regular representative of the PSB was Victor Larock, a younger sub-leader and editor of *Le Peuple*, who took part in the most important moments of the Socialist International in this period.

In the Western Occupied Zones of Germany, the SPD was rebuilt under the charismatic leadership of Kurt Schumacher. While he had ambitions to build the socialist movement as a cross-class alliance based on spiritual principles, he had to rely on the old party cadres for organisation and party traditions for legitimacy.[187] While he was involved in international contacts when the Germans had to win back their admission, he later delegated matters to Erich Ollenhauer. Ollenhauer had had long experience in international fraternal relations as a secretary of the Youth International and then in exile. In both the Belgian and German parties, continuity in international representation signalled the tight control of the dominant coalition.

In the post-war era, Dutch socialism completed its renewal, started in 1933 with the criticism of the SPD for failing to stop Hitler.[188] Indeed, the religious socialist Willem Banning used the SPD as the negative example of the socialism he fought at home: excessive emphasis on the working-class, which was not large enough to win power, while dismissing the middle class and ignoring nationalism and the spiritual values shaping the life of the common people. The march towards reformism and anti-communism was confirmed by a new programme with less ideological baggage in 1937. In 1938, Koos Vorrink backed Friedrich Stampfer's request for an ideological renewal of the SPD, another intersection of national and international spheres of socialism. After the war, Dutch socialism was under the dual leadership of Willem Drees and Koos Vorrink, dealing with government and party matters respectively. They employed their prestige to reshape socialism into a responsible force of government. In 1946, the Dutch Social Democratic Workers' Party fused with progressive liberals and Protestants to form the Dutch Labour Party (PvdA), following the British model. The new party abandoned references to Marxism and an exclusive working-class culture. It was an attempt to break the 'pillars' of Dutch society, the subcultures of religious, class or ideological nature, which commanded the loyalty of their members through a network of organisations that regulated every aspect of their life. While this ambitious goal fell short, ideological transformation made the PvdA 'respectable', allowing for the possibility of coalition governments with the confessional and bourgeois parties.

In addition to Vorrink, who made important contributions to international conferences, a regular representative was the sub-leader, Marinus Van der Goes van Naters, who succeeded Drees as chairman of the parliamentary group. He played a huge part in the Italian question and the debate over European integration. In 1948, the German exile Alfred Mozer became International Secretary, but Van der Goes was still responsible for international fraternal relations. However, in January 1951 Van der Goes clashed with Drees over the issue of New Guinea and he had to resign his chairmanship.[189] His role in international fraternal relations was reduced—he was still responsible for European questions—and Mozer represented the party at the Socialist International.[190] Due to shifting power relations, representation passed from a sub-leader to a party bureaucrat in the PvdA.

The Swedish Social Democratic Labour Party (SAP) had an arrangement similar to the Labour Party: both parties dominated their government and had a strong organisation. The SAP sent Gustav Möller, a veteran of international fraternal relations to the Clacton Conference—he attended the Berne International Congress in 1919 and was the SAP's representative at the LSI—who was also one of the great intellectuals of the party and as minister for social affairs, a designer of the Swedish Welfare State.[191] The SAP sent a signal of continuity and attention for international socialism but, above all, it showed its interest in proposing Sweden as a model to the movement. In the following years, however, the SAP kept a low profile because of differences with the pro-communist socialists of the East, the Marxist socialists of the Continent and the federalists. Another reason was Swedish neutrality, which managed to irritate anti-Germans and anti-communists in equal measure. In addition, the party had little interest in theory and foreign policy, having devoted all its attention to studying how to use the state machinery to achieve socialist goals in internal politics.[192] The SAP sent ministers and first-rate politicians as its representatives in the meetings of Nordic cooperation, as the other parties were close in ideology and government responsibilities, but at the international socialist meetings the party was represented by bureaucrats. In order to help the General secretary Sven Andersson, at the end of 1946 the party nominated an International Secretary, Kaj Björk, a minor functionary. Björk was very successful in having the International Socialist Conference accept the Swedish line on many issues and he enjoyed wide freedom of action in managing international fraternal relations because of the leadership's lack of interest. Things changed in the mid-1950s, when Prime Minister Tage Erlander and his young secretary, Olof Palme, took a more active role to fully exploit détente.

In Norway, the party secretary, Haakon Lie, chaired its international committee, whose members included the major figures of the party, trade unions and press, in addition to the Minister for Foreign Affairs.[193] Haakon Lie was fully in control of the international fraternal relations of the Norwegian Labour Party (DNA) and he became one of the most active players of the Socialist International. Björk was often available to represent all the Scandinavian parties, which did not have the means or the time to attend all the minor meetings. Thanks to regular contacts and ideological similarities, the Norwegian, Swedish and Danish parties formed a Scandinavian bloc on most issues—but not the Atlantic Treaty—and was one of the most influential centres of the socialist family.

In Austria, the SPÖ was rebuilt by older social democrats who had withdrawn from politics in 1934 and revolutionary socialists who had gone underground—though there was not an Austrian resistance movement. Karl Renner, who had become Prime Minister of the provisional government, established a privileged line with the Labour Party through Walter Wodak. Wodak had gone into exile in the 1930s and joined the British army, coming to Vienna as a member of the occupation forces. He got in touch with Renner and returned to London first as his quasi-official representative, then as press attaché of the newly established diplomatic representation. His position was peculiar, as his party mission had a secondary importance to his diplomatic activities to defend Austrian interests. The SPÖ created an international department in April 1946, with Julius Deutsch as secretary.[194] Wodak continued to act as the permanent representative in London and he could attend international meetings when the party did not have the money to send an envoy.[195]

For the first International Socialist Conference, the SPÖ decided to send the party president and vice-chancellor Schärf, Oscar Pollak, editor of the party newspaper, and Scharf, one of the joint secretaries. Because of the Labour Party decision to limit delegations to two members, Scharf was excluded,[196] although it was also a political choice, as Scharf was the leader of the leftist, pro-communist wing of the party. Oscar Pollak would have been the ideal person to conduct international fraternal relations: he had spent the war in Britain and the British knew him. The Foreign Office had helped him return to Vienna and they came to regret this choice: they considered Pollak 'a Bourbon'—a representative of pre-war left-wing socialism, an anachronism too distant from Renner and Schärf—a 'Viennese intellectual' with no links to the trade unions and one of the 'Jewish émigrés' who were not well received in Austria.[197] In addition, his violent anti-clericalism made coalition with the Christian Democrats turbulent and his violent anti-communism drew the hatred of the Soviet occupation forces, who did not lose any occasion to harass the social democratic newspaper.[198] The participation of the party leader, Schärf, at the international conferences was the only way to push Pollak to the sidelines.[199] Thus, Schärf found himself in a position where he had to control international fraternal relations to increase his preeminent position in the party, but also in Austria, since good relations with the Labour Government were prestigious. The Austrians gave a lot of publicity to the fact the Bevin's invitation of Schärf had been the first official visit by an Austrian to Great Britain after the war.[200] Wodak had a quarrel with Healey because the press release of the Bournemouth Conference had not mentioned Schärf.[201]

The next chapter will deal with the peculiar situation of Eastern European social democrats. The Italian case defies this classification, because party was less important than faction. Faction leaders employed their envoys to build their international standing and sabotage their opponents.

Notes

1. J. Price (1945) *International Labour Movement* (London: Oxford University Press), 167–173.
2. E. Pearce (2002) *Denis Healey: A Life in our Times* (London: Little Brown), 547.
3. W. Wodak to A. Schärf, 21 December 1945, W. Wodak (1980) *Diplomatie zwischen Parteiproporz und Weltpolitik: Briefe, Dokumente und Memoranden aus dem Nachlass Walter Wodaks 1945–1950* (Salzburg: Neugebauer), 23.
4. F. Malfatti to P. Nenni, 14 January 1946, Fondazione Pietro Nenni (FPN), Pietro Nenni, b.31, f.1547.
5. J. Polasky (1995) *The Democratic Socialism of Emile Vandervelde: Between Reform and Revolution* (Oxford: Berg), 191–199; 215–217.
6. Denis Healey, who won immediate likeability by just not being him, called Gillies 'a cantankerous Scot who distrusted foreigners and hated all Germans' D. Healey (1990) *The Time of My Life* (London: Penguin), 74.
7. C. Collette (1998) *The International Faith: Labour's Attitude to European Socialism* (Aldershot: Ashgate), 12–27; 46–62.
8. H.R. Winkler (2005) *British Labour Seeks a Foreign Policy, 1900–1940* (New Brunswick: Transaction), 38.
9. R. Vickers (2003) *The Labour Party and the World* (Manchester: Manchester University Press), 91–92; 113.
10. Collette, *The International Faith*, 87–92.
11. P.J. Noel-Baker. 'Memorandum concerning the "private and confidential" notes on the policy of German social democracy during the last world war and on the eve of the Third Reich', [November 1941]; H. Laski to P. Noel-Baker, 19 November 1941, Labour History Archive and Study Centre, People's History Museum, Manchester (LHASC), Labour Party (LP), International Sub-Committee, Minutes and Documents, 1941. Minutes of the meeting of the International Sub-Committee, 24 March 1942, LHASC, LP, International Sub-Committee, Minutes and Documents, 1942.
12. Laski and Gillies fought again in the 1943 ([William Gillies], 'Draft Circular'; Harold J. Laski, 'Comments on Mr. Gillies' Draft Circular', 22 August 1943; W. Gillies, 'Notes in Reply to Harold J. Laski', LHASC, LP, International Sub-Committee, Minutes and Documents, 1943).

13. Balthazar mentions the strengthening of the party officials (H. Balthazar (1972) 'L'Internationale Socialiste, Les debats de Londres en 1940–1941', *Cahiers d'histoire de la seconde guerre mondiale*, 2, 194).
14. B. Pimlott (1985), *Hugh Dalton* (London: Cape), 389–393.
15. [Hugh Dalton], 'Post-War Settlement', LHASC, LP, International Sub-Committee, Minutes & Documents, 1943. [Hugh Dalton], 'International Post-War Settlement', Second Draft; Minutes of the International Sub-Committee, 18 April 1944; 'Annual Conference'; 'Draft Resolution by the Rt. Hon. Hugh Dalton, MP on International Post-War Settlement for Annual Conference', LHASC, LP, International Sub-Committee, Minutes and Documents, 1944.
16. Minutes of the International Sub-Committee, 18 April 1944, LHASC, LP, International Sub-Committee, Minutes and Documents, 1944.
17. Entry, 13 and 14 November 1944; Entry, 16 January 1945, Ben Pimlott (ed.) (1986) *The Second World War Diary of Hugh Dalton 1940–45* (London: Jonathan Cape), 806–807; 823–824.
18. Malfatti, 'Conferenza dell'Internazionale Socialista, Londra 3–5 marzo 1945', Archivio Centrale dello Stato, Roma (ACS), Fondo Nicolò Carandini (NC), b.6.
19. Entry, 16 January 1945; 16 February 1945, Ben Pimlott *The Second World War Diary of Hugh Dalton*, 823–824; 831.
20. I. Kramnick, B. Sheerman (1993) *Harold Laski, A Life on the Left* (London: Hamilton), 483–496.
21. Kramnick and Sheerman, *Harold Laski*, 493.
22. Foreign Office to Brussels, 29 May 1945, The National Archives, Kew (TNA), FO 371/48988-Z5526.
23. Archivio Cinematografico Luce, Istituto Nazionale LUCE, Notiziario Nuova Luce NL010. http://patrimonio.archivioluce.com/luce-web/detail/IL5000094655/2/firenze-teatro-comunale-24-congresso-nazionale-del-partito-socialista-italiano-unita-proletaria.html (accessed 17 April 2018).
24. Kramnick and Sheerman, *Harold Laski*, 492.
25. 'Warschau – Bericht des polnischen Sozialisten S.Gross über den III. Parteitag der SPÖ in Wien', 30 October 1947, in P. Heumos (ed.) (2004), *Europäischer Sozialismus im Kalten Krieg: Briefe und Berichte 1944–1948* (Frankfurt: Campus), 21.
26. G. Devin (1993), *L'Internationale socialiste: histoire et sociologie du socialisme internationale: 1945–1990* (Paris: Presses de la Fondation national des sciences politiques), 328–329. D. Hanely (1983) 'Un socialisme aux couleurs de l'Angleterre : le parti travailliste et l'Internationale Socialiste depuis 1945', in H. Portelli (ed.), *L'Internationale socialiste* (Paris: Les Éditions Ouvrières). 59.

27. M. Van der Goes van Naters (1980) *Met en tegen de tijd* (Amsterdam: Arbeiderspers), 200.
28. Healey, *Time of my life*, 73–74.
29. A. Thorpe (2014) 'Locking out the Communists: The Labour party and the Communist party, 1939–46', *Twentieth Century British History*, 25, 2, 248–250.
30. A. Thorpe (2009) *Parties at War: Political Organization in Second World War Britain* (Oxford: Oxford University Press), 45–48.
31. Malfatti to Nenni, 14 January 1946, FPN, Pietro Nenni, b.31, f.1547.
32. Entry, 20 May 1946, B. Pimlott (1986) *The Political Diary of Hugh Dalton: 1918–40, 1945–60* (London: Cape), 372.
33. Minutes of the International Sub-Committee, 15 July 1947; Minutes of the International Sub-Committee, 18 November 1947, LHASC, LP, International Department (ID), Denis Healey's Papers (DH), 12.
34. J. Lee (1981) *My Life with Nye* (Harmondsworth: Penguin Books), 168–172.
35. 'Note on the International Department', July 1948, LHASC, LP, International Sub-Committee, Minutes and Documents, 1948.
36. Labour Party Annual Conference Report (LPACR) 1947, 18–19.
37. Lee, *My Life with Nye*, 168–172.
38. LPACR 1950, 23–28.
39. E. Randall, International exchange of party officials, *Labour organiser*, April 1950. E. Randall, A cheap holiday, *Labour organiser*, April 1950. A suggestion, *Labour organiser*, April 1950. E. Randall, International Socialist Solidarity, *Labour Organiser'*, May 1950.
40. Minutes of the International Sub-Committee 19 October 1948, LHASC, LP, ID, DH, 12.
41. A. Levi, Se tornerà il vento laborista, *La Stampa*, 5 April 1986.
42. E. Healey (2007) *Part of the Pattern: Memoirs of a Wife at Westminster* (Oxford : ISIS), 102.
43. Entry, 7 January 1952, Pimlott (ed.), *The Political Diary of Hugh Dalton*, 577.
44. H. Gotthelf to J. Middleton, 7 November 1952, LHASC, LP, James Middleton papers, M84.
45. Entry, 23 January 1952, Dalton, *The Political Diary of Hugh Dalton*, 578.
46. Healey, *Time of My Life*, 77.
47. Entry, 13 and 14 November 1944, Dalton, *The Second World War Diary of Hugh Dalton*, 806–807. A comparison between the drafts and the final version reveals that most changes were about language not content.
48. 'Notes for Mr Sam Watson 31 January 1949', LHASC, LP, ID, DH, 13, 03.

49. Entry, 16 June 1950, Dalton, *The Political Diary of Hugh Dalton*, 475–478. Pearce, *Denis Healey*, 128–138. R.M. Douglas (2004) *The Labour Party, Nationalism and Internationalism, 1939–1951* (London: Routledge), 247–248; 264.
50. Healey, *The Time of My Life*, 71.
51. Likewise, Christopher Mayhew, Parliamentary Under-Secretary for Foreign Affairs lost his seat in 1950 but received Bevin's seat as a reward for his work in the Foreign Office.
52. Healey, *The Time of My Life*, 78.
53. Entry, 7 January 1952, Dalton, *The Political Diary of Hugh Dalton*, 577.
54. Healey to H. Dalton, 12 February 1946, LHASC, LP, ID, DH, 03, 09.
55. Dalton to C. Attlee 10 August 1949, London School of Economics (LSE), Dalton, 2, 9, 7. Dalton to Attlee, 1 September 1950, LSE, Dalton, 2, 9, 9. Also Healey, *The Time of My Life*, 117.
56. Entries, 10 May 1951, 14 May 1951, P. Catterali (ed.) (2003) *The Macmillan Diaries, The Cabinet Years, 1950–1957* (London: Macmillan), 70–72.
57. M. Phillips to E. Bevin, 3 August 1945, TNA, FO 371/47442-N10124. Minutes of the International Sub-Committee, 20 November 1945, LHASC, ID, Minutes and Documents, 1945.
58. Minute, 8 November 1945, TNA, FO 371/47442-N15230.
59. V.A. Allen (1957) *Trade Union Leadership: Based on a Study of Arthur Deakin* (London: Longmans), 77–85.
60. Healey, *The Time of My Life*, 105.
61. Healey, *The Time of My Life*, 104.
62. 'Mr Denis Healey's speech at the Italian Unification Congress', TNA, FO 371/79301-Z8223.
63. A. Crosland (1975) *Social Democracy in Europe* (London: Fabian society), 1.
64. C.R. Ricotti (2005). *Il costituzionalismo britannico nel Mediterraneo* (Milano: Giuffrè). E. Capozzi (2002). *Le costituzioni anglosassoni e l'Europa. Riflessi e dibattiti tra '800 e '900* (Soveria Mannelli: Rubbettino).
65. H. Deutsch-Renner, Ende des Austromarxismus?, *Zukunft*, June 1946.
66. K. Czernetz, Probleme der Außenpolitik, *Zukunft*, August 1946.
67. E. Costa (2011) 'Il "campo sperimentale" del socialismo: la vittoria laburista del 1945 e i suoi riflessi sulla sinistra italiana', *Dimensioni e problemi della ricerca storica*, 24, 2, 20.
68. Stenogramme, 8 Juin, International Institute of Social History, Amsterdam (IISH), Socialist International (SI), 235.
69. SPD-Pressedienst, II/67, 20.8.1947, Ü: K.Schumacher, Großbritannien—von deutschen Sozialisten gesehen.

70. Quoted in K. Klotzbach (1982) *Der Weg zur Staatspartei : Programmatik, praktische Politik und Organisation der deutschen Sozialdemokratie 1945 bis 1965* (Berlin: Dietz), 117.
71. Quoted in M. Drögemöller (2008) *Zwei Schwestern in Europa. Deutsche und niederländische Sozialdemokratie 1945–1990* (Berlin: Vorwärts Buch), 46.
72. J. Texcier, The ideological development of democratic socialism in France, *Socialist International Information*, 14 January, 1956. Also M. Fulla (2016) *Les socialistes français et l'économie (1944–1981): une histoire économique du politique* (Paris: Presses de Sciences Po), 67–94.
73. M. Phillips, We talk with Stalin on the two roads to Socialism, *Daily Herald*, 22 August 1946.
74. See Chap. 5.
75. J. Nichols to C. Warner, 3 November 1945, TNA, FO 371/47109-N15361.
76. Circular 155/50, 'Report of the International Socialist Conference at Copenaghen, 1–3 June 1950', IISH, SI, 54.
77. LPACR 1944, 132. Dalton repeated the commitment in 1945 (LPACR 1945, 83).
78. LPACR 1943, 118.
79. Among the countries asking for help were France, Italy, Belgium, Austria, Bulgaria and the Faroe Islands (Minutes of the International Sub-Committee, 20 March 1945; Minutes of the International Sub-Committee 18 September 1945, LHASC, LP, ID, Minutes & Documents, 1945). Also Czechoslovakia (B. Vilim to M. Phillips, 22 November 1945, TNA, FO 371/47216-N16956).
80. J. Callaghan (2007) *The Labour Party and Foreign Policy: A History* (London: Routledge), 192.
81. For example, see Sam Watson's speech as chairman of the 1950 conference (LPACR 1950, 76); Dalton's speech at the 1950 conference (LPACR 1950, 166); Alice Bacon's speech, chairman of the 1951 conference (LPACR 1951, 74–75).
82. LPACR 1950, 131.
83. LPACR 1951, 131.
84. J.W. Russell to Attlee, 3 December 1946, TNA, FO 371/56359-N15741.
85. C. Mayhew to Prime Minister, 'Italian socialist parties', 14 June 1949, TNA, FO 371/79300-Z4298.
86. J. Hochfeld (1946) *An Open Letter from a Polish Socialist to a Friend of the Labour Party* (London: London Committee of the Polish Socialist Party), 3. Rome to Foreign Office, 29 November 1949, TNA, FO 371/79301-Z7767.

87. C. Norton to G.A. Wallinger, 7 January 1948, TNA, FO 371/72238-R953.
88. Rome to Foreign Office, 8 December 1949, TNA, FO 371/79301-Z7998.
89. 'I suppose it is a little difficult for Communists to understand how much argument and difference of opinion there can be amongst Socialists!' (R.B. Kirby to Healey, 28 November 1946, LHASC, LP, DH, 4, 14).
90. G. Procacci, (ed.) (1994) *The Cominform: Minutes of the Three Conferences 1947–1948–1949* (Milano: Feltrinelli), 795.
91. Procacci (ed.), *The Cominform*, 793.
92. P. Van Kemseke (2006) *Towards an Era of Development, The Globalization of Socialism and Christian Democracy: 1945–1965* (Leuven: Leuven University Press), 54.
93. L. Diamond (1991) *Multi-Track Diplomacy: A Systems Guide and Analysis* (Grinnel, Iowa: Peace Institute), 1. W. Kaiser and J.-H. Meyer (2013) 'Beyond Governments and Supranational Institutions: Societal Actors in European integration', in W. Kaiser, J.-H. Meyer (eds), *Societal actors in European integration: Polity-Building and Policy-Making, 1958–1992* (Basingstoke: Palgrave Macmillan), 1–6.
94. I. Parmar (2006) 'Conceptualising the state-private network in American foreign policy', in H. Laville and H. Wilford (eds), *The US Government, Citizen Groups and the Cold War: The State-Private Network* (London: Routledge), 13–25. G. Scott-Smith (2012) *Western Anti-Communism and the Interdoc Network: Cold War Internationale* (Basingstoke: Palgrave Macmillan), 10.
95. L. Van Dongen, S. Roulin and G. Scott-Smith (2014) 'Introduction', in L. Van Dongen, S. Roulin and G. Scott-Smith (Eds.) *Transnational Anti-Communism and the Cold War: Agents, Activities, and Networks* (Basingstoke: Palgrave Macmillan).
96. For two sides of the controversy see F. Stonor Saunders (2000) *Who paid the Piper?: The CIA and the Cultural Cold War* (London: Granta Books) and H. Wilford (2003) *The CIA, the British Left, and the Cold War* (London-Portland: F. Cass).
97. D.D. Kaye (2007) *Talking to the Enemy: Track Two Diplomacy in the Middle East and South Asia* (Santa Monica, CA: RAND National Security Research Division), 8; also xi–xix.
98. A. Defty (2004) *Britain, America and Anti-Communist Propaganda, 1945–53: The Information Research Department* (London: Routledge), 10–11.
99. E. Barker (1983) *The British between the Superpowers: 1945–50*, (Basingstoke: Macmillan), 232.

100. R.J. Aldrich (2001) *The Hidden Hand: Britain, America and Cold War Secret Intelligence* (London: John Murray), 151.
101. J.N. Henderson to Secretary of State, Minute, 9 August 1945, TNA, FO 371/50442-W11020.
102. Sir A. Clark-Kerr to Ernest Bevin, 6 September 1945, TNA, FO 371/47883-N12165.
103. A. De Gasperi to Carandini, 24 August 1945, ACS, NC, b.2.
104. M. Newman (2009) *Harold Laski: A Political Biography* (Pontypool: Merlin Press), 293–296.
105. T. Insall (2003) *Haakon Lie, Denis Healey and the Making of an Anglo-Norwegian Special Relationship 1945–1951* (Oslo: Oslo Academic Press), 76–83.
106. 'Policy in Eastern Europe', TNA, FO 371/65964-N4246.
107. Wilford, *The CIA, the British Left, and the Cold War*, 49.
108. *Italy: political situation*, 12 February 1948, TNA, FO 371/73156 -21359/G.
109. G. Gabrielli (2004) *Gli amici americani: i socialisti italiani dalla guerra fredda alle amministrative del 1952*, (Manduria: Lacaita), 189.
110. Signor de Gasperi Surmounts Another Crisis, *Economist*, Saturday, 14 April 1951.
111. Gainer to Warner, 22 December 1947, TNA, FO 371/71529-N425.
112. J. Lee, As I please, *Tribune* 31 August 1945. Warbey's speech in LPACR 1946, 162.
113. LPACR 1946, 162–169.
114. R.B. Kirby, 'Report by Labour attaché for period 20th October to 31st December 1946', TNA, FO 371/66218-N1283.
115. Healey, *The Time of My Life*, 83.
116. 'Gli addetti al lavoro nella diplomazia inglese', gennaio 1946, ACS, NC, b.6.
117. C. Mayhew (1998) *A War of Words: A Cold War Witness* (London: Tauris), 40–41.
118. *London information of the Austrian socialists in Great Britain*, 15 August 1945; [T.Williamson], 'Czechoslovakia', LHASC, LP, International Sub-Committee, Minutes and Documents, 1945. 'National Council of Labour delegation to Germany (British zone)', LHASC, LP, International Sub-Committee, Minutes and Documents, 1946. Vilim to M. Phillips, 22 November 1945, TNA, FO 371/47216-N16956. C.W.E. Duley, 'Visit to Argentina and Uruguay. 15th August to 30th Sept. 1947', 11 October 1947, TNA, BW 83/2.
119. I. Lukes (2012) *On the Edge of the Cold War, American Diplomats and Spies in Postwar Prague* (New York: Oxford University Press), 93. Nichols to Bevin, 20 August 1945, TNA, FO 371/47092-N11105.

120. Minutes of International Sub-Committee, 21 May 1946, LHASC, LP, International Sub-Committee, Minutes and Documents, 1946.
121. LPACR 1947, 168; 205.
122. Defty, *Britain, America and anti-communist propaganda*, 40–74.
123. Aldrich, *The Hidden Hand*, 151. Wilford shows the close relationship between the IRD and the Labour Party (Wilford, *The CIA, the British left, and the Cold War*, 48–49). Defty shows how pressure from the periphery encouraged the creation of a complex propaganda machinery (Defty, *Britain, America and Anti-communist Propaganda*, 40–52).
124. Healey to J.H. Watson, 8 December 1948, TNA, FO 1110/47-PR1211/G.
125. Minutes of the International Sub-Committee, 18 November 1947, LHASC, LP, ID, DH, 12.
126. Devin, *L'Internationale socialiste*, 320.
127. A. Carthy to F.J.C.Mennell, 9 January 1967, TNA, FCO 95/406.
128. Entry, Monday 24 July 1967, T. Benn (1988) *Out of the Wilderness: 1963–1967* (London: Arrow), 508.
129. Healey, *The Time of my life*, 76.
130. Wodak to Schärf, 21 December 1945, in Wodak, *Diplomatie zwischen Parteiproporz und Weltpolitik*, 21–24.
131. T.C. Imlay (2014) '"The policy of social democracy is self-consciously internationalist": The German Social Democratic Party's Internationalism after 1945', *The Journal of Modern History*, 86, 1, 86–97.
132. Insall, *Haakon Lie, Denis Healey and the Making of an Anglo-Norwegian Special Relationship 1945–1951*, 47–98; 227–272.
133. Healey to Kirby, n.d. [circa 24 December 1946], LHASC, LP, DH, 4, 14.
134. P. Dogliani (1985) 'La ricostituzione dell'Internazionale Socialista nel primo decennio postbellico (1918–1928). Le caratteristiche nuove di quadri e organizzazioni' in E. Collotti (ed.), *L'Internazionale Operaia e Socialista tra le due guerre* (Milano: Feltrinelli), 271–277.
135. E. Shaw (1988) *Discipline and Discord in the Labour Party: The Politics of Managerial Control in the Labour Party, 1951–87* (Manchester: Manchester university press), 22.
136. Shaw, *Discipline and discord in the Labour party*, 57–64.
137. What's happening, *Tribune*, 7 September 1945.
138. Mayhew, *A War of Words*, 107–108.
139. J. Lee, As I please, *Tribune*, 26 April 1946.
140. Minutes of the International Sub-Committee 19 March 1946, LHASC, LP, ID, Minutes and Documents, 1946.
141. See Chap. 4.
142. Healey to E.M. Donald, 10 October 1946, Heumos (ed.), *Europäischer Sozialismus im kalten Krieg*, 80.

143. Hankey, Minute, 18 April 1947, TNA, FO 371/65989-9821/G.
144. Nichols to C.F.A. Warner, 11 April 1947, TNA, FO 371/65989-9821/G.
145. The travels of John Mack in Eastern Europe can be found in TNA, FO 371/58611.
146. F.D. Warner, Minute, 23 May 1946, TNA, FO 371/58611-R7929.
147. P. Broomfield to H. White, 18 February 1946, TNA, FO 371/56765-N2793.
148. H. McNeil, Minute, TNA, FO 371/56459-N4914.
149. Hankey, Minute, 23 April 1947, TNA, FO 371/65989-9821/G.
150. 'Notes on Italy', LHASC, LP, ID, Harry Earnshaw, 1, 1–4.
151. H.B. Brenan, Minute 12 February 1948; Reddaway, Minute, 27 January 1948, TNA, FO 371/71448B-N1283.
152. Minutes of the International Sub-Committee, 16 November 1948, LHASC, LP, ID, DH, 12.
153. Healey to A.V. Clare (Fulham Central Labour Party), 11 September 1947, LHASC, LP, ID, DH, 07, 07.
154. M. Peterson to McNeil, 16 July 1946; McNeil to Peterson, 11 November 1946, TNA, FO 371/56766-N9529.
155. V. Cavendish-Bentinck to Hankey, 24 June 1946, TNA, FO 371/56356-N8441.
156. LPACR 1947, 18–19. LPACR 1948, 22.
157. See Chap. 6.
158. A. Bullock (1983) *Ernest Bevin: Foreign Secretary: 1945–1951* (London: Heinenmann), 552–553.
159. M. Jones (1992) *Michael Foot* (London: Gollancz), 145–162.
160. Entry, 13 September 1952, P. Nenni (1982) *Diari*, Vol. 1, *Tempo di Guerra Fredda: diari 1943–1956*, (Milano: SugarCo), 543.
161. Carandini to De Gasperi, 8 September 1945, ACS, NC, b.2.
162. Carandini to De Gasperi, 9 March 1946, ACS, NC, b.2. These rumours were repeated in 1947, but Dalton told W.J. Donovan that they were 'rubbish' (Dalton, *The Political Diary of Hugh Dalton*, 407).
163. LPACR 1947, 106–107. 'Bericht über die 46. Jahreskonferenz der britischen Arbeiterpartei', Wodak, *Zwischen Diplomatie und Parteiproporz*, 426–428.
164. See Chap. 6.
165. R.B. Murray, Minute, 9 January 1947, TNA, FO 371/61321-AS 804.
166. A.J. Montague, 'Report on visit of Mr C.E.W.Duley', 17 November 1947, TNA, BW 83/2.
167. C.L. Thomas to A.R.H. Kellas, 27 June 1950, TNA, LAB 13/487. ACS, Dipartimento Generale di Pubblica Sicurezza, Ufficio ordine pubblico, Servizio ordine pubblico, Categoria G (associazioni), b.146, f.100/25 (Associazione Italo-Britannica).

168. C. Tilly (1984) *Big Structures, Large Processes, Huge Comparisons* (New York: Russell Sage Foundation), 125.
169. B.D. Graham (1994) *Choice and Democratic Order: The French Socialist Party, 1937–1950* (Cambridge: Cambridge University Press), 262. A. Bergounioux and G. Grunberg (2005) *L'ambition et le remords: les socialistes français et le pouvoir (1905–2005)* (Paris: Fayard), 129–137.
170. H. Laski, Problems of the French Socialist Party, *Forward*, 17 July 1948, LHASC, LP, International Sub-Committee, Minutes and Documents, 1948.
171. R. Quilliot (1972) *La SFIO et l'exercise du pouvoir: 1944–1958*, (Paris: Fayard), 7.
172. Quilliot, *SFIO et l'exercise du pouvoir*, 377.
173. LPACR 1946, 197.
174. L. Levy to G. Valentin, 14 May 1947, L'Office Universitaire de Recherche Socialiste, Paris (OURS), Fonds Louis Lévy, APO 22, f. L. Lévy représentant du PS-SFIO à Londres 1946–1948.
175. J. Braunthal to R. Pontillon, 13 March 1952, IISH, SI, 605.
176. Quilliot, *SFIO et l'exercise du pouvoir*, 181. Also D. Lefebvre (1992) *Guy Mollet: le mal aimé*, (Paris: Plon), 180–181. Graham, *Choice and Democratic Order*, 333; 362.
177. Graham, *Choice and Democratic Order*, 84.
178. Imlay, '"The Policy of Social Democracy is Self-Consciously Internationalist"', 86–97.
179. Levy to Valentin, 21 May 1947, OURS, Fonds Louis Lévy, APO 22, f. L.Lévy représentant du PS-SFIO à Londres 1946–1948.
180. 'Relations between the PSLI (Partito Socialista Lavoratori Italiani) and the French socialists', 6 November 1947, CIA-RDP82-00457R001000660001-1, Central Intelligence Agency, Freedom of Information Act, Electronic Reading Room, https://www.cia.gov/library/readingroom/document/cia-rdp82-00457r001000660001-1 (accessed 29 December 2017).
181. G. Devin (1987) 'Guy Mollet et l'Internationale Socialiste', B. Ménager, P. Ratte, J.-L. Thiébault, R. Vandenbussche, C.-M. Wallon-Leducq, *Guy Mollet, Un camarade en république* (Lille: Presses Universitaires de Lille), 148.
182. Devin, *L'Internationale socialiste*, 289–300.
183. Imlay, 'The Policy of Social Democracy is Self-Consciously Internationalist', 86–97.
184. Lefebvre, *Guy Mollet*, 127–128.
185. Devin, 'Guy Mollet et l'Internationale Socialiste', 144.
186. N. Naïf (2008) 'Les partis socialistes de Belgique. Entre conquêtes, compromis et renoncements : 120 ans de réformisme', in C. Bougeard (ed.)

Un siècle de socialismes en Bretagne : De la SFIO au PS (1905–2005) (Rennes: Presses universitaires de Rennes), http://books.openedition.org/pur/4205, 135–151 (accessed 17 April 2018). Polasky, *The Democratic Socialism of Emile Vandervelde*, 220–252. M. Conway (2012) *The Sorrows of Belgium: Liberation and Political Reconstruction, 1944–1947*, (Oxford: Oxford University press), 177–189. D.S. White (1992) *Lost Comrades: Socialists of the Front Generation, 1918–1945* (Cambridge, Mass: Harvard University Press), 181–184.
187. Klotzbach, *Der Weg zur Staatspartei*, 54–69.
188. Drögemöller, *Zwei Schwestern in Europa*, 36–38; 44–48. D. Orlow (2000) *Common Destiny: A Comparative History of the Dutch, French, and German Social Democratic Parties, 1945–1969* (New York: Berghahn Books), 20–22; 45–55.
189. A.F. Mreijen, 'Goes van Naters, jhr. Marinus van der (1900–2005)', in *Biografisch Woordenboek van Nederland*. http://resources.huygens.knaw.nl/bwn1880-2000/lemmata/bwn6/goes, accessed 3 March 2017.
190. E.F. Albrecht to J. Braunthal, 1 June 1951, IISH, SI, 755. Also, F. Wielenga, 'Mozser, Alfred (1905–1979)', in *Biografisch Woordenboek van Nederland*. http://resources.huygens.knaw.nl/bwn1880-2000/lemmata/bwn6/mozser, accessed 3 March 2017. Drögemöller, *Zwei Schwestern in Europa*, 55–56.
191. K. Misgeld (1984) *Sozialdemokratie und Aussenpolitik in Schweden: Sozialistische Internationale, Europapolitik und die Deutschlandfrage 1945–1955* (Frankfurt: Campus Verlag), 11–13.
192. Misgeld, *Sozialdemokratie und Aussenpolitik in Schweden*, 17–26; 72–77.
193. Insall, *Haakon Lie, Denis Healey and the Making of an Anglo-Norwegian Special Relationship*, 76–77.
194. J. Deutsch to Wodak, 18 April 1946, Wodak, *Diplomatie zwischen Parteiproporz und Weltpolitik*, 113.
195. Schärf to Wodak, 28 December 1946, Wodak, *Diplomatie zwischen Parteiproporz und Weltpolitik*, 296–298.
196. Wodak to Schärf, 6 May 1946; F. Popp to Wodak, 7 May 1946, Wodak, *Diplomatie zwischen Parteiproporz und Weltpolitik*, 132–133; 135–137.
197. M.F. Cullis, Minute, 2 May 1946, TNA, FO 371/55282-C4727.
198. W.H.B. Mack to O. Harvey, 27 February 1946; M.F. Cullis, Minute, 12 March 1946, TNA, FO 371/55290-C3006.
199. Schärf to Wodak, 27 September 1946; Schärf to Wodak, 7 October 1946, Wodak, *Diplomatie zwischen Parteiproporz und Weltpolitik*, 226–227; 233.
200. M.F. Cullis, Minute, 9 March 1946, TNA, FO 371/55282-C2696.
201. Wodak to Schärf, 8 December 1946, Wodak, *Diplomatie zwischen Parteiproporz und Weltpolitik*, 274–275.

BIBLIOGRAPHY

Aldrich, R.J. (2001). *The hidden hand: Britain, America and Cold War secret intelligence*. London: John Murray.
Allen, V.A. (1957). *Trade union leadership: based on a study of Arthur Deakin*. London: Longmans.
Barker, E. (1983). *The British between the superpowers: 1945–50*. Basingstoke: Macmillan.
Balthazar, H. (1972). L'Internationale Socialiste, Les debats de Londres en 1940–1941. *Cahiers d'histoire de la seconde guerre mondiale*, 2, 191–210.
Bergounioux, A. & Grunberg, G. (2005). *L'ambition et le remords: les socialistes français et le pouvoir (1905–2005)*. Paris: Fayard.
Bullock, A. (1983). *Ernest Bevin: foreign secretary: 1945–1951*. London: Heinenmann.
Callaghan, J. (2007). *The Labour Party and foreign policy: a history*. London: Routledge.
Capozzi, E. (2002). *Le costituzioni anglosassoni e l'Europa. Riflessi e dibattiti tra '800 e '900*. Soveria Mannelli: Rubbettino.
Catterali, P. (Ed.). (2003). *The Macmillan diaries, The cabinet years, 1950–1957*. London: Macmillan.
Collette, C. (1998). *The International Faith: Labour's Attitude to European Socialism, 1918–39*. Aldershot: Ashgate.
Conway, M. (2012). *The sorrows of Belgium: liberation and political reconstruction, 1944–1947*. Oxford: Oxford University press.
Costa, E. (2011). Il "campo sperimentale" del socialismo: la vittoria laburista del 1945 e i suoi riflessi sulla sinistra italiana. *Dimensioni e problemi della ricerca storica*, 24 (2), 11–41.
Crosland, A. (1975). *Social democracy in Europe*. London: Fabian society.
Defty, A. (2004). *Britain, America and anti-communist propaganda, 1945–53: the Information Research Department*. London: Routledge.
Devin, G. (1993). *L'Internationale socialiste: histoire et sociologie du socialisme internationale: 1945–1990*. Paris: Presses de la Fondation national des sciences politiques.
Diamond, L. (1991). *Multi-Track Diplomacy: A Systems Guide and Analysis*. Grinnel and Iowa: Peace Institute.
Dogliani, P. (1985). La ricostituzione dell'Internazionale Socialista nel primo decennio postbellico (1918–1928). Le caratteristiche nuove di quadri e organizzazioni. In E. Collotti (Ed.). *L'Internazionale Operaia e Socialista tra le due guerre* (pp. 225–277). Milano: Feltrinelli.
Douglas, R.M. (2004). *The Labour Party, nationalism and internationalism, 1939–1951*. London: Routledge.

Drögemöller, M. (2008). *Zwei Schwestern in Europa. Deutsche und niederländische Sozialdemokratie 1945–1990*. Berlin: Vorwärts Buch.
Fulla, M. (2016). *Les socialistes français et l'économie (1944–1981): une histoire économique du politique*. Paris: Presses de Sciences Po.
Gabrielli, G. (2004). *Gli amici americani: i socialisti italiani dalla guerra fredda alle amministrative del 1952*. Manduria: Lacaita.
Graham, B.D. (1994). *Choice and democratic order: the French Socialist Party, 1937–1950*. Cambridge: Cambridge University Press.
Hanely, D. (1983). Un socialisme aux couleurs de l'Angleterre: le parti travailliste et l'Internationale Socialiste depuis 1945. In H. Portelli (Ed.). *L'Internationale socialiste* (pp. 57–66). Paris: Les Éditions Ouvrières.
Healey, D. (1990). *The time of my life*. London: Penguin.
Healey, E. (2007). *Part of the pattern: memoirs of a wife at Westminster*. Oxford: ISIS.
Heumos, P. (Ed.). (2004). *Europäischer Sozialismus im Kalten Krieg: Briefe und Berichte 1944–1948*. Frankfurt: Campus.
Hochfeld, J. (1946). *An open letter from a Polish socialist to a friend of the Labour party*. London: London Committee of the Polish Socialist Party.
Imlay, T.C. (2014). '"The policy of social democracy is self-consciously internationalist": The German Social Democratic Party's Internationalism after 1945', *The Journal of Modern History*, 86 (1), 81–123.
Insall, T. (2010). *Haakon Lie, Denis Healey and the making of an Anglo-Norwegian special relationship 1945–1951*. Oslo: Oslo Academic Press.
Jones, M. (1992). *Michael Foot*. London: Gollancz.
Kaiser, W. & Meyer, J.-H. (2013). Beyond Governments and Supranational Institutions: Societal Actors in European integration. In W. Kaiser & J.-H. Meyer (Eds.). *Societal actors in European integration: polity-building and policy-making, 1958–1992* (pp. 1–14). Basingstoke: Palgrave Macmillan.
Kaye, D.D. (2007). *Talking to the enemy: track two diplomacy in the Middle East and South Asia*. Santa Monica, CA: RAND National Security Research Division.
Klotzbach, K. (1982). *Der Weg zur Staatspartei : Programmatik, praktische Politik und Organisation der deutschen Sozialdemokratie 1945 bis 1965*. Berlin: Dietz.
Kramnick, I. & Sheerman, B. (1993). *Harold Laski, A life on the left*. London: Hamilton.
Lee, J. (1981). *My life with Nye*. Harmondsworth: Penguin Books.
Lefebvre, D. (1992). *Guy Mollet: le mal aimé*. Paris: Plon.
Lukes, I. (2012). *On the Edge of the Cold War, American Diplomats and Spies in Postwar Prague*. New York: Oxford University Press.
Mayhew, C. (1998). *A war of words: a Cold War witness*. London: Tauris.
Misgeld, K. (1984). *Sozialdemokratie und Aussenpolitik in Schweden: Sozialistische Internationale, Europapolitik und die Deutschlandfrage 1945–1955*. Frankfurt: Campus Verlag.

Naïf, N. (2008). Les partis socialistes de Belgique. Entre conquêtes, compromis et renoncements: 120 ans de réformisme. In C. Bougeard (Ed.). *Un siècle de socialismes en Bretagne: De la SFIO au PS (1905–2005)* (pp. 135–151). Rennes: Presses universitaires de Rennes, http://books.openedition.org/pur/4205
Nenni, P. (1982). *Diari*, Vol. 1, *Tempo di Guerra Fredda: diari 1943–1956*. Milano: SugarCo.
Newman, M. (2009). *Harold Laski: a political biography*. Pontypool: Merlin Press.
Orlow, D. (2000). *Common destiny: a comparative history of the Dutch, French, and German Social Democratic parties, 1945–1969*. New York: Berghahn Books.
Parmar, I. (2006). Conceptualising the state-private network in American foreign policy. In H. Laville & H. Wilford (Eds.). *The US Government, Citizen Groups and the Cold War: The State-Private Network* (pp. 13–28). London: Routledge,
Pearce, E. (2002). *Denis Healey: a life in our times*. London: Little Brown.
Pimlott, B. (1985). *Hugh Dalton*. London: Cape.
Pimlott, B. (Ed.). (1986a). *The political diary of Hugh Dalton: 1918–40, 1945–60*. London: Cape.
Pimlott, B. (Ed.). (1986b). *The Second World war diary of Hugh Dalton 1940–45*. London: Jonathan Cape.
Polasky, J. (1995). *The democratic socialism of Emile Vandervelde: between reform and revolution*. Oxford: Berg.
Price, J. (1945). *International labour movement*. London: Oxford University Press.
Procacci, G. (Ed.). (1994). *The Cominform: minutes of the three conferences 1947–1948–1949*. Milano: Feltrinelli.
Quilliot, R. (1972). *La SFIO et l'exercise du pouvoir: 1944–1958*. Paris: Fayard.
Ricotti, C.R. (2005). *Il costituzionalismo britannico nel Mediterraneo*. Milano: Giuffrè.
Scott-Smith, G. (2012). *Western Anti-Communism and the Interdoc Network: Cold War Internationale*. Basingstoke: Palgrave Macmillan.
Shaw, E. (1988). *Discipline and discord in the Labour party: the politics of managerial control in the Labour party, 1951–87*. Manchester: Manchester university press.
Stonor Saunders, F. (2000). *Who paid the piper?: the CIA and the cultural Cold War*. London: Granta Books.
Thorpe, A. (2009). *Parties at war: political organization in Second World War Britain*. Oxford: Oxford University Press.
Thorpe, A. (2014). Locking out the Communists: The Labour party and the Communist party, 1939–46. *Twentieth Century British History*, 25 (2), 226–250.
Tilly, C. (1984). *Big structures, large processes, huge comparisons*. New York: Russell Sage Foundation.
Van der Goes van Naters, M. (1980). *Met en tegen de tijd*. Amsterdam: Arbeiderspers.

Van Dongen, L., Roulin, S. & Scott-Smith, G. (Eds). (2014). *Transnational anticommunism and the cold war: agents, activities, and networks.* Basingstoke: Palgrave Macmillan.
Van Kemseke, P. (2006). *Towards an Era of Development, the globalization of socialism and Christian democracy: 1945–1965.* Leuven: Leuven University Press.
Vickers, R. (2003). *The Labour party and the world.* Manchester: Manchester University Press.
White, D.S. (1992). *Lost Comrades: socialists of the front generation, 1918–1945.* Cambridge, MA: Harvard University Press.
Wilford, H. (2003). *The CIA, the British left, and the Cold War.* London and Portland: F. Cass.
Winkler, H.R. (2005). *British Labour seeks a foreign policy, 1900–1940.* New Brunswick: Transaction.
Wodak, W. (1980). *Diplomatie zwischen Parteiproporz und Weltpolitik: Briefe, Dokumente und Memoranden aus dem Nachlass Walter Wodaks 1945–1950.* Salzburg: Neugebauer.

CHAPTER 4

The Labour Party and Eastern Europe, Social Democracy Behind the Iron Curtain

1 The New Social Democrats from Eastern Europe

At the end of the war, the Labour Party faced a continent divided by wartime experience and the rapidly falling Iron Curtain. The division of Europe made the unity of the socialist movement difficult and caused trouble for the Labour leadership. The relationship with the social democrats from Eastern Europe is the theme of this chapter. However, not all divisions were new; for a long time, the British and other Northern Europeans had seen Southern, Catholic Europe and Eastern Europe as alien, if not in opposition. As Labour leaders grappled with uncertainty, they resorted to rational analysis but also the preconceived notions of their culture.

The history of social democracy during the communist takeover of Eastern Europe—Heumos argues—is usually described as a tale of infiltration, terrorism and conspiracy.[1] The tale was developed by exiled socialists, spread by the Labour Party[2] and Western powers, later to become part of the mythology of Eastern European democracy.[3] However, it fails to tell the history of the social democrats, and 'as a result, their own ideological dilemmas and struggles to come to terms with the post-war reality have been at best ignored, at worst dismissed as irrelevant',[4] especially their relations with Western socialists.[5]

© The Author(s) 2018
E. Costa, *The Labour Party, Denis Healey and the International Socialist Movement*, Palgrave Studies in the History of Social Movements, https://doi.org/10.1007/978-3-319-77347-6_4

Until February 1948, the need to accommodate the socialist parties of Eastern Europe defined the development of the International Socialist Conference—in the following pages we refer particularly to the Polish Socialist Party (PPS) and the Czechoslovak Social Democratic Party (ČSSD).[6] Together with the Hungarians and the Italians, they formed an influential left-wing bloc. The British pursued two goals in their relationship with Eastern Europe: preparing the 'socialist roll-back of Eastern Europe'[7] and reaching a modus vivendi with pro-communist socialists and the Soviet Union. Until 1948 left-wing and right-wing socialists believed they all belonged to same movement and they had to win over the others, instead of eliminating them politically—in Eastern Europe, physically. Cohabitation and competition contributed to the internationalisation of domestic quarrels. The minority left-wing factions sought the help of Eastern parties, whose minority right-wing factions sought the help of the Labour Party—what Heumos calls the *Westoffensive* and the *Ostoffensive*.[8] The internal debates took place by making positive and negative references to Eastern Europe or Great Britain.

As Jan Gross explains, the 'revolutionary' transformation of the war preceded and made possible the radical political transformation of post-war Eastern Europe.[9] This included the restructuring of the socialist movements, Poland being emblematic. The German invasion of September 1939 and the flight abroad of the political élites of the regime (*Sanacja*) and the opposition created a crisis of legitimacy, which gave rise to a competition for power.[10] Especially radical was the transformation of the human material, as the systematic extermination and exile of political leaders shattered the normal mechanisms of the reproduction of the élite and the old system of values regulating the co-opting of new elements, replaced by what Anna Kriegel called the 'diabolical pedagogy'.[11]

Before the war, the Eastern European socialist movements were middle-sized, immobilised and in decline. Class consciousness was secondary to nationalism, working-class culture was defensive, preferring communitarian solutions to state interventions, and workers' organisations were sectorial.[12] The old reformist, anti-communist and nationalist leaders ended up either in exile or in concentration camps—whether German or Soviet. While avoiding a moralistic denunciation of opportunism, understanding Eastern European history requires stressing how war and reconstruction provided pre-war heretics and upwardly mobile youths with the opportunity to advance their careers and ideals. Out of 75 members of the PPS's Supreme Council, 36 died during the war and 11 remained in exile. Adam

Ciolkosz spoke of more than 700 party leaders killed in the Resistance.[13] In 1945, only six members of the PPS Executive Committee elected by the 1937 Congress were left in Poland and only one was immediately co-opted into the new party. The June 1945 Congress elected an Executive Committee with only one person who had been part of the pre-war Executive Committee: Jan Stańczyk, just returning from exile. No post-war socialist leader had been a leading figure before the war, except Józef Cyrankiewicz and only locally:

> The new PPS leadership was recruited from the middle ranks of the party, the trade unions, the cooperative movement, the Society of Workers' Universities, and the Youth Organization of the Society of Workers' Universities.[14]

The destruction of the old élite was partially self-inflicted. During the invasion, the socialist party was dissolved, according to Prazmowska,[15] to prevent new leaders from challenging the exiled leadership. The underground socialist organisation WRN barred access to leftists and young people without previous experience in the party. Since the old socialists were compromised with the *Sanacja* regime, lacked a radical programme and were reluctant to undertake military operations, their ties with the working-class were weakened:

> This in turn created preconditions for certain sections of the pre-war left-wing community and the younger generation, which had no loyalty to pre-war organisations, to develop their own groups and formulate a vision of a post-war reality, something the PPS-WRN would not countenance.[16]

Left-wing socialists, especially the young people radicalised by the war, formed independent organisations proposing radical programmes. Conversely, the newly formed communist party (Polish Workers' Party, PPR) was moderate and nationalist to better serve Soviet interests. The siege of Warsaw destroyed the main centre of left-wing socialism and the Red Army suppressed the WRN. A group led by Edward Osobka-Morawski was the largest to survive and in September 1944 it held the first congress in liberated Poland, absorbing exiles returning from the Soviet Union and the West. Most delegates were members of left-wing socialist groups without ties to the WRN or the pre-war party, thus the congress condemned the reformist tradition. Their organisation was completely dependent on the communists and the Soviet Army, so they backed the Lublin government and broke relations with the Polish Government in exile in London.

Czechoslovak socialism took a similar road, with the Munich Agreement discrediting two decades of reformist leadership among the rank and file.[17] In exile, left-wing social democrats—Zdeněk Fierlinger, Bechyne and Bohumil Laušman—accepted communist offers for a Popular Front, but a group of right-wingers defended party traditions, to the point of splitting. With the mediation of Moscow and Beneš, who wanted all socialists to ally with the communists, some right-wingers, like Holub and Vaclav Majer, rejoined the party, while the veteran Belina, a member of the Dallas Committee, refused any cooperation, dying in isolation and exile in 1948. By 1944, left-wing socialists had taken over the party, thanks to international events and help from the communists. Majer, who lacked a following in the party, was made a minister only as a concession to Beneš. Fierlinger, a secondary figure before the war, had a meteoric rise as the man of Moscow. The congress of October 1945 indicated a break with the party of 1938. Some party cadres, industrial workers and leaders joined the communist party, because of their radicalisation in the concentration camps and rumours about an immediate fusion upon liberation. The ČSSD kept the pre-war territorial organisation, only trying to develop industrial sections when it was too late.

While the Eastern European socialist parties were committed to a Popular Front, disagreement was allowed on the role of social democracy in the new state and the degree of cooperation with the communists. The model for the factional struggle in the ČSSD drawn by Karel Kaplan has a general applicability. The left-wing faction—or the Ultra-Left[18]—systematically backed working-class unity under communist leadership. They received help from the communists, with many cases of entryism. In Poland the leader was Matuszewski, in Czechoslovakia Němec. The right-wing faction did not openly ask to break with the communists but for the party to develop its identity and policies, to ally with other parties as well and to accept pre-war members. The leading figures were Bolesław Drobner and Julian Hochfeld in Poland, Majer in Czechoslovakia. Most party members belonged to a wide Centre or Centre-Left that wanted cooperation with the communists on equal terms instead of fusion. In Poland and Czechoslovakia this faction was led by the party leaders, respectively Osobka-Morawski and Fierlinger at the beginning, later Cyrankiewicz and Laušman, when the parties wanted more autonomy.[19] The socialist mass genuinely desired to preserve its identity and traditionally distrusted the communists but was also convinced that rebuilding the nation and securing democracy required working-class unity against capitalists and reactionaries, especially German revanchists. Socialists had the probably correct impression that the other classes were not socialist or democratic. In addition, socialists—as indeed other politicians and Western diplomats—believed that communists could not govern alone and Stalin would be forced to compromise to safeguard Soviet security. As Stańczyk said, they trusted that the Soviets understood that the Poles were 'good neighbours and loyal allies' but 'exceedingly unsuitable material for subjects or slaves'.[20]

Despite the loosening of the idealistic and human connections with pre-war reformism, the desire to regain a degree of autonomy from the communists soon emerged. While in April 1945 most PPS members had no ties with pre-war socialism, old socialists joined the party and by the beginning of 1946 they were the majority. The PPS and the Polish Popular Party (PSL), born as stooge parties, became genuine forces offering tentative resistance to communism.[21] Social conflict also encouraged autonomy. The Polish government lacked strong popular support and relied on the Polish army trained in the USSR.[22] Its strategic goal was the elimination of independent social organisations and the atomisation of society, enabling the creation of the new society and the 'New Man'. This conflicted with the working-class tradition of horizontal solidarity and independence from the state. Workers also desired industrial self-management, putting them in conflict with an economic policy of centralisation and increased productivity.[23] Resistance emerged in traditional working-class communities like Lodz, where the socialists were strong. The communists and the secret police worried about minor socialist officials backing spontaneous strikes.[24] Indeed, the failure of the socialists was their inability to exploit the instincts of their base by giving a social content to the struggle against communism, linking political aspirations to everyday struggles.[25] This was to be discovered by the Catholic trade unionists of *Solidarność* decades later. The socialist leaders were interested in high politics, thus their leverage to increase power was acting as mediators with the West.

2 The Choice Between London and Lublin

Even though they were not familiar with these new socialist leaders, the British Labour Party was willing get information and establish contacts and spent the second half of 1945 doing so.[26] Morgan Phillips attended the Congress of the ČSSD. He reported back that the alliance with the communists was consensual.[27] The social democrats made professions of independence,[28] which their secretary Vilim matched with his battle to have an independent socialist party in Slovakia.[29] Phillips also believed in the communist commitment to democracy, which president Beneš confirmed. The Labour Party understood the situation and simply wanted to encourage contacts with the West. Indeed, Czechoslovak socialists were relieved to observe Labour's interest in them.[30] Every faction respected and admired the Labour Party, was lukewarm towards the SFIO—because of the Munich Agreement—and unanimously hated the German social democrats.

The Polish situation was embarrassing, because there were two competing groups: the PPS in exile in London, familiar faces, and the Lublin PPS, strangers claiming to represent the Polish workers. The exiled socialists called the Lublin people crypto-communist usurpers imposed by the Russians,[31] the Lublin people said the exiles lacked a following and were compromised with reactionaries. Pre-war socialist leaders were often persecuted in Poland. The Labour Party juggled its contradictory obligations: the war had begun to restore a 'free and independent Poland' and they had worked together with the Polish exiles on the propaganda. However, the *Post-war settlement* demanded friendship with the Soviet Union and cooperation with European socialists—without specifying of what kind. There was also the old argument of working only with living parties, not exiles.

Considerations of foreign policy were important. Western diplomats and moderate Polish exiles argued that Poland had to accept losing territory beyond the Curzon line and being in the Soviet sphere of influence, as the price to preserve pluralism and sovereignty. The Yalta Agreement recognised the Lublin government in exchange for the pledge to include ministers from among the émigrés and to hold free elections. The leader of the PSL, Mikołajczyk and some socialists returned to Poland, but most leaders stayed in London.

At the London socialist conference of March 1945, Poland was still represented by the exiled leader Adam Ciolkosz. The socialists returning from exile or the underground hoped to conquer the Lublin Party from within, being encouraged to do so by Dalton and *Tribune*.[32] However, the Soviet authorities persecuted resistance fighters to demoralise their opponents and to compromise moderates and Western nations giving assurances. Ciolkosz said that the Labour Party had failed in its duty to defend Polish socialists, who trusted them.[33] Morgan Phillips took a wait-and-see attitude to help the conciliation between the two groups.[34] When Labour's newspaper called the PPS in exile a non-representative rump, Ciolkosz replied:

> It has to be stated most emphatically that the position and authority of bodies appointed by the Party is subject to decisions of the Party alone and not to any views or comments made by sources outside the Party, however friendly.[35]

The Lublin PPS resented that the Western socialists undermined their legitimacy. They justified admitting former members of the WRN this way: 'We wanted to put an end to this legend [that the true socialists were outside the PPS], so that our friends in the West could not say any longer that there is a second Polish Socialist Party'.[36]

Morgan Phillips used Jerzy Szapiro from the Polish embassy as a channel of communication.[37] Szapiro probably wrote a document expressing the point of view of the right-wing of the PPS. The argument was that the PPS in Poland was no longer the Lublin PPS, as the old socialists were taking over the party from within. Openly condemning the communists would have been romantic, but the war had made the Poles realist. Reducing the power of the communists required patience, internal cohesion and ending banditry. Poland had to keep friendship with the Soviet Union and act as a bridge between the East and the West. Britain should not have provoked counterproductive tensions. Embracing this document, the Labour Party made a choice for the PPS in Poland,[38] though not a public one yet. Despite some distortions to convince the British, the centre-left faction actually became stronger with the nomination of Cyrankiewicz as party secretary in July 1945. Cyrankiewicz had been a local organiser before the war and a member of the WRN. In addition to the return of old party cadres and the resistance of socialist workers, demands for autonomy grew stronger, according to Gomułka, because of the success of international socialism.[39]

When the first International Socialist Conference convened in Clacton (17–19 May 1946), the Labour Party definitely chose the PPS in Poland, since it was decided to admit only living parties and one party per nation.[40] Healey said that even if the Polish socialists were communist stooges, they would report the content of the conference, showing to the Soviets that there was nothing to be suspicious of. Ciolkosz read the situation with greater clarity: 'You are strengthening the position of those people whom you consider to be Communist stooges and who now will be able to claim the blessing of the Labour Party'.[41] The Labour Party was breaking with the traditions of internationalism by throwing its weight behind one group in a factional struggle:

> Under these circumstances, the invitation of the leadership of the 'official' PPS to the Clacton Conference may easily create an impression of an official recognition and blessing by the British Labour Party to a group of usurpers, to the detriment of those genuine democratic Socialists, who are waging a hard and solitary struggle for freedom, democracy and socialism in Poland.[42]

In Britain the change of attitude towards the PPS took place under the same leadership, as a concession to the demands of the minority to preserve party unity. In contrast, the SFIO's attitude towards the Warsaw PPS was a point of contention between factions and the ascent to power of Guy Mollet provoked discontinuity.

In May 1946, the Polish socialist Debniki visited France to form a Franco-Polish Friendship Committee, convince French socialist to break relations with the London PPS and encourage Poles in France—former soldiers, POWs and migrants—to return to Poland. Debniki gained the sympathy of the leftist Bracke, who confessed his impotence, since he thought the party was influenced by British policies.[43] Later, Debniki met and quarrelled with the deputy secretaries of the SFIO Gérard Jaquet and Robert Verdier, close to Blum and Ciolkosz.[44] The French criticised the Poles for the persecution of old socialists and said that if the Debniki was there to ask for the SFIO's help, he could not complain about undue interferences. Debniki said that the PPS was a mass party of 300,000 members and the Poles would not be treated like children; also, they would not listen to suggestions on how to run elections, after the SFIO had lost a referendum. The French should have believed what their comrades said, not what the reactionary French Foreign ministry, the no less reactionary British Foreign Office and the reactionary and traitorous Polish socialists in exile said. What if the PPS had welcomed Paul Faure as a guest?

In September 1946 a Polish delegation led by the right-wing socialist Hochfeld attended the SFIO Congress.[45] Hochfeld resented the typically paternalistic treatment of Eastern Europeans by the French. However, the victory of Mollet and the left-wing faction changed party policy and the attitude towards the PPS as well. Mollet assured Hochfeld that his anti-communism was a concession to the right-wing of the party, but he intended to take control over the party machinery; he promised to help the PPS convince Polish refugees to return, that the party newspaper, *Populaire*, would pay more attention to news from Poland and to send a delegation to Poland. In addition, the left-wing socialist delegates of many parties discussed the possibility of creating an international journal with an editorial board of leftist socialists.

After the admission of the PPS to the International Socialist Conference, the Polish socialists in exile, led by Ciolkosz and Zaremba, continued to defend their cause[46] but their old friends ignored them and treated them as an embarrassment,[47] because they were resentful of the West, they allied with Polish nationalists and they condemned nationalisations.[48]

3   NATIONAL CHARACTER AND SOCIALISM

In 1981, Denis Healey warned that what a politician could do was limited. The socialist was not an engineer but a gardener: 'You have to respect the nature of the soil. You must know that certain plants will grow in certain places and not in others'.[49] The image of 'socialist as a gardener'—taken from Attlee[50]—summed up the assumptions that influenced how British socialists perceived politics in Eastern Europe and the Mediterranean. Only some nationalities were fit for socialism. This did not depend on social and economic factors but on a vaguer and more permanent 'national character', which made the actions of individuals predictable. This had major implications for Labour's attitude to an active Socialist International and European integration. British socialists imagined Europe crossed by two invisible lines—the Iron Curtain and the Olive Line—creating three spaces—Northern Europe, Southern Europe, Eastern Europe. Only Northern Europe was fit for socialism. Political phenomena could be explained by exploiting long-term preconceptions ingrained in British culture. The people on whom this discourse was 'imposed' could reject it or turn it to their advantage.

G.D.H. Cole wrote that introducing democratic socialism in the wrong country was difficult if not impossible, only countries where liberal tolerance and government by consent were already the norm were suitable.[51] In 1957 Healey said 'Socialism is a social response by human beings to their economic and political environment. It must differ from place to place and time to time'.[52] Geography determined the national character and politics:

> All over the world the people, like us, are human beings—but they are not human beings like us. Different landscapes tend to produce different people. [...] So if you want to understand the nature—or even the politics of a people, it is useful to meet them in their natural environment.[53]

Imaginary lines and mental mapping were not simply a shorthand, they were prescriptive. Geographic determinism justified essentialism—'Historical speculators from Hegel through Spengler to George Kennan have ascribed regime types to geographic factors'.[54] Values, actions, and feelings of the people could be explained by their national character or genius or spirit (*Volksgeist*). As Italian historian and leading anti-fascist intellectual Gaetano Salvemini explained:

> We agree that in a given time every section of humanity possess its defining—not just physical, but also psychological—features. We disagree with the idea that a historical process can be explained with an 'instinct' or *Volkgeist* or a 'national character.' Every time a lazy mind fails to discover the cause of the events, it fills the gap with one of these words. We cannot delude ourselves to have solved a historical question when we just hide our ignorance behind the cover of a false tautological explanation, which often is born out of self-congratulatory nationalism.[55]

Not all national characters were equal. As Labour embraced Whig historiography,[56] it accepted the notion that Britain, unlike the Continent, was naturally suited for parliamentary democracy.[57] This was how Trevelyan and Dalton explained fascism. According to Salvemini, it had racist assumptions:

> There is a brutal Nazi theory of the Nordic race. There is another, more flexible racist theory, which can be found in this suave and condescending refrain: 'You are unworthy of being equal to us in dignity. We possess a parliamentary nature; we have the genius of parliament. You have to settle with dictatorship.' Concepts like 'nature', 'genius', and 'instinct' require something primitive, permanent, and immutable as a basis: the 'race'.[58]

The language of culture and national character—like *Vansittartismus*—was used to dismiss Marxism and other explanations involving social or economic factors. A.J.P. Taylor gave theoretical foundation to the *Sonderweg* interpretation of German history by indicating the 'permanence of German geography' as the first factor shaping the German character.[59] In the debates over German rearmament the notion of a German character played a part,[60] but generally speaking the invisible line drawn by Vandervelde to explain fascism was no longer useful after the war.

In the post-war era a new imaginary line cut Europe in two, an iron curtain from Stettin in the Baltic to Trieste in the Adriatic. The defining of the identity of the civilised West exploited a widely accepted identification of Eastern Europe with backwardness and barbarism:

> It was Western Europe that invented Eastern Europe as its complementary other half in the eighteenth century, the age of Enlightenment. It was also the Enlightenment, with its intellectual centres in Western Europe, that cultivated and appropriated to itself the new notion of 'civilisation', an eighteenth-century neologism, and civilisation discovered its complement, within the same continent, in shadowed lands of backwardness, even barbarism.[61]

Eastern Europe was the transitional stage between Asia and Europe, thus Soviet rule could be presented as an Asiatic domination. The socialists did not invent the division of Europe, but they adopted the contrast. The Polish right-wing socialist Ludwik Grosfeld mentioned his desire 'to carry out Socialist revolution in Poland on Western not totalitarian lines'.[62] The two couple of adjectives in binary opposition (East-West, totalitarianism-democracy) were interchangeable. Mollet's most famous statement was that the communists 'looked neither Right nor Left, but to the East.'[63] Karl Czernetz explained that Soviet socialism did not suit Central and Western Europe[64] and Soviet expansionism was in continuity with Tsarist geopolitics.[65] For many socialists choosing the West meant choosing democracy. As the Hungarian communist Mihály Farkas complained, in people's democracies anti-communism was disguised under the idea of building a bridge between East and West—'the conflict between freedom and imperialism is reduced to a question of geography'"[66] The Italian communist Togliatti, turned the image to its head: the West was once the vanguard, but 'the centre of gravity of the civilised world has migrated since then', eastward.[67]

In the first two years of the International Socialist Conference, geographical essentialism was used not to highlight the contrast but to paper over the differences. East was economic democracy, West was political democracy; by their marriage, full socialism would be born.[68] In 1946 Nenni invoked the synthesis between East and West to keep Europe united—and above all, to keep his party united:

> What does the West mean for us? It is the region where the struggle of the vanguard men consolidated the freedom of thought, freedom of conscience, individual freedom [...]
> What does the East mean for us? It is the region that thirty years ago realised one of the greatest revolutions in history, defending it against the capitalist world.[69]

Socialist World, the journal of the International Socialist Conference, warned the reader to take local conditions, history and national character into consideration before judging too harshly the socialists of the East.[70] Different conditions made socialism diverse, but 'the essential socialist principles remain the same in all countries'.[71] Future Foreign Secretary, Patrick Gordon Walker said 'Berlin [...] is the front line between the eastern and western conception of democracy in Germany and in Europe'.[72] Czernetz asked for cooperation between Russia and Britain, 'between the victorious dictatorial socialism in the East and the only continuous democratic socialist experiment in the West'.[73]

Socialists exploited the notion about the 'barbaric' East to reinforce cohabitation. Polish[74] and Czechoslovak[75] socialists asked not to be judged by Western European standards. Western socialists would not allow massive expropriation, ethnic cleansing and persecution of dissenters in the civilized West, but these things could happen in Eastern Europe because of the environment and the character of the people. It served to deny the responsibility of the Eastern socialists and to absolve the Western socialists for their complicity.

Geographical determinism could justify a pro-Soviet stance—not by arguing that it was an ideal model but by saying that it was unreasonable to expect the USSR to meet Western European standards. The West also had undemocratic governments, civil strife and weak rule of law in a previous historical stage. Stalin was nothing more than what Cromwell had been—a comparison he encouraged.[76] Bevan warned not to be self-righteous about British civilisation, given that democratic government was very recent.[77] 'No elections east of the Elbe have ever been fair by British standards',[78] said a letter to the *New Statesman and Nation*; it was ignorant and insular to pretend from the East the same democracy that had taken centuries for Britain to develop.[79] John Ennals said that in Britain democracy meant rule of law, but in the East it meant majority rule, which had to be defended by reactionary enemies.[80] Some justified the Prague Coup with the Czechoslovak road to socialism,[81] while Zilliacus said that the Labour Party had to cooperate with the leaders the European workers had chosen, not 'the leadership that Transport House or anyone else might think they ought to choose'.[82]

The communists appropriated this rhetorical strategy, like the communist governor of Gdansk, who told British diplomats that the Western model of democracy suited English genius, but it was wrong for Poland, where it had brought about the dominations of capitalists and landowners.[83] It was no different from what Giovanni Papini—the ultra-nationalist Italian intellectual who anticipated many of the cultural themes of fascism—said: parliament suited the English genius, but in the hot climate had become 'rotten' and 'foul-smelling'.[84]

This cultural relativism while claiming to reject the hegemonic Western model was problematic, because, as Salvemini said, respecting the traditions of the local culture implied that tyranny and backwardness were integral part of the experience of being non-Western. As the *Tribune* said:

> In particular, [rebuilding] an International would depend on the crystallisation of zones of influence which would sacrifice the Eastern Socialist parties to Russia. The comfortable assumption that people living east of fourteen degrees latitude [sic, longitude] have no right to desire the western type of democracy is one which no socialist cannot afford to make.[85]

Ciolkosz the Polish socialist imprisoned by the *Sanacja*, driven into exile by Nazism and kept there by Communism, made a passionate appeal to Laski, asking him to judge the Polish experience through his own experience. In Britain, Laski enjoyed complete freedom of expression in words and writings, political freedom, he could vote for whomever he wanted and could engage in a political battle without putting his life in jeopardy:

> I am sure, Professor Laski cannot visualise for himself any other existence. And since he denies to others—to his fellow-men and fellow-Socialists—all these things which he enjoys, I am left with no alternative but to regard it as a sickeningly 'colonial' approach [...] Speaking of Poland, Professor Laski seems to be speaking of 'natives'. To hear this language, after the military

defeat of Nazism with its theories of inequality, national or racial superiority, contempt for the weak—is sinister. But I refuse to believe this voice to be the voice of British Socialism.[86]

This rhetoric of geography led to a paradox: people like Nenni and the left-wing socialists had criticised the geographical and essentialist arguments to justify fascism before the war, but they later embraced them to justify the communist regimes. During the Cold War, Healey explained that the values of democracy and socialism were not just the values of European culture but the values of 'the brotherhood of all men on this earth'.[87]

4 'THE DISLOYAL MPS'

During the war Gillies had warned that the International would be reborn in a climate of intense nationalism and anti-German feelings.[88] Tension with the PPS was not just ideological but nationalist and even ideological issues were expressed in a nationalistic language. In pre-war Poland, the strong Ukrainian, German and Jewish minorities resisted the hegemonic pretensions of the slim Polish majority. During the resistance all political forces, including the socialists, demanded Poland for the Poles, with minorities marginalised. Mass extermination by the Germans, ethnic cleansing of Germans and Ukrainians after the war and the flight of the Holocaust survivors due to pogroms led to an ethnically homogenous Poland where the self-expression of minorities was not tolerated. This was the only legitimacy that People's Poland had.[89] The communism of the PPR was in line with the 'national Bolshevism' developed in the 1930s in the Soviet Union: unity of the people in place of social contradictions, the myth of the nation in place of the myth of social revolution, nationalism as the unifying factor, the struggle of the national communities in place of class struggle.[90] The enemies of the new order were germs and allies to the Germans. The occupation of the new western territories was a permanent *casus belli* with Germany, which made the alliance with the Soviet Union essential, especially given the ambiguity of Western powers about the Oder-Neisse Frontier and their desire to revive Germany. On this issue, there was no real difference between the socialists in Warsaw and the socialists in exile. Ciolkosz always supported the collective guilt of the Germans[91] and denied their right to self-determination.[92] He wanted international socialism to approve Polish claims extending to Brandenburg, while rejecting the annexation of Eastern territories to the Soviet Union.[93] French socialists feared that the Poles would provoke the Third World War and fall into the hands of the Soviet Union to defend themselves from Germany. All Western socialists wanted some realistic compromise by Poland with its neighbours.

Polish socialists also backed an internal policy of national unity. They wished to avoid polarisation and civil war, which put them at odds with Mikołajczyk, whose party was backed by the Western governments. The PSL wanted free elections to build an alternative to communist power. Despite some enthusiasm for the Labour victory in 1945 by socialists and even communists,[94] the argument that Bevin's policy was a continuation of Churchill's soon took hold. At this stage, the factional struggle fully exploited international references. The leader of the Ultra-Left Matuszewski explicitly requested to follow the Yugoslav way—that is, immediate takeover and social revolution. The right-wing socialist intellectuals (Jan Topiński, Hochfeld and Jan Strzelcki) took Britain as a model of humanist socialism independent from communism.[95] The communists wanted complete nationalisation and centralisation, as Gomułka believed the workers were not mature enough and needed external authority.[96] Conversely, the socialists wanted workers' self-management and a mixed economy with three sectors—private, state, co-operative.

The Ministry of Information, controlled by Matuszewski encouraged regular anti-British propaganda, which hurt right-wing socialists the most. Consequently, right-wing socialists were particularly insistent that the British government avoided provocations. Hochfeld, published an imaginary letter to the Labour Party to plead his case. He rejected accusations from *Tribune* that Polish socialists accepted a single list of government parties at the elections under blackmail.[97] Continental socialism was different from British monarchical and traditional socialism. Like England under Cromwell, Poland was at the historical stage of repressing of the enemies of democracy, as recommended by Otto Bauer. The Polish way was not ideological but simply the pragmatic adaptation of socialism to national conditions. Grosfeld repeated the appeal for comprehension and support at the Clacton Conference.[98] Conversely, Cyrankiewicz had the impression that Western socialists did not understand that Eastern socialists needed unity with the communists: 'As European political life became polarized by the Cold War, Polish socialists felt both abandoned and misunderstood by their West European counterparts'.[99]

Tension with the Poles threatened the unity of the Labour Party, giving dissenters opportunities to oppose Bevin's policy. This played into the hands of the Poles, who exploited the internationalisation of domestic quarrels. Leftist public opinion in Britain feared anti-communism legitimising the return of bourgeois and reactionary forces—as was then happening in Greece. As Denis Healey, then a radical, warned the Labour Annual Conference in 1945, 'Socialist revolution has already begun in Europe' and Britain had to choose the right side, because 'The upper classes in every country are selfish, depraved, dissolute, and decadent'.[100] Although the *New Statesman and Nation* actually believed communist propaganda[101] and *Tribune* criticised repression by the regime, both journals condemned reactionaries in Poland and abroad, particularly the Polish Armed Forces organised by the Allies and not yet disbanded after the war.[102] The British government organised the Polish Resettlement Corps to discharge the soldiers and a civil bureaucracy of Polish civil servants providing cultural, education and welfare services to Poles in Britain. The Polish Government, backed by the Labour left-wing, demanded to be given control of the organisation or at least its dissolution, as it was a subversive centre and legitimised the existence of a White Poland, backed by Britain, an alternative to Red Poland. Nenni also asked Bevin to disband the Anders Army,[103] as the Polish soldiers disturbed social life and elections.[104] British trade unions harshly condemned Polish troops in Scotland as well.[105] The arguments of the British and Italians were the same: the Poles accepted former members of the Wehrmacht, were hostile to any form of socialism, took part in the black market, corrupted the virtue of young women, lived off state hand-outs and sought to build a state within the state.[106]

The Polish government exploited visits by British MPs and trade unionists to Poland to encourage dissent in the Labour Party and gain legitimacy.[107] The biographer of the British ambassador to Poland, Victor Cavendish-Bentick, argues that they undermined the British policy of resisting communism.[108] Labour Party members came from the working-class and they listened to the words of Polish socialists and communists, who came from the same social milieu; conversely, they distrusted the upper classes, whether conservative Poles or British diplomats.[109] A visit abroad was also the opportunity to express discontent about Bevin's policy, which was not exclusive of the Labour left.[110] In some cases, the Polish Ministry of Information took Labour members who had never been abroad and did not speak foreign languages, organised guided tours, waited for them to make a press statement in favour of the Polish Government and then abandoned them at the British embassy.[111] At the end of 1945 Bevin had tried to block these visits[112] and in April 1946 he blocked a delegation of the Labour Party,[113] after a parliamentary delegation—over which he had less control—irritated the Foreign Office[114] and pro-British Poles opposing communism.[115] The Foreign Office repeated its opposition to sending a delegation for the elections of January 1947: 'Surely the delegation will inevitably be nobbled by communists and fellow-travellers and used for electoral propaganda?'[116]

In Czechoslovakia the problem was the same, as the Ministry of Information invited British speakers who could embarrass the British Government, like the communist leader Pritt, Zilliacus and the historian of the Soviet Union E.H. Carr.[117] The Foreign Office could only react by 'exporting reliable citizens and reliable information'.[118] The embassy had the Minister of Health, not a communist, invite reliable speakers, including Labour MPs with a medical background.[119]

Press statements made by Labour visitors criticising the Government were reused in the Soviet, Polish and even British press.[120] The Foreign Office talked about a 'fifth column' in the British press that repeated propaganda from the Polish embassy, often unwillingly, as many newspapers could not afford foreign correspondents.[121] There was an on-going triangulation so that articles published in Britain and inspired by the Polish embassy were reprinted in Poland as indicative of the British public opinion:

> Szapiro and Co. are very pleased with the Left Wing Labour Members of Parliament whom they think they have nobbled, and have been much annoyed when Strasburger [the ambassador, a career diplomat] has pointed out that these individuals have little influence and that it would be far better to make friends with other elements.[122]

5 'A Mark of Special Favour to the Polish Socialist Party'

Denis Healey left a description of Labour's policy towards Eastern European social democrats that deserves to be quoted in full:

> While endeavouring to assist our Eastern European colleagues to the fullest extent in their crucial struggle, it has nevertheless been the policy of the

Labour Party up till now to encourage Social Democratic parties wherever possible to fight within the country concerned and if necessary within a National coalition, rather than be forced into opposition or exile. Moreover in order to avoid being accused of 'splitting the unity of the workers', they have always attempted [to] co-operate with the Communists rather than be identified with any anti-Communist or anti-Soviet blocs. In view of this the Labour Party, which always hopes that some basis of understanding may yet be achieved with Russia and Eastern Europe, has been very chary of recognising dissident and avowedly anti-Soviet growls in exile, including the Polish Socialist Party's Delegation for Abroad [Ciolkosz] (although during the war, when it was one of the Resistance groups, we did co-operate with it closely).

[...]

In conclusion, it must be stated that our foreign policy at the present time, though it may appear sometimes to be illogical and indecisive, is based on the conviction that Social Democracy can provide a third alternative to Russian Communism on the one hand and American free-for-all capitalism on the other—and further, that this third way, though attacked from both Right and Left, is the only way if democracy, as we understand it, is to survive. By fighting continually for our ideals and working for the collaboration of all socialist parties, we still hope to prevent the irrevocable division of Europe into two.[123]

Labour's policy perfectly matched that of right-wing Eastern socialists (Hochfeld, Majer, Böhm in Hungary), who from liberation had asked for preferential treatment from the British Governments because of their socialist identity and ability to block the communist takeover. In January 1947, the Foreign Office adopted the official policy 'to encourage any anti-Communist tendencies inside the Government blocs'.[124] It could be questioned whether the Foreign Office was exploiting informal socialist diplomacy to play power politics or the Labour Party was exploiting diplomatic channels to serve its goals or the Eastern socialists were using international connections to fight their factional struggle. Indeed, this cooperation worked only in the small window of time when the interests of the three groups coincided.

The initial British policy was to support the forces openly opposing the communist takeover. They supported popular parties (Mikołajczyk's PSL in Poland and the Smallholders in Hungary) or 'independent socialists' who had broken with the pro-communist leadership of the official socialist parties. The Foreign Office tried to convince the Labour Party to support these parties, especially dissident Romanian and Bulgarian social democrats—Petrescu and Lulchev.[125] Healey bluntly refused, saying these splinter parties lacked a working-class following and were not free to organise. For Healey, the following of the working-class was a better weapon against communism than ideological clarity, so he believed it was possible to encourage official social democrats to regain independence from the communists.[126] The diplomats were not convinced.[127]

In Poland, Mikołajczyk allied with dissident socialists—heirs to the prewar party and in contact with Ciołkosz. One of their leaders toured Europe seeking help from their Western comrades.[128] Mikołajczyk wanted the Labour Party to convince the PPS to break with the communists and to refuse to run in elections in a single list of all Government parties. He asked for the intervention of *Tribune*.[129] McNeil had to ask this as a personal favour to Jennie Lee—the Foreign Office did not have contacts with leftist papers.[130] *Tribune* was already criticising the Polish Government and Zilliacus as a mouthpiece of Polish propaganda,[131] so it was cooperation rather than subordination. The published article[132] irritated the right-wing of the PPS, which accepted the single list and expected the Labour Party and the British Government to appreciate their efforts. This was the catalyst for Hochfeld to write his pamphlet to the Labour Party.[133] Already in December 1945, the socialist prime minister Osóbka-Morawski told diplomats that the PPS was indispensable to avoid a communist monopoly of power, so it merited British help.[134] He repeated these arguments when Morgan Phillips visited Warsaw on his way back from Moscow.[135]

In Czechoslovakia, the Foreign Office trusted Beneš to resist communist penetration,[136] but Beneš wanted the Labour Party to drive the ČSSD towards anti-communism and help the faction contesting the pro-Soviet and pro-communist line of Fierlinger.[137] The Foreign Office urged Attlee to send a telegram of encouragement to the ČSSD Congress in October 1945.[138] The diplomats also prepared a propaganda campaign to present Great Britain as a model of ordered progress.[139] When the secretary of the ČSSD, Vilím, asked for magazines, newspapers and information material from the Labour Party, Morgan Phillips asked the Foreign Office to provide air transport.[140]

Since 1945, the rank and file of the ČSSD had been pressuring the leadership to break the alliance with the communists, and so, starting in 1946, they tried to decelerate the revolution without openly breaking away.[141] The abysmal election result in May 1946 strengthened those, like

Majer and Görner, who wanted more autonomy and to be treated as equals by the communists.[142]

The terror campaign against Mikołajczyk's party during the election of January 1947 caused the PPS to worry about its fate. In addition, the leaders knew the 1946 referendum had been a fraud, so they assumed that the communists needed their help to govern and also that those opposing communism would gather around them. The basis of this new self-confidence was the belief that they were indispensable, which was nothing less than the delusion that the people's democracy was actually different from a one-party system. A planned coup at party headquarters by the ultra-left—foreshadowing what would happen to the ČSSD in 1948—was prevented in September 1946, strengthening Cyrankiewicz and the centrist faction. According to Kersten, this episode was read as a warning discouraging autonomy,[143] while according to Prazmowska, Cyrankiewicz exploited the episode to repress the ultra-left and strengthen the position of the PPS.[144] In addition, Cyrankiewicz met Stalin, who led him to believe that the USSR would support the PPS if it was loyal to Moscow in foreign policy. The PPS was in a strong bargaining position when negotiating for more seats in the single list and positions in the state bureaucracy.

While negotiations took place, elements of the PPS asked the British Government to switch its support to them. The British embassy had recently introduced a labour attaché, Kirby, which gave the Polish socialists a direct channel.[145] Grosfeld explained that it was chimerical to expect impartial elections in Poland and Western protestations were counterproductive, but the PPS could play a central role.[146] Détente and reassurance about the Oder-Neisse frontier would make the PPS the dominant force in politics and among the working-class.[147]

British diplomats could not agree on whether the socialists could become an autonomous force.[148] It is hard to say whether their private pledges about independence were sincere, since Polish socialists said different things to different people. Osobka-Morawski told the British Ambassador that the pact of unity of action with the PPR was a temporary measure that would have allowed the socialists to gain a foothold and overtake the communists,[149] but he told the Italian Ambassador, the communist Eugenio Reale, that it was unthinkable that the communists and socialists could have different opinions on vital issues and that the supporters of an independent PPS were a minority.[150]

In December 1946, Osobka-Morawski told the British Ambassador that Britain had to stake everything on the PPS. A contentious issue was the return of the gold deposited in London during the war, which the British had promised to return if the Poles abided by the Yalta Agreement and stopped persecuting the PSL. Osobka-Morawski said frankly that he could not save the PSL, as he already had enough problems keeping socialists out of jail. He asked for the restitution of the Polish gold 'as a mark of special favour to the Polish Socialist Party',[151] complaining about an absence of socialist solidarity on the British side. The Foreign Office considered this appeal pathetic, as Osobka-Morawski was a socialist in words, but his actions indicated otherwise.[152]

Ten days later, after meeting Cyrankiewicz, the secretary of the PPS and prime minister from January 1947, the British Ambassador Cavendish-Bentinck completely changed his mind.[153] Cyrankiewicz's policy was the same as Osobka-Morawski's: to strengthen the autonomy of the party while maintaining the alliance with the communists. Cyrankiewicz said that the Soviets made it clear they would not accept a Government without the communists, but it was possible for the Polish and Czechoslovak socialists to avoid the Yugoslav way. He had already excluded crypto-communist socialists and received guarantees against communist interferences. The Western powers had to accept the lesser evil and back the socialists discreetly; one way was returning the Polish gold and having the treaty signed by a socialist minister, who would receive the acclaim.

Cavendish-Bentinck was impressed by Cyrankiewicz's personality and asked for a completely new policy.[154] Elections would not remove the communists; Cavendish-Bentinck knew that president Bierut had told Reale that the Italian communists had the masses, but the Polish communists had the power and they would keep it. The only way was 'to support the Socialist Party very discreetly and encourage any opposition it may make to the Soviet-sponsored Communists'.[155] Cavendish-Bentinck had confidence in the new generation of socialist leaders and the industrial workers, who, unlike the inert peasants, could mobilise and paralyse the nation with a general strike. Britain had to accept the Oder-Neisse frontier, return the Polish gold and end discrimination against Polish workers in Great Britain.[156] The Polish socialists increased their contacts with Kirby[157] and Hochfeld promised to celebrate Labour's achievements in the party newspaper.[158] The British embassy also opened a reading room filled with material provided by the Labour Party.[159]

Cavendish-Bentinck was naïve in many ways, particularly about the power and intentions of the socialists, but he predicted how the communist regime would fall: a new generation of determined political activists would organise the workers in a permanent mobilisation that would make the country ungovernable. This new generation, however, would come from the Catholics, not the socialists, and it took 30 years to start, not three.

Cavendish-Bentinck's enthusiasm encouraged a complete revision in January 1947; the new policy for Eastern Europe was to spread Western social democracy as a bulwark against communism.[160] The plan included visits by parliamentarians, trade unionists, officials of the co-operative movement, spreading positive information about social democracy and influencing foreign correspondents. The groundwork for the creation of the IRD was laid down.

Prazmoswka argues that this policy was short-lived and the socialists showed few signs of independence, but the matter is complex.[161] Indeed, by February, Cavendish-Bentinck was less optimistic, but still repeated the same recommendations and Foreign Office officials, although sceptical, clung to this policy as *faute de mieux*, with no better alternative,[162] or to avoid creating a precedent of voluntary capitulation.[163] In addition, Kirby and Healey had faith in the Polish socialists to the very last and thus ensured that they received special attention from the Foreign Office. Even Bevin, who was hardly soft on communists, was confident enough of being able to help the Polish socialists.[164] For example, when he went to Warsaw in April 1947, he refused to discuss the return of the Polish gold with the communist foreign minister[165] and he had a private meeting with Cyrankiewicz.[166] They agreed on the compensation of British shareholders for the nationalisations and the return of the gold. Bevin said that he would not force the Polish soldiers to return to Poland, because he was a trade unionist and he would not abandon those who had fought at his side. Bevin explained that he was working to create a bridge between the East and the West, and Cyrankiewicz said he would prefer Bevin to build it rather than Truman. Grosfeld was enthusiastic about the meeting and thanked the British.[167] Bevin praised Cyrankiewicz in the Commons[168] and at the Annual Conference of the Labour Party, repeating his famous statement of 1945, that 'left can talk to left' in foreign affairs.[169] The Foreign Office was satisfied with the results, which had as a consequence a reduction of anti-British propaganda in the socialist press,[170] and they defended the choice with the Americans.[171]

In June, the embassy considered the policy a reasonable success: Bevin's visit increased the prestige of the socialists, who showed some resistance in rejecting the communist proposal for a united party.[172] A future commercial treaty would increase the prestige of Grosfeld, the undersecretary for foreign trade. In conclusion, Britain would have a reduced role, but at least it could have helped the socialists through the exchange of visits and providing information material. While Prazmowska is right that the Foreign Office was sceptical about this policy of favouring Polish socialists, they continued enforcing it for many months. This détente between Poland and Great Britain concealed the fragility of this friendship amidst international tensions and the inexorable pace of the communist takeover.[173]

6 THE BEGINNING OF THE COLD WAR

In June, Cyrankiewicz told the new ambassador Gainer that Bevin's visit opened a new era for Anglo–Polish relations, but he was worried about the renewed communist offensive and Marshall's Harvard speech.[174] In the first half of 1947, the Polish socialists had become stronger, which Gomulka explained with the Reaction's backing of the socialists, particularly right-wing socialists, whom he considered 'wilful and unhesitating Anglo-Saxon agents'.[175] The Industry Minister Minc started the takeover of the distribution of consumer goods, harming the co-operatives, a socialist stronghold, and delegitimising the three-sector economy.[176] This was accompanied by a witch hunt hitting socialists. At the International Socialist Conference in Zurich (6–9 June 1947), the Polish socialists explained the situation to Healey, who promised to send a delegation from the British Co-Operative Alliance to help them.[177] Healey was employing all the 'soft power' at his disposal, but it was completely unsuited to go up against the power of the communist-controlled police and army.

Minc's action was the turning point for power relations inside the party. Cyrankiewicz marginalised the resurgent ultra-left and the right-wing of the party,[178] whose demand for a specifically socialist economic policy was rejected and whose representatives lost their positions in the party. The principle of 'no enemy to the left' was enshrined. Healey did not care for Osobka-Morawski, whose journey from the Left to the Right made him suspicious, but he still trusted Cyrankiewicz and wanted the British secret services to extract him if possible.[179] A greatly misplaced trust, as he would continue as Prime Minister of communist Poland until 1970, with a brief interruption of just two years! Healey disliked Hochfeld: 'He is a rather histrionical person who regularly offers his resignation when crossed'.[180] These words reveal an attitude typical of the British Labour movement, a strong hostility towards the right-wing elements in the Continental socialist parties, whom they considered petit bourgeois intellectuals, opportunists and hysterical. Healey used similar words for Saragat and there was a widespread hostility to the SFIO, radical in words and opportunist in its deeds. The strength of the Labour Party was its following among the working-class, which gave them a majority to govern alone and to implement a radical programme, the only alternative to communism for the disheartened masses. Centrists ready to make compromises with the conservatives were as much a threat to unity as communists.

In July, the new ambassador concluded that British policy in Poland had failed and the socialists only wanted to save their lives. The fusion had not yet taken place so as to not frighten socialists abroad.[181] Under these conditions, any gesture of goodwill would have been useless. When Bevin asked whether the return of Polish gold had helped the socialists, the ambassador said that the communists had taken the credit, because they controlled the press. In August 1947, the Foreign Office informed the Labour Party that 'the Socialist horse is no longer a good bet'.[182] This change also signalled the political turnaround made possible by the Marshall Plan. As Bevin explained to the Polish minister Rusinek, Britain would no longer propose general plans for European reconstruction, but it would go on alone with the willing nations.[183]

Healey still had faith in the PPS.[184] The Fabian Society hosted a socialist delegation from Poland—which published a series of articles celebrating the reforms of the Labour Government[185]—and Kirby continued to recommend privileged treatment for the PPS. It was the Polish socialists who started to shun the attentions of the British, and Cyrankiewicz made it clear that being linked with the West had become a burden[186] and stressed how Polish socialism was completely different to the British kind.[187] When Kirby tried to organise a visit of British co-operatives to Poland, he discovered that the communists had taken over the organisation and blocked the contacts.[188]

The situation was the same in Czechoslovakia, as the power struggle became a life-or-death confrontation in the middle of 1947.[189] The political players deliberately assumed an intransigent position, as international tension made a coalition impossible and the democratic parties understood that the communists would have to resort to subversive measures. The political climate was tainted by threats of violence and accusations of aiding German revanchism through the Marshall Plan. The anti-communist parties rallied the enemies of the revolution with accusations of 'terror', but they failed to offer any positive content.[190] The impression that anti-communism was identical to anti-socialism made an alliance with the social democrats impossible.

In the ČSSD, the right-wing became stronger and bet on Laušman as an alternative to Fierlinger.[191] While originally leftist, Laušman spoke in favour of socialism in the Czechoslovak form and an alliance with socialist Britain. The British embassy was not satisfied with the slow evolution: reliable leaders, like Majer, were gutless and the leaders contesting Fierling, like Vilim and Laušman, unreliable. When the National Socialists—a non-Marxist socialist party with an unfortunate name—asked for direct help from the Labour Party, the Ambassador encouraged the Foreign Office to support this request, as British policy was to encourage all socialists confronting the communists.[192]

When Healey visited Czechoslovakia in 1947, he explained to the National Socialists that the Labour Party could not formally initiate international contacts with them, though the National Socialists were not interested in an affiliation to the 'informal Socialist International'.[193] The difference was that the Foreign Office saw support of the anti-communist forces as merely instrumental, but the Labour Party had to develop international fraternal relations in accordance to its principles and its social democratic identity. The transnational socialist network was more about identity than individual issues. As in other countries, the Foreign Office could count on the occasional help of the Labour Party but could not issue orders.

In October 1947, the Soviet leadership created the Cominform as a new international organisation for the communist parties of Europe and Zhdanov imposed the new doctrine: the parliamentary road to socialism had been overrated and state control was necessary to save the people's democracy. There were two-camps: the Western imperialist camp and the USSR-led democratic camp. The only relationship with the social democrats was their submission and fusion in a working-class unity party; those who refused were complicit with imperialism. The only choice for the social democrats was to accept or to resist. The former was the Polish way, the latter the Czechoslovak, and both led to the disappearance of social democracy in Eastern Europe:

> They [the social democratic leaders] had gone out of their way to co-operate with the Communists, to prove their friendship towards the Soviet Union and to promote a programme of social transformation as radical as anything

demanded by the Communists. That was not enough. Nothing short of complete emasculation through fusion with the Communists was considered satisfactory.[194]

International tension led to the escalation of the internationalisation of domestic quarrels. Fierlinger and the ČSSD press continuously defamed German social democracy, while right-wing social democrats were more sympathetic.[195] When the time came to decide on the Marshall Plan, Fierlinger conceded that the Labour Party recognised the need of the Czechoslovaks to cooperate with the communists, but when Molotov forced the Prague Government to withdraw its acceptance, Fierlinger embraced the Soviet arguments, while Majer found himself isolated in the party and the Government for his support of the Marshall Plan. Fierlinger and Erban said that the Cominform was merely a response to the International Socialist Conference and they started openly criticising the Labour Party. At the Antwerp Conference, the ČSSD broke for the first time with the Poles and Italians and voted for the creation of Comisco. At the Executive Committee of January 1948, Fierlinger said that the International Socialist Conference was the continuation of the Second International and an organisation with anti-Soviet intentions devoted to preserving capitalism. He asked to leave the organisation, but the other members of the executive rejected the proposal in very harsh terms.

The deteriorating political climate in Czechoslovakia and the encouragement of the Ultra-Left by the communists increased the internal convulsions, culminating in the party congress in Brno on 14–16 November 1947.[196] Although everyone accepted cooperation with the communists, Laušman proposed strengthening the party and demanding equal dignity, Fierlinger emphasised the need to fight the reaction backed by Western capital. Though almost 80% of delegates criticised Fierlinger, only 61% went as far as voting for Laušman as an alternative. It was also unclear how many rejected cooperation entirely and how many were seeking a stronger bargaining position. As in Poland, the centrist elements allied with the right-wing against the ultra-left backed by the communists. Even the leader of the Czechoslovak communists, Gottwald, said the congress was a success for the right-wing, backed by national and international Reaction and a failure for the socialist left-wing. For Healey this was enough—in addition to professions of democracy and denunciations of communist terror—to diagnose a victory for socialist autonomy. He believed that a more confident attitude would force the communists to caution, as they could not reach their goal of 51% of votes at the elections. In an ominous gesture, Healey wrote in the margin the words: 'without open terrorisation'.[197]

Healey's comments at the Congress of the PPS in December were similar. The alliance of centrist and right-wing factions prevailed and the congress strove to demonstrate the irreplaceable role of the PPS in Poland and Europe, in order to reject the proposal for unification.[198] Hochfeld's programme offered a synthesis between communism and social democracy. Cyrankiewicz defended the unique role of the PPS at the international level—'The Polish road to socialism must be a bridge between the Russian revolution and the future social revolution in the West'.[199] Oskar Lange condemned sectarian Internationals working against the united front—meaning Comisco but also Cominform.[200] The task of the PPS was to work for the creation of a unitary International maintaining contacts with the revolutionary elements in the West. Drobner even dared to defend Leon Blum.[201]

Healey still trusted the Eastern European socialists and believed they had a role in the Soviet sphere of influence. They were defending their principles and independent organisation, biding their time until the end of the Cold War, which he expected to be over soon. The audience booed the speeches of Gomułka and Grumbach, but they cheered Healey when he explained how the Labour Party defeated the steel industry and House of Lords, two strongholds of Reaction.[202] He said the Poles envied the Labour Party, but feared replicating the weakness of French socialism.

By the start of 1948, the conditions for independent social democracy in Poland and Czechoslovakia no longer existed. Cyrankiewicz made his contribution by working with the Hungarian social democrats to oust the autonomous leadership of the ČSSD.[203] The Czechoslovak communists helped in the creation of a secret organisation of the social democratic left-wing: 'The "left" had been entirely organised, led, financed and manipulated by the communists [...] It was not a classic "left-wing opposition" so much as a communist faction inside social democracy'.[204]

The Prague coup was started by the resignation of National Socialist and Popular ministers in an attempt to block the communist ascendancy. The communists had control of the centres of power and the trade union movement, a better organisation and were willing to use force.[205] The social democrats stayed neutral, divided between Majer's request to dissolve the Gottwald Government and the left-wing request for a Government of only communists and social democrats. While on 24

February the presidium of the ČSSD was still debating the issue, extremist social democrats, encouraged by the communists, organised assault squads that took over party headquarters and newspapers, with the help of the security forces. The full-out assault wrong-footed the social democrats, whose only concern became saving the lives of their militants. Right-wing social democrats like Majer and Vilim were excluded and the centre accepted yielding and saving whatever influence it was able to.

After 25 February the ČSSD was completely purged from the inside and when the communists were not satisfied, they purged it from the outside as well.[206] The centrists lost power, substituted by the Ultra-Left. Another working-class party could not exist, so fusion was forced with urgency. However, local social democratic organisations were liquidated to prevent the infiltration of right-wing social democrats in the new party. In Poland there was no need to persecute the leaders, who remained in charge until the fusion, gaining important positions in the new unified party:

> If, adhering to contemporary public opinion [...], we consider the PPS as a defeated army, then the commanders of this army really strove to obtain the best possible terms of surrender.[207]

The Polish centrist socialists did not lose political agency and they personally took care of eliminating the right-wing elements resisting communism. Although the Western socialists were surprised, there was continuity. At the December 1947 congress, the PPS wanted to show it was irreplaceable and later the leaders wanted to demonstrate that their cooperation was more useful than their resistance. The imminent fusion changed the relations of power in the party and consequently its international alliances: five days after approving fusion in March 1948, the PPS broke with the Western socialists.[208] The end of Czechoslovak social democracy was tragic, but, as the Bundist Lucien Blijt noted: 'Even so, if only for the sake of the future, there is an enormous difference between capitulation and defeat'.[209]

NOTES

1. P. Heumos (1991) 'Die Sozialdemokratie in Ostmitteleuropa 1945–1948. Zum gesellschaftlichen Potential des demokratischen Sozialismus in Polen, der Tschechoslowakei und Ungarn', in H. Lemberg (ed.) *Sowjetisches Modell und nationale Prägung. Kontinuität und Wandel in Ostmitteleuropa nach dem Zweiten Weltkrieg* (Marburg/Lahn: J.G.Herder-Institut), 51–70.

2. D. Healey (ed.) (1951) *The Curtain Falls: The Story of the Socialists in Eastern Europe* (London: Lincolns-Prager).
3. A. Applebaum (2013) *Iron Curtain: The Crushing of Eastern Europe 1944–1956*, (London: Penguin Books), Chapter 9.
4. A.J. Prazmowska (2000) 'The Polish Socialist Party 1945–1948', *East European Quarterly*, 34, 3, 337.
5. P. Heumos (2004) 'Einleitung' in P. Heumos (ed.) *Europäischer Sozialismus im Kalten Krieg: Briefe und Berichte 1944–1948* (Frankfurt: Campus), 13–17.
6. For the Hungarian social democrats see U. Jodah (2003), *The Hungarian Social Democrats and the British Labour Party, 1944–8* (PhD Thesis: University of West England, Bristol).
7. P. Heumos, 'Einleitung', 33.
8. P. Heumos, 'Einleitung', 37.
9. J. Gross (1997) 'War as Revolution', in N. Naimark, L. Gibianskii (eds), *The Establishment of Communist Regimes in Eastern Europe, 1944–1949* (Boulder: Westview press), 17–35. Also P. Kenney (1997) *Rebuilding Poland: Workers and Communists, 1945–1950* (Ithaca: Cornell University Press), 1–23.
10. A.J. Prazmowska (2004) *Civil War in Poland, 1942–1948* (Basingstoke: Palgrave), 1–23.
11. V. Tismaneanu (2009) 'Diabolical Pedagogy and the (Il)logic of Stalinism in Eastern Europe', in V. Tismaneau (ed.) *Stalinism Revisited: The Establishment of Communist Regimes in East-Central Europe* (Budapest: Central European University Press), 25–34.
12. Heumos, 'Die Sozialdemokratie in Ostmitteleuropa 1945–1948', 54–57.
13. A. Ciolkosz (1946) *The Expropriation of a Socialist Party*, (New York: Polish Socialist Alliance).
14. K. Kersten (1991) *The Establishment of Communist Rule in Poland, 1943–1948* (Berkley: University of California Press), 177.
15. Kersten, *The Establishment of Communist Rule in Poland*, 14–117. Prazmowska, 'The Polish Socialist Party 1945–1948', 338–341. Ciolkosz denied this decision in Ciolkosz, *The Expropriation of a Socialist Party*.
16. Prazmowska, *Civil War in Poland*, 40.
17. K. Kaplan (1984) *Das Verhängnisvolle Bündnis. Unterwanderung, Gleichschaltung und Vernichtung der Tschechoslowakischen Sozialdemokratie 1944–1954* (Wuppertal: Pol-Verlag), 36–40. M. Myant (1981) *Socialism and Democracy in Czechoslovakia, 1945–1948* (Cambridge: Cambridge University Press), 46–52.
18. Kaplan, *Das Verhängnisvolle Bündnis*, 140–143.
19. The communists employed this interpretative scheme as well (Kersten, *The Establishment of Communist Rule in Poland*, 185).

20. Congress of the Socialist Party in Warsaw, *Polpress*, 6 July 1945.
21. Kersten, *The Establishment of Communist Rule in Poland*, 143.
22. J. Micgiel (1997) '"Bandits and reactionaries": The Suppression of the Opposition in Poland, 1944–1946' in Naimark, Gibianskii (eds), *The Establishment of Communist Regimes in Eastern Europe*, 93–104.
23. Kenney, *Rebuilding Poland*, 40–57.
24. Kenney, *Rebuilding Poland*, 118.
25. Heumos, 'The Sozialdemokratie in Ostmitteleuropa 1945–1948', 63–65.
26. P. Heumos (1983) 'Die britische Labour Party und die sozialistischen Parteien Ostmitteleuropas, 1944–1948' *Bohemia*, 24, 319–322. Heumos, 'Einleitung', 24–37.
27. M. Phillips, 'Czechoslovakia', Labour History Archive and Study Centre, People's History Museum, Manchester (LHASC), Labour Party (LP), International Sub-Committee, Minutes & Documents, 1945.
28. Nichols to Bevin, 27 October 1945, The National Archives, Kew (TNA), FO 371/47094-N14763. Nichols to Bevin, 26 October 1945, TNA, FO 371/47094-N14858.
29. Kaplan, *Das Verhängnisvolle Bündnis*, 50–54; 111–116.
30. [T. Williamson], 'Czechoslovakia', LHASC, LP, International Sub-Committee, Minutes & Documents, 1945.
31. 'A Statement by the PPS', 8 January 1945 1/4, LHASC, LP, ID, CORR, POL.
32. Prazmowska, *Civil War in Poland*, 131. What's happening, *Tribune* 5 January 1945. What's happening, *Tribune* 26 January 1945. What's happening, *Tribune* 23 March 1945. What's happening, *Tribune*, 9 November 1945.
33. A. Ciolkosz to M. Phillips, 15 May 1945 1/10; Labour Party to PPS, 21 June 1945 1/17; M. Phillips to Ciolkosz, 1 June 1945 1/12, LHASC, LP, ID, CORR, POL.
34. Howie to A.S. Moyse, 29 June 1945, LHASC, LP, Denis Healey's Papers (DH), 4, 13.
35. Ciolkosz to W.N. Ewer (Daily Herald), 17 June 1945 1/15, LHASC, LP, ID, CORR, POL.
36. Ciolkosz, *The Expropriation of a Socialist Party*, 11.
37. 'Memorandum on Certain Anglo-Polish problems', 28 September 1945 1/46, LHASC, LP, ID, CORR, POL.
38. 'Conditions in Poland, September 1945', LHASC, LP, JSM, INT, 13, Poland 1945. There is no signature, but it is clearly the product of Polish socialists. Huemos does not identify any particular group (Heumos (ed.), *Europäischer Sozialismus im kalten Krieg*, 115–123). The decision to circulate the document in the International Sub-committee – under the heading 'International Department' – indicates a clear choice for the socialist in

Poland over the Party in exile, which kept sending a lot of material, which was not circulated.
39. Kersten, *The Establishment of Communist Rule in Poland*, 184.
40. 'Note on the possible reconstruction of the Socialist International', January 1946, 27/4/17, LHASC, LP, LSI.
41. 'Aufzeichnung eines Gesprächs zwischen dem polnischen Sozialisten A. Ciolkosz und dem britischen Sozialisten D.Healey', 6 May 1946, in Heumos (ed.), *Europäischer Sozialismus im Kalten Krieg*, 142.
42. Ciolkosz to M. Phillips, 13 May 1946, Heumos (ed.), *Europäischer Sozialismus im Kalten Krieg*, 145–146.
43. K. Debniki to the International Department of the PPS Executive, 17 May 1946, b, Heumos (ed.), *Europäischer Sozialismus im Kalten Krieg*, 151–153.
44. K. Debniki to the International Department of the PPS Executive, 17 May 1946, c, Heumos (ed.), *Europäischer Sozialismus im Kalten Krieg*, 153–162.
45. 'Bericht des polnischen Sozialisten J.Hochfeld über die internationale sozialistische Konferenz über das Franco-Regime und den XXXVIII Parteitag der SFIO in Paris', September 1946, Heumos (ed.), *Europäischer Sozialismus im Kalten Krieg*, 165–182.
46. Delegation abroad of the Polish Socialist Party (Adam Ciolkosz) to the delegates of the International Socialist Conference (Bournemouth), 7 November 1946, Heumos (ed.), *Europäischer Sozialismus im Kalten Krieg*, 193–197.
47. P. Noel-Baker to D. Healey, 27 January 1947; Ciolkosz to Noel-Baker, 9 January 1947, LHASC, LP, DH, 9, 5.
48. Bialas, Zaremba to Partie Socialiste Belge, 21 October 1947, Heumos (ed.), *Europäischer Sozialismus im Kalten Krieg*, pp.207–209.
49. 'Healey's Socialism – an Interview with Austin Mitchell' in G. Radice (ed.) (1981) *Socialism with a Human Face*, (London), 4–5.
50. J.H. Brookshire (1995) *Clement Attlee* (Manchester: Manchester University Press), 11.
51. G.D.H. Cole, Democratic Socialism for Europe, *New Statesman and Nation*, 17 January 1948.
52. D. Healey, 'European socialism today', *New Leader*, 16 September 1957 in D. Healey (1990) *When Shrimps Learn to Whistle: Signposts for the Nineties* (London: Penguin), 64–65.
53. D. Healey (2002) *Healey's World: Travels with my Camera* (Lewes: Book Guild), 236.
54. C.S. Maier (1988) *The Unmasterable Past: History, Holocaust, and German National Identity* (Cambridge, Mass: Harvard university press), 117.

55. G. Salvemini, 'Monarchia o Repubblica' in G. Salvemini (1969) *L'Italia vista dall'America* (Milano: Feltrinelli), 217–218 On this argument see A. Lyttelton (1973) *The Seizure of Power: Fascism in Italy, 1919–1929* (London: Weidenfeld and Nicolson), 2.
56. S. Berger and P. Lambert (2003) 'Intellectual Transfers and Mental Blockades' in S. Berger and P. Lambert (eds.), *Historikerdialoge: Geschichte, Mythos und Gedächtnis im deutsch-britischen kulturellen Austausch 1750–2000*, (Göttingen: Vandenhoeck & Ruprecht), 58.
57. M. Spiering (2015) *A Cultural History of British Euroscepticism* (Basingstoke: Palgrave Macmillan) 23–29. A. Berselli (1971) *L'opinione pubblica inglese e l'avvento del fascismo* (Milano: Franco Angeli), 120.
58. G. Salvemini, '"Natura" o "Civiltà"' in G Salvemini, *L'Italia vista dall'America*, 141. First published in *The Nation*, 27 March 1943.
59. A.J.P. Taylor (1988) *The Course of German History: A Survey of the Development of German History since 1814* (London: Rutledge), 2. Originally published in 1945.
60. R. Crowfort (2008) 'Labour Party Factionalism and West German Rearmament 1950–4', in P. Corthorn, J. Davis (eds), *The British Labour Party and the Wider World* (London: Tauris), 141.
61. L. Wolff (1994) *Inventing Eastern Europe: The Map of Civilization on the Mind of the Enlightenment* (Stanford: Stanford University Press), 4. For the use of the Other in the construction of the Western identity see E.W. Said (1979) *Orientalism* (New York: Vintage books).
62. Warsaw to Foreign Office, 29 April 1947, TNA, FO 371/66155-N4984.
63. R. Tiersky (1974) *The French Communism, 1920–1972* (New York: Columbia University Press), 180.
64. K. Czernetz, Die österreichischen Sozialisten und Sowjetrussland, *Zukunft*, June 1946.
65. K. Czernetz, Probleme der Außenpolitik, *Zukunft*, August 1946.
66. Minutes of the First Conference of the Cominform, 25 September 1947, G. Procacci (ed.) (1994) *The Cominform: Minutes of the Three Conferences 1947–1948–1949* (Milano: Feltrinelli).
67. P. Togliatti, L'umanità al bivio, *Rinascita*, November 1951.
68. M. Buset, A New Socialist International, *Socialist World*, September–November 1947.
69. 'Discorso di Pietro Nenni al XXV congresso del PSIUP' in A. Benzoni, V. Tedesco (eds) (1968) *Documenti del socialismo italiano* (Padova: Marsilio), 32–33.
70. Reviews, *Socialist World*, September–November 1947.
71. Antwerp and After, *Socialist World*, March–May 1948.
72. P. Gordon Walker, 'Visit to Berlin', *Tribune*, 29 March 1946.

73. K. Czernetz, Probleme der Außenpolitik, *Zukunft*, August 1946. The Austrian socialists often stressed the role of their country at the centre of the overlapping circles of Europe (K. Waldbrunner, Socialism and planning in Austria, *Socialist World*, September–November 1948. Oscar Pollak, The Third Force, *Socialist World* 4, March–May 1948).
74. L. Blit, The Bund – A Jewish socialist movement, *Socialist World*, June–August 1947.
75. A member of the Research Department, Czechoslovak Social Democratic Party, Czechoslovakia on the road to socialism, *Socialist World*, June–August 1947.
76. I. Deutscher (1967) *Stalin* (New York: Oxford University Press), 569–570. Stalin-Wells Talk, *The New Statesman and Nation*, December 1934.
77. Labour Party Annual Conference Report (LPACR) 1950, 131.
78. Correspondence, *New Statesman and Nation*, 8 February 1947.
79. T. Paine, About Liberty, *New Statesman and Nation*, 9 August 1947.
80. Correspondence, *New Statesman and Nation*, 22 June 1946.
81. LPACR 1948, 115–119.
82. LPACR 1948, 186–187.
83. C.N. Ezard (Consul, Gdansk) to V. Cavendish-Bentinck, 1 January 1947, TNA, FO 371/66218-N1288.
84. G. Papini, I deputati, *Lacerba*, 13 March 1915 in G. Papini (1963) *Tutte le opere di Giovanni Papini*, Vol. 8, *Politica e civiltà* (Milano: Mondadori), 1052.
85. Special correspondent, Britain and World Socialism, *Tribune*, 7 June 1946. Healey likely inspired the article.
86. Ciolkosz to the editor of Forward, 3 October 1946, Heumos (ed.), *Europäischer Sozialismus im Kalten Krieg*, 185–193).
87. D. Healey (1951) 'Socialism' quoted in Healey, *When Shrimps Learn to Whistle*, 57.
88. W. Gillies, 'The International – Points for Consideration', 20 July 1944, LHASC, LP, International Sub-Committee, Minutes and Documents, 1944.
89. Prazmowska, *Civil War in Poland*, 190.
90. S. Pons (2014) *The Global Revolution: A History of International Communism, 1917–1991* (Oxford: Oxford University Press), 118–132.
91. Ciolkosz to Laski, 28 April 1944, Heumos (ed.), *Europäischer Sozialismus im Kalten Krieg*, 98.
92. Ciolkos to M. Phillips, 15 May 1945, Heumos (ed.), *Europäischer Sozialismus im Kalten Krieg*, 106–108.
93. F. Malfatti to N. Carandini, 'Conferenza dell'Internazionale Socialista', 16 March 1945, Archivio Centrale dello Stato, Roma (ACS), Fondo Nicolò Carandini, b.6, f. 'Conferenza dell'Internazionale Socialista.'

94. Warsaw to Foreign Office, 28 July 1945, TNA, FO 371/50442-W11020.
95. For a synthesis of the ideas of right-wing Polish socialists see A Polish Correspondent, Poland's Three year plan, *Socialist World*, December 1947–February 1948.
96. Kersten, *The Establishment of Communist Rule in Poland*, 366.
97. Retreat from Potsdam, *Tribune*, 1 March 1946.
98. 'Under these circumstances our Polish democracy must have other weapons to protect herself than the British democracy' ('International Socialist Conference at Clacton – May 17th–20th, 1946', International Institute of Social History, Amsterdam (IISH), Socialist International (SI), B.234).
99. Prazmowska, *Civil War in Poland*, 206.
100. LPACR 1945, 104; 114.
101. No Magic overnight, *New Statesman and Nation*, 19 January 1946. Operation Joseph, *New Statesman and Nation*, 15 June 1946.
102. What's happening, *Tribune*, 1 February 1946.
103. Malfatti to P. Nenni, 18 febbraio 1946, Fondazione Pietro Nenni, Roma (FPN), Pietro Nenni, b.31, f.1547.
104. Polacchi, Cetnici ed altra gente agli ordini di Anders, *Unità*, 23 febbraio 1946. Al nord il commercio della droga è in gran parte nelle mani di militari polacchi, *Unità*, 18 agosto 1946. Le prodezze dei criminali di Anders che uccisero una crocerossina, *Unità*, 8 agosto 1946.
105. AEU condemns Plan for 'Invasion' of Polish 'Fascist' troop, *Manchester Guardian*, 27 June 1946. Similar arguments were repeated in 1947 (E.H.G. McLaren to Morgan Phillips, 14 December 1947, LHASC, LP, DH, 9, 4).
106. Similarities with the arguments right-wing parties would use against immigrants decades later are evident.
107. Warsaw to Foreign Office, 14 November 1945, TNA, FO 371/47442-N15630.
108. P. Howarth (1986) *Intelligence Chief Extraordinary: The Life of the Ninth Duke of Portland* (London: Bodley Head), 215–217.
109. Cavendish-Bentinck to C.F.A. Warner, 19 January 1946, TNA, FO 371/56459-N1456.
110. Cavendish-Bentinck to Warner, 21 January 1946, TNA, FO 371/56459-N1935.
111. Cavendish-Bentinck to R.M.A. Hankey, 25 January 1947, TNA, FO 371/66091-N1442.
112. Foreign Office to Warsaw, 16 November 1945, TNA, FO 371/47442-N15630.

113. C. Johnson to H. McNeil, 3 April 1946; D. Allen, Minute, 5 April 1946; R.M.A. Hankey, Minute, 5 April 1946; Hector McNeil, Minute, 8 April; McNeil to Johnson, 9 April 1946, TNA, FO 371/56459-N4914.
114. C.F.A. Warner, Minute, TNA, FO 371/56459-N2810.
115. Warsaw to Foreign Office, 15 January 1946, TNA, FO 371/56432-N696.
116. Warsaw to Foreign Office, 13 November 1946, TNA, FO 371/56358-N14561.
117. Carr's travels around Europe particularly annoyed the Foreign Office (TNA, FO 371/64085).
118. P.B.B. Nichols to Warner, 10 October 1947; Warner to Nichols, 14 November 1947, TNA, FO 371/65802-N13056.
119. A. Rumbold (Prague) to Hankey, 4 December 1947; N. Reddaway, Minutes, 8 January 1948; Hankey to Rumbold, 13 January 1948, TNA, FO 371/65802-N14020.
120. Moscow to Foreign Office, 14 March 1946, TNA, FO 371/56459-N3594.
121. Cavendish-Bentinck to W. Ridsdale (News Department), 6 June 1946, TNA, FO 371/56439-N6709. Mikołajczyk's lost opportunity, *Economist*, 25 May 1946.
122. Cavendish-Bentinck to Hankey, 23 August 1946, TNA, FO 371/56357-N11016.
123. Denis Healey or Morgan Phillips to R.E. Tennyson (Hull City Labour Party), 12 November 1947, LHASC, LP, DH, 9, 5. Heumos published this letter with an attribution to Morgan Phillips, but the draft is not signed and the attribution to Healey is more likely. (Heumos (ed.), *Europäischer Sozialismus im kalten Krieg*, 147–148).
124. 'Policy in Eastern Europe', TNA, FO 371/65964-N4246.
125. Williams, Minute, 2 November 1946, TNA, FO 371/59823-UN2938. Bucharest to Foreign Office, 3 May 1946, TNA, FO 371/59203-R6728.
126. Williams, Minute, 4 November 1946; C. Mayhew, Minute, 4 November 1946, TNA, FO 371/59203-R16225.
127. Attlee's secretary to A. Holman, 8 November 1946, TNA, FO 371/59203-R16225.
128. C.F.A. Warner, Minute, 12 February 1946, TNA, FO 371/56434-N2154.
129. Warsaw to Foreign Office, 15 January 1946, TNA, FO 371/56432-N702.
130. J.E. Galsworthy, Minute, 17 January 1946; W.D. Allen, Minute, 17 January 1946, J. Rob, Minute, 22 January 1946, I.A. Ridson (?), Minute,

25 January 1946; J. Rob, Minute, 11 February 1946, TNA, FO 371/56432-N695.
131. What's happening, *Tribune*, 11 January 1946. What's happening, *Tribune*, 3 May 1946. What's happening, *Tribune*, 12 April 1946.
132. Retreat from Potsdam, *Tribune*, 1 March 1946.
133. J. Hochfeld (1946) *An Open Letter from a Polish Socialist to a Friend of the Labour Party* (London: London Committee of the Polish Socialist Party), 4–5.
134. Cavendish-Bentinck to Warner, 16 December 1945, TNA, FO 371/56354-N20.
135. M. Zborowska to Healey, 10 September 1946, LHASC, LPA, DH, 4, 14.
136. Nichols to Bevin, 28 November 1945, TNA, FO 371/47096-N16797.
137. Nichols to Warner, 12 October 1945, TNA, FO 371/47093-N14093.
138. F.T.R. Giles to J.M. Addis, 31 October 1945; Foreign Office to Prague, 4 November 1945, TNA, FO 371/47094-N14477.
139. Overseas Planning Committee, 'Plan of propaganda for Czechoslovakia – Aims and objectives', 3 December 1945, TNA, FO 371/47100-N16910.
140. B. Vilim to M. Phillips, 22 November 1945; M. Phillips to Bevin, 30 November 1945, TNA, FO 371/47216-N16956.
141. Heumos, 'Die Sozialdemokratie in Ostmitteleuropa 1945–1948', 67.
142. Myant, *Socialism and Democracy in Czechoslovakia*, 125–130. Kaplan, *Das Verhängnisvolle Bündnis*, 62–80.
143. Kersten, *The Establishment of Communist Rule in Poland*, 293–301.
144. Prazmowska, 'The Polish Socialist Party 1945–1948', 349–351. Mikołajczyk informed the Foreign Office (Warsaw to Foreign office, 27 November 1946, TNA, FO 371/56451-N15239).
145. R.B. Kirby, 'Report by Labour attaché for period 20th October to 31st December 1946', TNA, FO 371/66218-N1283.
146. Kirby, 'Memorandum by Labour Attache on conversation with Dr Grosfeld', 4 November 1946, TNA, FO 371/56359-N15646.
147. Barchard, 'Note of a conversation with Dr Wilder of the Polish embassy, held on Wednesday, the 4th December, 1946', TNA, FO 371/56359-N15645.
148. P.F. Hancock, Minute, 30 November 1946; R.M.A. Hankey, Minute, 2 December 1946, TNA, FO 371/56451-N15295.
149. J.W. Russell to C. Attlee, 3 December 1946, TNA, FO 371/56451-N15793.
150. 'Visita di congedo al presidente del consiglio e al maresciallo di Polonia', 26 November 1946, ACS, Eugenio Reale, b.1.
151. Russell to Attlee, 3 December 1946, TNA, FO 371/56359-N15741.

152. P.F. Hancock, Minute, 17 December 1946, TNA, FO 371/56452-N15949.
153. Cavendish-Bentinck to Attlee, 11 December 1946, TNA, FO 371/56359-N16227.
154. Cavendish-Bentinck to Hankey, 13 December 1946; Foreign Office to Warsaw, 25 December 1946, TNA, FO 371/56359-N16232.
155. Cavendish-Bentinck to Attlee, 13 December 1946, TNA, FO 371/56359-N16232.
156. Cavendish-Bentinck to Bevin, 27 December 1946, TNA, FO 371/66152-N143.
157. Cavendish-Bentinck to Hankey, 28 December 1946, TNA, FO 371/66152-N143.
158. Cavendish-Bentinck to Hankey, 10 January 1947; Kirby, Record of conversation, 9 January 1947, TNA, FO 371/66152-N836.
159. Kirby to Healey, 6 January 1947, LHASC, LP, DH, 09, 04. A. Bay to Kirby, 16 January 1947, LHASC, LP, DH, 9, 5.
160. 'Policy in Eastern Europe', TNA, FO 371/65964-N4246.
161. Prazmowska, 'The Polish Socialist Party, 1945–1948', 349–352.
162. Cavendish-Bentinck to Bevin, 28 February 1947; Hancock, Minute, 12 March 1947; Warner, Minute, 15 March 1947, TNA, FO 371/66092-N2811.
163. Warner, Minute, 11 February 1947, TNA, FO 371/66153-N1985. Warsaw to Foreign Office, 6 February 1947; Foreign Office to Warsaw, 19 February 1947, TNA, FO 371/66153-N1724. Warsaw to Foreign Office, 21 February 1947, TNA, FO 371/66154-N2360.
164. 'Brief for Secretary of State to take to Moscow – Poland', TNA, FO 371/66092-N2555.
165. Warsaw to Foreign Office, 29 April 1947, TNA, FO 371/66155-N4993.
166. Hankey, Minute, 3 May 1947; 'Record of a conversation between the Secretary of State and the Polish Prime Minister at the Presidency of the Council of Ministers, Warsaw on 27th April, 1947', TNA, FO 371/66155-N5579.
167. Warsaw to Foreign Office, 29 April 1947, TNA, FO 371/66155-N4984.
168. Foreign Office to Warsaw, 5 May 1947, TNA, FO 371/66156-N6390.
169. F. Savery, Minute, 31 May 1947, TNA, FO 371/66156-N6392.
170. Warner, Minute, 15 May 1947, TNA, FO 371/66155-N5836.
171. Hankey to D. Allen (Washington), 20 May 1947, TNA, FO 371/66175-N4729.
172. P. Broad to Bevin, 3 June 1947, TNA, FO 371/66093-N6707.
173. Hancock, Minute, 24 June 1947, TNA, FO 371/66093-N6707.

174. Gainer to Bevin, 12 June 1947, TNA, FO 371/66156-N7060.
175. Kersten, *The Establishment of Communist Rule in Poland*, 359.
176. Kersten, *The Establishment of Communist Rule in Poland*, 374.
177. Healey to M. Phillips, 23 June 1947, LHASC, LP, DH, 9, 4.
178. Kersten, *The Establishment of Communist Rule in Poland*, 372–378.
179. Hankey, Minute, 26 August 1947, TNA, FO 371/66094-N9823.
180. Broad to Warner, 14 August 1947, TNA, FO 371/66094-N9823.
181. Gainer to Bevin, 11 July 1947, TNA, FO 371/66094-N8301.
182. Warner, Minute, 1 August 1947, TNA, FO 371/66094-N9082.
183. Bevin to Broad, 1 October 1947, TNA, FO 371/66157-N11419.
184. Hankey, Minute, 26 August 1947, TNA, FO 371/66094-N9082.
185. Warsaw to Foreign Office, 20 August 1947, TNA, FO 371/66156-N10018.
186. 'Memorandum by Mr M.B.Winch – Cyrankiewicz on Socialist Position', 29 August 1947, TNA, FO 371/66095-N10396.
187. Warsaw (Broad) to Foreign Office, 2 September 1947, TNA, FO 371/66094-N10285. Even at this stage some diplomats believed that the socialists kept away from the embassy to prepare the final confrontation.
188. 'Copy Minute from Mr R.B.Kirby, dated 19th Nov. 1947', TNA, FO 371/66096-N13896.
189. Myant, *Socialism and Democracy in Czechoslovakia*, 160–161.
190. Myant, *Socialism and Democracy in Czechoslovakia*, 113–120.
191. I. Lukes (2012) *On the Edge of the Cold War, American Diplomats and Spies in Postwar Prague* (New York: Oxford University Press), 162–182.
192. Nichols to Hankey, 30 October 1947, TNA, FO 371/65802-N12557.
193. Healey to Bevin, 20 November 1947, TNA, FO 371/65802-N13414. A. Meyer, Minutes, 3 December 1947, TNA, FO 371/65802-N13662.
194. What's happening, *Tribune*, 27 February 1948.
195. Kaplan, *Das Verhängnisvolle Bündnis*, 107–116.
196. Kaplan, *Das Verhängnisvolle Bündnis*, 132–140.
197. Healey to Bevin, 20 November 1947; 'Report on the visit of Mr Denis Healey, International secretary of the Labour Party, to the Biennial congress of the Czechoslovak Social Democratic Party at Brno, 14–16 November 1947', TNA, FO 371/65802-N13414.
198. Kersten, *The Establishment of Communist Rule in Poland*, 326.
199. 'XXVII Congres du Parti Socialiste Polonais – 2ème journée', TNA, FO 371/66097-N14824. He insisted it did not mean a third way between capitalism and revolution.
200. Speech by Oskar Lange, TNA, FO 371/66097-N14824.
201. Gainer to Bevin, 22 December 1947, TNA, FO 371/66097-N14846.

202. D. Healey, 'Report on the 27th Congress of the Polish Socialist Party in Wroclaw', TNA, FO 371/71529-N572.
203. A. Szakasits to Cyrankiewicz, 23 December 1947, Heumos (ed.), *Europäischer Sozialismus im Kalten Krieg*, 234.
204. Kaplan, *Das Verhängnisvolle Bündnis*, 145.
205. Myant, *Socialism and Democracy in Czechoslovakia*, 208–218- Kaplan, *Das Verhängnisvolle Bündnis*, 149–158. 'Notes on the coup in the Czechoslovak Social Democratic Party', LHASC, LP, International Sub-Committee, Minutes & Documents, 1947.
206. Kaplan, *Das Verhängnisvolle Bündnis*, 159–162.
207. Kersten, *The Establishment of Communist Rule in Poland*, 436.
208. Warsaw to Foreign Office, 24 March 1948, TNA, FO 371/71529-N3595.
209. L. Blit, The Art of Suicide, *Tribune*, 23 April 1948.

Bibliography

Applebaum, A. (2013). *Iron curtain: the crushing of Eastern Europe 1944–1956*. London: Penguin Books.

Berger, S. & Lambert, P. (2003). Intellectual transfers and mental blockades. In S. Berger & P. Lambert (Eds.). *Historikerdialoge: Geschichte, Mythos und Gedächtnis im deutsch-britischen kulturellen Austausch 1750–2000*. Göttingen: Vandenhoeck & Ruprecht.

Benzoni, A. & Tedesco, V. (Eds.). (1968). *Documenti del socialismo italiano*. Padova: Marsilio.

Berselli, A. (1971). *L'opinione pubblica inglese e l'avvento del fascismo*. Milano: Franco Angeli.

Brookshire, J.H. (1995). *Clement Attlee*. Manchester: Manchester University Press.

Ciolkosz, A. (1946). *The expropriation of a socialist party*. New York: Polish Socialist Alliance.

Crowfort, R. (2008). Labour Party Factionalism and West German Rearmament 1950–4. In P. Corthorn & J. Davis (Eds.). *The British Labour Party and the Wider World* (pp. 127–144). London: Tauris.

Deutscher, I. (1967). *Stalin*. New York: Oxford University Press.

Gross, J. (1997). War as Revolution. In N. Naimark & L. Gibianskii (Eds.). *The Establishment of Communist Regimes in Eastern Europe, 1944–1949* (pp. 17–35). Boulder: Westview Press.

Healey, D. (Ed.). (1951). *The Curtain falls: the Story of the Socialists in Eastern Europe*. London: Lincolns-Prager.

Healey, D. (1990). *When Shrimps learn to whistle: signposts for the nineties*. London: Penguin.

Healey, D. (2002). *Healey's World: travels with my camera*. Lewes: Book Guild.
Heumos, P. (1983). Die britische Labour Party und die sozialistischen Parteien Ostmitteleuropas, 1944–1948. *Bohemia*, 24, 317–334.
Heumos, P. (1991). Die Sozialdemokratie in Ostmitteleuropa 1945–1948. Zum gesellschaftlichen Potential des demokratischen Sozialismus in Polen, der Tschechoslowakei und Ungarn. In H. Lemberg (Ed.). *Sowjetisches Modell und nationale Prägung. Kontinuität und Wandel in Ostmitteleuropa nach dem Zweiten Weltkrieg* (pp. 51–70). Marburg and Lahn: J.G.Herder-Institut.
Heumos, P. (Ed.). (2004a). *Europäischer Sozialismus im Kalten Krieg: Briefe und Berichte 1944–1948*. Frankfurt: Campus.
Heumos, P. (2004b). Einleitung. In P. Heumos (Ed.). *Europäischer Sozialismus im Kalten Krieg: Briefe und Berichte 1944–1948*. Frankfurt: Campus.
Hochfeld, J. (1946). *An open letter from a Polish socialist to a friend of the Labour Party*. London: London Committee of the Polish Socialist Party.
Howarth, P. (1986). Intelligence chief extraordinary: the life of the ninth Duke of Portland. London: Bodley Head.
Jodah, U. (2003). *The Hungarian Social Democrats and the British Labour Party, 1944–8*. PhD Thesis: University of West England, Bristol.
Kaplan, K. (1984). *Das Verhängnisvolle Bündnis. Unterwanderung, Gleichschaltung und Vernichtung der Tschechoslowakischen Sozialdemokratie 1944–1954*. Wuppertal: Pol-Verlag.
Kenney, P. (1997). *Rebuilding Poland: workers and communists, 1945–1950*. Ithaca: Cornell University Press.
Kersten, K. (1991). *The establishment of communist rule in Poland, 1943–1948*. Berkley: University of California Press.
Lukes, I. (2012). *On the Edge of the Cold War, American Diplomats and Spies in Postwar Prague*. New York: Oxford University Press.
Lyttelton, A. (1973). *The seizure of power: Fascism in Italy, 1919–1929*. London: Weidenfeld and Nicolson.
Maier, C.S. (1988). *The unmasterable past: history, holocaust, and German national identity*. Cambridge, MA: Harvard University Press.
Micgiel, J. (1997). 'Bandits and reactionaries': The Suppression of the Opposition in Poland, 1944–1946. In N. Naimark & L. Gibianskii (Eds.). *The Establishment of Communist Regimes in Eastern Europe, 1944–1949* (pp. 93–104). Boulder: Westview Press.
Myant, M. (1981). *Socialism and Democracy in Czechoslovakia, 1945–1948*. Cambridge: Cambridge University Press.
Papini, G. (1963). *Tutte le opere di Giovanni Papini*, Vol. 8, *Politica e civiltà*. Milano: Mondadori.
Pons, S. (2014). *The global revolution: a history of international communism, 1917–1991*. Oxford: Oxford University Press.

Prazmowska, A.J. (2000). The Polish Socialist Party 1945–1948. *East European Quarterly*, 34 (3) 337–359.
Prazmowska, A.J. (2004). *Civil War in Poland, 1942–1948*. Basingstoke: Palgrave.
Procacci, G. (Ed.). (1994). *The Cominform: minutes of the Three conferences 1947–1948–1949*. Milano: Feltrinelli.
Radice, G. (Ed.). (1981). *Socialism with a human face*. London.
Said, E.W. (1979). *Orientalism*. New York: Vintage Books.
Salvemini, G. (1969). *L'Italia vista dall'America*. Milano: Feltrinelli.
Spiering, M. (2015). *A cultural history of British Euroscepticism*. Basingstoke: Palgrave Macmillan.
Taylor, A.J.P. (1988). *The course of German history: a survey of the development of German history since 1814*. London: Rutledge.
Tiersky, R. (1974). *The French Communism, 1920–1972*. New York: Columbia University Press.
Tismaneanu, V. (2009). Diabolical Pedagogy and the (Il)logic of Stalinism in Eastern Europe. In V. Tismaneau (Ed.). *Stalinism revisited: the establishment of communist regimes in East-Central Europe* (25–34). Budapest: Central European University Press.
Wolff, L. (1994). *Inventing Eastern Europe: the map of civilization on the mind of the enlightenment*. Stanford: Stanford University Press.

CHAPTER 5

The Institutional Development, from the International Socialist Conference to Comisco (1946–48)

1 Formal and Informal Socialist Internationalism

After the death of the LSI, international socialism did not have a permanent organisation with formal rules and a bureaucracy until the Clacton Conference (17–19 May 1946), which established the skeleton of the new institution: regular conferences (the International Socialist Conference) and a permanent office (the Socialist Information and Liaison Office, SILO). Six months later, a committee to convene conferences, supervise the office and debate urgent issues was added (the Consultative Committee). Later, the conferences became an annual event, the Consultative Committee was replaced by an organ with greater political authority, the Comisco (Committee of the International Socialist Conference), and the secretariat assumed more responsibilities. However, the basic structure of the Socialist International—'the embryo' according to De Brouckère—was already there in 1946. The Frankfurt Congress of 1951 simply formalised it and it would remain the same for the decades to come.

The Labour Party set the pace of the reconstruction of the Socialist International:

> The European socialists were at the mercy of the concessions and limitations which the BLP conceded them or imposed upon them. In other words, it was the BLP and no other party which determined the rhythm of postwar transnational cooperation.[1]

The Labour Party had the assets indispensable for the rebirth of the Socialist International: a network of contacts, permanent offices, prestige and material resources. The Labour Party enjoyed its leadership position and showed no interest in a strong, independent institution. At the beginning, the International Socialist Conference was dependent on the Labour Party, lacking autonomy and a complex organisation—what Panebianco calls 'institutionalisation'.[2] The hegemony of the Labour Party was an inverse function of the institutionalisation of the Socialist International.

The informal network centred on the Labour Party best served the need for control of the Labour leaders, but it could not last indefinitely. Socialist ideals, binding even Labour leaders, called for the creation of an organisation where all parties were members on an equal basis. Major steps to rebuild an independent International—the creation of Comisco, at the end of 1947, the creation of the anti-communist propaganda machinery in 1948, the decision to recreate the International in 1951—came after severe setbacks for the Labour Party, respectively, the convertibility crisis of the Pound, the Sovietisation of Eastern Europe, the narrow victory at the elections of February 1950. Dissatisfaction with the excessive power of Labour found a window of opportunity. In addition, these events redefined the context in which the international organisation and the national parties operated. The ideological struggle of the Cold War called for strengthening the social democratic identity, with an explicit charter of principles, enlargement of the organisation and a greater involvement of all the parties. The transition of practice and informality to an institution meant common rules limiting the freedom of individual parties. International socialist cooperation followed its own logic, beyond what the party that had restarted it originally intended.

The institutional history of the Socialist International is not just made up of reactions to contingency, it must be also understood through the debate over the plans and goals of internationalism. Before the war, the plans for reforming the International included abandoning the pretence to command the national parties and concentrating on exchanging information and opinions. Decisions would be taken in a small Bureau with the most important parties. These proposals were still valid, but a World War in between demanded further reflection. Before the war, the right-wing factions wanted a retrenchment, while after, the reformists saw in international debates the possibility to give intellectual coherence to their policies. There was also a practical side of internationalism, as international fraternal relations could provide assets for factional struggle and even electoral campaigns.

The plans of the Labour Party were a result of competing intellectual forces. Denis Healey and Morgan Phillips were central in defining the strategy, but, at least in the first period, depended on others. Until February 1948, two opposite principles guided Labour's strategy for international fraternal relations: the ambition to reach a global agreement with the world communist movement and the ambition to develop an organisation of parties united by the same values, which would have cooperated for practical goals without embarrassing the Labour Government. Harold Laski gave a theoretical foundation to the first ambition and John Price wrote the guidelines to realise the second.

2 'Co-operation, or at Least Mutual Tolerance'

While social democrats and communists strove to emphasise their reciprocal differences, left-wing socialists believed in mending the divide in the working-class movement and that the Socialist International could act as a bridge between the two sides.[3] In April 1922, Friedrich Adler convened a joint meeting of the Second International, the Vienna Union and the Comintern, but plans for cooperation failed because of suspicion and the attempt to impose conditions on the communists.[4] Left-wing socialists like Nenni saw the reluctance of the LSI to embrace the Popular Front as a failure.[5] Socialists wanted a global agreement for the Popular Front, so as to restore working-class unity but also to avoid local agreements, which the communists would have ruthlessly exploited; thus they wanted acceptance of democracy and a new attitude towards social democratic parties as conditions. For the communists what mattered were local agreements on practical actions against fascism, while a global agreement would have curtailed their freedom of action; they considered the Popular Front a tactical rather than strategic change, since the crisis of capitalism and social democracy was irreversible.[6] In the 1930s, Blum, Otto Bauer, and Nenni wanted agreements on common action with the Comintern; Adler, De Brouckère and Vandervelde made an agreement on principles a prerequisite. The policy of Gillies and Albarda prevailed: tolerance of local agreement, but no high-level negotiations.

In the brief period after the Molotov-Ribbentrop Pact, the identification of communism with totalitarianism and the equivalence with Nazism laid its foundation, although they were shelved with the invasion of the

Soviet Union, encouraging supporters of working-class unity, like Laski.[7] In January 1943 he wrote in *Left News* a fourteen-point proposal that had 'An approach to the Soviet Union with the purpose of ending the schism between the Internationals before hostilities cease' as its first point.[8] The staunchest supporters of rebuilding the International, De Brouckère and Max Buset, gave their approval. The task of the new International was to help socialist Governments and prevent the return of fascism. The consultative committee of the *International Socialist Forum*, led by Braunthal, was the coordinating centre of the early attempts to rebuild the International.[9] Laski was confident he could convince Stalin to affiliate to this International, but Eden forbade the visit of a party delegation to Moscow, Huysmans refused to be involved in an attempt to bypass the Labour Party[10] and even the Soviets were not enthusiastic about the proposal and doubted its sincerity.[11]

After the 1945 elections, Laski wanted the Labour Party to take the lead in the world socialist movement in ideological opposition to communism, since it had grown more confident and was firmly resolved to strengthen its autonomy.[12] During his visits to France, Italy and Sweden, Laski warned local socialists to avoid fusion with the communists and to rebuild the Socialist International. His help was well received: a newspaper close to Beneš reprinted Laski's article that discouraged Nenni from fusion.[13] However, rejection of communist sabotage did not preclude a pro-Soviet foreign policy or an agreement with the communist movement. In February 1946, Laski told Braunthal that Russian isolationism put Europe at risk of falling into the hands of monopoly capitalism,[14] adding that no Socialist International should have been built until cooperation with the USSR was secured. This would turn Europe socialist in 20 years. Laski's initiative represented the contradictions of the British Labour movement: the need to reconcile friendship with the Soviet Union with a strong hostility towards communism, valuing individual communists for their important trade union work without making concessions to the communist party.[15] Laski's plan found a counterpart in 'Nenni's dream of a great progressive and revolutionary world front',[16] in which Western socialists would find a natural ally in the Soviet Union and reclaim their revolutionary mission. The left-wing French socialists wanted to rebuild the Socialist International in a hurry, as they saw the opportunity to lead the European socialist movement along the revolutionary road.[17] At the August 1947 SFIO congress, the party was divided between left-wing motions—calling for the Socialist International to be the united front of all the workers—and Mollet's motion—calling for the International to be a mediating influence between the two blocs.[18] All left-wing socialists believed in the revolutionary agency of the Socialist International and in a general agreement between Labour Britain and the Soviet Union. They acted on the incorrect assumption that the Great Alliance would continue to be the cornerstone of global affairs.[19]

The issue at stake in the first International Socialist Conference (Clacton, 17–19 May 1946) was finding a modus vivendi with the world communist movement and their allies, the left-wing socialists. The Labour Party wanted the national communist parties to stop sabotaging their socialist allies.[20] Even Dalton feared that a Third World War would force him to side with reactionaries and the Catholic Church.[21] If Stalin had ceased to consider the social democrats as enemies, he could have ordered the communists to work with them, maybe even forming a genuine united working-class party. The Soviet Union would have reaped benefits, because, as Laski had already explained in 1943, the united working-class would have led to Governments around Europe that were friendly to the Soviet Union. Some even spoke of a top-level summit between Attlee, Blum and Stalin to reach the great compromise between the two working-class blocs.[22]

Laski denied that the Clacton conference was an attempt to rebuild the Second International or to coordinate the socialist forces against communism. He said that these meetings had to reach a consensus on how to achieve friendship and cooperation with the Soviet people, while keeping the socialist movement united against any division of Europe. Referring to the creation of the SED in the Soviet Occupation Zone, he said that forced fusion of socialists and communists hindered true unity of action, which could be only free and consensual. Laski warned that political problems required global solutions, as technology was rapidly transforming transport, financial markets and warfare, rendering the national dimension obsolete. Unity and vigilance were necessary against clericalism and reaction under the guise of Christian democracy. As for the Socialist International:

> In my own judgement, it is of primary importance that no attempt was made to create a definite structure, or to issue a definite code of principles [...] Above all, if we can, we must try to find a form of relationship which enables Russia and the Social Democratic Parties to co-operate for the great ends they have in common.[23]

Healey informed Larock that Laski did not speak for the Labour Party and the connection between cooperating with Russia and rebuilding the International was his personal opinion.[24] However, Laski expressed widespread albeit confused aspirations. Indeed, soon after, the Labour Party approved sending a party delegation to the Soviet Union. Bevin approved; though he had previously blocked the mission, he saw some potential benefits, if the delegates avoided being taken advantage of.[25] Morgan Phillips and Laski believed that their common faith in socialism could be a sound foundation for friendship between Britain and the Soviet Union.[26] The central event of the visit was the meeting with Stalin at the Kremlin, who gave some satisfaction to Laski. Stalin expressed sincere appreciation for the radical reforms and the nationalisations of the Labour Government and opened the door to another road to socialism. The passage deserves to be fully quoted:

> There were two roads to Socialism, [Stalin] said, the Russian way and the British way—and it was clear that we both intended to reach the Socialist goal in our own fashion. The Russian road was shorter but more difficult, and had involved bloodshed—but he wanted us to remember that Marxist-Leninists did not think that theirs was the only way to Socialism. The Parliamentary method involved no bloodshed, but it was a longer process. Whatever the differences between us might be at the moment, the great and historic fact remained that Britain and Russia, two of the greatest countries in the world, were both moving in the direction of socialism.
>
> In Britain, through the Parliamentary electoral method, Stalin went on, it was possible to sound the opinion of every responsible person in the country as to whether they wanted Socialism or not; but in Russia in the early days there was a very low level of culture, and the peasants, who were a great problem, did not even want to hear about Socialism. It was essential that we should understand these indigenous questions.
>
> We were, in the nature of things, going about our business in different ways, but since we both had the same ultimate object, it would be truly amazing if there were no friendship between our two countries.[27]

Still, Stalin mentioned that the British bourgeoisie could be tougher than the Russian aristocracy, so the final transition to socialism could force the British Labourites to smash the enemy.[28] Morgan Phillips chose to concentrate on the brighter side of the speech. If Communists in Europe realised that there were two ways to socialism, 'it would go a long way towards ending the internecine conflicts which are holding up progress in some countries because of a desire to create a one-party State'.[29] In private, Morgan Phillips was more sceptical:

> As apparently the purpose of the delegation's visit was to see what possibility of co-operation, or at least mutual tolerance, existed between social democracy and Communism in Europe, this confirmed their feeling that there was nothing to be done.

This confirmed Labour's belief that socialism needed to be the alternative to communism:

> [In] the success of British socialism lay[s] the only hope for Europe which was definitely seeking a new economic and political approach and which might well succumb to Communism unless Britain could show a more congenial and equally effective answer to the problems of today.[30]

As Healey reported to Wodak, the visit had caused wide disappointment, although the British did not understand the true reasons. The Labourites got the impression that the Soviets would not make concessions on security because they feared the return of the conservatives and that Stalin was growing weaker and Zhdanov stronger.[31] It was a typical Soviet tactic to have different people espouse different attitudes, giving the impression that some were flexible and some hard-liners.

In fact, Stalin had already said things of this sort. He was rehashing themes from his famous interview with H.G. Wells in 1934.[32] In January 1945, Stalin told Dimitrov and the Yugoslav and Bulgarian communists that the Soviet way was the best, but it was not the only one that brought to socialism[33] and, in April 1945, Stalin told Tito that socialism was possible even under the British monarchy.[34] In 1946, he repeated the same concept to the Polish and Czechoslovak communists and the PPS. In the same year Gottwald, the prime minister and communist leader of Czechoslovakia, employed Stalin's words to justify the parliamentary road to socialism, although this did not stop him seizing power in a coup the very next year.[35] In September 1946 Stalin had told Dimitrov that the Bulgarian communists should have created a labour party to unite all the workers on a minimum programme but this was just a façade to avoid international condemnation.[36] The Soviets read Labour's delegation as a sign of weakness: the Labourites had promised too much to the British workers and they would soon clash with the British bourgeoisie and American imperialism:

It is obvious that Laski was trying to find out whether Moscow would conduct a policy of 'sovietizing' England [...] It was also clear that the Labourites wanted to prepare the ground for the moment when, should they be in a tight spot, they would have some support from the Sov[iet] Union.[37]

At the Zurich Conference (6–9 June 1947), the Belgians proposed an agreement with the Soviet Union for the unity of the global working-class movement. Buset proposed the integration of East and West as the ideological foundation of European socialism: Russia had laid the foundation of economic and social democracy, the West had advanced political democracy. The difference was due to historical conditions, but by the end of the century Russia and the West would develop political democracy and economic democracy respectively, making unity possible.[38]

The approaches of the Labour Party and the International Socialist Conference shows that a general agreement between social democracy and communism was impossible even before the Cold War. The Soviets had little interest in a new global order on a consensual basis, as territorial security and spheres of influence shaped their interpretation of world affairs. The deradicalisation of the communist movement was a mere deferment of the revolutionary conflict. The ideological assumptions were still the inevitability of war and the uniqueness of the Soviet model, while international affairs were still seen through the prism of revolution as civil war and binary struggle.[39]

The global Popular Front was never a practical solution, rather a myth to keep the International Socialist Conference united and allow cohabitation with Eastern European socialists. Thus, in 1946 and 1947 the Western parties, particularly the Labour Party, did everything they could to encourage the social democrats and strengthen their autonomy in the national system, even in alliance with the communists. Even the Scandinavians, who barely tolerated the other Continental socialists, did not want to prematurely exclude Eastern socialists.[40] When, in 1947, Buset repeated the need of an agreement with the Soviet Union and that the Socialist International was the means to this end, Morgan Phillips said he did not believe the Soviets were interested.[41]

For many, every hope of compromise died in February 1948, when the Prague Coup forced them to face reality. Some, especially members of the older generation like Braunthal, kept the door open even after this: 'a basis of agreement between the Socialist Western Europe and the Communist East may be found'.[42]

3 JOHN PRICE'S BLUEPRINTS FOR THE SOCIALIST INTERNATIONAL

Through John Price, Ernest Bevin's worldview shaped the internationalism of the Labour Party. Price was a docker and a worker-intellectual like Bevin, who was his patron and trusted him totally.[43] Price organised international aid for Austria in 1934 and worked for the LSI. In 1937, Bevin called him to the Transport and General Workers' Union (TGWU), putting him in charge of the Research and Education Department and later the Political Department and International Department. Like Healey, he was a talented young man whose career was helped by Bevin. During the war, Price helped socialist exiles with radio propaganda and the Dallas Committee, travelled to meet Swedish and Swiss trade unionists and contributed to the international section of the Labour post-war programme.

Before joining the International Labour Organisation, Price wrote a memorandum for the International Department[44] and a book[45] where he explained his position on the Socialist International, internationalism and international fraternal relations. He recognised and fully embraced that reformism was completely state-centred. Direct action, such as general strikes, self-help or revolutions, was no longer the way to socialism, only national Governments could make the difference.[46] Some still believed in the romantic struggle of oppressed against oppressors and the state as an instrument of bourgeois oppression, but protest and opposition had to give way to cooperation and integration.[47] The more social tasks and economic power the State assumed, the more the workers identified with the State, as the guarantor of their welfare.[48] The only function of parties was formulating policies and winning elections: 'In the international, no less than in the national, sphere the parties must behave as if they believed in their capacity to govern and not as if they expected to remain permanently in opposition'.[49]

Past Internationals were too doctrinal[50] and their only successes were in stopping Governments from implementing damaging policies. The delusion that the Socialist International could directly influence international affairs or give orders to the national parties was dangerous. Price accepted the principle of liberal internationalism about the natural harmonisation of national interests. There was no need to impose disinterested internationalism on nationalist parties; once the national parties acquired objective information about international affairs and became aware of the legitimate interests and concerns of their counterparts, international cooperation would appear evidently in their own best interests.

Reformist internationalism required the International to adopt strict criteria for admission—in the LSI 'the door of eligibility was opened very wide'.[51] Only parties agreeing on parliamentary action and operating legally could act together; mixing with others would lead to a paralysed organisation like the LSI. Price refused a broad church with a vague definition of socialism, he wanted agreement about peace, democracy and revolution:

> With a view to the establishment of a sound international organisation, capable of effective action, the attempt should be made to formulate such a statement of aims and objects. The future organisation should be confined at the beginning to parties which accept it.[52]

Imposing a 'strict test of admission' was problematic, as it made a competing International possible, but that was preferable to an organisation paralysed by dissent. Action demanded agreement, otherwise the International would produce just vague and useless manifestos. Price had reservations about admitting the communists, because their goals and methods differed from the socialists' faith in democracy. In the private memorandum, Price accepted Laski's proposal to start high-level negotiations with Moscow to resolve their differences, but he opposed the admission of the national communist parties, as they were disruptive, except for the Communist Party of the Soviet Union, which truly represented the Russian working-class—a common idea among British trade unionists.

Price's model for the International was Bevin's TGWU: an emphasis on internal cohesion, the removal of dissenting elements, the ability of the leadership to make rapid and effective decisions.[53] Price also recommended a specialised and professional staff, like the TGWU had, for international contacts.

However, the strength of the Socialist International was not its bureaucracy but the national parties. The problem was how to make the parties abide by jointly made decisions without any means of enforcement. The only sanction was expulsion, which could be employed for associating with an enemy organisation not a lack of zeal—removing a part would damage the whole.[54] If the International wanted to be 'more than a post office or a debating society',[55] it had to influence the decisions of the national parties, as international action consisted of the parallel actions of the national parties, coordinated by the international secretariat. Respecting national autonomy made action slow, but it prevented mistakes and embarrassments; international cooperation was successful not only when parties took positive action, but also when it prevented parties from taking actions harmful to others. A national party would not enforce a harmful or embarrassing international resolution. The continuous exchange of information and opinion would make socialist leaders aware of the priorities and needs in other countries.

The central task of the Socialist International was to 'collect, digest, and disseminate this information'[56] and keep the spotlight on international affairs. This was an elitist approach. There was little illusion about the naturally internationalist working-class. Indeed, for Prince even the leaders failed to appreciate the international dimension of most political problems. There were few issues around which the masses would mobilise and even then only for a short period. Celebrating May Day or International Women's Day could be useful to remind people about internationalism. The only actors exercising a continuous influence on international affairs were the national Governments. The Socialist International would serve the socialist leaders as a regular channel of information and a forum to meet with their colleagues from other nations. Frank discussion could help ministers make informed choices, but this had to be confidential rather than in public.

Healey read and approved Price's memorandum and book. Unlike the trade unionist Price, Healey doubted the power of organisations to dominate and shape the situation and he was more concerned not to 'let slip the possible through clutching at the ideal',[57] as each party lived in and was conditioned by its historical and political context. Healey particularly appreciated Price's observation that the main task of an international organisation was preventing a member from taking actions that could damage another. As International Secretary, he followed this principle to reconcile the desires and fears of European socialists.

Price possessed the intellectual clarity to appreciate the features of socialism in his time: the integration of the labour movement in the state and society, the growing technocratic and elitist dimension of politics, the contradiction between the international system and the national dimension of democracy. Despite the widely held opinion that the Cold War had radically altered the evolution of democratic socialism, the Socialist International created in 1951 was a faithful realisation of Price's blueprints, written while the war was still ongoing. It bears witness to the power of the Labour Party to impose its plan on the socialist community, against the objections of the French and Belgians. It also proves that Price's plan was realistic and based on objective assessments. Credit for realising it, however, lies with Healey, who exploited the divisions in the European socialist movement.

4   The Three Blocs of European Socialism: Planners, Leftists and Federalists

After the war, with emerging differences among socialists, three distinct groupings took shape: the 'planners', the 'federalists' and the 'leftists'.

The leftist group was easy to identify: they rejected bourgeois democracy, emphasised the revolutionary nature of socialism and wanted unity of action with the communists and the Soviet Union. While this brand of left-wing socialism had been common before the war, after the war it gave way to social democracy as the only form of democratic socialism. After the elimination of Eastern European socialism and the expulsion of the PSI, the group disappeared.

Planners were the socialist parties which, thanks to their hegemony over the working-class and strong organisation, could form majority Governments or coalition Governments from a position of strength. They were in a position to fully exploit the power of the nation-state to plan the economy and enact social reforms. Since the realisation of socialism was possible within the nation state, they were suspicious of any international organisation that could limit its power and of international commitments that could make them unpopular. The leader of the group was the British Labour Party and it included the Swedish, Norwegian and Danish parties.

Federalist were those socialist parties that operated in coalition Governments and could not convert the state machinery to socialist goals. Therefore, they were open to sacrificing the power of the nation state to supra-national institutions—whether they clearly recognised the limits of state power to influence the economy and foreign affairs or they wanted to achieve at international level what they could not achieve at national level or both, is debatable. They linked achievement of socialist goals with supranationality—which they first identified with socialist internationalism and later with European unification. The most representative members were the French, Belgian and Dutch parties.

Only the federalists wanted the Socialist International to be swiftly reborn, but until February 1948, they were blocked by the joint opposition of planners and leftists, as the Socialist International would have been an embarrassment for them.[58]

The Nordic parties (Scandinavians and Finland, a peculiar case) shared policies and cultural attitudes, while they were suspicious of the other Continentals.[59] In 1945, they decided together to oppose communism and reject the reconstruction of an International able to tell national parties what to do, while endorsing international contacts.

The leftist group agreed with many of these objections, though from a different perspective. Lelio Basso, the intellectual force of left-wing Italian socialism, systematically criticised the Socialist International. It was utopia to expect Government parties to follow the line of a supranational organisation; even then, it would work only if international socialism completely identified with Great Britain, as the communists did for the USSR. The Socialist International was a demagogic myth of anti-communism 'to prepare the Western Bloc as an anti-Soviet weapon and as a tool to divide the working-class and Europe'.[60]

The PPS also saw in the creation of a Western International the petrification of the division of Europe and the schism of the labour movement; they wanted a unitary International of all the workers.[61] The ČSSD agreed that a Socialist International would consolidate the division of the world and hinder cooperation with the communists. True unity required the recognition of differences, as a divided International forced into unity would have been ineffective.[62] In the two 1947 conferences, the ČSSD tried to have a debate on basic ideological questions—like the relationship with capitalism and the differences between Western and Eastern Europe.

It needs to be noted that leftist socialists formed a solid left-wing bloc that cooperated, especially on the refusal to admit the Germans. The ČSSD was reluctant and when its leftist leadership was deposed at the end of 1947, it left the Italians and Poles on their own.[63] Leftists also had contacts with left-wing Labour members and the left-wing of the SPÖ.[64] The Eastern European socialists organised two Danubian conferences where all the parties, except the Austrians, were leftist.[65] They wanted to signal both their difference from the Western socialists and independence from the communists.[66] At the end of 1947, there were rumours about a Socinform, a permanent office for left-wing socialists. Healey considered it communist-inspired propaganda,[67] but there were actually plans to coordinate the leftists inside the International Socialist Conference, not to create an alternative Socialist International.[68]

Healey suspected that the PPS exploited its contacts with Western leftists not only against Western socialists but also to impress the communists.[69] Eastern socialists wanted to cultivate their identity through their relations with the western comrades.[70] 'They seemed to be following a middle course of limited internationalism, strengthening their position without calling down the wrath of the communists'[71]:

> The conclusion seems to be that both the Communists and Socialist Parties in countries behind the 'Iron Curtain' are anxious to foster their own international links and organisations but that neither wishes to come out in the open so strongly as to provoke the other to action ...[72]

In addition to stopping the Socialist International, leftist socialists slowed the admission of the SPD,[73] because of their war-time experience and their refusal to legitimise an anti-Soviet Germany.

The goal of the federalists from the start was the rebirth of the Socialist International. The PSB regularly renewed the demand. Max Buset requested to put the rebuilding of the Socialist International on the agenda of the Clacton Conference.[74] At the Zurich Conference (6–9 June 1947), he presented his detailed list of arguments.[75] The first argument was keeping the torch of internationalism alive for future generations: the practice of international debates had created past socialist leaders and it would create the socialists of the future. The second argument was ideological: socialism was either international or it could not exist. Contemporary political problems required support from global public opinion, it was impossible to build socialism in one country—a jibe at the Soviet Union and the Labour Party. The third argument was tactical: the adversaries of socialism were already international. The communists identified with the USSR, the conservatives with American imperialism, the Catholics, the foe of socialism, with the Vatican. Even Liberals, a relic of the previous century, and military veterinarians had their international meetings! 'Are we, the pioneers of internationalism, the first to practise international action, too much afraid now to take up our international tradition?'[76] Buset said that the practice would help the socialists to become closer and not embarrass their comrades. Only a lack of will explained the failure of internationalism.

The SFIO was the only other party to strongly back the Belgian proposal for an active International to coordinate the national parties: it had committed itself to rebuilding the International in national congresses and international meetings since 1944.[77] For Mollet, economic and social problems required international solutions. While the Labour Party sought a close identification with the Labour Government, for Mollet the role of the socialist party was not just to support the Government but to act as a bridge between the national and international spheres.[78] Mollet backed the restoration of the Socialist International to present himself as a guardian of orthodoxy and to answer his critics. At the 1947 SFIO congress, the left-wing factions proposed the Socialist International as an alternative to the Marshall Plan. Mollet accepted the Marshall Plan and proposed the Socialist International as a guarantor for the autonomy and unity of the international working-class and as an instrument for denazification in Germany.[79] At the congress, Marianne Pollak, the SPÖ delegate, helped Mollet by speaking of the Third Force as a global influence and a guarantee against the extremes. Even after the Cominform Conference, Blum and Mollet used the cohabitation of different socialist parties in the International Socialist Conference to prove that the Socialist International was a Third Force resisting bipolar division. This evident misreading of events helped appease their left-wing minority.

The SPÖ was committed to the Socialist International—'Never was the International more sorely missed'[80]—despite some caution over their geopolitical position. Like Buset, they wanted international coordination of the socialists.[81] Oscar Pollak said that the very idea of socialism was a mediation between extremes, the Third way between communism and capitalism.[82] Without socialism to mediate, communism would stir a Catholic reaction, slicing Europe in two.[83]

5 The Creation of New Institutions

Having won the elections, Morgan Phillips finally picked up the thread of rebuilding the International in August 1945. The Preparatory Committee set up by the March 1945 conference had done nothing and no party—except the Swiss—had answered the call to send proposals for the International. The initiative fell once more to the Labour Party.[84]

The first international event of democratic socialism after the war was the SFIO Congress in August 1945. Envoys from Great Britain (Laski and Morgan Phillips), Italy (Nenni and Silone), Belgium (De Brouckère and Huysmans) and Spain (Llopis) attended, strengthening the sense of belonging to the socialist family in the delegates, whose self-confidence was boosted by Labour's victory. This made Blum's appeal to be true to socialist traditions and reject fusion with the communists much stronger. 'The vote of the Paris congress makes it certain that the Socialist International will be revived'.[85] On the margins of the congress, the envoys debated the Socialist International and charged a committee of Morgan Phillips, Laski and Levy with drafting a proposal.[86]

The proposal envisioned an organisation in London, open to all socialist parties which were not in exile and met the criteria set by a conference.[87] There would be one party per country and one vote per party. The governing body would be a seven-member Bureau, with permanent seats for the British and the French. Resolutions would not be binding, but each party had to publicise them. Publications and resolutions from every party would be circulated. The Bureau could form investigative committees and expert commissions for specific issues, in addition to a commission responsible for spreading socialist literature and publishing an international journal. A fund would finance legal assistance and relief for socialists in difficulty. A lesser form of membership was envisioned for parties with the right to be informed and helped but no right to vote. The Austrians and Italians, formerly enemies, and the Swedes and Swiss, formerly neutrals, would be members from the start, but not the Germans, as this was too controversial. The International had to go beyond Europe, involving the parties from the Commonwealth and Latin America. Any initiative demanded caution, as the International would not have survived a third failure.

After Healey took up office in December 1945, he discussed the committee's proposal with the other socialists. Eventually, most socialists agreed to postpone the rebuilding of a new International and to form a liaison office, to maintain contacts and circulate news.[88] This makeshift solution agreed with Price's idea for the International—in Dalton's words: 'I should not be broken-hearted if we did simply fall back on a liaison committee!'[89] The Labour leadership exploited the resistance of Scandinavian and Eastern socialists to drop internationalist commitments included by Laski and Levy. Healey thought a liaison committee was 'less embarrassing and of more immediate value'[90]: parties under Soviet domination or allied with a large communist party would have found an International under British leadership embarrassing; the Scandinavians did not trust an International passing 'inflammatory but ambiguous resolutions' and did not want problems with the USSR. The Austrians and French, who wanted an International, objected to the exclusion of parties in exile, the admission of ministers, the treatment of the Jewish Labour Party of Palestine and the condemnation of past Internationals. Healey naively believed that thorny issues, like Spain and Palestine, would solve themselves in a few years. Furthermore, a liaison committee did not have to operate in public and express opinions about every issue.

The Labour Party called for an international socialist conference on its own authority, without claiming the cumbersome mantle of the LSI.[91] The Belgian and French parties were strongly opposed to abandoning the restoration of the International.[92] Dutch socialists, before the war very critical, urgently demanded an international organisation.[93] Other than that, the Scandinavians and the parties in the Soviet sphere of influence approved the minimalist plan.[94] Backed by Nenni[95] on the left and the Scandinavians on the right, the Labour Party was in full control of international socialism.

Appropriately, the first International Socialist Conference in Clacton (17–19 May 1946) was 'a meeting which took place throughout in a blaze of obscurity'.[96] Dalton spoke about the dialectics of continuity and renewal of socialism during the ordeal of the world war: the survivors of the old generation testified to endurance, the new faces renewal.[97] The presence of ministers in office, broke with the anti-ministerialist tradition and emphasised the centrality of Government. Dalton presented the Labour Party as a model of democratic renewal and social reform, while stressing the need to preserve friendship with all great powers and eliminate the 'iron curtain of suspicion'. He still criticised the communists and proposals for fusion. The other delegates described their internal situation.

Grumbach (SFIO) tried to put the rebuilding of the Socialist International on the agenda, as this was a prerequisite for any successful socialist policy. He was backed by the Belgians, Austrians, and Swiss, but Aake Ording (DNA) argued that this was not the right moment. He said that international contacts were necessary because a trial period was needed to build familiarity, exchange ideas and create a common ideology. Language was a central point of contention; Ording was particularly concerned with the vague definition of social democracy: did it stand for what the Scandinavians called 'democratic socialism' or a third way between American capitalism and the Soviet system? Eastern European socialists requested a unitary International like the World Federation of Trade Unions (WFTU), although they probably did not expect success and they simply wanted to highlight their concern about the division of Europe. The conference approved the Norwegian proposal to create a permanent information office with a full-time secretary. The International Department of the Labour Party would be responsible for hiring the staff, administering the office and covering the initial costs, which later would be shared among the parties.

The article in the *Tribune* about the Clacton conference, inspired by the Labour Party report, argued that the Socialist International of the past was 'immediately impossible and ultimately undesirable'[98]: the majority of parties did not want the International and those who wanted it disagreed on the form:

> Moreover, the parties with the experience of power are reluctant to limit their freedom by obligations to a body which in the past failed to produce anything but magniloquent and equivocal manifestos and was always subject to the extravagances of impotent idealism.[99]

The Clacton conference was the beginning of the association that regularly convened under the name International Socialist Conference. It also established the first permanent office to maintain contacts between conferences, the Socialist Information and Liaison Office (SILO), with German exile Edith Loeb as its administrative secretary. SILO would convene conferences and produce a bulletin with contributions from all parties. The Bournemouth Conference (8–10 November 1946) added a Consultative Committee tasked with advising SILO but without any authority to settle political questions.[100]

Already in Bournemouth the skeleton of the organisation was defined: a plenary congress, a committee meeting regularly and a permanent secretariat. The weakness of the Consultative Committee in the beginning did not signal strong control from the assembly but rather the decisive influence of the Labour Party between conferences. The key question was whether the Socialist International would be a loose organisation of parties with different outlooks, cooperating towards a common goal, or a community of like-minded parties that excluded dissenters. The contradiction of ideas would only be resolved by events.

The year 1947 and the first 3 months of 1948 were a turning point for socialist internationalism. The incoming Cold War made relations with pro-communist socialists difficult. The unresolved question on the nature of the International Socialist Conference came to the fore. Labour's primacy was challenged on two fronts: the federalists renewed their request to rebuild the Socialist International and the leftists opposed the admission of the SPD and the Italian social democrats. At Clacton and Bournemouth, the Labour Party was in charge, but in Zurich the Swiss party rejected Labour's directions and the agenda of the Consultative Committee, allowing the debating of questions that embarrassed the British, like Greece and Palestine.[101] Healey was not satisfied:

But in the general atmosphere one detected a tendency to revert to the amiable irresolution of the pre-war International, to escape from the small opportunities for constructive initiative into equivocal or meaningless declarations of general intention.[102]

Grumbach manoeuvred the conference's agenda to his advantage. Healey called him a cunning troublemaker, since the Labour leadership was used to control annual conferences by exploiting procedural rules and presenting dissent as disorder.[103] The Conference empowered the Consultative Committee to prepare a binding agenda for the next meeting[104]—Buset commenting that it was an Executive Committee that dared not say its name.[105]

For the first time, rebuilding the International was discussed openly. Buset moved his proposal to rebuild the International, putting forward his arguments in favour.[106] He reassured the Eastern socialists that a synthesis of East and West would naturally emerge from the evolution of socialism. He also said that there was no intention of embarrassing the Labour Government. Like Mollet, Buset rejected the complete identification of the socialist party with the Government; the party had to conceive ideas and convince public opinion. The Executive of the SFIO instructed its delegation to champion of the rebirth of the Socialist International and Mollet reported on the pressing demands of the workers in France, no less than in Belgium, for internationalism.[107] World socialism needed a doctrine and a policy of its own, the time had come to rebuild an International that—again—'dared not say its name'.

The Hungarian socialist Antal Ban appreciated Buset's arguments, but he doubted their feasibility. The South African socialist Macpherson was strongly opposed, as the International would represent only Europe. Morgan Phillips took a dilatory stance, approving the proposal in principle with a number of qualifications. Repeating Price's arguments, Morgan Phillips said that there were two roads to rebuild the International. The first road was to admit everyone who shared the final goal, welcoming labour parties, socialist parties and communist parties:

> The second possibility is to set up an International whose members would be chosen very carefully. Then we will face the need to define exactly the goal and the conditions in which we are going to work.[108]

The International needed unity to act effectively, but the parties were divided, for example on communism. Morgan Phillips disagreed with

Buset on the role of the political party: the task of a party was to win elections and shield the conquests of the workers from the return of the Conservatives. He referred to Stalin's words to justify his attitude: following the longer British road forced the party to keep on winning elections.

Buset held out an olive branch, arguing that the immediate task was not rebuilding the International but studying the question. A committee was formed to study the ideological principles and the problems of organisation. At the request of the Romanian socialists, it was made explicit that the committee would not act under the assumption that rebuilding the International was the only solution,[109] although Healey was convinced that the committee would not produce any result.[110] The left-wing Belgian socialist Isabelle Blume chaired two committees to study the reconstruction of the international women's secretariat and the international relief organisation.[111]

The committee for the rebuilding of the International met in Paris in August.[112] Two proposals emerged: the Franco-Belgian proposal to rebuild the International and the British proposal to reform the Consultative Committee.[113] Buset's plan for the International was similar to the LSI: the federated parties would be committed to enact strategic decisions taken by a two-thirds majority, while free to decide on tactics.[114] Like the LSI, the votes would depend on the number of members. The president, two vice presidents, a secretary and an administrative secretary, with the addition of 16 elected members would form the Executive, responsible for enacting the decisions of the Conference, the information service and relief. The financial commitment of the parties would be in line with the needs of the Conference. The Belgian proposal would turn the International into an independent player with autonomous power over international affairs—with its own representation at the UN. Distance between party and Government was necessary, otherwise the International would replicate the policy of national Governments. To increase cohesion, every party would adopt a declaration of principles, while deciding autonomously about relations with the communists. It was a return to Adler's International.

Conversely, the British proposal continued a trend started by Dalton and Gillies to concentrate power in the hands of the bigger parties. This meant strengthening small committees over the plenary assembly. Morgan Phillips brought back the idea of 'socialist ambassadors', who would have a full mandate and enough information to take political decisions in the

Consultative Committee. This would prevent turning every conference into a free and chaotic discussion.

The committee, meeting in October, adopted Morgan Phillips' memorandum.[115] Conditions were not ripe for the Socialist International, what was needed was to reform the International Socialist Conference as the main liaison organisation. The committee suggested the creation of an International Committee for Socialist Conferences made up of delegates with a full mandate and empowered to realise the decisions of the conferences. The rules would allow the summoning of regional conferences, like those organised in Eastern Europe, in order to accommodate the needs of the socialists of the Soviet sphere of influence. Special sub-committees would study specific issues. Doubling party fees would finance the expansion. The Swiss Humbert-Droz said that it was an improvement and the maximum the Labour Party could accept. He understood that as long as the Eastern Europeans were members, there would be no progress but at least they would avoid the division of the continent.

At the Antwerp Conference (28 November–1 December 1947), Buset, who had proposed to rebuild the International at Zurich, introduced the compromise solution to reform the Consultative Committee. He levelled some criticism at the Labour Party and the management of the Consultative Committee, which blurred the line between political and administrative decisions, especially involving socialists in London without political authority. He suggested longer meetings for the new Consultative Committee, to meet in cities other than London and to increase the financing. On Buset's suggestion, the new committee was called Committee of International Socialist Conferences, soon shortened to Comisco—probably in imitation of Cominform.

The creation of Comisco had little symbolic value but important political consequences. Office and staff were separate from the Labour Party[116] and it took full responsibility for calling conferences and meetings. The Belgians considered Comisco as foreshadowing the Executive Committee.

When Comisco first met on 10 January 1948, Larock wanted to adopt a short constitution to make it similar to the Executive Committee of the LSI, but the Dutch Martin Bolle argued against a detailed constitution and in favour of a sub-committee of socialists residing in London to deal with administrative questions. In the end, Healey proposed and Comisco approved electing a sub-committee lasting one year to call the meetings of Comisco and supervise the finances of SILO. This sub-committee originally included representatives from Great Britain (Morgan Phillips), the

Netherlands (Bolle), Belgium (Larock), Austria (Wodak) and Czechoslovakia.[117] After the Prague Coup, Levy (SFIO) substituted the Czechoslovak representative.

In this period there were also efforts to rebuild the ancillary organisations. The SPÖ wanted to restore the Socialist Educational International, for the children's organisations, as it was before 1934.[118] However the Scandinavian parties had developed a network of their own children's organisations and refused a central organ with the power to interfere in their internal decisions. 'The Scandinavian organisations want an organ for collaboration and won't help to build an international organisation with supreme power in the actual [sic] situation'.[119] In October 1947, the children's organisations from Scandinavia, Great Britain, France, Belgium, Germany and Switzerland did away with the pre-war statute and started the liaison organisation proposed by the Swedes from scratch. The basic conflict among European social democrats was acted out in miniature for the children's organisations.

The two committees chaired by Isabelle Blume[120] proposed rebuilding the Women's Secretariat to the Antwerp conference—with only the mild opposition of the British.[121] The Conference also approved the formation of a Relief Committee and an International Women's Committee. Before every international conference, the International Socialist Women' Conference would meet, and so each delegation was required to include at least one woman.[122]

6 Breach and Restructuring

The Antwerp Conference signalled the crisis of the International Socialist Conference as an instrument for cohabitation and mediation between the very different tendencies in European socialism. Centrist compromises made by the supporters of the Third Force (Belgians, French, Labour left) or just the realists (Labour right, Czechoslovaks) forfeited any practical action and relied on verbal vagueness to hide divisions. In addition, the PvdA from the right and the PSI and PPS from the left encouraged polarisation to bring about the split.

Laski's speech in Antwerp was his last meaningful political action. He presented the Labour Party as a guarantor of the unity of Europe and the socialist movement, highlighting the difference with the imperialist USA. He made openings to the Eastern European socialists and asked them simply for loyalty to democratic socialism.[123] Nonetheless, he accepted that the economic rebirth of Germany and the Marshall Plan without political conditions were necessary to revitalise the European economy and prevent misery, the breeding ground of communism. Revived trade would benefit Eastern Europe as well. For the Polish socialists, however, German revanchism was the paramount preoccupation.

Vorrink—who, according to Nenni, 'spoke like Truman'[124]—said that it was impossible to rebuild the International without free socialism to the East and it was impossible to take a position without offending the Eastern socialists. Hochfeld took offence, as the PPS was independent and it would not allow a communist monopoly of power. Larock proposed a vague resolution on world peace that satisfied nobody. The PvdA voted against, saying they wanted to condemn the repression of independent socialists in Eastern Europe. The PPS put forward an alternative resolution blaming the intensified class struggle and counterrevolution for international tensions, calling for the defence of European independence and truly popular Governments. The Czechoslovak Kraus proposed an economic resolution demanding increased productivity and international economic cooperation on a socialist basis. As critics noted, it was an intellectual piece ignoring political reality—the Marshall Plan—and the actual problem of Europe—the dollar deficit. Morgan Phillips complained that the Eastern Europeans demanded respect for their situation but would not allow the Western socialists to solve the problems with the instruments they chose. The Conference voted the two vague resolutions, leaving their implementation to the newly created Comisco.

The Cominform conference marked the end of the idea that the Socialist International could negotiate a global agreement between social democracy and communism. It was no longer possible to imagine a summit of Stalin with Attlee and Blum when they were described as traitors and tools of imperialism. While the parties were still quarrelling over Cominform and the admission of the SPD, the first meeting of Comisco, on 10 January 1948, had to implement the Antwerp resolution.[125] The Norwegians, Dutch and Belgians insisted that the Marshall Plan was central and required cooperation between willing parties, which they hinted would be more productive than the Antwerp conference. The Poles argued it was an attempt to split Europe. The compromise was that it would not be Comisco but the SFIO and the Labour Party to call a conference to study the Marshall Plan. Not long before French and British socialists had decided to develop 'more regular and intimate contact than heretofore'[126] to confront together issues involving the Great Powers, such as the international control of the Ruhr.

The Prague Coup forced an end to a relationship that neither Western nor Eastern socialists wanted to break. In 1947, the SFIO and the Labour Party still believed they could save the unity of Europe, but some parties had already come to terms with the new situation. Just before the Prague Coup, Haakon Lie told the other Nordic parties that the division of Europe and Germany was unavoidable and the Western Europeans should have pursed economic and military cooperation. Italian and Polish obstructionism had made socialist cooperation impossible from Clacton onwards.[127]

Few periods have benefited socialist internationalism as much as the 2 years between the Vienna Conference (4–7 June 1948) and the Copenhagen Conference (1–3 June 1950). The Prague Coup might have been a tragedy, but it also undid the Gordian knot: divisions in opinion and strategy no longer mattered, as the socialists faced a common enemy. Bolle argued that SILO had failed in the provision of information and propaganda because it was paralysed by differences between Western socialists and appeasers of communism, but things were now different:

> The position therefore is now that the International Socialist Conference and Comisco are made up of independent parties of a purely social democratic character.[128]

Clarity engendered activism and optimism: if socialists finally agreed on what to do, surely they could act and act effectively. This was confirmed in the Italian election of 1948, where the Comisco parties backed dissident social democrats, since the official Italian socialist party had an electoral alliance with the communists. The Popular Front coalition suffered an astounding defeat, which cast doubt on the possibility of communists and their allies winning in Western democracies; as Nenni said, 'How can I help but face that under the communist banner, direction or inspiration—whether apparent or real—you cannot win in the West?'[129] Other episodes testified to the fact that socialists could resist. The Vienna Conference (4–7 June 1948) celebrated the resistance of the Austrian workers to Soviet occupation forces, a continuation of their resistance to fascism in 1934.[130] During the Berlin blockade, the city led by a social democratic city council became 'the moral capital of Europe'[131] and the mayor Ernst Reuter provided a living example of resistance without concessions to any form of totalitarianism.[132]

When in 1948[133] and 1949[134] the time came to reassess the organisations of international socialism (SILO, Comisco, International Socialist Conference), socialists were confident they could reorganise them to promote socialism and intervene where needed. The Labour Party, which had blocked the rebuilding of the Socialist International, carried the political and financial burden for expanding the responsibilities and organisation of Comisco, while expanding its International Department.[135] Morgan Phillips promised £1000 to turn Comisco into a propaganda machine for socialism—in addition to £300 to help refugees.[136] In 1948, the Labour Party covered one-third of the budget of the entire organisation, which had just lost funding from Eastern Europe, allowing it to survive and even expand.[137]

The Labour leadership believed that it had a responsibility to lead by example. As Dalton said, 'We shall be lighting fires of hope and we shall be kindling sympathy and generous emulation in many other countries in Europe and in other continents of the world'.[138] The International Socialist Conference would play a large part. It did not have the resources or the ambition of the Comintern, but it was 'at least a moral symbol through which the policy of its members can be influenced'; 'In particular, the Labour Party could use it as a platform from which to publicise the British approach to problems of democratic socialism'.[139]

On 20 March 1948, Comisco decided to give a coordinated response to its enemies—especially communists. Plans to relaunch *Socialist World* as a journal with wide distribution were dashed by technical and political issues, so SILO decided to replace it with a newsletter and single-issue pamphlets.[140] In reality the Information Research Department (IRD) had taken over the task of circulating articles, news, and propaganda among the socialist forces of Europe and it could do the job with greater efficiency than a small socialist office.[141] The Vienna Conference approved Bolle's plan to overhaul the organisation, doubling affiliation fees to finance it.[142] The goal was to give the small organism which met more often the power to make rapid political decisions to answer communist attacks. Despite opposition from the PSB to make official the transformation of the Sub-Committee of Comisco into the centre of the organisation, it actually acquired juridical personality, a chairman (Morgan Phillips) and a secretary (Bolle himself).[143] SILO became 'Secretariat of the International Socialist Conference'.[144] Finally, international socialism had an organism to take decisions and an office to enforce them. However, resources were still the weak point.

Among the obstacles to the ability of Comisco to influence the development of socialism in individual countries, the limited ability to grant financial help was the most important, as the Greek and Italian cases will show. In 1945, Morgan Phillips proposed that the International should grant relief and legal assistance,[145] but the needs of the organisation went beyond the means of a political party. During the war the Labour Party gave Continental socialist exiles £300 for propaganda—though it might have come from the Government.[146] In 1944, the TUC and Bevin, with Eden's blessing, offered to help the French trade union federation (CGT) to rebuild, especially to keep the communists in a minority. Citrine, the chairman of the TUC, gave officials of the CGT £2000, after receiving assurances that the communists were a minority and would not organise a faction.[147] He was bewildered that the French were not anxious to receive the money. He thought they received enough from the resistance, but the British ambassador knew better: the communists were giving much bigger sums. Predictably, the CGT would come under communist domination and it was only thanks to the American trade unions that the socialist trade unionists managed to build up their federation, *Force Ouvriere*. When, in 1945, the Belgian, Dutch and Italian parties asked for help to rebuild their organisations, the Labour Party found it could not even promote an appeal fund, as it would have diverted funds from the General Election Appeal Fund—though they asked the Fabian Society to find other financiers.[148] When eighty-two Labour MPs asked for a relief fund for the German and Austrian socialists,[149] the International Sub-Committee answered that only the Government could sustain costs of such magnitude.

This does not mean that the contribution of the Labour Party to international socialism was small. In the 1920s, there were complaints about its limited financial commitment to the LSI[150] and the decision to retrench in the late 1930s was also an attempt to scale back the considerable cost—in 1939 the Labour Party paid £1000 but refused further payments without reform.[151] When it was time to restart the international socialist community, the British took on the administrative costs.[152]

The income of the International Socialist Conference in 1947 was £1634 19 s.[153] Labour's contribution was substantial—£350, around one-fifth of the total budget. Also fundamental was the contribution from Eastern socialists—£350 from Poland and Czechoslovakia each—which explains their enormous influence on the International Socialist Conference. The other big contributor was Sweden (£300), a strong party unaffected by the war.

1948 was a year of radical change: the Eastern socialists left and the organisation was to enlarge to carry out propaganda and relief for the refugees. SILO did not even have enough money to support current activities, despite the decision in Antwerp to double fees.[154] The money Morgan Phillips promised to the Vienna Conference was nothing but providential. The Scandinavian parties remained substantial contributors: £500 from the Swedes, £300 from the Danes, £150 from the Norwegians. The Austrian party returned to being a major contributor: £750, more than a fifth of the total income. The following year the SPD contributed £800.[155] With the persecution of socialists in Eastern Europe, the larger parties contributed to a Refugee Organisation Fund.[156]

In 1950, the income of Comisco rose to £5699 7 s. 4d. While Labour's contribution was fixed at £1000, it was still 17%—not counting the Refugee fund of £1263, where Labour covered a quarter of the total. In 1952, Labour agreed to raise its contribution from £1300 to £2000, solving the financial problems of Comisco.[157] When the Socialist International set up a special fund to reach out to Asian socialists, the British offered £1000.[158] In 1950, the fees of Belgium and France increased to only £100 and £400 respectively. These figures explain why the opinion of the French and Belgian parties carried so little weight on important political issues.

It is clear that the rich parties did not lack a financial commitment to international socialism, and the pre-war attempt to reduce the organisation and cut expenses was overwhelmed by events. However, these parties had priorities of their own. When the Greek socialists asked for financial help for their 1951 and 1952 elections, the French, British and Dutch could not contribute, since they also had elections.[159]

By the end of 1948, the International Socialist Conference and Comisco were much closer to what the Socialist International would be at its rebirth. The need to take an active part in foreign affairs and ideological struggles drove the rebuilding of the institution. However, while some political issues were settled, other questions would soon emerge.

Notes

1. P. Van Kemseke (2006) *Towards an Era of Development, The Globalization of Socialism and Christian Democracy: 1945–1965* (Leuven: Leuven University Press), 18.
2. A. Panebianco (1988) *Political Parties: Organization and Power* (Cambridge: Cambridge University Press), 47–68.

3. S. Pons (2014) *The Global Revolution: A History of International Communism, 1917–1991* (Oxford: Oxford University Press), 24.
4. H. Steiner (1985) 'Die Internationale Arbeitsgemeinschaft Sozialisticher Parteien (2 ½ Internationale) 1921–1923', in E. Collotti (ed.), *L'Internazionale Operaia e Socialista tra le due guerre* (Milano: Feltrinelli) 56–59.
5. B. Tobia (1985) 'Pietro Nenni e la politica dell'Internazionale Operaia e Socialista (1930–1939)'; M. Mancini (1985) 'L'IOS e la questione del fronte unico negli anni Trenta', in Collotti (ed.), L'Internazionale Operaia e Socialista tra le due guerre, 159–175; 184–198.
6. Pons, *The Global Revolution*, 98–112.
7. I. Kramnick and B. Sheerman (1993) *Harold Laski, A Life on the Left* (London: Hamilton), 467–471; 503–509.
8. H.J. Laski, 'The Need of International Labour Unity, Suggestion for a Discussion', *Left News*, January 1943.
9. J. Braunthal to P. Nenni, 21 October 1944, Fondazione Pietro Nenni, Rome (FPN), Fondo Pietro Nenni, b.20, f.1159.
10. 'An Exchange of Letters between Julius Braunthal and Camille Huysmans', [December 1942–February 1943], International Institute of Socialist History, Amsterdam (IISH), Friedrich Adler, 83.
11. Entry, 5 May 1942, G. Dimitrov (2003) *The Diary of Georgi Dimitrov, 1933–1949* (New Haven: Yale University Press), 214–215.
12. A. Thorpe (2014) 'Locking out the Communists: The Labour party and the Communist party, 1939–46', *Twentieth Century British History*, 25, 2, 242–248.
13. 'Weekly information summary for period 8th–14th September', The National Archives, Kew (TNA), FO 371/47093-N12334.
14. M. Newman (1993) *Harold Laski: A Political Biography* (Basingstoke: Macmillan), 296–301.
15. A. Thorpe (2009) *Parties at war: political organization in Second World War Britain* (Oxford: Oxford University Press), 40.
16. G. Sabbatucci (1991) 'Il Mito dell'Urss e il socialismo italiano', *Socialismo Storia: Annali della Fondazione Giacomo Brodolini*, 3, 69–70.
17. K. Debniki to the International Department of the PPS Executive, 17 May 1946, in P. Heumos (ed.) (2014) *Europäischer Sozialismus im Kalten Krieg: Briefe und Berichte 1944–1948* (Frankfurt: Campus), 151–153.
18. B.D. Graham (2000) 'Choix atlantique our Troisième force internationale?' in S. Bernstein (ed.) *Le Parti socialiste entre Résistance et République* (Paris: Publications de la Sorbonne), 161–165.
19. G. Arfé (1978) 'Pietro Nenni, libertario e giacobino' in P. Nenni, *Vento del Nord* (Torino: Einaudi), xxvii–xxviii.
20. Carandini to De Gasperi, 9 March 1946, Archivio Central dello Stato, Roma (ACS), Fondo Nicolò Carandini (NC), b.2.

21. Entry, 29 February 1948, B. Pimlott (1986) *The Political Diary of Hugh Dalton: 1918–40, 1945–60* (London: Cape), 427.
22. 'Conferenza internazionale dei partiti socialisti (Clacton-on-Sea 17–20 maggio 1946)', 28 February 1946, ACS, NC, b.6.
23. H. Laski, 'A note on the socialist conference at Clacton', [May 1946], Labour History Archive and Study Centre, People's History Museum, Manchester (LHASC), Labour Party (LP), International Department (ID), Denis Healey's papers (DH), 03, 11.
24. D. Healey to V. Larock, 31 May 1946, LHASC, LP, ID, DH, 03, 11.
25. M. Phillips to E. Bevin, 23 May 1946; J.H.Lambert, Minute, 24 May 1946, TNA, FO 371/56766-N7301.
26. Moscow Embassy to Northern Department, 16 August 1946, TNA, FO 371/56767-N10686.
27. M. Phillips, We talk with Stalin on the two roads to Socialism, *Daily Herald*, 22 August 1946.
28. F. Roberts to C.F.A. Warner, 23 August 1946, TNA, FO 371/56768-N10977. A. Bacon, H. Clay, H. Laski, M. Phillips, 'Goodwill mission to the USSR', LHASC, LP, International Sub-Committee, Minutes & Documents, 1946.
29. M. Phillips, We talk with Stalin on the two roads to Socialism, *Daily Herald*, 22 August 1946.
30. Roberts to Warner, 23 August 1946, TNA, FO 371/56768-N10977.
31. Wodak to Schärf, 4 October 1946, W. Wodak (1980) *Diplomatie zwischen Weltpolitik und Parteiproporz* (Graz: Styria 1980), 228–230.
32. Stalin-Wells Talk, *The New Statesman and Nation*, December 1934.
33. Entry, 28 January 1945, Dimitrov, *The Diary of Georgi Dimitrov*, 357–358.
34. Pons, *The Global Revolution*, 137.
35. M. Myant (1981) *Socialism and Democracy in Czechoslovakia, 1945–1948* (Cambridge: Cambridge University Press), 137–143.
36. Pons, *The Global Revolution*, 186–200. K. Kaplan (1984) *Das Verhängnisvolle Bündnis. Unterwanderung, Gleichschaltung und Vernichtung der Tschechoslowakischen Sozialdemokratie 1944–1954* (Wuppertal: Pol-Verlag), 69–74. Entry, 2 September 1946, Dimitrov, *The Diary of Georgi Dimitrov*, 411–414.
37. Entry, 4 September 1946, Dimitrov, *The Diary of Georgi Dimitrov*, 415.
38. Stenogramme, 8 Juin, IISH, Socialist International (SI), 235.
39. Pons, *The Global Revolution*, 98–112.
40. L. Misgeld (1984) *Sozialdemokratie und Aussenpolitik in Schweden: Sozialistische Internationale, Europapolitik und die Deutschlandfrage 1945–1955* (Frankfurt: Campus Verlag), 76.
41. Misgeld, *Sozialdemokratie und Aussenpolitik in Schweden*, 100–110.

42. J. Braunthal (1949) 'The Rebirth of Social Democracy', *Foreign Affairs*, 27, 4, 600.
43. J. Fisher (2005) *Bread on the Waters: A History of TGWU Education, 1922–2000* (London: Lawrence & Wishart), 21; 45–88.
44. Price, 'International Socialist Action, Problems of Organisation', February 1945, LHASC, LP, International Sub-Committee, Minutes and Documents, 1945.
45. J. Price (1945) *International Labour Movement* (London: Oxford University Press).
46. Price, *International Labour Movement*, 258–261.
47. The debate in the SPÖ between social democrats and left-wing socialists on this issue is enlightening (F. Weber (1986) *Der kalte Krieg in der SPÖ: Koalitionswächter, Pragmatiker und revolutionäre Sozialisten, 1945–1950* (Wien: Verlag für Gesellschaftskritik), 45–46).
48. For a contemporary lucid analysis see I. Silone (2002) 'Missione europea del Socialismo', in N. Novelli (ed.), *Per Ignazio Silone* (Firenze: Polistampa), 90–92 (originally published in 1947).
49. Price, 'International Socialist Action, Problems of Organisation', February 1945, LHASC, LP, International Sub-Committee, Minutes and Documents, 1945.
50. Price, *International Labour Movement*, 12.
51. Price, 'International Socialist Action, Problems of Organisation', February 1945, LHASC, LP, International Sub-Committee, Minutes and Documents, 1945.
52. Price, 'International Socialist Action, Problems of Organisation', February 1945, LHASC, LP, International Sub-Committee, Minutes and Documents, 1945.
53. Price, *International Labour Movement*, 167–173.
54. Price, *International Labour Movement*, 191–200.
55. Price, 'International Socialist Action, Problems of Organisation', February 1945, LHASC, LP, International Sub-Committee, Minutes and Documents, 1945.
56. Price, 'International Socialist Action, Problems of Organisation', February 1945, LHASC, LP, International Sub-Committee, Minutes and Documents, 1945.
57. D. Healey, The Workers' Internationals, *Tribune*, 15 February 1946.
58. G. Devin (1993) *L'Internationale socialiste: histoire et sociologie du socialisme internationale: 1945–1990* (Paris: Presses de la Fondation national des sciences politiques), 19–29. Misgeld, *Sozialdemokratie und Aussenpolitik in Schweden*, 61.
59. Misgeld, *Sozialdemokratie und Aussenpolitik in Schweden*, 43–54.

60. L. Basso, Il dialogo riprende II, *Quarto Stato*, 15–30 dicembre 1946. Also, S. Merli (1981) *Il Partito nuovo di Lelio Basso: 1945–1946* (Venezia: Marsilio), 73–82.
61. J. Hochfeld (1946) *An Open Letter from a Polish Socialist to a Friend of the Labour Party* (London: London Committee of the Polish Socialist Party), 16–17. 'Bericht des polnischen Sozialisten J. Hochfeld über die internationale sozialistische Konferenz über das Franco-Regime und den XXXVIII Parteitag der SFIO in Paris', September 1946, Heumos (ed.), *Europäischer Sozialismus im Kalten Krieg*, 168.
62. V. Bernard, International socialist co-operation, *Socialist World*, March–May 1948. Also Kaplan, *Das Verhängnisvolle Bündnis*, 111–116.
63. Entry, 30 November 1947, P. Nenni (1982) *Diari*, Vol.1, *Tempo di Guerra Fredda: diari 1943–1956* (Milano: SugarCo), 402.
64. 'Warschau – Bericht des polnischen Sozialisten S.Gross über den III. Parteitag der SPÖ in Wien, 30. Oktober 1947', Heumos (ed.), *Europäischer Sozialismus im Kalten Krieg*, 210–221.
65. P. Heumos (ed.) (1985) *Die Konferenzen der sozialistischen Parteien Zentral- und Osteuropas in Prag und Budapest 1946 und 1947: Darstellung und Dokumentation* (Stuttgart: F. Steiner).
66. Warsaw to Foreign Office, 20 December 1946, TNA, FO 371/56707-N15990.
67. Kirby to Healey, 17 November 1947, LHASC, LP, ID, DH, 9, 5.
68. Vecchietti to Nenni, n.d. [October 1947], FPN, Fondo Pietro Nenni, b.42, f.1959.
69. Healey to Kirby, 3 November 1947, LHASC, LP, ID, DH, 9, 5.
70. Kirby to Healey, 20 December 1946, LHASC, LP, ID, DH, 4, 14.
71. T. Brimelow, Minute, 7 January 1947, TNA, FO 371/56707-N15990.
72. Waterfield, Minute, 6 January 1947, TNA, FO 371/56707-N15990.
73. R.M.A. Hankey, Minute, 14 November 1946, TNA, FO 371/56244-N14860.
74. M. Buset to M. Phillips, 9 April 1946, LHASC, LP, ID, DH, 03, 09.
75. Stenogramme, 8 Juin, IISH, SI, 235. A summary can be found in M. Buset, A new Socialist International, *Socialist World*, September–November 1947.
76. Buset to M. Phillips, 9 April 1946, LHASC, LP, ID, DH, 03, 09.
77. P. Buffotot (1983) 'Le Parti Socialiste SFIO et l'Internationale Socialiste (1944–1969)', in H. Portelli (ed.) *L'Internationale socialiste* (Paris: Les Éditions Ouvrières), 89–92.
78. V. Larock (1977) 'L'internationaliste', *Témoignages: Guy Mollet, 1905–1975* (Paris: Fondation Guy Mollet), 60–62. G. Devin (1987) 'Guy Mollet et l'Internationale Socialiste', B.Ménager, P.Ratte, J.-L. Thiébault, R.Vandenbussche, C.-M. Wallon-Leducq, *Guy Mollet, Un camarade en république* (Lille: Presses Universitaires de Lille), 146.

79. Graham, 'Choix atlantique ou Troisième force internationale?', 162.
80. The International, *London information of the Austrian socialists in Great Britain*, 21 November 1945.
81. B. Kautsky, Die internationale Arbeitbewegung, *Zukunft*, January 1947.
82. O. Pollak, The Third Force, *Socialist World*, March–May 1948. On the SPÖ's position on the Marshall Plan and the Third Force see Weber, *Der kalte Krieg in der SPÖ*, 122–128.
83. Oscar Pollak, Europa – 50:50, Zukunft, July 1946.
84. Minutes of the International Sub-Committee, 1 August 1945, LHASC, LP, ID, Minutes & Documents, 1945.
85. What's happening, *Tribune*, 17 August 1945.
86. Minutes of the International Sub-Committee, 18 September 1945, LHASC, LP, ID, Minutes & Documents, 1945. Misgeld, *Sozialdemokratie und Aussenpolitik in Schweden*, 43–48.
87. 'Note on the possible reconstruction of the Socialist International', January 1946, LHASC, LP, Minutes & Documents, 1946.
88. Malfatti to Nenni, 30 January 1946, FPN, Fondo Pietro Nenni, b.31, f.1547.
89. H. Dalton to Healey 18 February 1946, LHASC, LP, ID, DH, 03, 09.
90. Healey to Dalton, 12 February 1946, LHASC, LP, ID, DH, 03, 09.
91. M. Phillips to the secretaries of the socialist parties, 16 February 1946, LHASC, LP, ID, DH, 03, 10.
92. Buset to M. Phillips, 9 April 1946; D. Mayer to M. Phillips, 16 April 1946; LHASC, LP, ID, DH, 03, 09.
93. C. Woudenberg to Labour Party, 6 March 1946, LHASC, LP, ID, DH, 03, 12.
94. H. Hedtoft to Labour Party, 29 March 1946; B. Vilim to M. Phillips, 15 March 1946; U. Varjonen to M. Phillips, 26 March 1946, LHASC, LP, ID, DH, 03, 12. H. Lie to Healey, 13 February 1946, LHASC, LP, ID, DH, 03, 12.
95. Entry, 21 January 1946, Nenni, *Tempo di Guerra fredda*, 176.
96. Special correspondent, Britain and World Socialism, *Tribune*, 7 June 1946.
97. 'International Socialist Conference at Clacton May 17th–20th 1946', LHASC, LP, ID, DH, 03, 10. Misgeld, *Sozialdemokratie und Aussenpolitik in Schweden*, 59–71. R. Steininger (1979) *Deutschland und die Sozialistische Internationale nach dem Zweiten Weltkrieg, Darstellung und Dokumentation* (Bonn: Neue Gesellschaft), 47–48.
98. Special correspondent, Britain and World Socialism, *Tribune*, 7 June 1946.
99. Special correspondent, Britain and World Socialism, *Tribune*, 7 June 1946.

100. 'Minutes of the International Socialist Conference, Bournemouth, November 8–10', IISH, SI, 234.
101. Stenogramme, 6 Juin, IISH, SI, 235.
102. D. Healey, 'Notes on the minutes of the Zurich conference', LHASC, LP, International Sub-Committee, Minutes and Documents, 1947.
103. L. Minkin (1978) *The Labour Party Conference: A Study in the Politics of Intra-Party Democracy* (London: Allen Lane).
104. Minutes of the International Socialist Conference, Krongresshaus, Zurich, 6–9 June, 1947, IISH, SI, 235.
105. Stenogramme, 6 Juin, IISH, SI, 235.
106. Stenogramme, 8 Juin, IISH, SI, 235. Steininger, *Deutschland und die Sozialistische Internationale nach dem Zweiten Weltkrieg*, 52–57.
107. Buffotot, 'Le Parti Socialiste SFIO et l'Internationale Socialiste (1944–1969)', 91.
108. Stenogramme, 8 Juin, IISH, SI, 235.
109. Minutes of the International Socialist Conference, Krongresshaus, Zurich, 6–9 June, 1947, IISH, SI, 235.
110. D. Healey, 'Notes on the minutes of the Zurich conference', LHASC, LP, International Sub-Committee, Minutes and Documents, 1947.
111. E. Loeb to I. Blume, 17 November 1947, IISH, SI, 236. Socialist International Women (2007) *The First Hundred Years: A Short History of Socialist International Women* (Berlin: Vorwärts Buch), 31–34.
112. Steininger, *Deutschland und die Sozialistische Internationale nach dem Zweiten Weltkrieg*, 58–59.
113. M. Phillips, 'Memorandum on the Consultative Committee of the International Socialist Conference', attached to a letter of 29 August, LHASC, LP, International Sub-Committee, Minutes and Documents, 1947.
114. 'Digest on Belgian Proposals on the Reconstitution of an International', December 1947, IISH, SI, 535, Belgium 1946–1954.
115. 'Draft resolution unanimously voted by the International Preparatory Commission, Brussels, 29th October 1947', LHASC, LP, International Sub-Committee, Minutes and Documents, 1947.
116. Circular 80, 'Summarised report of the first meeting of the Committee of the International Socialist Conference, 10 January, 1948', IISH, SI, 47.
117. Circular 47, 'Report on the activities of Silo since the Antwerp International Conference', 27 May 1948, IISH, SI, 47.
118. 'Notes and proposals by the Austrian Socialist Party concerning the Socialist Education International', LHASC, LP, International Sub-Committee, Minutes and Documents, 1947.
119. K. Björk to Loeb, 10 November 1947, IISH, SI, 236.
120. Blume to Loeb, 19 November 1947, IISH, SI, 236.

121. 'Meeting of the Provisory Committee in charge of examining the possibilities of reconstructing the international socialist women's Committee', 28 November 1947, IISH, SI, 236.
122. Circular 88, 'Summary of proceedings, International Socialist Conference, Antwerp 28 November–2 December, 1947', IISH, SI, 47.
123. Circular 88, 'Summary of proceedings, International Socialist Conference, Antwerp 28 November–2 December, 1947', IISH, SI, 47.
124. Entry, 29 November 1947, Nenni, *Tempo di Guerra Fredda*, 401.
125. Circular 80, 'Summarised report of the first meeting of the Committee of the International Socialist Conference, 10 January, 1948', IISH, SI, 47. 'Notes on the first meeting of the Conference of International Socialist Parties, London, January 10th 1948'; 'Note on the projected Conference of Western Socialist Parties, March 21–22 in London', LHASC, LP, International Sub-Committee, Minutes and Documents, 1948.
126. 'Note on a conference between Mr. Morgan Phillips and Monsieur Salomon Grumbach on Friday, 9th January, 1948', LHASC, LP, International Sub-Committee, Minutes and Documents, 1948.
127. Misgeld, *Sozialdemokratie und Aussenpolitik in Schweden*, 110–131.
128. M.C. Bolle, 'Statement of the activities and finance of the Socialist Information and Liaison Office and the Sub-Committee of Comisco in charge of it', 27 May 1948, IISH, SI, 47.
129. Entry, 30 April 1948, Nenni, *Tempo di Guerra Fredda*, 426.
130. Notes on the quarter, *Socialist World*, June–August 1948.
131. 'Report to the International sub-committee on visit to German SPD Congress in Berlin, 8th May 1948, and the Swedish Social Democratic Party Congress in Stockholm, May 9–14th, 1948 by Mr. Harold Earnshaw', LHASC, LP, International Sub-Committee, Minutes and Documents, 1948.
132. Berlin – City of decision, *Socialist World*, September–November 1948.
133. M.C. Bolle, 'Statement of the activities and finance of the Socialist Information and Liaison Office and the Sub-Committee of Comisco in charge of it', 27 May 1948, IISH, SI, 47.
134. Circular 30/49, 21 June 1949, IISH, SI, 48.
135. 'Note on the International Department', July 1948, LHASC, LP, International Sub-Committee, Minutes & Documents, 1948.
136. Van Kemseke, *Towards an Era of Development*, 37.
137. Circular 22/49, IISH, SI, 48.
138. Labour Party Annual Conference Report (LPACR) 1945, 103.
139. Memorandum on international socialist policy, LHASC, LP, International Sub-Committee, Minutes and Documents, 1948.
140. Circular 121, Comisco Meeting (3 December 1948); Circular 122, Publications, (17 December 1948), IISH, SI, 47.

141. T. Insall (2010) *Haakon Lie, Denis Healey and the Making of an Anglo-Norwegian Special Relationship 1945–1951* (Oslo: Oslo Academic Press), 218–223.
142. Circular 103, 'Report of the Third meeting of the committee of International Socialist Conference, Vienna, 3 June 1948', IISH, SI, B.47.
143. Circular 117, 'Report by M.C. Bolle (Holland) on activities since Vienna Meeting of Comisco (3 June 1948)', IISH, SI, 47.
144. 'Summary of the decisions of the COMISCO meeting at Clacton, 3rd December 1948', LHASC, LP, International Sub-Committee, Minutes and Documents, 1948.
145. 'Note on the possible reconstruction of the Socialist International', January 1946, LHASC, LP, International Sub-Committee, Minutes and Documents, 1946.
146. Minutes of the International Sub-Committee, 19 June 1942, LHASC, LP, International Sub-Committee, Minutes and Documents, 1942.
147. D. Cooper to A. Eden, 5 October 1944, TNA, FO 371/42066-Z6739.
148. Minutes of the International Sub-Committee, 18 April 1945, LHASC, LP, International Sub-Committee, Minutes and Documents, 1945.
149. Minutes of the International Sub-Committee, 15 January 1946, LHASC, LP, International Sub-Committee, Minutes and Documents, 1945.
150. E. Collotti (1985) 'Appunti su Friedrich Adler segretario dell'Internazionale Operaia e Socialista', E. Collotti (ed.) *L'Internazionale Operaia e Socialista tra le due guerre* (Milano: Feltrinelli), 65–73.
151. Minutes of the International Sub-Committee, 13 July 1939, LHASC, LP, International Sub-Committee, Minutes and Documents, 1940.
152. Minutes of International Sub-Committee, 20 March 1945, LHASC, LP, International Sub-Committee, Minutes and Documents, 1945.
153. 'Minutes of the consultative committee meeting of the International socialist conference', Sixth meeting, 26 September 1947, LHASC, LP, International Sub-Committee, Minutes and Documents, 1947.
154. Circular 47, 'Report on the activities of SILO since the Antwerp International Conference', 27 May 1948, IISH, SI, 47.
155. Circular 17/51, 'Annual Report of the Activities of the International Socialist Conference, 1 January–31 December 1950', 12 February 1951, IISH, SI, 58.
156. 'Minutes of the meetings of the Comisco Sub-committee January 6, 1949', LHASC, LP, International Sub-Committee, Minutes and Documents, 1949.
157. Braunthal to Mollet, 6 March 1952, IISH, SI, 605.
158. Van Kemseke, *Towards an Era of Development*, 71.

159. Circular 186/50, Report of activities of Comisco, from June to September 1950, 30 September 1950, IISH, SI, 55. 'Minutes of the meeting of the International Socialist Conference Sub-Committee, 20 October 1950'; 'Report of activities and correspondence 7 November–11 December 1950', IISH, SI, 57.

Bibliography

Arfé, G. (1978). Pietro Nenni, libertario e giacobino. In P. Nenni (Ed.). *Vento del Nord* (pp. vii–lx). Torino: Einaudi.

Buffotot, P. (1983). Le Parti Socialiste SFIO et l'Internationale Socialiste (1944–1969). In H. Portelli (Ed.). *L'Internationale socialiste* (pp. 89–100). Paris: Les Éditions Ouvrières.

Collotti, E. (1985). Appunti su Friedrich Adler segretario dell'Internazionale Operaia e Socialista. In E. Collotti (Ed.). *L'Internazionale Operaia e Socialista tra le due guerre* (pp. 65–103). Milano: Feltrinelli.

Devin, G. (1987). Guy Mollet et l'Internationale Socialiste. In B. Ménager, P. Ratte, J.-L. Thiébault, R. Vandenbussche & C.-M. Wallon-Leducq (Eds.). *Guy Mollet, Un camarade en république* (pp. 143–168). Lille: Presses Universitaires de Lille.

Devin, G. (1993). *L'Internationale socialiste: histoire et sociologie du socialisme internationale: 1945–1990*. Paris: Presses de la Fondation national des sciences politiques.

Dimitrov, G. (2003). *The diary of Georgi Dimitrov, 1933–1949*. New Haven: Yale University Press.

Fisher, J. (2005). *Bread on the waters: a history of TGWU education, 1922–2000*. London: Lawrence & Wishart.

Graham, B.D. (2000). Choix atlantique our Troisième force internationale?. In S. Bernstein (Ed.). *Le Parti socialiste entre Résistance et République* (pp. 157–165). Paris: Publications de la Sorbonne.

Heumos, P. (Ed.). (1985). *Die Konferenzen der sozialistischen Parteien Zentral- und Osteuropas in Prag und Budapest 1946 und 1947: Darstellung und Dokumentation*. Stuttgart: F. Steiner.

Heumos, P. (Ed.). (2004). *Europäischer Sozialismus im Kalten Krieg: Briefe und Berichte 1944–1948*. Frankfurt: Campus.

Hochfeld, J. (1946). *An Open Letter from a Polish Socialist to a Friend of the Labour Party*. London: London Committee of the Polish Socialist Party.

Insall, T. (2010). *Haakon Lie, Denis Healey and the making of an Anglo-Norwegian special relationship 1945–1951*. Oslo: Oslo Academic Press.

Kaplan, K. (1984). *Das Verhängnisvolle Bündnis. Unterwanderung, Gleichschaltung und Vernichtung der Tschechoslowakischen Sozialdemokratie 1944–1954*. Wuppertal: Pol-Verlag.

Kramnick, I. & Sheerman, B. (1993). *Harold Laski, A life on the left*. London: Hamilton.
Larock, V. (1977). L'internationaliste. In *Témoignages: Guy Mollet, 1905–1975* (pp. 60–62). Paris: Fondation Guy Mollet.
Mancini, M. (1985). L'IOS e la questione del fronte unico negli anni Trenta. In E. Collotti (Ed.). *L'Internazionale Operaia e Socialista tra le due guerre* (pp. 184–198). Milano: Feltrinelli.
Merli, S. (1981). *Il Partito nuovo di Lelio Basso: 1945–1946*. Venezia: Marsilio.
Minkin, L. (1978). *The Labour party conference: a study in the politics of Intra-Party Democracy*. London: Allen Lane.
Misgeld, K. (1984). *Sozialdemokratie und Aussenpolitik in Schweden: Sozialistische Internationale, Europapolitik und die Deutschlandfrage 1945–1955*. Frankfurt: Campus Verlag.
Myant, M. (1981). *Socialism and Democracy in Czechoslovakia, 1945–1948*. Cambridge: Cambridge University Press.
Nenni, P. (1982). *Diari*, Vol.1, *Tempo di Guerra Fredda: diari 1943–1956*. Milano: SugarCo.
Newman, M. (2009) *Harold Laski: A political biography*. Pontypool: Merlin Press.
Panebianco, A. (1988). *Political parties: organization and power*. Cambridge: Cambridge University Press.
Pimlott, B. (Ed.). (1986). *The political diary of Hugh Dalton: 1918–40, 1945–60*. London: Cape.
Pons, S. (2014). *The global revolution: a history of international communism, 1917–1991*. Oxford: Oxford University Press.
Price, J. (1945). *International Labour Movement*. London: Oxford University Press.
Sabbatucci, G. (1991). 'Il Mito dell'Urss e il socialismo italiano'. *Socialismo Storia: Annali della Fondazione Giacomo Brodolini*, 3, 45–78.
Silone, I. (2002). Missione europea del Socialismo. In N. Novelli (Ed.). *Per Ignazio Silone* (pp. 87–95). Firenze: Polistampa.
Socialist International Women. (2007). *The first hundred years: a short history of Socialist International Women*. Berlin: Vorwärts Buch.
Steiner, H. (1985). Die Internationale Arbeitsgemeinschaft Sozialisticher Parteien (2 ½ Internationale) 1921–1923. In E. Collotti (Ed.). *L'Internazionale Operaia e Socialista tra le due guerre* (pp. 45–61). Milano: Feltrinelli.
Steininger, R. (1979). *Deutschland und die Sozialistische Internationale nach dem Zweiten Weltkrieg, Darstellung und Dokumentation*. Bonn: Neue Gesellschaft.
Thorpe, A. (2009). *Parties at war: political organization in Second World War Britain*. Oxford: Oxford University Press.
Thorpe, A. (2014). Locking out the Communists: The Labour party and the Communist party, 1939–46. *Twentieth Century British History*, 25 (2), 226–250.

Tobia, B. (1985). Pietro Nenni e la politica dell'Internazionale Operaia e Socialista (1930–1939). In E. Collotti (Ed.). *L'Internazionale Operaia e Socialista tra le due guerre* (pp. 159–175). Milano: Feltrinelli.

Van Kemseke, P. (2006). *Towards an Era of Development, The Globalization of Socialism and Christian Democracy: 1945–1965.* Leuven: Leuven University Press.

Weber, F. (1986). *Der kalte Krieg in der SPÖ: Koalitionswächter, Pragmatiker und revolutionäre Sozialisten, 1945–1950.* Wien: Verlag für Gesellschaftskritik.

Wodak, W. (1980). *Diplomatie zwischen Parteiproporz und Weltpolitik: Briefe, Dokumente und Memoranden aus dem Nachlass Walter Wodaks 1945–1950.* Salzburg: Neugebauer.

CHAPTER 6

The Labour Party and Italy, Social Democracy Below the Olive Line

1 The Mediterranean Character

Inside the international socialist movement, Italian socialism was the opposite of the Labour Party. While the Labour Party was the leader of Socialist International, the Italian Socialist Party was expelled. While the Labour Party represented Cold War social democracy—meaning reformism and anti-communism—Italy had the only European socialist party without a reformist and anti-communist leadership. Italian socialism shaped the international socialist movement by opposition and negation.

The reasons why social democracy was successful in Britain but not in Italy are complex and involve socio-economic factors and political contingency. A much simpler reading was common among contemporaries and later historians: the Italian national character, unlike the British, was not suited for social democracy. Like in Eastern Europe, the explanation for comparable political phenomena rested on preconceived notions ingrained in British culture. For contemporary British diplomat John Pilcher, it was evident that geography had made the Italian character the opposite of the British character:

This chapter partly reuses concepts and quotations from E. Costa (2018). 'The Socialist International and Italian Social Democracy (1948–50): Cultural Differences and the "Internationalisation of Domestic Quarrels"', *Historical Research*, 90, 251, 160–184.

© The Author(s) 2018
E. Costa, *The Labour Party, Denis Healey and the International Socialist Movement*, Palgrave Studies in the History of Social Movements, https://doi.org/10.1007/978-3-319-77347-6_6

> Indeed the conclusion forged on the Anglo-Saxon is that the chief feature of the Italian character is the absence of those Nordic virtues of grit, staying power in adversity and steadfastness in unpopularity, which the English understand by the very world character.[1]

For Healey, the 'Olive line' was more important than the 'Iron Curtain' and differences between Northern and Southern Europe more significant. Below the Olive line—Italy, Spain, Greece and sometimes France—socialism was not possible.[2] A socialist foreign policy was impossible because only Northern European workers held socialism as their faith—for American workers it was capitalism, for French and Italian workers communism.[3] In 1957, he even had doubts about the continuous existence of a Socialist International: 'For even in Europe there are national differences so radical as to defy any useful generalisation'.[4] Difference in race, temperament, political and economic institutions made a European federation impossible.[5]

According to Healey, it was not that Southern Europeans did not know the techniques of planning and economic management with which British and Scandinavians had achieved prosperity; they could not replicate their success because of the national character of the population. Socialism required 'a level of civic responsibility and administrative competence which scarcely exists outside the Anglo-Saxon world and northern Europe.'[6] In France and Italy, planning had failed because the people refused to pay their taxes.[7] In 1945, Healey warned about the 'depraved, dissolute, decadent' ruling classes of the Continent.[8]

What was the character of the people below the Olive line? In the global hierarchy, the Mediterranean is an intermediate position between 'Modernity' and the 'Primitive world'. According to Michael Herzelf, the Mediterranean is an imperialist category that has been interiorised. He argues that Edward Said provided a static image of the Orient, without considering its practical use: stereotypes may be false, but they served a tactical purpose and they carried out a social practice. Thus, British culture could employ the Mediterranean as an object of exoticism for commercial or academic purposes. At the same time, people from Greece or Italy—very different countries merged in the category of Mediterranean—could invoke their 'Mediterranean temperament' to justify actions and attitudes that could be taken negatively, like lack of work discipline, corruption and machismo. Self-stereotyping provides a short-term advantage that implicitly undermines their desire to be taken seriously by the Northern peoples:

> For, by conforming to a model of Mediterranean peoples as unreliable, imprecise, and spontaneous—all virtues that are highly regarded in the inside spaces of Greek cultural intimacy—[the Greeks] are also providing both an excuse for their own failures in the larger spheres of competition and an excuse for others to despise them. And so the self-fulfilling quality of earlier stereotypes, once again, may all too easily fulfil itself.[9]

Italians have interiorised the dialectical opposition between Europe north of the Alps and the Mediterranean character, which defines Italian identity and explains regional differences. Europe is the ideal of civilisation and rationality, an unreachable aspiration to strive for; the Mediterranean is the true nature—like Conrad's Darkness—that needs to be kept in check constantly to avoid degradation to the African level. As Ugo La Malfa warned: 'We climbed up the Alps to glance at Europe. Beware not to break the rope, because we could fall into the Mediterranean. This is not a pleasant alternative and it is I, a Sicilian, saying this'.[10] People from Milan consider theirs the most European city in Italy, which Romans would concede because they think of themselves as less Mediterranean than people from Calabria. Stereotypes are polysemous, with a meaning assigned according to the tactical need: 'When a Roman wishes to justify doing nothing, this is "Mediterranean"; when the same Roman wishes to justify a furious reaction, this, too, is "Mediterranean"?'[11]

The characterisation of Mediterranean countries was the result of interaction with the more powerful countries, especially with young British aristocrats undertaking the Grand Tour. Given the strength of anti-Catholicism in eighteenth-century Britain, Continental Europe, especially Italy was the Other against which British identity was defined. Later, Byron 'discovered' Greece and the Balkans, making it the new Other. Unlike Britain, Catholic countries had tyranny, superstition and corruption, which produced the poverty of the many and the opulence of the few.[12] Virtue, vigour and prosperity were strictly linked, with the common contrast being between rich and egalitarian Switzerland and poor Italy.[13] To others, however, French absolutism best suited the culture and climate of the country. Many embraced the Malthusian theory that unrestrained sexuality was the cause of overpopulation, making saving and investments impossible.

In addition to economic failures, Italians were unfit for parliamentary democracy because of their preference for sentimental and dramatic politics, which left little room for cold, pragmatic common sense. As mentioned earlier, this was the reason invoked to explain fascism. For Healey the distinctive feature of Italy[14] and Greece was the chasm between the 'corrupt, self-seeking and shallow'[15] middle class, compromised with fascism, and the workers living in miserable conditions. Thus, after the fall of Mussolini, the democratic rebirth was presented as a moral battle against the old unreconstructed national character. The backward South was inhabited by poor people in miserable conditions, corrupt middle classes tainted by fascism and prostitutes.[16] People in Northern Italy bore their poverty with dignity and a level of hygiene, they tried to raise themselves by joining the Resistance movements and organising co-operatives. Poverty was a consequence of the vices of the dictatorship and the Resistance a moral struggle to regain civilisation, which required the dehumanisation of the signs of past corruption, such as prostitutes. Healey's descriptions used literary references as much as direct witnesses.

This idea of the democratic renewal of Italy was encouraged by the Italians themselves, wanting better terms for the Peace Treaty.[17] Italian socialists stressed how Northern Italy was modern and European—justifying their claim to belong to the European club—while Southern Italy was backward—to excuse their shortcomings.[18] The Greek socialists also asked leniency for their country lagging behind Western Europe.[19] The Italian argument to defend Trieste from Yugoslav claims was that Tito's regime was progressive for the Slovene peasants, but it was unfit for an urban and complex society 'accustomed to Western traditions of freedom'.[20]

Anti-Catholicism was an important feature of British post-war culture, even among socialists, who saw Continental socialists squeezed between reactionary clericalism and totalitarian communism.[21] They argued that political Catholicism tried to become progressive after the war, but the Church rejected cooperation with the socialists and used its propaganda machinery and its sway over women to legitimise the return of conservatism and elements compromised with fascism. A continental conservative bloc with the addition of Spain and Portugal was a threat. Only Britain and Northern Europe were immune from the conservative comeback—implicitly because they were protestant.

2 Italian Social Democracy in the Era of Cohabitation

Italian socialism went from being a major player in socialist internationalism to a civil war between pro-communist and anti-communist factions to a civil war among the anti-communist social democrats. As divisions increased, the internationalisation of domestic quarrels called for foreign intervention: the State–private network was most effective in Italy but also most problematic. As influence is a two-way road, divisions over Italian socialism exposed divisions inside the International Socialist Conference and between the Labour Party and the British Foreign Office.

From the beginning, the Italian socialist movement had been heterogeneous and rife with ideological divisions. During the war, old and new socialists formed the Italian Socialist Party of Proletarian Unity (PSIUP), an uneasy coalition of factions with opposing strategies.[22] Although at the elections of 1946 it still emerged as the biggest party of the left, the PSIUP spent most of that year engulfed in intense factional struggle. The largest faction, led by veteran leader Pietro Nenni called for the Popular Front with the communists to fight fascism, imperialism and capitalism, believing that the division of the working-class was the reason for past defeats. For left-wing socialists, bourgeois democracy and the managed economy were transitional stages to be overcome in a socialist society. Conversely, Italian right-wing socialists emphasised the autonomy of socialism from communism and the superiority of the ideals of freedom and democracy. Alliance with the communists could only be tactical; indeed, socialism was the alternative to capitalism and totalitarianism.

Lelio Basso, the leading theoretician and organiser of Italian left-wing socialism, worked to marginalise old socialists loyal to reformist traditions and to have left-wing ideas and people take over the party.[23] Basso argued that Italian socialism had to choose between Great Britain and Eastern Europe and needed to choose the latter. Basso supported the Bolshevisation of the party, while the reformists wanted a federal party on the British model.[24] He rejected the reformist traditions and the Western example and took the Soviet Union and the people's democracies as his model.[25] Basso warned that capital and reaction wanted socialists to renounce Marxism and embrace an intellectual, middle class, sentimental socialism he identified with '*laburismo*'.[26] He argued that the prosperity Labourism promised derived from imperialist exploitation.[27] Nenni warned not to believe that Labourism was viable in Italy:

> Must we really take seriously those who wants us to choose between the West and the East? Between socialism with freedom and socialism without freedom? [...]
> The roads are not the same everywhere; but do you believe, comrades, that it depends on free will of the people, the socialists, the communists, the working-class organisations?[28]

Left-wingers successfully coordinated with Zilliacus in Britain[29] and Polish[30] and Czechoslovak socialists.[31] Even before their split in 1947, the Italian social democrats wanted a special relationship with the European social democrats,[32] claiming to be their true Italian counterparts. The Cold War was not the reason for their break, as they made the first approach in 1945. Ignazio Silone—the writer and centrist socialist leader—had a letter delivered to the Labour Party through the British Embassy, in order to avoid the communists' notice.[33] He asked the Labour Party to build at least a liaison office—if they were reluctant to rebuild the Socialist International—to allow the socialists to coordinate their policies as the communists did:

> Forgive me if I take the liberty of insisting on this point [coordination between socialists], because, in our effort to give Italian Socialism a democratic and European trend, it is of decisive importance for us to adhere to the Socialist International. Only it is difficult to adhere to something that doesn't exist.[34]

The group around *Critica Sociale*, the reformist journal edited by Giuseppe Faravelli, also wanted a special relationship with the Labour Party to fight Nenni.[35] The journal constantly wrote about Britain to educate the public about the socialist experiments in Western Europe. Faravelli asked for the open support of his group by the Labour Party, expressed through a public endorsement or a permanent supply of articles from a Labour leader—especially Laski—for the journal. 'We ask you'—he wanted to say to the Labourites—'to give us your moral and political support, which is going to be a source of prestige and strength inside the party'.[36] In September 1945, Laski addressed an article to Nenni, calling a fusion of socialists and communists a prelude to dictatorship.[37] Even Francesco Malfatti, labour attaché at the Italian embassy in London, suggested the possibility of encouraging the evolution of the PSIUP according to the example of the Labour Party.[38] However, the British Labour Attaché in Rome, Braine, whom Bevin trusted, advised against a direct intervention into the internal affairs of the PSIUP,[39] since the Labour Party was reluctant to become attached to the social democratic factions of Italian socialism.

This tension culminated in January 1947. Saragat—the former second in command to Nenni and the respectable face of Italian socialism—concluded that it was impossible to resist pro-communist encroachment and led the desertion of two anti-communist factions,—*Critica Sociale* and the radical leftists of *Iniziativa Socialista*—to form the Italian Workers' Socialist Party (PSLI). This left the pro-communist faction in charge of the mainstream socialist party, which took the old name of Italian Socialist Party (PSI). Many centrist socialists stayed in the old party. From then, by Italian social democrats we refer to the anti-communist socialists outside the mainstream party, who, however, claimed to be the only true socialists in Italy.

With division came the involvement of other parties. The British had little sympathy for the pro-communist socialists but they also disliked the social democrats, whom they considered to be middle class intellectuals. The Labour Party's line was to back centrist elements trying to preserve party unity. In January 1946, Nenni told Bevin he would not carry out the fusion with the communists without a general agreement between Great Britain and the Soviet Union.[40] At the 1946 Congress, Nenni said that the Italian socialists would not choose between Great Britain and Eastern Europe but seek a synthesis.[41] The Congress confirmed a centrist compromise, with Laski's blessing.[42] The linkage to international socialism was strong, but not strong enough to avoid Nenni's alignment with the Soviet Union or to favour the social democrats in a split.[43] Healey strongly disapproved of the January 1947 split, as the workers would stay loyal to the old party, the Italian Communist Party (PCI) would become the stronger party and the unchecked pro-communist factions would take over.[44]

The PSLI claimed European socialism as a model, particularly the British version[45] and asked for recognition from the Labour Party and the International Socialist Conference, arguing it was the only true socialist party.[46] Since only one party per nation was allowed and there were two parties claiming to speak for Italian socialism, the International Socialist Conference had to intervene. Admission corresponded to a recognition that could be employed against other pretenders. For example, in Zurich the Spanish question was not how to coordinate policies to depose Franco, but which Spanish socialist party in exile to recognise, much to Nenni's frustration.[47] As Price and Morgan Phillips understood, the central question in rebuilding the International was who was to be included, who was to be excluded and according to which principle.

Facing numerous cases in addition to the Italian one, the Zurich Conference (6–9 June 1947) established a general principle.[48] According to Buset, the spirit and tradition of the International was to intervene to avoid division, especially for illegal parties, where it was impossible to know the orientation of the workers. The status of observer party (without the right to vote) was introduced to admit the parties not operating legally. Healey's policy was also to mediate divisions and restore unity. He came up with a plan with Malfatti and the centrist Ivan Matteo Lombardo, to have the International Socialist Conference mediate reunification.[49] As he said at the Zurich Conference, 'the question is whether we, with our prestige of international organisation, can restore the unity between the two parties.'[50] Pointless ideological squabbles produced chatter, not action; Italian socialists needed to reunite for the sake of socialism in Italy and Europe.

A committee of the Zurich Conference was to examine how to help achieve this goal, but divisions in Italian socialism revealed the divisions in the European socialist movement. The PSI argued that the Italian question did not exist. The PSLI was a splinter party and only their unconditional return could produce reunification. The PSI would not tolerate their invitation as official members.[51] The other leftist parties agreed, arguing that an intervention would legitimise any splits provoked by an alliance with the communists. Hochfeld explained that, in the presence of a strong communist party, socialists had to be united to preserve democracy and socialism:

> The Italian comrades who broke unity must repent. We cannot award any prize to those who break unity, because tomorrow we could find ourselves in a difficult situation. Any minority inside a socialist party could claim that there is no internal democracy. Then it will break unity and say that it wants to re-join the party, but on better terms.[52]

While the committee on the Italian question suggested intervention, the PSI won a procedural victory with the decision that minority parties from a nation already represented could not be admitted as observers. In the plenary assembly, Nenni used his prestige and rhetorical ability—for once he could speak in French.[53] Nenni blamed the strength of communism on the anti-fascist credentials of the USSR and the faults of the West. Italian socialists needed unity of action and radicalism to win the trust of workers, who would see them as an alternative to communists. Nenni struck a chord with the British, explaining that all the chatter about the absence of internal democracy was really about the creation of industrial cells where the workers could debate problems without the involvement of lawyers and journalists, who dominated the local parties with their eloquence. It was not the responsibility of the International to designate the party of the Italian workers: almost one million chose the PSI, only 150,000 the PSLI. 'We cannot substitute the sovereignty of a congress with, if I may so, the non-existent and inadmissible sovereignty of the International'.[54]

Healey noted the importance of personal relations in the International: Nenni carried the day thanks to his friendship with Grumbach—as well as Mollet, Buset and Jarblum.[55] The proposal to intervene was withdrawn and Nenni was satisfied with having blocked Saragat's attack and Silone's intrigues.[56] His old friend De Brouckère however warned him not to abuse his victory, a warning that felt on deaf ears, as evidenced by the gloating article in the PSI newspaper.[57] Healey was not satisfied with the results of the conference, which had disappointed the responsible, centrist members of the PSI who were working for unity.

The SFIO was particularly affected by the internationalisation of domestic quarrels.[58] Before the split, Mollet had close relations with leftist, but anti-communist *Iniziativa socialista*. He disapproved of *Iniziativa socialista* joining the PSLI, since he considered Saragat a tool of the Vatican and the USA. The socialist French prime minister Ramadier had broken with the communists and formed a coalition Government with the Christian Democrats, Mollet regarded him as the French Saragat. Actually, at the time, the PSLI preferred to stay in opposition in order to appear as a serious alternative to the PSI, though there were talks of them joining a centrist government. At the Zurich conference, the French delegation was divided between Grumbach, who backed Nenni, and Boutbien, who backed Saragat, so it could not use all its influence to help the PSLI. After the Zurich conference, Mollet reconsidered his position and cultivated relations with the Italian left-wing social democrats, hoping to build a leftist Western group inside the International Socialist Conference. 'The truth of the matter is that Mollet is using the PSLI to sharpen his dealings with the faction led by Ramadier, which he is known to oppose'.[59]

Conversely, the right-wing faction of the SFIO—Ramadier and Blum—supported efforts to unite the PSLI and PSI, as they preferred a broad-church party with the right-wing faction in charge, isolating leftist social democrats and Nenni's pro-communist faction. Blum wrote to Saragat to encourage reunification and Ramadier sent Henri Ribière, head of the Service de Documentation Extérieure et de Contre-Espionnage (SDECE) intelligence agency, who said that a Government of socialists and Christian Democrats backing the Marshall Plan, like Ramadier's, 'would enjoy much international support' from Ramadier and other socialist parties. This might imply funding, which the PSLI desperately needed. The American trade unionists pressured the right-wing elements of the PSLI, to which they supplied the funds they needed to survive,[60] to follow Ramadier's example.[61]

Just before the Antwerp Conference, the Foreign Office warned the Labour Party to treat the Italian and Polish socialists as tools of the Cominform.[62] Saragat explained that recognition by the British and the International Socialist Conference provided a cover to the pro-communist PSI while the communists were rebuilding their International.[63]

At the Antwerp Conference (28 November–1 December 1947), the question was whether the International Socialist Conference had a right to intervene. Buset and Boutbien proposed a commission to mediate between PSI and PSLI.[64] Nenni repeated that intervention would infringe the sovereignty of the congress, but Buset and Grumbach protested that this decision would sanction the idea that the International could not intervene in internal affairs. Laski asked the conference to pass over the question, which led to lasting resentment against him among Italian social democrats. However, even right-wing socialist Van der Goes van Naters—a future ally of Saragat—argued that the Conference would be authorised to intervene only by the request of the two parties.

Nenni told the conference that the socialists had to fight the counter-revolutionary threat strengthened by the Truman Doctrine, which found practical application in Spain and Greece and maybe Italy and France soon—France even more so, as the French socialists had mistakenly split the working-class.[65] On the other hand, he praised beneficial Soviet interference. By then, Nenni aligned with the Zhdanov Doctrine of two camps—he discussed the issues before the conference with Malenkov.[66]

The Prague Coup changed everything. Without socialists behind the Iron Curtain, Italian socialism was no longer a bridge with Eastern Europe, but an embarrassment.[67] In January 1948, the PSI decided to present a joint list with the communists at the elections. The centrist figures the Labour Party trusted—Silone and Lombardo—joined other independent socialists to form the Union of Italian Socialists (USI). Together with the PSLI, they would present the list 'Socialist Unity' at the elections. The British Ambassador wrote that recruiting the Labour Party against Nenni was essential for 'keeping Italy on the right side of the iron curtain'.[68] On 13 March, Healey and Morgan Phillips issued an ultimatum to the PSI to end the alliance with the communists. Then, they promised support to Socialist Unity and invited them to the international conference on the Marshall Plan, which Nenni opposed.[69] The Labour Party intervened directly in the electoral campaign, denouncing the PSI as a false socialist party. Healey made a direct appeal by radio to the Italian socialists.[70] Morgan Phillips' telegram wishing success to Lombardo 'was reproduced as an election poster and stuck on the walls all over Italy'.[71]

3   Italian Social Democracy in the Era of Anti-communism

In 1948, international socialism was finally unified and had a sense of purpose. Even the once reluctant Labour Party expressed a commitment to intervention. Action followed, but results were mixed. Socialists were like-minded about democracy and anti-communism, but when everyone became anti-communist, divisions emerged, especially regarding the strategies to fight communism.

According to Redvaldsen, there were two paths for social democrats, which were already evident in the 1930s.[72] In most European countries the working-class vote was not enough to win a majority—especially with proportional representation—thus, socialist parties had to reach out to other social groups—farmers, other wage-earners, the middle classes—or form coalitions with the parties representing these groups.[73] In Sweden and Norway this strategy was successful and it strengthened the reformist and inter-classist character of the socialist parties.[74] After the war, it was the PvdA that carried this project to its logical conclusion, transforming socialism into the left-wing of a centrist coalition of democratic forces, including Christian Democrats and liberals. In what we call here 'Coalition Strategy', reforms would come from negotiation and compromise, not winning a majority, so a coalition with moderates was more important than winning more votes.

The British Labour Party followed another path because of the different conditions it operated under. As Redvaldsen notes, the Norwegian electoral system turned the 40.1% votes for the DNA into a plurality of seats, but the same share of votes under the first-past-the-post method would have given the British Labour Party a majority of seats.[75] Also, the nature of British society was such that the Labour Party did not need the sympathetic middle classes to win, just a majority of the working-class.[76] The Labour Party identified itself as 'the only effective bulwark against reaction and revolution'[77] and during the war it confirmed that only a 'virile and fighting policy of socialism'[78] was an antidote to communism. Socialists had to appear like an alternative Government to the bourgeois parties and an alternative working-class party to the communists. The 'Alternative Strategy' aimed at winning over workers from communism to protect democracy and gain a majority. The party needed to emphasise its working-class character and ties with the trade unions.

The socialists did not give much thought to this difference, they were more concerned about where to intervene. A survey of the Labour Party, probably written by Healey, located the strong and weak points of European socialism.[79] Socialist parties in Great Britain, Scandinavia, the Netherlands and Austria had a solid organisation, a strong following among the working-class and a stable share of votes between 30% and 50%. The British felt they were in harmony with these parties, especially the DNA[80] and the SPÖ.[81] They also liked the PvdA,[82] although differences emerged later. The British admired Swedish socialism, but did not understand their neutrality.[83] Their worries were about France, Germany and Italy. The SFIO was in an impossible situation: to keep extremists out, they formed a coalition Government with parties that had quite different economic policies. They could not enact the radical economic policies the French economy needed. Despair and contempt for French socialism was typical of Labour culture: disorganisation, verbal radicalism and practical opportunism, devotion to ideology and a middle class nature were ascribed to the French.[84] Despite there being some truth in this, the British did not know French political culture and did not empathise with a party facing proportional representation and communist competition. However, they formed a committee to help the SFIO win over the French workers.

Healey was not optimistic about German social democracy, with its mediocre leaders and weak ties with trade unions. It was impossible to accept the laissez-fair economic policies of the occupation forces as a condition to join the Government. 'Thus the SPD, despite its past electoral successes, faces a decline as disastrous as that of the SFIO'.[85] Others, like Harry Earnshaw[86] and Sam Watson[87] were more optimistic. There was also disagreement about the Saar and international controls over the Ruhr, with the British viewing Schumacher as nationalist and uncooperative.[88]

Paradoxically, with hindsight, Healey was hopeful about Italy, the country where international socialism had just successfully intervened. He expected that Comisco would soon detach centrist socialists from Nenni and help their unification. Then, they would win 20% of votes and gain bargaining power in Government. The future of social democracy was in Southern Europe. In January 1949, Healey said that he hoped to see the Latin countries soon become not just democratic but social democratic.[89] As we have seen from his comments in the 1950s, his ideas would change.

The 18 April 1948 Italian elections seemed to confirm the success of the social democrats and the confidence of Comisco: the combined vote of socialists and communists collapsed from 40% to 31% and 'Socialist Unity' collected a not small part of their fleeing votes, 7.1%. What elections did not resolve was whether the social democrats had to join a coalition Government with the Christian Democrats. This was the crux of the matter for all socialist parties: choosing between the Coalition Strategy and the Alternative Strategy. The communist offensive and a lack of funds forced the PSLI to abandon the opposition strategy and to join the Christian Democratic Government in December 1947. However, the election had given the Christian Democrats a majority of seats, so the question was whether joining the Government was necessary, especially if their conditions of having a socialist economic policy were not met. We call left-wing social democrats those supporting the Alternative Strategy and right-wing social democrats those supporting the Coalition strategy.

Another divisive issue was party organisation. Healey offered support to Socialist Unity on the condition that they would form a unified party after the election. The PSLI was already a structured organisation, with a right-wing majority and a left-wing minority, the latter politically close to other social democratic groups. In a new party, left-wing social democrats would have been in control. Saragat's position was that all social democrats should have joined the already organised PSLI, where he was in charge. Postponing the creation of a new party would leave left-wing social democrats without an organisation, buildings or money. The more they stayed out, the greater Saragat's bargaining power, since in opposition the left-wing social democrats had to rely on their meagre finances, while in Government Saragat could dispense patronage and receive illicit funds.

Healey was the stumbling block on Saragat's path. The recognition of Comisco—especially of Labour—was the strongest argument the social democrats had for their claim of being the true socialist party in Italy, but a recognition granted could also be rescinded. The International Socialist Conference in Vienna (4–7 June 1948) did not admit the PSLI as a full member but gave the seat to Socialist Unity, waiting for a new unified party.[90] The PSI was suspended, with the expectation that the anti-communist elements would either purge pro-communist socialists or leave the party.[91]

The problem was that Healey—backed by Mayhew—supported the Alternative Strategy and the creation of a new unified party. He argued that the priority of social democrats was to win over the workers from communism by opposing the conservative and Jesuitical Government. This placed him in conflict not only with Saragat but also with the UK Foreign Office and the US State Department. The Foreign Office believed in the Coalition strategy—'it is always British policy to support a third force in the centre'.[92] Britain had to support social democratic Governments when possible, but also collaboration with the Christian democrats when necessary.[93] In addition, a Government without social democrats would have been 'less amenable to British influence'.[94] The Americans also resented that left-wing social democrats refused to support the Atlantic Treaty and a trade union federation that would have included all non-communist forces—since Catholic trade unionists would have been dominant.[95]

The PSLI—divided in two wings—and the USI having failed to agree on unification, a third player entered the field in May 1949. The disaster of April 1948 led to the fall of Nenni and the takeover of the PSI by a centrist faction wanting socialist autonomy. In the factional struggle, the pro-communist faction of Nenni and Basso defined its identity by continuously attacking Comisco and making rapprochement impossible.[96] Helped by the communists, they reasserted their control in the congress of May 1949, causing a final wave of social democrats, led by former minister Romita, to leave the party. Boutbien, sent there to monitor the situation, had many left-wing social democrats commit to 'a constituent assembly for socialism'.[97] The International Socialist Conference in Baarn (14–16 May 1949) definitively expelled the PSI. As Boutbien's intervention was considered too leftist, the conference set up a commission chaired by Van der Goes van Naters to aid the unification—De Brouckère refused the position because of his personal friendship with Nenni.[98]

With the PSLI deeply divided over the Atlantic Treaty, its left-wing tried to turn the PSLI conference in June into a unification conference, by admitting representatives of the USI and Romita's group as delegates with voting rights.[99] While the Labour Party backed this attempt, Van der Goes van Naters did not press the issue; instead he negotiated to have the unification congress to take place in the future, after the census of the members of the three groups.[100]

The unification congress was to take place in December 1949, with the census ending in October. As it was clear that left-wing social democrats had a majority, on 31 October Saragat announced the PSLI would not take part in the congress, since left-wing social democrats recruited crypto-communists and did not recognise the Atlantic Treaty. This provoked the split of the left-wing of the PSLI. In addition, while his grumbling about the Labour Party had been private until then, Saragat openly accused the Labour Party of trying to lord it over other socialists and pitting factions against each other.[101] In his campaign against the Labour Party, Saragat exploited the nationalistic resentment of the Italian public towards Britain.

For Healey, this manoeuvre meant that the social democrats had forfeited the chance to become the socialist party Italy needed because of Saragat's wish to stay in Government 'as a sort of Ramsay MacDonald'[102]—in addition to being 'mutable' and 'paid by USA'.[103] Healey's position was that the Labour Party and Comisco would support the unification conference, as they had produced the agreement Saragat had betrayed. Not only that, but Healey used the overseas service of the BBC to directly address the Italian public, stating that Saragat's accusations were a 'hysterical fantasy' and accepting the Atlantic Treaty was not a precondition for being part of Comisco—the great SAP was neutral.[104]

The unification congress in Florence (4–8 December 1949) created the Unified Socialist Party (PSU), uniting USI, Romita's group and the left-wing of the PSLI (Faravelli).[105] The new party embraced the Alternative Strategy by demanding a socialist economic policy and a trade union federation without Catholic or communist trade unionists. The Atlantic Treaty was accepted as a *fait accompli*, but only as a defensive agreement limited to Europe. Healey endorsed this strategy and encouraged the Italian social democrats to follow Labour's example. His actions had some cover since Mayhew supported the Alternative Strategy and affirmed the right of the Labour Party to help other socialist parties. However, he warned that the Labour Party was neither completely identifiable with the Government nor completely independent, so Healey should have had to 'walk the tight-rope', instead he 'jumped unhesitatingly into the abyss'.[106] When in June and December 1949 the British diplomats called Bevin to stop Healey from sabotaging their policy, he did not openly censure him and simply asked him to act as a 'reasonable' person.[107]

Saragat's attacks on Healey were meant to expose him and he successfully provoked a reaction from the British Foreign Office, enraged about the commotion in Italian public opinion: 'Not since Gladstone wrote his fiery letters about the state of prisons in the Kingdom of Naples has a British official representative let so many sparks fly as did Mr. Denis Healey'.[108] In 1948, it was the diplomats who encouraged Labour's intervention in Italy and again in 1949 they asked Labour to convince the Italian social democrats to approve the Atlantic Treaty—at request of the Italian Government.[109] However, they did not like it when Labour took a different position over Italy and reminded them of its independence. Healey replied that 'he would be very ready to listen to our advice but did not undertake to follow it'; the diplomats said 'The Foreign Office has no control at all, over what Mr Healey does'.[110] This was the main problem of the State–private network. The diplomats felt they were robbed of their job of representing Britain abroad—'I fear we cannot for long continue to speak in this country with two voices'.[111] The distinction between party and government was often lost to the public, as it was the difference between Labour Party, *Tribune* and Comisco.

In June and December 1949, the Italian Government accused Healey of a 'treacherous foreign intervention in our internal politics'[112] for trying to force the social democrats to leave the Government.[113] Through various channels, Prime Minister De Gasperi tried to have the British Government rein Healey in.[114] More worryingly, the Americans wanted the Italian social democrats to stay in Government and asked the British Government to force the TUC and the Labour Party to help their policy, an intervention that even British diplomats found 'heavy-handed'.[115]

Pressure on the British mounted after the creation of the PSU, when Comisco had to take a position. After a week, Comisco approved the unification conference and recommended the admission of the PSU as full members at the next conference in the middle of 1950. The PSLI would have time until then to disband and join the PSU. Van der Goes van Naters said that it was only through his intervention that the PSLI was not expelled immediately.[116] In a purely material sense, the PSLI had the upper hand: a functioning organisation, more Senators and Deputies, Government patronage, and so on. However, the biggest socialist party in Italy was not the PSLI, it was the PSI; the only way the PSLI could claim to truly represent Italian socialism was through confirmation from Comisco. Thus, Comisco could force its conditions on the PSLI or even provoke its collapse. Until March 1950, Healey was sure this was the right way:

> Healey is convinced PSU will then gain in strength and constitute a real and growing opposition, and an alternative to Communism without weakening De Gasperi. Saragat will apparently be finished for [the] time being at any rate and PSLI [a] rump of no account in the Government.[117]

However, Saragat had a major ally inside Comisco in Van der Goes van Naters. The head of the Comisco commission for Italy resented Healey's unilateral actions, showing that the British thought they alone were Comisco. Labour's power was also reduced by the British general election of February 1950, which gave it a majority of only a few seats—it was said that a landslide would have forced Saragat out of Government.[118] The Dutchman did not like 'the Labour-minded PSU' because they rejected the Atlantic Treaty and the Coalition strategy.[119] He offered to support Saragat and when he attended the PSLI congress in January 1950 he reasserted his authority as a mediator.[120] At the Comisco Sub-Committee in March, Van der Goes van Naters presented Saragat's proposal not to expel anyone by having the PSU and PSLI share the Italian seat.[121] The French proposal to recommend the admission of the PSU alone was approved with the backing of the Labour Party.

Finally, Van der Goes van Naters wrote to Bevin that the PSLI was essential to Italian stability and social reforms. Using information from Bolle, he claimed the PSLI still had a working-class following.[122] Bevin, who was already anxious about the situation, was finally convinced to ask Healey to revise his position.[123] Surprisingly, Healey said he had already changed opinion on his own—probably Bevin informed him in advance, to avoid humiliating him before the civil servants.[124]

The Copenhagen Conference (1–3 June 1950) finally settled the question by admitting both PSLI and PSU. Comisco would not intervene, unless asked to do so by both parties, which would decide unification on their terms.[125] Saragat was 'purring with pleasure'.[126] Healey justified this choice as a division of labour:

> PSLI as a tame instrument of De Gasperi in his continual war with the Right wing of the Demo-Christian Party and PSU as an opposition force which may be able to cut into the disillusioned or apathetic workers and in particular into the present adherents of PSI and PCI.[127]

These events had a paradoxical conclusion. When in November 1951 the Labour Party lost the election, Saragat privately expressed relief, as he had been misunderstood and mistreated.[128] Conversely, Nenni regretted the defeat and still considered the Labour Party the only hope for socialism in Europe.[129]

4   The Debate Inside Comisco

Comisco intervened in Italy to help unite the social democrats, but the divisions of the Italian social democrats divided Comisco. In Eastern Europe the only course was supporting the forces resisting the communist takeover. In Italy the socialists were spoiled for choice; anti-communism was not enough to be considered a brother party, the party had to be socialist. Healey said that Comisco had to take 'positive action on questions of socialist credentials'.[130] What was 'respectable' for the Foreign Office was not necessarily 'respectable' for the socialists: the Labour Party preferred 'the purer milk of socialist doctrines'.[131] Labour's definition of socialism was not the only one: as Van der Goes van Naters said, 'Comisco does not have to become a copy of the Labour Party'.[132] What makes the debate inside Comisco about the Italian question interesting is that the inclination of the parties revealed their strategic decisions and political culture.

Central to Labour's culture was Arthur Henderson's belief that the Labour Party was 'the only effective bulwark against reaction and revolution'. At the 1949 conference, celebrating the 50 years' jubilee of the founding of the party, Jim Griffiths repeated that 'democratic Socialism is the only bulwark against the spread of totalitarian Communism' and the Labour Party had to offer an alternative to unbridled capitalism 'for totalitarian Communism is born of chaos and nurtured on despair'.[133] Griffith supported the Beveridge Plan during the war and helped build the Welfare State, believing that misery and despair had produced fascism and would produce communism. Dalton said 'It is full employment and social justice in a democracy which destroy communism, and that is why it is such a miserable and contemptible force in our country'.[134] Bevan would later apply this principle to the Third World: 'If help for the so-called backward areas was not given, they would become breeding grounds for war and all sorts of other horrors'.[135]

The Labour Party was the political voice of the working-class and only the workers could save democracy. An article in the *Economist*—probably written by Healey[136]—explained that revelations about the communist purges would only affect the intellectuals:

> The hard core of French and Italian labour will remain loyal to the [communist] party as long as prices are high, food is scarce and unemployment threatens. And it is on the indoctrinated party cadres and the industrial masses that Moscow relies to keep western Europe seething.[137]

The socialists needed to offer a real alternative to the workers, but to be credible they had to refuse association with the bourgeois Governments, worse if associated with reactionary churches.[138] Healey often repeated—backed by Mayhew and Foot—that the 'best hope for Italian socialism lies in the wilderness as recommended by the PSU'.[139] The betrayal of MacDonald, who abandoned the movement and socialist policies to form a Government with the 'respectable' parties, was still burning. The episode of the Nenni Telegram, the most serious insubordination during the Attlee Government, was evidence of Labour's queasiness about Italian social democrats. Among the signatories were not just regular fellow travellers, but also centrists confused by so sudden a switch of alliances. Zilliacus called the Italian and French social democrats 'Macdonaldite Socialists' in public, but Healey used the term in private.

It must be noted that Healey believed in this strategy more than the people enacting it. He criticised the PSU leadership for being intellectuals with not enough ties with the trade unions.[140] According to Healey, the problem with Italian politicians was that they wanted power immediately and 'they will not reconcile themselves to the long period of organisation and propaganda to develop the strength on which effective action could be built'. Too much time was spent on doctrinal minutiae, which damaged party unity:

> Only the Communist and Catholic parties possess both the *faith* to unite divergent tendencies and the long-term view which enables them to pass from tactic to strategy.[141]

'Faith' was the emotional, pre-rational element that subsumed the individual members—divided by trade, region, religion—into the movement and made them strive together towards the common goal. There was an element of non-conformist religion, as shown by Griffith's language: he celebrated the pioneers who sacrificed and suffered in hard times, with nothing but faith assuring victory.[142] The influence of the trade unions—strengthened after MacDonald's betrayal—made loyalty a moral imperative. Dissent could be tolerated, threatening the integrity of the organisation and the decision of the majority was not up for challenge.[143] Not one member of the Labour Party forgave Saragat for the capital crime of splitting the party.

The Dutch socialists would not call Saragat a traitor or 'hysterical', as Healey did.[144] Van der Goes van Naters commended Saragat's bravery for splitting the party in January 1947, giving the workers an alternative to Catholics and communists.[145] He also appreciated the break with socialist traditions—such as abandoning the hammer and sickle as a symbol[146]—as the Dutch socialists had done earlier. The PvdA was conceived less as a workers' party and more as a party for all those who recognised socialism as a moral duty, including Catholics, the middle classes and intellectuals. Although the PvdA's share of the vote did not increase dramatically, the strategic goal was forming coalitions with other parties. This required accommodation with the centrist parties and avoiding embarrassments, like being associated with Marxism. The debate about the Frankfurt Declaration showed the ideological proximity between Saragat and the PvdA.[147] When Healey came against European integration and Van der Goes van Naters in favour, the Italians sided with the latter.[148]

Anti-Catholicism was an important factor in Labour's rejection of European integration—Michael Young spoke of 'the Catholic "black reaction" behind the Council of Europe'.[149] Healey blamed the 'Jesuit-controlled' Catholic Action for splitting the Italian trade union movement[150] and said that Italian Christian Democracy was not a true labour party, but merely an arm of the Catholic Church.[151] Traditional socialists appreciated Healey's 'anti-clerical feeling',[152] but Saragat and the PvdA considered anti-clericalism an obstacle to their alliance with the Catholics. Indeed, the biggest contribution of the PvdA to the Socialist International was having a special conference of the Socialist International, held in Bentveld in 1953, declare a positive attitude to religion.[153]

Foreign policy was also contentious. Bevin and the Labour Party did not originally want Italy in the Atlantic Treaty, so Healey could side with left-wing social democrats in opposing it. Conversely, the Dutch considered approval of the Atlantic Treaty as not negotiable; indeed, Van der Goes van Naters had fought to win over neutralists in his party, so he had sympathy for Saragat.[154] Also, the Dutch did not forgive the British for failing to help to reclaim Indonesia, so they could sympathise with the

Italian resentment over losing their colonies.[155] The French favoured the PSU because they shared the idea of Europe as a Third Force alternative to the Atlantic Community—while Saragat and the PvdA considered Europe part of the Atlantic Community.[156]

5　The Results and Limits of Intervention

Despite its early optimism, Comisco had little to show after its intervention in Italy. In 1948, Silone[157] and Healey[158] were confident that Italian social democracy could be the start of something great, but a long period in opposition was required.[159] When Saragat joined the Government in 1947, Salvemini said it was just 'another miscarriage'[160]:

> I think that by joining the De Gasperi Government [Saragat] wasted a position which was not electoral, but moral and political and which could have borne precious fruits in the next ten years. The man has cut down the tree to eat the fruit.[161]

In 1951 Saragat and Romita agreed on unification, forming the Italian Democratic Socialist Party (PSDI).[162] The Italian Government once again asked the British to block unification, but the Labour Party stayed neutral after the 'unfortunate experience' of December 1949 and the Foreign Secretary refused to become involved.[163] At the Frankfurt Conference (30 June–3 July 1951), Romita announced socialist unity in Italy and thanked Comisco, but by the end of 1951 the new party was already divided and without money.[164]

By 1951, pessimism was widespread and justified: 'Italian socialism has been, is, and will remain for the foreseeable future a broken reed. The reasons are deep-rooted, ineradicable and familiar'.[165] For the rest of its existence the PSDI remained a small party of the progressive middle class and Government cronies, never winning workers over from communism. The party was a permanent coalition member with the Christian Democrats; according to Saragat it tempered their reactionary tendencies and it probably encouraged De Gasperi's progressive reforms in 1950–51. Even so, its contribution was marginal.

Comisco's confidence proved misplaced, at least in the short-term. The long-lasting effect of Comisco's intervention was the socialisation of socialist leaders, creating an international network. Healey always denied that he was involved in intrigues with Italian socialists and pushing them in a certain direction. Saragat accused Healey of being in regular contact with Ignazio Silone through his wife and Paolo Vittorelli, but he had no evidence to prove this.[166] Van der Goes van Naters confirms Labour's preference for Silone and Romita. Silone contributed to Crossman's *The God that Failed* and was friends with Mary Saran. Silone was on the steering committee of the Congress for Cultural Freedom with Haakon Lie and the German Carlo Schimdt.

The most fruitful relationship was between Healey and Vittorelli, then international secretary of the PSU, whom Alfred Robens called 'a great personal friend of Denis Healey'.[167] Vittorelli visited London in the summer of 1949 and had contacts with Michael Foot.[168] Vittorelli, who had wartime experience with Labour and the SOE, became responsible for the international relations of the PSI in 1959 because he enjoyed the trust of the Labour Party, which wanted to verify Nenni's conversion to Western-style socialism.[169]

Saragat was right after all: the Labour Party had a preferred faction and they worked together to create an independent democratic socialist party able to enact the Alternative Strategy. Healey still believed it was the right path in 1956 and from then the Labour Party helped the evolution of the PSI towards social democracy.[170] In doing so, they followed the trail blazed by the PSU. The programme of the PSU was different than Saragat's, but it was acceptable, as Healey had endorsed its foreign policy. In 1952 the PSI mocked Romita for proposing unification on three conditions: refusing cooperation with the communists; recognition of the principles of the Socialist International; acceptance of the Atlantic Treaty as a defence agreement limited to Europe.[171] It was the same conditions the PSI would come to accept. In 1963, Vittorelli wrote the foreign policy of the PSI and accompanied Nenni to his meeting with Harold Wilson, where they agreed on a coordinated foreign policy regarding the US proposal for a nuclear Multi-Lateral Force (MLF).[172]

Tristano Codignola, another member of the PSU, owned the publishing house *Nuova Italia* and he was the liaison for transmitting the CIA funds to Italy for cultural propaganda.[173] *Nuova Italia* worked with the Information Research Department (IRD) until 1952 and probably even after that date.[174] Another PSU member was Piero Calamandrei, whose journal *Il Ponte* published a special feature 'The Socialist Experience in England'.[175] Important British socialists—probably indicated by Silone— wrote contributions: G.D.H. Cole, Roy Jenkins, George Brown, Healey, Zilliacus. Like the contemporary *New Fabian Essays*, it was an attempt to reflect on the years of the Attlee Government and to learn a lesson for the future. Calamandrei took Britain as 'the only positive example democratic socialists can claim for their own, the proof that democracy allowed the destruction of privilege without resorting to dictatorial measures'.[176] He even tried to convince Togliatti, with little success.[177]

This contact too had effects. Piero's son, Franco was a communist who in 1951 condemned the Labour Party,[178] but later became close to the party's right-wing leader Amendola. They both met Healey in London in April 1959—he had accepted by accident, as he believed the son to be the father. Franco Calamandrei and Amendola proposed an amicable and unofficial liaison between the Labour Party and the PCI, to discuss problems of foreign policy. Healey dismissed the affair as Khrushchev's ploy.[179] However, it was part of the faction's strategy to stress their similarities with the European socialist movement. In the 1960s and 1970s, Italian communists worked to establish international contacts with social democrats.[180] In the 1980s, the affiliation to the Socialist International became a point of factional struggle. In 1985, the Italian Communist Party prepared a congress resolution asserting that the party was 'an integral part of the European Left'. The pro-Soviet ultra-left contested the expression, seeing it as the precondition to enter the Socialist International. Enrico Morando, one of right-wing leaders, asked to establish a permanent link with the European parties. The drafting committee laughed at the proposal, since no one was crazy enough to join the Socialist International.[181] However, after the leadership of the Italian Communist Party opted to change its name in 1989, they decided to apply to the Socialist International.[182]

Even the leader of the Italian Republican Party, Ugo La Malfa, had tried to convince Healey to create a looser and more flexible organisation than the Socialist International, with the inclusion of other progressive, but not socialist forces.[183] Thus, all the political groups of the Italian left—social democrats, socialists, republicans and communists—considered the affiliation to the Socialist International an important feature in defining their identity and Denis Healey had a part in all these attempts.

Even if in the long term it had some influence, the problem remains of why the intervention of Comisco did not pay dividends in the short term. As mentioned, answering the question why social democracy failed in Italy is too ambitious, but an analysis of the intervention of Comisco offers important insights.

Some marginal effects could be seen. The appeal of the Labour Party in Italy might have convinced some workers to desert the communist-dominated trade union federation.[184] In the elections of 1948, Vittorelli described how poor peasants were impressed that an international organisation with a magical name cared for them: 'International Socialist solidarity was the one trump card with which the Left among the democratic Socialists could win an audience [...].'[185]

Nenni's socialists believed Labour support was important so they publicised any Labour heretics supporting them, no matter how marginal.[186] In 1946, the Italian communists feared Laski's prestige and diagnosed that the strength of the socialists was their traditional following in the working-class and the perception that they had the support of Great Britain.[187] When both factors were in play, as in 1948, it produced results.

The Foreign Office argued that the Italian social democrats would not stay in opposition because 'the Italians are most impressed by results and would be unlikely to back in any force a party which never held office',[188] blaming the national character. Healey's comment on the lack of faith is instructive, but it is not enough. Rather, we should follow the money. Poverty was always the main obstacle to the development of a truly autonomous socialist movement in post-war Italy. The communists dominated the organisations of the labour movement—trade unions, co-operatives, cultural associations—that could finance the party in opposition—in addition to the money from Moscow. The Christian Democrats had access to the Catholic organisations and state power; they also controlled the levers of patronage and corruption. The socialists had to stay independent between two rich competitors that could entice them with the money their party needed to survive. When the centrists ousted Nenni in 1948, they found the party close to collapse. The Soviets and communists prevented this in exchange for continuing the Popular Front.[189] When Nenni really broke with the communists after 1956, he had to find new financers—including Yugoslavia and the Labour Party—before inevitably falling into the arms of the Christian Democrats.[190] The freedom to take part in politics required money that put the politicians in debt with their financiers. This was even worse because Italian socialism was deeply divided, so any money first went to the faction and then to the party.[191]

From the start the unbalance in the left was strong: the PSLI spent only 2 million lire for the 1947 Sicilian elections, compared to the 6 to 7 million of the PSI, and the communists' 30 million.[192] The American trade unionists were among the major financers of the social democrats, but they applied conditions. In 1946, they promised $25,000 if the Italian socialists rejected fusion.[193] Later they pressured the PSLI to join a coalition Government with the Christian Democrats and a trade union federation with the Catholics.[194] This went against the strategy of their representative in Italy, Faravelli, who argued that by embracing 'anti-Bolshevism of any kind, even clerical anti-Bolshevism'[195] it was impossible to win over the workers—so they simply financed someone else.[196]

One of the reasons the left-wing social democrats were competitive in 1949 and recruited more people for the Florence Conference was a contribution that Romita received from the CEO of FIAT, Valletta, who hoped that a unified socialist party would be able to destroy the PSI by encouraging defections.[197] Among Romita's contributors there were also entrepreneurs to whom he had given Government contracts while he was Minister for Public Works. Romita was also eager to go back to the Government to distribute Government jobs to get more votes than the PSI, which disgusted Healey.[198]

The Comisco budget for 1950 reveals the poor state of the finances of the PSU: just £30, closer to an exile party than a party from a large nation.[199] As Silone confessed at the end of 1950:

> The search for funds to pay for our extremely limited expenses become every month more difficult, more precarious, more humiliating. I repeat … I do not mean we have to liquidate the PSU and accept unification at any cost, but we have to say that we can no longer go on this way.[200]

By January 1951 regular party activities had to stop due to a lack of money—despite receiving funds from Yugoslavia.[201] The Comisco parties collected donations to rebuild the party headquarters, damaged by a neo-fascist terrorist attack.[202]

Nationalism was another obstacle to effective intervention by the Labour Party and the Socialist International, because of grievances with Great Britain. Socialist internationalism was accused of being a cover for British imperialism—the same charge made against the League of Nations—by both fascists and communists.[203] The Italians and Dutch read the struggle between the PSLI and the PSU as a proxy war between the Americans and the British.[204] In post-war Italy, nationalism and revanchism greatly influenced the political climate, due to the territories lost to Yugoslavia, the uncertain status of Trieste under Anglo-American occupation and the loss of the colonies. The arguments that Yugoslav demands were illegitimate and that the western powers were using self-determination as a cover for imperialism had continuity with fascist propaganda, although they predated fascism and were not confined to it. Great Britain received the brunt of the criticism because it was traditionally seen as the defender of the Slavs against the Italians. As Salvemini explained in 1917 to Robert Seton-Watson, defender of the oppressed nations in the Austro-Hungarian empire, by encouraging Slav extremists they were weakening Italian moderates.[205] The fascist criticism of power politics and imperialist hypocrisy was similar to contemporary Bolshevik denunciations, but, in a typical fascist fashion, denouncing the formality of values and laws served to get rid of any obstacle to indiscriminate acquisition. The same problem was present during the Second World War, when Vladko Velebit, Tito's envoy abroad, commissioned A.J.P. Taylor to justify the Yugoslav claim on Trieste, provoking a very harsh reaction from Salvemini.[206] Salvemini was one of the most important voices of liberal and pluralist socialism, parliamentary democracy and anti-fascism; the fact that even he had an axe to grind with Britain was hardly auspicious. Nenni tried to explain to Bevin that Trieste was for the Italians what Strasbourg was for the French[207] and *Critica Sociale*, the journal that actively took the Labour Party as a model, openly contested the stance of the Labour Government on the Italian colonies.[208] The Italians were not the only sensitive ones: the decision to leave South Tyrol to Italy enraged Austrian socialists.[209]

When the PSLI broke with the Florence congress, they openly attacked the British Labour Party employing nationalist rhetoric. Saragat said he admired the Labour Government, but the loss of Italian colonies and the Peace Treaty showed that the British had no great love for the Italians.[210] The newspaper of the PSLI published an editorial cartoon with Bevin ready to use the Atlantic Charter as toilet paper.[211]

In 1952, the Socialist International held its second congress in Milan, the working-class capital of Italy, to show its interest in Italy and increase the prestige of the PSDI before the election. However, police reports showed that Milanese workers were not won over: they considered the PSDI a group of petit bourgeois who wanted a red social democracy without the popular masses.[212] They mocked Paolo Treves for addressing the congress in English, as he did when the RAF was bombing the city—during the war he did broadcasts on the BBC. They also resented the discrimination against Italian miners in Great Britain and the 'theft' of the colonies. They said that the Labourites controlled the International, compensating for their lost imperial power, and the Italian social democrats were useful idiots.

6 Tactical Stereotypes

As Salvemini said, the national character implies something 'primitive, permanent, and immutable'.[213] As a rhetorical tool, it evokes inevitability and justifies a policy of non-intervention. Fascism was fit for backwards countries, communism was appropriate for Eastern Europeans, so any sense of responsibility was to be thrown off. Healey brilliantly explained the abuse of geography in politics:

> I often think it is a mistake to talk, as we so often do over here, of the struggle between Western democracy and Eastern totalitarianism. Inevitably, this presentation of the Cold War, as a conflict between two political ideals which have precise geographical locations, encourages the tendency to write off everything east of the Iron Curtain as somehow belonging to totalitarianism by birth. So the agony of Eastern Europe is taken for granted as the natural fate of peoples who have never known freedom and therefore cannot feel its loss. I imagine this attempt to rationalise another's suffering conceals a profound sense of guilt.[214]

And yet Healey himself often employed geography to deduce the character of the peoples. How can we reconcile this? Too much attention is paid to the degree to which stereotypes limited the perception of contemporary players. Herzelf explains that stereotypes are flexible and have a practical use. They can be repurposed to different goals.

For example, the British made regular comparison of foreigners with the Irish, but the meaning changed according to the speaker and the occasion. A fellow traveller compared the Poles to the Irish to justify communism: 'the Irish characteristics of superstition and a certain mental and physical untidiness being redeemed in Poland by a (perhaps new) dogged energy and sturdy commonsense'.[215] Healey explained his sympathy for Poland 'which had so much in common with my Irish ancestors'.[216] A British diplomat, more neutrally, argued that Russia had to find with Poland a reasonable compromise between security and freedom, as Britain had done with the Republic of Ireland.[217] We have one reference with three different meanings, but which one can be deduced only from its tactical use. Images, metaphors, analogies, prejudices have a strong presence in culture and are difficult to change, but they are always available and politicians and opinion-makers can bend them into new configurations to fit their ends. In different situations the same person could use the same reference to draw up opposing arguments.

A study of Healey's autobiography is enlightening, for what is reveals and even more for what it conceals about his involvement with Italian socialism. While the events of 1946 and 1947 are mentioned, his most important intervention between 1948 and 1950 is only alluded obliquely. He mentions his attack to Saragat in 1949, the protest of the diplomats and Bevin's reaction,[218] but he does not mention what the attacks were about. When he mentions the Copenhagen conference, when Comisco had to choose between the PSU and the PSLI, Healey spoke about two Italian socialist parties, 'both were undeniably democratic, and both had split from Nenni's party over relations with the Communists'.[219]

> On this occasion the British argued pragmatically that we should admit both, while insisting that this should not create a precedent. The French argued furiously against such a constitutional breach, and finally gave in—strictly on the condition that the meeting simultaneously passed a *motion prealable* stating that under no circumstances should there be more than one party from a single country.[220]

The lesson Healey takes from this experience is that many of the problems with Continental socialists depended on 'mental and linguistic patterns' and had little to do with the concrete issues. He rehearses the common theme of British down-to-earth pragmatism and French abstract ideology but fails to mention that at that conference the French were backing a position Healey himself had supported until 2 months earlier, before embracing the Dutch proposal. His language seems to imply that the two socialist parties were equal, but this is not what he said at the time:

> In Mr Healey's views the press, including 'The Times', had been wrong in concluding that there was no difference between the two groups except a clash of personalities. There was a fundamental difference of opinion between them as to how preserve Socialism in Italy.[221]

The differences between the French and British national character are a cover to hide the political differences at stake, the Coalition Strategy and the Alternative Strategy. Probably Healey was not proud of letting himself be exposed, allowing Saragat and Van der Goes van Naters to outmanoeuvre him—he was similarly evasive about Greece. When the outcome was still uncertain, Healey refrained from a language of national character, but after the result had been settled, he hid behind the cover of the immutable nature of the people. Thus, stereotypes served a practical purpose.

While the British employed tactically the stereotypes about the Mediterranean people, the tactical response of the Mediterranean people was equally important. How did they react to the inferiority assigned to them by British culture? Did it made them consider Northern social democracy a more advanced model than their own local traditions? For example, in Italy and Greece, the main forces of the Left held the Socialist International in contempt at the beginning and later they presented their application enthusiastically. Donald Sassoon employs this explanation:

> International prestige in the countries of Southern Europe is an important political currency. The craving to be assimilated into the efficient, civilized, prosperous and, above all, modern world of Northern Europe, the fear of backwardness and underdevelopment, the memories of dependency—all this created, particularly among the urban classes, an attitude of deferential respect towards anyone supported by rich and modern foreigners.[222]

There is undeniable truth in this statement, but it is not the whole story. For example, Italian diplomats who admired the Labour Government's ability to stop communism and wanted the Italian Government to adopt its policies,[223] resented Labour's prejudices and preferred the Conservatives in Government:

> At least they do not have the ideological prejudices the Labourites have against us: 1) Italy is unable to have a socialist Government as the LP means it; 2) Italy is governed by reactionaries; 3) worst of all, they are under the influence of the Vatican.[224]

The Socialist International mattered because of the internationalisation of domestic quarrels. In Greece and Italy, the mainstream leftist cultures had a powerful anti-reformist, and anti-Western character. Communists were the majority and even socialists embraced the myth of revolution, rejected 'managing capitalism' and aspired to an alternative modernity to the Western model. The 'modernisers' in the Left adopted the myth of the Socialist International and northern social democracy to compete with their adversaries. The Socialist International was important to them because it was an object of hate for communists and left-wing socialists. This was not a new phenomenon: in 1931, Rosselli[225] and Wertheimer[226] were already hailing British Labour as an alternative to their local Marxist tradition. It was no different from what Crosland did: employing Scandinavian and American examples to counter the admiration for Soviet physical planning.[227]

The tactical use of the stereotype also explains the use of nationalism by those opposing Healey. The Italian Minister for Foreign Affairs told Bevin in 1950 that a speech from a Rhodesian minister saying that Italian immigrants were at the same level as African natives was souring Anglo-Italian relations.[228] When the PSLI attacked the Labour Party over the Florence Congress, it was more direct:

> So in Florence [Healey] addressed some Italian socialists with words that Negro socialists—if they exist—might find bearable, since maybe the London Government can claim some merit in civilising them. They are absolutely unbearable for a country that has been for years a suffering victim of lasting English hatred.[229]

Regarding the loss of the Italian colonies, Britain was more exposed to the accusation of hypocrisy, but there was another level. Colonisation was conceived as the right of the superior race,[230] thus many Italians read being denied colonies as being branded as an inferior race. Von Tirpitz too accused the British of not recognising anyone as their equal and treating the Germans as blacks.[231] Resentment towards Britain was a sign of resistance to the dominant discourse—the inferiority of the Mediterranean races—but the reaction mimicked what they considered the feature of a superior race, that is, the right to colonise. However, while the indignation was sincere, the backlash against a stereotype was tactical. Both the minister and the PSLI actually backed the British model of socialism.

The episode showed the limits of the Socialist International. First, it did not have the financial power to help weaker parties, as the member parties had limited resources and they lacked a rich patron state, like the USSR. Secondly, to be effective the Socialist International had to be identified with a successful example of actually existing socialism—in this case the British Labour Party—but thus it carried over all the negative connotations associated with its model—Healey privately conceded this.[232] Italians who would have otherwise admired the British Labour Party and taken it as a model, found the superiority complex off-putting, whether they were diplomats, socialist leaders or Milanese workers.

The year 1950 proved to be a turning point in socialist internationalism. Under Cold War pressure, there were more opportunities for international cooperation, the socialists experimented with new kinds of action and tested their limits. Boutbien complained that the Italian matter was the only occasion in which international socialism intervened in internal socialist matters.[233] The intervention in Italy was ambitious, but it revealed that direct intervention was dangerous, as it provoked rejection in the local parties and engendered divisions among the stronger parties. As 1950 came to a close, Healey drew the conclusion that this kind of international socialist activity would not be repeated:

> In general 1950 showed marked progress in the development of the International Socialist Conference and its ancillary bodies as a discussion forum. But by abdicating responsibility for the unification of Italian Socialism the Conference surrendered its last claim to direct influence over the affairs of a member Party.[234]

Notes

1. J. Pilcher, 'Friends, Romans, and Countrymen? (A Study of the Italian outlook)', 8 January 1951, The National Archives, Kew (TNA), FO 371/96226-WT1015/2.
2. D. Healey, 'Britain and Europe', 10 November 1987 in D. Healey (1990) *When Shrimps Learn to Whistle: Signposts for the Nineties* (London: Penguin), 78.
3. D. Healey (1952) 'Power politics and the Labour Party' in Healey, *When Shrimps Learn to Whistle*, 6–9.
4. D. Healey, European socialism today, *New Leader*, 16 September 1957, in Healey, *When Shrimps learn to whistle*, 65.
5. Labour Party (1948) *Feet on the Ground, A Study of Western Europe* (London: Labour Party), 20.
6. Healey, 'Power politics and the Labour Party', 14. Already mentioned in D.W. Healey (1950) 'The International Socialist Conference 1946–1950', *International Affairs*, 26, 3, 365.
7. D. Healey, Great Britain and European federation, *Comisco Information Service*, 23 June 1951.
8. Labour Party Annual Conference Report (LPACR) 1945, 114.
9. M. Herzfeld (2005) 'Practical Mediterraneanism: Excuses for Everything, from Epistemology to Eating', in W.V. Harris (ed.), *Rethinking the Mediterranean* (Oxford: Oxford University Press), 57.
10. E. Biagi, Dicono di Lei, La Malfa, *La Stampa*, 19 December 1972.
11. Herzfeld, 'Practical Mediterraneanism', 59–60.
12. J. Black (1992) *The British Abroad: The Grand Tour in the Eighteenth Century* (Stroud: Alan Sutton), 234.
13. Black, *The British Abroad*, 228. Also, C. Dickens, North Italian Character, *All the year round*, 10 September 1859, 467.

14. D. Healey (1990) *The Time of My Life* (London: Penguin), 59.
15. Healey, *The Time of My Life*, 41.
16. M. Hyde, The People of Romagna, *Tribune*, 23 March 1945. L. Ause, Note from Rome, *Tribune*, 13 July 1945.
17. Carandini a Bonomi, 27 November 1944, *I documenti diplomatici italiani*, Decima Seria: 1943–1948, Vol. 1, 627–628. For positive mentions in parliamentary debates Hansard, HC Deb 03 August 1943 vol 391 cc2233-2237; Hansard, HC Deb 28 September 1944 vol 403 cc561-566.
18. An Italian Correspondent, Italy – Political battleground, *Socialist World*, September-November 1947.
19. A. Gregoroyannis, The Socialist Movement in Greece, *Socialist World*, March-May 1948.
20. A correspondent recently in Trieste, Watch on the Adriatic, *Tribune*, 10 May 1946.
21. What's happening, *Tribune*, 24 May 1946. The Pope steps out, *Tribune*, 7 June 1946.
22. F. Taddei (1984) *Il socialismo italiano del dopoguerra: correnti ideologiche e scelte politiche (1943–1947)* (Milano: Franco Angeli), 28.
23. S. Merli (1981) *Il Partito nuovo di Lelio Basso: 1945–1946* (Venezia: Marsilio), 43–71.
24. L. Basso, L'aspetto politico dei nuclei aziendali, *Quarto Stato*, 30 June 1946. N. Tursi, Per la democrazia interna, *Critica Sociale*, 15 November 1945. N. Tursi, L. Preti, Per uno statuto democratico del partito, *Critica Sociale*, 30 November 1945.
25. Merli, *Il partito nuovo di Lelio Basso*, 83–93.
26. O dittatura borghese o democrazia socialista, intervento di Lelio Basso al Congresso Nazionale del Partito, *Quarto Stato*, 15 January 1947.
27. L. Basso, Socialismo Europeo, *Quarto Stato*, 15 September 1946.
28. 'Discorso di Pietro Nenni al XXV congresso del PSIUP' in A. Benzoni, V. Tedesco (eds) (1968) *Documenti del socialismo italiano* (Padova: Marsilio), 32–33.
29. K. Zilliacus to P. Nenni, 6 February 1948; Zilliacus to Nenni, 25 February 1948, Fondazione Pietro Nenni, Roma (FPN), Fondo Pietro Nenni, b.43, f.2005.
30. T. Vecchietti a Nenni, n.d. [1947], FPN, Pietro Nenni, b.42, f.1959. J. Cyrankiewicz, J. Rosner to Nenni, 7 April 1948, FPN, Pietro Nenni, b.23, f.1263. Warsaw to Foreign Office, 20 September 1947, TNA, FO 371/66250-N10617.
31. J. Hàjek to Nenni, 8 January 1949, FPN, Fondo Pietro Nenni, b.28, f.1449.
32. G. Arfè (1984) 'Introduzione' in Taddei, *Il socialismo italiano del dopoguerra*, 11–14.

33. N. Charles to C.C. Harvey, 30 December 1945, TNA, FO 371/60613-ZM130.
34. I. Silone to M. Phillips, 11 December 1945, Labour History Archive and Study Centre, People's History Museum, Manchester (LHASC), Labour Party (LP), International Department (ID), Denis Healey's Papers (DH), 03, 09.
35. Faravelli to Pertini, 9 November 1945; Faravelli to Saragat, 4 December 1945, P.C. Masini and S. Merli (eds) (1990) *Il socialismo al bivio: l' archivio di Giuseppe Faravelli, 1945–1950* (Milano: Fondazione Giangiacomo Feltrinelli), 56; 63.
36. Faravelli to Piero Treves, Milano, 21 December 1945, Masini and Merli (eds), *Il socialism al bivio*, 72–73.
37. Taddei, *Il socialismo italiano del dopoguerra*, 153; 167.
38. Rome to Foreign Office, 13 October 1945, TNA, FO 371/50037-ZM5214.
39. W.H. Braine, 'The Socialist Party in Italy', 14 August 1946, TNA, LAB 13/247.
40. Entry, 16 October 1945, P. Nenni (1982) *Diari*, Vol.1, *Tempo di Guerra Fredda: diari 1943–1956* (Milano: SugarCo), 151.
41. 'Discorso di Pietro Nenni al XXV congresso del PSIUP' in Benzoni, Tedesco, *Documenti del socialismo italiano*, 32–33.
42. Il Congresso socialista che si apre oggi a Firenze, *La Stampa*, 11 aprile 1946.
43. S. Colarizi (2005) 'I socialisti italiani e l'internazionale socialista: 1947–1958', *Mondo contemporaneo*, 2, 5–7.
44. 'Memorandum on Visits of Labour Party Delegation to Rome', LHASC, LP, ID, 08, 08. A. Varsori (1988) 'Il Labour Party e la crisi del socialismo italiano (1947–1948)', *Socialismo Storia. Annali della Fondazione Giacomo Brodolini e della Fondazione di Studi Storici Filippo Turati*, 2.
45. J.J. Schreider, L'esperimento laburista, *Critica Sociale*, 16 January–1 February 1947.
46. 'Conference Socialiste Internationale, Zurich, 6/8 Juin 1947 – Commission italienne', International Institute of Social History, Amsterdam (IISH), Socialist International (SI), 235. Also Varsori, 'Il Labour Party e la crisi del socialismo italiano', 174–177.
47. 'I get the impression that in the last few years we have repeated the errors we made in 1937 and 1938. We gather from time to time, we write some resolutions and we say important things, then we do not follow up our statements of principle with any action' (Stenogramme, 7 June, IISH, SI, 235).
48. Stenogramme, 7 June, IISH, SI, 235.
49. 'Programme for mending split in the Italian Socialist Party agreed with Lombardo and Malfatti, 3rd May 1947', IISH, SI, 235.

50. Stenogramme, 7 June, IISH, SI, 235.
51. C. Spinelli to D. Healey, 18 May 1947, IISH, SI, 235.
52. Stenogramme, 7 June, IISH, SI, 235.
53. Stenogramme, 6 June, IISH, SI, 235.
54. Stenogramme, 6 June, IISH, SI, 235.
55. D. Healey, 'Notes on the minutes of the Zurich conference', LHASC, LP, International Sub-Committee, Minutes and Documents, 1947.
56. Entry, 9 June 1947, Nenni, *Tempo di Guerra Fredda*, 167.
57. E. Caporano, Figure dell'Internazionale, *l'Avanti!*, 20 June 1947.
58. E. Loeb to G. Mollet, 17 November 1947, IISH, SI, 236.
59. 'Relations between the PSLI (Partito Socialista Lavoratori Italiani) and the French socialists', 6 November 1947, CIA-RDP82-00457R001000660001-1, Central Intelligence Agency, Freedom of Information Act, Electronic Reading Room, <https://www.cia.gov/library/readingroom/document/cia-rdp82-00457r001000660001-1> (accessed 29 December 2017).
60. Rapporto, 7 August 1947, Archivio Centrale dello stato, Roma (ACS), Dipartimento generale di pubblica sicurezza (DGPS), Direzione Servizi Informativi Speciali (SIS), Affari Generali, b.45, f. PSLI.
61. V. Montana a G. Faravelli, 4 maggio 1947, Masini and Merli, *Il socialismo al bivio*, 256.
62. C.F.A. Warner, Minute, 24 October 1947, TNA, FO 371/67767-Z9237.
63. G. Saragat to M. Phillips, 28 October 1947, quoted in Varsori, 'Il Labour Party e la crisi del socialismo italiano', 184–185.
64. Circular 88, 'Summary of proceedings, International Socialist Conference, Antwerp 28 November–2 December, 1947', IISH, SI, 47. Varsori, 'Il Labour Party e la crisi del socialismo italiano', 189–190.
65. Entry, 29 November 1947, Nenni, *Tempo di Guerra Fredda*, 401.
66. Varsori, 'Il Labour Party e la crisi del socialismo italiano', 190. Colarizi, 'I socialisti italiani e l'internazionale socialista', 7–17.
67. Varsori, 'Il Labour Party e la crisi del socialismo italiano', 191–202.
68. 'Italy: political situation', 12 February 1948, TNA, FO 371/73156-21359/G.
69. 'Quarterly report'; TNA, FO 371/73193-Z2449. 'Fortnightly report 1st–15th March', TNA, FO 371/73160–Z3549.
70. Fortnightly review, 1st–18th April, TNA, FO 371/73193-Z3503.
71. Letters to the Editor, *The Manchester Guardian*, 6 January 1954.
72. D. Redvaldsen (2011) *The Labour Party in Britain and Norway: Elections and the Pursuit of Power between the World Wars* (London: I.B. Tauris), 10–11.
73. S. Berger (1995) 'European Labour Movements and the European Working Class in Comparative Perspective', in S. Berger, D. Broughton

(eds), *The Force of Labour: The Western European Labour Movement and the Working Class in the Twentieth Century* (Oxford: Berg), 252.
74. Redvaldsen, *The Labour Party in Britain and Norway* 115–123. G. Esping-Andersen (1992) 'The Making of a Social Democratic Welfare State', in K. Misgeld, K. Molin and K. Åmark (eds) *Creating Social Democracy: A Century of the Social Democratic Labor Party in Sweden* (University Park: Penn State Press), 41–47.
75. Redvaldsen, *The Labour Party in Britain and Norway*, 11.
76. R. McKibbin (2010) *Parties and People: England 1914–1951* (Oxford: Oxford University Press), 180–183.
77. A. Thorpe (1989) '"The only Effective Bulwark against Reaction and Revolution": Labour and the Frustration of the Extreme Left' in A. Thorpe (ed.), *The Failure of Political Extremism in Inter-War Britain* (Exeter: University of Exeter), 19.
78. A. Thorpe (2014) 'Locking out the Communists: The Labour Party and the Communist Party, 1939–46', *Twentieth Century British History*, 25, 2, 235.
79. 'Memorandum on international socialist policy', LHASC, LP, International Sub-Committee, Minutes and Documents, 1948.
80. H. Earnshaw, 'Report on the Congress of the Norwegian Labour Party, Oslo, 17–18 Feb. 1949', LHASC, LP, International Sub-Committee, Minutes and Documents, 1949.
81. H. Douglass, 'Report on Austrian socialist party congress, Graz, 2nd November, 1950', LHASC, LP, International Sub-Committee, Minutes and Documents, 1950.
82. H. Earnshaw, 'Report of Dutch Labour Party Congress, Rotterdam, 8–10 Feb. 1951', LHASC, LP, International Sub-Committee, Minutes and Documents, 1951.
83. 'Report to the International sub-committee on visit to German SPD Congress in Berlin, 8th May 1948, and the Swedish Social Democratic Party Congress in Stockholm, May 9–14th, 1948 by Mr. Harold Earnshaw', LHASC, LP, International Sub-Committee, Minutes and Documents, 1951. J. Aunesluoma (2003) *Britain, Sweden and the Cold War, 1945–1954: Understanding Neutrality* (Basingstoke: Palgrave Macmillan).
84. H. Laski, Problems of the French Socialist Party, *Forward*, 17 July 1948, LHASC, LP, International Sub-Committee, Minutes and Documents, 1948.
85. 'Memorandum on international socialist policy', LHASC, LP, International Sub-Committee, Minutes and Documents, 1948.
86. 'Report to the International sub-committee on visit to German SPD Congress in Berlin, 8th May 1948, and the Swedish Social Democratic Party Congress in Stockholm, May 9–14th, 1948 by Mr. Harold

Earnshaw', LHASC, LP, International Sub-Committee, Minutes and Documents, 1948.
87. S. Watson, 'Report on the German Social Democratic Party, Dusseldorf, September 10th–15th, 1948', LHASC, LP, International Sub-Committee, Minutes and Documents, 1948.
88. D. Healey, 'Visit to Germany – Report by Secretary', March 1950; Percy Knight, 'Report on the German Social Democratic Party Conference, Hamburg 20th–26th May, 1950', June 1950, LHASC, LP, International Sub-Committee, Minutes and Documents, 1948.
89. Reuniting Italian Socialists, *The Manchester Guardian*, 24 January 1949.
90. Rome to Foreign Office, 17 June 1948, TNA, FO 371/73162-Z4979.
91. 'Report to the National Executive Committee on International Socialist Conference, Vienna, June 4/7 1948', LHASC, LP, International Sub-Committee, Minutes and Documents, 1948.
92. A.D.F. Pemberton-Pigott, 'Italian socialist parties, Points of discussion with the Times representative', TNA FO 371/79299-Z3930.
93. I. Mallet, Minute, 27 May 1949, TNA, FO 371/79299-Z3908.
94. Rome to Foreign Office, 6 June1949, TNA, FO 371/79299-Z4133.
95. F. Romero (1992) *The United States and the European Trade Union Movement* (Chapel Hill: University of North Carolina press), 153–172. Faravelli to Simonini, Canini, Saragat, 29 September 1948, Masini and Merli, *Socialismo al bivio*, 350–351.
96. Colarizi, 'I socialisti italiani e l'internazionale socialista', 17–22.
97. 'Supplement to report on PSLI Conference, Milan 1949, 1 June 1949', TNA, FO 371/79300-Z4297. M. Nardini (2012) 'La SFIO et la réunification du socialisme italien. La naissance du PSDI, la mission Commin et la rencontre de Pralognan (1949–1957)', *L'Ours, hors série Recherche Socialiste*, 60–61, 147–162.
98. D. Healey, 'Report on the International Socialist Conference, Baarn, Holland', LHASC, LP, ID, ITA, 9. Healey to M. Van der Goes van Naters, 26 May 1949; L. De Brouckère to Van der Goes van Naters, 3 June 1949, IISH, Archief Marinus van der Goes van Naters, 11.
99. Healey to Van der Goes van Naters, 13 June 1949, IISH, Archief Marinus van der Goes van Naters, 11.
100. Rome to Foreign Office, 20 June 1949, TNA, FO 371/79300-Z4457. 'Report of the Italian commission of Comisco', LHASC, LP, ID, ITA, 9.
101. G. Saragat, Discordanze, *Umanità*, 16 ottobre 1949. Lettera aperta al compagno Leon Blum, *l'Umanità*, 22 novembre 1949.
102. 'The crisis in Italian socialism', TNA, FO 371/79300-Z7452.
103. Healey's notes, n.d [circa Nov. 1949], LHASC, LP, ID, ITA, 9. Healey to Mayhew, 16 December 1949, TNA, FO 371/79301-Z8223.
104. 'BBC Italian Broadcast', 23 Nov. 1949, LHASC, LP, ID, ITA, 9.

105. D. Healey, 'Report on the Italian Socialist Unification Congress', TNA, FO 371/89636–WT1015/5. V. Mallet to Foreign Office, 10 January 1950, TNA, FO 371/89636–WT1015/3.
106. C.P. Mayhew, Minute, 15 December 1949, TNA, FO 371/79301-Z8071.
107. I. Mallet, C. Mayhew, E. Bevin, Minutes, 8 June 1949, TNA, FO 371/79300-Z4297.
108. Labour Party washes its hands of Saragat, *The Manchester Guardian*, 8 December 1949.
109. Rome to Foreign Office, 5 March 1949, TNA, FO 371/79299-Z1994. Rome to Foreign Office, 12 March 1949, TNA, FO 371/79299-Z2218.
110. G. Jebb, Minute, 2 December 1949, TNA, FO 371/79301-Z7772.
111. Rome to Foreign Office, 8 December 1949, TNA, FO 371/79301-Z7998.
112. Gallarati Scotti to Sforza, 10 June 1949, in *I documenti diplomatici italiani, Undicesima serie 1948–1953*, Vol. 2, 1107.
113. V. Mallet to I. Mallet, 26 May 1949, TNA, FO 371/79299-Z4200. Rome to Foreign Office, 22 June1949, TNA, FO 371/79300-Z4477.
114. R.B.H. Baker, Minute, 29 October 1949, TNA, FO 371/79300-Z7159.
115. C.B. Shuckburgh, Minute, 31 January 1949, TNA, FO 371/89636-WT1015/8.
116. 'International socialist conference (Paris), Summary of speeches', LP, ID, ITA, 11. Van der Goes van Naters, 'De Positie van het Italiaanse Socialisme', 22 January 1951, IISH, Archief Marinus van der Goes van Naters, 11B.
117. E. Davies, Minute, 21 March 1950, TNA, FO 371/89637-WT1015/23.
118. Rome to Foreign Office, 5 February 1950, TNA, FO 371/89636-WT1015/9.
119. M. van der Goes van Naters (1980) *Met en tegen de tijd* (Amsterdam: Arbeiderspers), 259. Van der Goes van Naters to Saragat, 22 December 1949, IISH, Archief Marinus van der Goes van Naters, 11B.
120. Van der Goes van Naters to Comisco Sub-Committee, 15 January 1950, IISH, Archief Marinus van der Goes van Naters, 11C. J.W. Russell, Minutes, 9 February 1950; Rome to Foreign Office, 14 January 1950, TNA, FO 371/89636-WT1015/4.
121. Saragat to Van der Goes van Naters, 25 February 1949, IISH, Archief Marinus van der Goes van Naters, 11C. Circular 65/50, IISH, SI, 51.
122. M.C. Bolle, 'Unification of Italian democratic socialism', 3 May 1950, LHASC, LP, ID, ITA, 11.
123. E. Bevin, 25 March 1950, TNA, FO 371/89637-WT1015/27. E. Bevin, Minute, 15 May 1950, TNA, FO 371/89637-WT1015/29.

124. A.R. Moore, Minute, 23 May 1950, TNA, FO 371/89637-WT1015/32.
125. D. Healey, 'Report on the International Socialist conference, Copenhagen', LHASC, LP, International Department, ITA, 11.
126. Rome to Foreign Office, 29 June 1950, TNA, FO 371/89637-WT 1015/33.
127. Healey to Davies, 8 June 1950, TNA, FO 371/89638-WT1016/2.
128. V. Mallet to G.W. Harrison, 3 November 1951, TNA, FO 371/96226-WT1015/13.
129. Entry, 22 September 1952, Nenni, *Tempo di Guerra Fredda*, 544.
130. 'International socialist conference (Paris), Summary of speeches', Circular 3/50, 4 January 1950, LHASC, LP, International Department, ITA, 11.
131. G.P. Young, Minute, 5 April 1950, TNA, FO 371/89637-WT 1015/24.
132. Van der Goes van Naters to M.C. van Bolle, 29 November 1949, IISH, Archief Marinus van der Goes van Naters, 11B.
133. LPACR 1949, 110.
134. LPARC 1950, 167.
135. P. Van Kemseke (2006) *Towards an Era of Development, The Globalization of Socialism and Christian Democracy: 1945–1965* (Leuven: Leuven University Press), 70.
136. At the time Healey wrote unsigned articles for *The Economist*. Given the themes and the language, the attribution to him is reasonable (E. Pearce (2002) *Denis Healey: A Life in Our Times,* (London: Little Brown), 96–102).
137. [D. Healey?], A year of Titoism, *Economist*, 2 July 1949. The Italian diplomats read the article and they agreed with it. Sofia to Rome, 18 October 1947, Archivio storico diplomatico del Ministero degli Affairi Esteri, Roma (MAE), Rappresentanza diplomatica d'Italia a Budapest, b.8, f.4: Comunismo, Cominform (1947–1952).
138. D. Healey, Mediterranean impressions-1, *Tribune*, 11 February 1949.
139. Moore, Minute, 20 March 1950, TNA, FO, 371/89637-WT1015/23. Also 'Appendix to supplement on report of PSLI congress', 13 June 1949; Christopher Mayhew to Prime Minister, 'Italian socialist parties', 14 June 1949, TNA, FO 371/79300-Z4298. R.B.H. Baker, Minute, 29 October 1949, TNA, FO 371/79300-Z7159.
140. D. Healey, 'Report on the Italian Socialist Unification Congress', TNA, FO 371/89636–WT 1015/5.
141. D. Healey, 'Report on the Italian Socialist Unification Congress', TNA, FO 371/89636–WT 1015/5.
142. LPACR 1949, 107.
143. E. Shaw (1988) *Discipline and Discord in the Labour Party: The Politics of Managerial Control in the Labour Party, 1951–87* (Manchester: Manchester university press), 26–30.

144. Van der Goes van Naters described Saragat as emotional but reliable, in a deliberate contrast with Healey's words (Van der Goes van Naters, *Met en tegen de tijd*, 256).
145. Van der Goes van Naters to Saragat, 22 December 1949, IISH, Archief Marinus van der Goes van Naters, 11B. J.A.W. Burger to Marinus van der Goes van Naters, 3 January 1950, IISH, Archief Marinus van der Goes van Naters, 11C.
146. Van der Goes van Naters to het Partijbeatuur van de Partij van de Arbeid, 30 January 1949, IISH, Archief Marinus van der Goes van Naters, 11B.
147. Circular 87/51, 'Report of the meeting of the Committee of the International Socialist Conference at Frankfort-on-Main, 28–29 June 1951', IISH, SI, 60.
148. Circular 55/51, Report on Comisco Meeting, 2–4 March 1951, IISH, SI, 59.
149. R. Broad (2001) *Labour's European Dilemmas: From Bevin to Blair* (Basingstoke: Palgrave), 24.
150. D. Healey, 'Report on the Italian Socialist Unification Congress', TNA, FO 371/89636–WT1015/5.
151. Gallarati Scotti to Sforza, 10 June 1949 in *I documenti diplomatici italiani, Undicesima serie 1948–1953*, Vol. 2, 1107.
152. M.B. Jacomb, Minute, 26 January 1950, TNA, FO 371/89636–WT1015/5.
153. J. Braunthal (1980) *History of the International*, Vol. 3, *World Socialism 1943–1968* (London: Gollancz), 207–209.
154. J.A.W. Burger to van der Goes van Naters, 3 January 1950, IISH, Archief Marinus van der Goes van Naters, 11C. Van der Goes van Naters to Bolle, 29 November 1949, IISH, Archief Marinus van der Goes van Naters, 11B. G. Scott-Smith (2008) *Networks of Empire: the US State Department's Foreign Leader Program in the Netherlands, France and Britain: 1950–70* (Bruxelles: Peter Lang), 109.
155. W. Mallinson (2010) *From Neutrality to Commitment: Dutch Foreign Policy, NATO, and European Integration* (London: Tauris), 56–59.
156. Telespresso ministero affari esteri to Presidenza del consiglio, 31 May 1950, ACS, Presidenza del consiglio, Gabinetto, 1948–1950, b.15-2, f.42270. G.Devin (1987) 'Guy Mollet et l'Internationale Socialiste', in B.Ménager, P.Ratte, J.-L. Thiébault, R.Vandenbussche, C.-M. Wallon-Leducq (eds), *Guy Mollet, Un camarade en république* (Lille: Presses Universitaires de Lille), 148.
157. G. Vassalli, Il Piave, *l'Umanità*, 21 April 1948.
158. Healey to I.V. Lombardo, 25 May 1948, TNA, FO 371/73161-Z4339.
159. W.H. Braine to Stewart and Pilcher, 3 January 1950, TNA., LAB 13/457.
160. T. Borgogni (1998) 'Il carteggio Codignola-Silone negli anni 1947–1951', in L. Mercuri (ed.) *L'azionismo nella storia d'Italia, 1946–1953*,

(Ancona: Lavoro editoriale), 389. Salvemini had high hopes for the PSU (Qualche sasso in capponaia, *Il Mondo*, 24 dicembre 1949).
161. Salvemini to Angelica Balabanoff, 9 February 1948, IISH, Anželika Balabanova Papers, 130.
162. Mallet to Morrison, 5 April 1951, TNA, FO 371/96227-WT1016/19.
163. E. Davies, Minute, 2 March 1951; Sforza to Morrison, 23 March 1951; Morrison to Sforza, 31 March 1951, TNA, FO 371/96227-WT1016/17.
164. Circular 100/51, 'Report of the First congress of the Socialist International held at Frankfort-on-Main, 30 June–3 July 1951', IISH, SI, b.60.
165. G.P. Young, Minute, 8 August 1951, TNA, FO 371/96226-WT1015/7.
166. Rome to Foreign office, 26 November 1949, TNA, FO 371/79301-Z7903.
167. A. Robens to H. Gaitskell, 4 April 1960, University College London (UCL), Gaitskell Archive, C204.
168. P. Vittorelli to M. Foot, 2 July 1949, LHASC, Michael Foot Papers, Tribune papers (2).
169. TNA, HS 6/821. L. Nuti (1999) *Gli Stati Uniti e l'apertura a sinistra, Importanza e limiti della presenza americana in Italia* (Roma-Bari: Laterza) 275–277.
170. Healey to Gaitskell, 'Earthquake in Italy' n.d. [probably June 1956], UCL, Gaitskell Archive, C310(2).
171. Un fatto compiuto, *L'Avanti!*, 21 maggio 1952.
172. Entry, 25 September 1963, P. Nenni (1982) *Diari*, Vol.2, *Gli anni del centro-sinistra: diari 1957–1966* (Milano: SugarCo), 294–295.
173. F. Stonor Saunders (2000) *Who Paid the Piper?: The CIA and the Cultural Cold War*, (London: Granta Books), 107.
174. Rome information department to IRD, 16 November 1953, TNA, FO 1110/569, PR G22/76.
175. L'esperienza socialista in Inghilterra, *Il Ponte*, maggio-giugno, 1952.
176. P. Calamandrei, Questa Democrazia, *Il Ponte*, maggio-giugno 1952.
177. E. Costa (2011) 'Il "campo sperimentale" del socialismo: la vittoria laburista del 1945 e i suoi riflessi sulla sinistra italiana', *Dimensioni e problemi della ricerca storica*, 24, 2, 11–41.
178. F. Calamandrei, Come il partito laburista ha perduto le elezioni, *Rinascita*, November 1951.
179. Healey to Gaitskell 1 April 1959, UCL, Gaitskell, C313.
180. M. Di Donato (2015) *I comunisti italiani e la sinistra europea: il PCI e i rapporti con le socialdemocrazie (1964–1984)* (Roma: Carocci).

181. E. Morando (2010) *Riformisti e comunisti?: dal PCI al PD: i "miglioristi" nella politica italiana*, (Roma: Donzelli), 46–49.
182. M. Gervasoni (2011) 'Una guerra inevitabile: Craxi e I comunisti dalla morte di Berlinguer al crollo del muro', G. Acquaviva and M. Gervasoni (eds), *I socialisti e i comunisti negli anni di Craxi* (Venezia: Marsilio), 87–99.
183. N. Jucker to Healey, 10 January 1960, LHASC, LP, ID, ITA, 3.
184. Braine to Gee 19 April 1948, TNA, LAB 13/457.
185. P. Vittorelli, Lift the Hunger Curtain, *Tribune*, 2 May 1952.
186. Largo raduno in piazza Baiamonti alla presenza dell' On. Valiani e del laburista Cadogan, *Avanti!*, 16 April 1948.
187. 'Direzione, 9–10 aprile 1946' in R. Martinelli, M.L. Righi (des) (1992), *La politica del Partito comunista italiano nel periodo costituente: i verbali della Direzione tra il 5. e il 6. Congresso, 1946–1948*. Roma Editori riuniti., 179–180; 191.
188. Moore, Minute, 26 January 1950, TNA, FO 371/89636–WT1015/5.
189. 'Extract from SIS report re Italy', 28 September 1948; Rome to Western Department, 26 October 1948, TNA, KV 2/2025. Entry, 18 May 1949, Nenni, *Gli anni del centro-sinistra*, 487.
190. Nuti, *Gli Stati Uniti e l'apertura a sinistra*.
191. Basso to Nenni, 25 September 1945, Fondazione Pietro Nenni (FPN), Fondo Pietro Nenni, b.18, f.1093. Bellanca to Nenni, 18 December 1946, FPN, Fondo Pietro Nenni, b.18, f.1098.
192. Faravelli to L. Antonini, 26 April 1947, in Masini and Merli, *Il socialismo al bivio*, 255.
193. Molinari to Nenni, 28 March 1946, FPN, Fondo Pietro Nenni, b.33, f.1651.
194. Montana to Faravelli, 4 May 1947; Faravelli to Antonini 7 October 1948, Masini and Merli, *Il socialismo al bivio*, 256; 363.
195. Faravelli to Montana 13 October 1948, Masini and Merli, *Il socialismo al bivio*, 365.
196. Montana to Faravelli 18 December 1948, Masini and Merli, *Il socialismo al bivio*, 386–387.
197. 'Financing of Giuseppe Romita', 13 January 1950, Central Intelligence Agency, Freedom of Information Act, Electronic Reading Room, CIA-RDP82-00457R004100340014-8, <https://www.cia.gov/library/readingroom/document/cia-rdp82-00457r004100340014-8> (Accessed 29 December 2017).
198. Healey to Davies, 8 June 1950, TNA, FO 371/89638-WT1016/2.
199. Circular 17/51, 'Annual report on activities of the International Socialist Conference', 12 February 1951, IISH, SI, 58.

200. Borgogni, 'Il carteggio Codignola-Silone negli anni 1947–1951', 393.
201. Rapporto, 25 June 1951, ACS, DGPS, Divisione affari Generali, 1951, b.31, f. Partito socialista (Siis). Rapporto questura di Roma, 11 Januart 1951, ACS, DGPS, Divisione affari Generali, 1951, b.31, f. Partito socialista unitario.
202. Circular 8/51, 'Minutes of the meeting of the International Socialist Conference Sub-Committee, 25 January 1951'; Circular 28/51, 'Minutes of the meeting of the International Socialist Conference Sub-Committee, 1–2 March 1951', IISH, SI, 58. Circular 63/51, 'Minutes of the meeting of the International Socialist Conference Sub-Committee, 21 May 1951', IISH, SI, 58.
203. The extreme left in Italy systematically associated the Labour Party and the Socialist International to British imperialism to delegitimise the social democratic way in Italy (Costa, 'Il "campo sperimentale del socialismo"', 11–41).
204. Dietro il sipario, *L'Avanti!*, 28 marzo 1951. Van der Goes van Naters, 'De Positie van het Italiaanse Socialisme', 22 January 1951, IISH, Archief Marinus van der Goes van Naters, 11B.
205. G. Salvemini to R.W. Seton-Watson, 10 February 1917 quoted in R. Vivarelli (2012) *Storia delle origini del fascismo: l'Italia dalla Grande Guerra alla Marcia su Roma*, Vol. 1 (Bologna: Il Mulino), 591–593.
206. C.J. Wringley (2006) *A.J.P. Taylor: Radical Historian of Europe* (London: Tauris), 147–149. Salvemini's answer in G. Salvemini, Trieste and Trist, *Free Italy*, 16 April 1945, collected in G. Salvemini (1969) *L'Italia vista dall'America* (Milano: Feltrinelli), 651–661.
207. Nenni to Bevin, 5 September 1945, FPN, Fondo Pietro Nenni, b.19, f.1118.
208. U.G. Mondolfo, L'Italia e le potenze vincitrici, *Critica Sociale*, 30 settembre 1945. U.G. Mondolfo, Dopo la conferenza di Londra, *Critica Sociale*, 1 marzo 1946.
209. J. Deutsch to W. Wodak, 25 June 1946, in W. Wodak (1980) *Diplomatie zwischen Parteiproporz und Weltpolitik: Briefe, Dokumente und Memoranden aus dem Nachlass Walter Wodaks 1945–1950* (Salzburg: Neugebauer), 176–177.
210. G. Saragat, Discordanze, *Umanità*, 16 October 1949.
211. *Umanità*, 5 October 1949.
212. Fiduciaria da Milano, 23 October 1952, ACS, DGPS, Divisione affari riservati, 1951–1953, b.54, f.p-50.
213. G. Salvemini, '"Natura" o "Civiltà"' in Salvemini, *L'Italia vista dall'America*, 141.
214. D. Healey (1953) 'Socialism', *The Unity of European Culture*, quoted in Healey, *When Shrimps Learn to Whistle*, 57.

215. A. Vallance, Thumbnail Sketch of Poland, *New Statesman and Nation*, 31 July 1948.
216. Healey, *The Time of my life*, 61.
217. Moscow to Foreign Office, 17 May 1946, TNA, FO 371/56439-N6471.
218. Healey, *The Time of my Life*, 105.
219. Healey, *The Time of my Life*, 93.
220. Healey, *The Time of my Life*, 93.
221. Moore, Minute, 20 March 1950, TNA, FO 371/89637-WT1015/23.
222. D. Sassoon (2010) *One Hundred Years of Socialism: The West European Left in the Twentieth Century* (London: Tauris), 599.
223. Lettera ambasciata di Londra, 13 September 1949, MAE, Serie affari politici 1946–1950, Gran Bretagna, b.36 Rapporti politici e partiti politici 1949, f.7.
224. Anzilotti to Zoppi, 3 June 1949, MAE, Serie affari politici 1946–1950, Gran Bretagna, b.36 Rapporti politici e partiti politici 1949, f.7.
225. 'I am explicitly in favour of reorganizing the socialist movement on similar basis to the British Labour Party' (C. Rosselli (2009) *Socialismo liberale* (Torino: Einaudi), 141).
226. E. Wertheimer (1930) *Portrait of the Labour Party* (London: Putnam's sons).
227. R. Toye and N. Lawton (2008) '"The Challenge of Co-existence": The Labour Party, Affluence and the Cold War, 1951–64' in P. Corthorn, J. Davis (eds), *The British Labour Party and the Wider World* (London: Tauris), 145–166.
228. Sforza to V. Mallet, 2 February 1949, in *I documenti diplomatici italiani, Undicesima serie 1948–1953*, Vol. 4, 14.
229. C.A. [Carlo Andreoni], 'Due Discorsi', *L'Umanità*, 9 dicembre 1949.
230. On the relationship between freedom and owning slaves in classical liberalism see D. Losurdo (2014) *Liberalism: A Counter-history* (London: Verso).
231. G. Radice (1992) *Offshore, Britain and the European idea*, (London: Tauris), 76.
232. 'Memorandum on international socialist policy', LHASC, LP, International Sub-Committee, Minutes and Documents, 1948.
233. L. Boutbien, *Aspect International de l'Idée du Mouvement Socialiste*, [around Copenhagen Conference], L'Office Universitaire de Recherche Socialiste, Paris (OURS), Fond Guy Mollet, AGM 53: Internationale Socialiste, 1949–1957, f. Comisco 1950.
234. D. Healey, 'Socialist Movement', *Encyclopedia Britannica*, November 1950 in LHASC, LP, ID, DH, 14, 01.

Bibliography

I documenti diplomatici italiani, Decima Seria: 1943–1948, Vol. 1.
I documenti diplomatici italiani, Undicesima serie: 1948–1953, Vol. 2.
Arfé, G. (1978). Pietro Nenni, libertario e giacobino. In P. Nenni (Ed.). *Vento del Nord* (pp. vii–lx). Torino: Einaudi.
Aunesluoma, J. (2003). *Britain, Sweden and the Cold War, 1945–1954: Understanding Neutrality*. Basingstoke: Palgrave Macmillan.
Benzoni, A. & Tedesco, V. (Eds.). (1968). *Documenti del socialismo italiano*. Padova: Marsilio.
Berger, S. (1995). European Labour Movements and the European Working Class in Comparative Perspective. In S. Berger & D. Broughton (Eds.). *The Force of Labour: The Western European Labour Movement and the Working Class in the Twentieth Century* (pp. 245–261). Oxford: Berg.
Black, J. (1992). *The British abroad: the Grand Tour in the eighteenth century*. Stroud: Alan Sutton.
Borgogni, T. (1998). Il carteggio Codignola-Silone negli anni 1947–1951. In L. Mercuri (Ed.). *L'azionismo nella storia d'Italia, 1946–1953* (pp. 384–393). Ancona: Lavoro editoriale.
Braunthal, J. (1980). *History of the International*, Vol. 3, *World Socialism 1943–1968*. London: Gollancz.
Broad, R. (2001). *Labour's European dilemmas: from Bevin to Blair*. Basingstoke: Palgrave.
Colarizi, S. (2005). I socialisti italiani e l'internazionale socialista: 1947–1958. *Mondo contemporaneo*, 2, 1–62.
Costa, E. (2011). Il "campo sperimentale" del socialismo: la vittoria laburista del 1945 e i suoi riflessi sulla sinistra italiana. *Dimensioni e problemi della ricerca storica*, 24 (2), 11–41.
Costa, E. (2018). The Socialist International and Italian social democracy (1948–50): cultural differences and the 'internationalisation of domestic quarrels'. *Historical Research*. 90 (251), 160–184.
Devin, G. (1987). Guy Mollet et l'Internationale Socialiste. In B. Ménager, P. Ratte, J.-L. Thiébault, R. Vandenbussche & C.-M. Wallon-Leducq (Eds.). *Guy Mollet, Un camarade en république* (pp. 143–168). Lille: Presses Universitaires de Lille.
Di Donato, M. (2015). *I comunisti italiani e la sinistra europea: il PCI e i rapporti con le socialdemocrazie (1964–1984)*. Roma: Carocci.
Esping-Andersen, G. (1992). The making of a social democratic welfare state. In K. Misgeld, K. Molin & K. Åmark (Eds.). *Creating social democracy: a century of the Social Democratic Labor Party in Sweden* (pp. 35–66). University Park: Penn State Press.

Gervasoni, M. (2011). Una guerra inevitabile: Craxi e I comunisti dalla morte di Berlinguer al crollo del muro. In G. Acquaviva and M. Gervasoni (Eds.). *I socialisti e i comunisti negli anni di Craxi* (pp. 87–99). Venezia: Marsilio.

Healey, D. (1990). *The time of my life*. London: Penguin.

Herzfeld, M. (2005). Practical Mediterraneanism: Excuses for Everything, from Epistemology to eating. In W.V. Harris (Ed.). *Rethinking the Mediterranean* (pp. 45–63). Oxford: Oxford University Press.

Labour Party. (1948). *Feet on the ground, A study of Western Europe*. London: Labour Party.

Losurdo, D. (2014). *Liberalism: A Counter-history*. London: Verso.

McKibbin, R. (2010). *Parties and people: England 1914–1951*. Oxford: Oxford University Press.

Mallinson, W. (2010). *From neutrality to commitment: Dutch Foreign Policy, NATO, and European Integration*. London: Tauris.

Martinelli, R. & Righi, M.L. (Eds.). (1992). *La politica del Partito comunista italiano nel periodo costituente: i verbali della Direzione tra il 5. e il 6. Congresso, 1946–1948*. Roma: Editori riuniti.

Masini, P.C. & Merli, S. (Eds.). (1990). *Il socialismo al bivio: l' archivio di Giuseppe Faravelli, 1945–1950*. Milano: Fondazione Giangiacomo Feltrinelli.

Merli, S. (1981). *Il Partito nuovo di Lelio Basso: 1945–1946*. Venezia: Marsilio.

Morando, E. (2010). *Riformisti e comunisti?: dal PCI al PD: i "miglioristi" nella politica italiana*. Roma: Donzelli.

Nardini, M. (2012). La SFIO et la réunification du socialisme italien. La naissance du PSDI, la mission Commin et la rencontre de Pralognan (1949–1957), *L'Ours, hors série Recherche Socialiste*, 60–61, 147–162.

Nenni, P. (1982a). *Diari*, Vol.1, *Tempo di Guerra Fredda: diari 1943–1956*. Milano: SugarCo.

Nenni, P. (1982b). *Diari*, Vol.2, *Gli anni del centro-sinistra: diari 1957–1966*. Milano: SugarCo.

Nuti, L. (1999). *Gli Stati Uniti e l'apertura a sinistra, Importanza e limiti della presenza americana in Italia*. Roma-Bari: Laterza.

Pearce, E. (2002). *Denis Healey: a life in our times*. London: Little Brown.

Radice, G. (1992). *Offshore, Britain and the European idea*. London: Tauris.

Redvaldsen, D. (2011). *The Labour Party in Britain and Norway: Elections and the pursuit of power between the world wars*. London: I.B. Tauris.

Romero, F. (1992). *The United States and the European trade union movement*. Chapel Hill: University of North Carolina press.

Rosselli, C. (2009). *Socialismo liberale*. Torino: Einaudi.

Salvemini, G. (1969). *L'Italia vista dall'America*. Milano: Feltrinelli.

Sassoon, D. (2010). *One hundred years of socialism: the West European Left in the twentieth century*. London: Tauris.

Scott-Smith, G. (2008). *Networks of Empire: the US State Department's Foreign Leader Program in the Netherlands, France and Britain: 1950–70*. Bruxelles: Peter Lang.

Shaw, E. (1988). *Discipline and discord in the Labour party: the politics of managerial control in the Labour party, 1951–87*. Manchester: Manchester university press.

Taddei, F. (1984). *Il socialismo italiano del dopoguerra: correnti ideologiche e scelte politiche (1943–1947)*. Milano: Franco Angeli.

Thorpe, A. (1989). "The only effective bulwark against reaction and revolution": Labour and the frustration of the extreme left. In A. Thorpe (Ed.). *The failure of political extremism in inter-war Britain* (pp. 11–27). Exeter: University of Exeter.

Thorpe, A. (2014). Locking out the Communists: The Labour party and the Communist party, 1939–46. *Twentieth Century British History*, 25 (2), 226–250.

Toye, R. & Lawton, N. (2008). "The Challenge of Co-existence": the Labour Party, Affluence and the Cold War, 1951–64. In P. Corthorn & J. Davis (Eds.). *The British Labour Party and the Wider World* (pp. 145–166). London: Tauris.

Van Kemseke, P. (2006). *Towards an Era of Development, The Globalization of Socialism and Christian Democracy: 1945–1965*. Leuven: Leuven University Press.

Varsori, A. (1988). Il Labour Party e la crisi del socialismo italiano (1947–1948). *Socialismo Storia. Annali della Fondazione Giacomo Brodolini e della Fondazione di Studi Storici Filippo Turati*, 2, 159–211.

Vivarelli, R. (2012). *Storia delle origini del fascismo: l'Italia dalla Grande Guerra alla Marcia su Roma*, 1. Bologna: Il Mulino.

Wertheimer, E. (1930). *Portrait of the Labour Party*. London: Putnam's Sons.

Wodak, W. (1980). *Diplomatie zwischen Parteiproporz und Weltpolitik: Briefe, Dokumente und Memoranden aus dem Nachlass Walter Wodaks 1945–1950*. Salzburg: Neugebauer.

Wringley, C.J. (2006). *A.J.P. Taylor: Radical Historian of Europe*. London: Tauris.

CHAPTER 7

'The Little Foreign Office of Transport House', British Foreign Policy and Socialist Internationalism

1   South Tyrol: A Case of Triangular Socialist Diplomacy

The cases of Eastern Europe and Italy have shown that Denis Healey stood at the nexus of national foreign policy and socialist internationalism, where informal socialist diplomacy took place. The transnational socialist network allowed state and non-state actors to communicate concerns and interests, negotiate decisions and coordinate their policies. This informal interaction made decision-making over foreign policy issues smoother—'governance' enhanced 'government'. It proved useful with contentious issues such as South Tyrol. As Healey recalls:

> The Italian and Austrian Government appointed socialists to their embassies in London, who used me as a vehicle for conducting their relationship with the British Government as well as with the Labour Party.[1]

Between the wars, Austrian and Italian socialism included left-wing and social democratic tendencies, but after the war their conflict had divergent results: the marginalisation of left-wing socialists in Austria and the flight and expulsion of social democrats from the PSI. The SPÖ was rebuilt after Liberation as a compromise between the old social democratic cadres and the revolutionary socialists. One of new secretaries of the party was Erwin

Scharf, who supported integral socialism and cooperation with the communists, holding up Italy, France and Belgium as examples.[2] In 1946 and 1947, Scharf defended Austromarxism against right-wing degeneration and asked to attack the Christian democrats instead of the communists. Unlike Basso, Scharf proved unable to stop control over the party going back to the reformist party cadres who formed the social fabric and solidarity network of the Austrian socialist movement.

In the SPÖ, references to international socialism shaped the factional struggle. Scharf was said to owe his position to his special relationship with the Soviets and the Yugoslavs.[3] Like Basso, Scharf argued that '*Labourismus*'[4] was false socialism with which capitalists and reactionaries wanted to convince the workers to abandon Marxism and class struggle. Scharf wanted the SPÖ to strengthen ties with Eastern European and left-wing socialists. Even if Labourism was the correct road for the British workers, Scharf offered the same warning as Nenni: it was mistaken to assume that the Austrian workers could choose that road:

> We talk a lot about democratic socialism and dictatorial socialism, where we stress the 'democratic' and 'dictatorial' word, thus giving the impression that we are saying: socialism is just a secondary interest [...]
> We can then make some effort and actually say what we mean, i.e. the democratic road and the dictatorial road to socialism! Of course the problem is that the socialists cannot always choose which road to take.[5]

On the other side, former exiles Czernetz and Pollak kept contacts with the British and defended the Labour model.[6] Schärf, the leader of the SPÖ, explicitly asked Bevin to give the Austrian socialists a preferential treatment, since they were the first target of the Soviets.[7] The Foreign Office issued more invitations to Austrian socialists to Britain to increase their prestige.[8] Pollak, who before the war was a revolutionary socialist, became the editor of the daily *Arbeiter Zeitung* and a member the party executive. He kept an anti-communist editorial line that influenced the attitude of right-wing socialists.[9] In September 1945, Pollak brought a message from the Labour Party to the party executive that explicitly said to reject the united front with the communists and accept a coalition between SPÖ and ÖVP (the Christian democrats). When Schärf visited Bevin in London, the Foreign Secretary insisted on the importance of preserving a coalition with the ÖVP,[10] a commitment Schärf made publicly some months later.[11]

In 1948, Scharf denounced the leadership by publishing confidential documents in an explosive pamphlet. He said—backed by the communist Franz Honner—that Pollak had received detailed instructions from Bevin. There was some truth in this: the Foreign Office had told Pollak to provide information about the Renner government—which the British government did not initially trust—but Pollak said that he had only relayed to the party the point of view of the Labour Party, not the Labour Government. The expulsion of Scharf started a brief but intense campaign to remove dissenting elements from the party. However, this was no shady manoeuvring from abroad to try to direct Austrian politics but a classic case of the internationalisation of domestic quarrels:

> The Labour Party suggested to the SPÖ the repression of the communists and the strengthening of the bourgeois influence over Austrian politics. This well-meaning advice was fully consistent with the political inclinations of the majority faction of right-wing socialists.[12]

Austrian socialists saw in the Labour Party not just a model of reformist socialism, but an important patron for foreign policy issues, such as the occupation of the country and the nationalisation of German-owned industries. The case of South Tyrol involved the participation of Italian, Austrian and British socialists in a triangular exchange of influences.

South Tyrol is a region on the Southern slope of the Alps with a German majority, which was assigned to Italy after the First World War. After the Second World War, Austria and Italy, former enemy countries, were in the ambiguous situation of being both victims and accomplices of Nazi Germany. Their new Governments hoped for benevolence from the Labour Government by using their anti-fascist and socialist credentials. The Austrian and Italian Governments delegated their socialist members to win over the progressive opinion-makers in Britain and Labour politicians by exploiting ideological similarities and personal contacts. Diplomatic weakness pushed the Austrians and Italians to rely on informal socialist diplomacy. The Italian ambassador in London, Nicolò Carandini, had at his service a 'social observer', Francesco Malfatti, chosen by Nenni. Nenni wanted to replicate the role of the British labour attaché to maintain contacts with organised labour, but they were introduced only in London, Washington and Paris, not Eastern Europe, where socialists were less trustworthy.[13] When Carandini arrived in London, he found the organisation 'Friends of Free Italy' and MPs like Ivor Thomas and Vernon Bartlett, who defended Italy in the House of Commons. Carandini considered Malfatti a valuable collaborator:

> In many occasions I took advantage of him to have my point of view presented to the Labour movement and to exercise pressure, in those circles where my direct intervention would have been difficult and inappropriate.[14]

The Austrians did the same. While the ambassadors were usually career diplomats favoured by the Christian Democrats, a socialist with the qualification of press attaché was assigned to the embassy to maintain contacts with the local labour movement: Walter Wodak held this office in London, Bruno Kreisky in Stockholm, Ernst Lemberger in Paris.[15] Thus began the induction of socialists into the diplomatic corps and a foreign policy based on socialist contacts, which would peak with Kreisky. Wodak established important contacts with Government officials, such as M.F. Cullis, and Labour members, such as Jennie Lee and Barbara Ayrton Gould. When Adolf Schärf visited London in 1946, their friendship worked as an 'open sesame' to all the official circles.[16] Lee, Gould, Gordon-Walker, Blenkinsop and William Warbey created—encouraged by Wodak—a pro-Austrian lobby of MPs to pressure Bevin and John Hynd.[17] Socialists and liberals with an interest in defending Austria formed the Anglo-Austrian Democratic Society.[18]

Nenni also relied on Riccardo Luzzatto, a socialist who had lived between Italy and Vienna, belonged to both the Austrian and Italian parties and was in contact with Karl Renner.[19] During the Second World War, Luzzatto worked for the BBC, represented Italy at the Huysmans Committee and lobbied for Italy through writings and contacts with important Labour personalities like Hynd, Ivor Thomas, Laski and Stafford Cripps.[20]

In their lobbying efforts, Wodak and Malfatti had two important successes: the visit of the socialist leaders to London and the debate by proxy in the House of Commons. Nenni had optimistic expectations for the international role of the Labour Government.[21] He wrote to Bevin to explain how a nationalistic reaction to the loss of Trento and Trieste could endanger Italian democracy, asking for a meeting in person.[22] Bevin asked the Labour Party to invite Nenni as a party member, not as a minister. He hoped to clear up any misunderstanding, but the invitation was also a concession to the Labour left—Laski had already invited Silone and wanted to invite Nenni, because they agreed on the alliance with the

Soviet Union.[23] Nenni was disappointed by the visit, because Labour members did not want to make promises before the peace conference and they underestimated Nenni's commitment to keeping South Tyrol. Nenni saw first-hand the popularity of Austrian arguments in Labour circles, especially after the defeat of the Austrian communists at the November 1945 elections.[24] Nenni found Bevin warm and genial but 'evasive'. Actually Bevin did not say South Tyrol was lost, but the Foreign Office argued that if Nenni had received this impression, it would have been very useful.[25]

The Austrian socialists demanded a visit for their leader Schärf as well.[26] Wodak argued that the fate of South Tyrol and Carinthia—for which Yugoslavia was staking a claim—was the most important problem to discuss with the Labour Party.[27] The visit gave a boost to the morale of the SPÖ, which claimed to be 'regarded abroad as the only really representative body of the Austrian republic'.[28] However Bevin was non-committal and Schärf got the impression that South Tyrol was lost.[29] After the peace conference left South Tyrol to Italy, he said that his impression was right,[30] but Bevin had offered Nenni the same vague words.

The Austrians and Italians also mobilised their friends in politics and public opinion.[31] Some Labour MPs prepared a plan to share the hydroelectric resources of South Tyrol in a joint Austrian and Italian administration, which Wodak leaked to the press with the help of the *New York Times*. However, coordination between Austrian conservatives and socialists was often difficult[32]: Wodak sometimes took initiatives independently of the Christian Democrat Foreign Minister[33] and vice-chancellor Schärf acted on his own.[34] On this issue De Gasperi, Nenni, and Carandini had a better level of cooperation—for example, Bevin approved the postponement of the Italian election to spring 1946 because Nenni had accepted it as well.[35] The Italian ambassador was free to cultivate good relations on a wider range, with both the Labour leader Hugh Dalton and Conservative leader Harold Macmillan.[36] Dalton supported the Italian claim on South Tyrol[37] and encouraged the Foreign Office to back the Italian line[38] while most diplomats backed the Austrians.[39] At the Clacton Conference, Dalton praised Italy and promised a fair treatment.[40]

The Austrian argument was that by ethnicity and tradition South Tyrol belonged to Austria and a plebiscite would confirm this.[41] Otherwise, it would remain a constant source of diplomatic strife. Conversely, the Italians employed arguments similar to the Czechoslovaks and Poles: they needed a border as the first line of defence against a possible Pan-Germanic menace. The Italians would not expel the Germans, while the Austrians would not protect the Italian minority.[42] In addition, the Italian Government had made extensive investments in the hydroelectric industry in South Tyrol, essential for economic reconstruction.

A key argument was that the Italians had redeemed themselves of fascism through the Resistance and co-belligerence in the last 2 years of the war—using Churchill's words, Italy had 'worked her passage home'. On the contrary, the Austrians and South Tyrolese had welcomed the Nazi regime, did not have a resistance movement, fought to the last for the Third Reich and committed war crimes in Italy. As Riccardo Luzzatto wrote for the British public:

> Only those Governments who were dangerously near the Nazi line and accordingly far from the feelings of their own people, show an aggressive nationalism; and the more they were inclined to come to terms with Nazism, the more violent is their nationalism and their request for other people's land.[43]

The strongest argument was the same for both Governments: humiliation over South Tyrol would have undermined the legitimacy of democracy in their country, strengthening fascists and communists. Both used their weakness as leverage to extract concessions from the great powers.

While Italy and Austria had no opportunity for a public confrontation, a debate by proxy took place in the House of Commons on 25 July 1946. Conservative MP Robert Boothby presented a motion signed by 150 MPs across party lines—with the contribution of the friends of the Austrian embassy—denouncing the concession of South Tyrol to Italy as a violation of the spirit of the Atlantic Charter.[44] He rehearsed the Austrian arguments, which the former Austrian ambassador, Georg Franckenstein, had supplied to the Conservatives. Wodak gave similar documents to Jennie Lee.[45] The Labour MP John Paton spoke in favour of Austria; he had been a member of the parliamentary delegation to Austria, which Wodak had advised his Austrian comrades to cultivate.[46]

When Carandini was informed of Boothby's motion, he asked Macmillan and other MPs to defend Italy in Parliament, supplying documents with the arguments to employ.[47] Macmillan accepted the task and also agreed with Bevin—who had accepted that South Tyrol would remain part of Italy to preserve the balance of power—to employ arguments that did not exacerbate nationalist feelings and to highlight the importance of interdependence to solve the problems in a European framework. After Macmillan supported the Italian cause, Bevin closed the debate by reminding the House with blunt honesty that it was impossible to invoke the ethnic principle for South Tyrol and its 250,000 German-speaking inhabitants at the same time as 13 million Germans were being expelled westwards to satisfy the security demands of the Eastern Europeans. He added that restoring Austria to its 1938 frontiers was an imperfect solution, but it was the only guarantee to preserve the territorial unity and independence of the country while Soviet troops were there. Bevin closed his speech with an appeal to rely less on independence and more on interdependence in the future. The debate was very tense and emotional: Bevin suffered a heart attack immediately after it.[48]

The Austrians and Italians were not simply competing for the favour of the British Government, they also tried direct contacts at party level to resolve their disagreement. The socialist *prefetto* of Bolzano, De Angelis, pursued a policy of autonomy and cooperation with the moderate German-speaking elements.[49] He also wanted bilateral negotiations with Renner, against the wishes of the Italian Government, which pursued a centralist policy.[50] In December 1945, Luzzatto went to Vienna to discuss with the SPÖ the establishment of an autonomous region for South Tyrol.[51] Renner and the other Austrian socialists refused to discuss it and said they would raise the question at the next international socialist conference. Luzzatto told the British that the Austrian masses did not care about South Tyrol, that the Austrian Government had a Nazi mentality and that foreign minister Gruber was a creature of the OSS (the wartime intelligence agency of the USA).[52] It was true that Austrian socialists like Schärf and Deutsch did not consider South Tyrol a priority and wanted a direct approach with the Italian socialists and Christian Democrats to achieve tangible goals like linguistic autonomy.[53] In September 1947, the PSI and the SPÖ agreed on a number of ongoing issues.[54] While there were some attempts of international conciliation through socialist contacts, they did not ease the tension and it was not the socialists who paved the way for future reconciliation. Even in this case, international Christian Democratic networks were more effective.

The practice of lobbying the Labour Government might not have influenced the final decision of the Peace Conference, but it created long-term contacts between the Austrian and British socialist movements.[55] Conversely, MPs—like Dalton and Macmillan—came to sympathise with Italy because of their war experience, not out of any socialist inspiration. As in other cases, socialist familiarity merely provided the opportunity to develop contacts.

Furthermore, Bevin knew how to cut off undesired influences when he wished to. When Schärf visited London and tried to raise the question of South Tyrol, Bevin said that the issue would have to wait.[56] When Nenni came to London in January 1946, Bevin did not speak to him privately, but, to mark the distance between party and Government, he received him together with his civil servants and the Italian ambassador:

> In that moment he was not speaking as one of the great leaders of the Labour Party—and he wanted to make it clear. He was *His Majesty's Foreign Secretary* [English in the original] duly armoured and safeguarded by his official role against the pitfalls of a meeting with a member of the same political church [...] To my recollection, in no other meeting had he been so cautious, wary, generic in words and unwilling to promise.[57]

2 Admitting the Germans

The admission of the SPD was the most important issue in the first 2 years of the Conference. During wartime, the marginalisation of the Germans was the foundation principle of the social democratic community, as the role of recognition became the exclusion of the enemy. While former enemies and neutrals—Italians, Austrians, Swedes and Swiss—were admitted, the Germans were excluded from the informal and formal socialist conferences in 1945 and 1946.

Schumacher's conception of the SPD was a national and international party, the guarantor of German democracy.[58] Like the SPÖ, he hoped for a special treatment from the British government, since the SPD was the main tool for the democratisation of Germany. He wanted to discourage a recognition of the SED, presented as nationalist and communist. He also hoped that the Labour Party could convince the Labour Government to alleviate hunger and misery, which were feeding extremism, and shelve policies encouraging revanchism, like dismantling and foreign control over the industries of the Ruhr.[59] According to Steininger, the German social democrats had ill placed their hopes: the British government's policy was not ideological and did not favour the SPD. In addition, the distinction between Labour Party and Labour Government was strong, as Bevan explained: 'We must try and maintain a distinction between the Labour Government and the Labour Party, and by insisting upon it, it would be more possible for us to take a strong, determined action as a Party which will not involve the government'.[60] The Labour Party lobbied in Schumacher's favour, obtaining his invitation to Britain, the first German leader abroad after the war.[61] However, they trusted the German social democrats less than the Austrian socialists.

The Clacton Conference (17–19 May 1946) encouraged the parties to investigate the situation in Germany and the Bournemouth Conference (8–10 November 1946) debated the German problem.[62] Two opposing strategies emerged. The British Labour Party, the PvdA and the DNA had contacts with the SPD and believed in their goodwill; with Mollet as secretary, even the SFIO abandoned its anti-German position.[63] Despite mistrust and past grievances, those parties believed the SPD could be the instrument of democratisation and denazification of Germany, thus it needed material and moral support. Morgan Phillips argued that since the International Socialist Conference was an informal body, aiding Schumacher would not embarrass the other parties in front of their electors. The PPS took the opposite position: the SPD would not solve the German question, rather the German question had to be solved before admitting the SPD. Grosfeld doubted that the millions of votes for the SPD were socialist votes. He did not want to encourage revanchism and offend the USSR, as he feared the Germans would pit the Allies against each other, as they had done before. As Grosfeld duly noted, belonging to the International Socialist Conference was a political asset:

> Though the Conference was not a formal body, the admission of the SPD could have political significance, and would militate against agreement among the United Nations.[64]

The PPS opposed the SPD for nationalist reasons, but it was also a ploy to gain legitimacy as the main anti-German socialist party. As they told the British, attacks against the Germans served to reassure the communists, who considered the International Socialist Conference a British tool.[65] In Bournemouth, it was clear that a majority of socialist parties were in favour of admitting the SPD, but there was also a very hostile minority, consisting of the Eastern European parties, the Jewish party from Palestine and the Swiss party. To save the unity of the conference, it was decided to invite the German social democrats at the next conference to state their case and answer questions. Schumacher was anxious, but Healey was confident about admission.[66] Indeed, the question set an important procedural point, namely that admission of new members would not require unanimity but a two-thirds majority, not counting abstentions.[67]

The real issues at stake were the criteria with which to judge whether a party was truly socialist. In Zurich (6–9 June 1947), Schumacher repeated that the SPD would defend democracy in Germany. Socialism was not an economic idea but a moral one as well, inspired by freedom and democracy. The party of the working-class was the only one immune from the infiltration of the bourgeoisie, opportunists and former Nazis. Quoting Morrison, he said that true unity of the working-class would not come from a popular front, but from ending communist sabotage. A modus vivendi with the USSR was necessary, but cooperation with the communists and deference to Moscow were not the criteria to judge the adherence of the SPD to socialism: the only evidence they needed were the years its leaders spent in prison and concentration camps. As Nenni noted, Schumacher's mangled body covered in scars was a living symbol of wartorn Germany and his best argument.[68] Schumacher said:

> The question for the socialists is: do they want a free anti-totalitarian Socialism to live or do they want to leave us alone? For us international socialists the Social-Democrats are the defenders of human rights on German soil. Can we international socialists rely on the SPD to be a loyal, trustworthy and equal member of our partnership? Comrades, we ask you today for an answer to this question.[69]

While Western socialists backed Schumacher—particularly Grumbach, who greeted the Germans as old comrades despite all his relatives who had been murdered—the Eastern European socialists rejected Schumacher's arguments and questioned the socialist credentials of the SPD.[70] Hochfeld said the leaders of the SPD were true anti-fascists, but they were objectively helping Nazism, with their nationalism and hatred for communism and the USSR. He demanded harsh conditions: interrupting nationalist propaganda, denazification, re-education and a united front of the German workers. The Czechoslovak Vilem Bernard wanted the SPD to concentrate on economic issues and abandon nationalist propaganda, even if a drop in popularity was the price to pay. Diplomacy and socialist internationalism were mixed: the debate over the admission of the SPD was a confrontation by proxy over different readings of the international situation, the reconstruction of Europe and the role of the Soviet Union.

Two peculiar positions deserve mention. Van der Goes van Naters questioned why the SPD kept its old name, despite past failures, and why it did not renounce Marxism and demands for material goods to embrace an ideology of equality—doing what the Dutch socialists had been doing since 1937. Indeed, some German social democrats wanted a complete renovation of the party,[71] but old party cadres clung to tradition. As Schumacher said, the old banner was better than the new to gather the militants—who could be tempted by communism. History—particularly resistance to Nazism and persecution—was a source of legitimacy among party cadres, electors and fraternal socialist parties. As Drögemöller notes, this interaction showed the diverse strategy of the two parties and the eventual overcoming of differences in the late 1950s.[72] The International Jewish Bund and the Jewish Labour Party of Palestine questioned the credentials of the SPD not for their present political role, but for the responsibility of German workers in the Holocaust. Decades later, genocide would dominate the representation of Nazism, but then it was just one element among others, even for other Jewish socialists.[73]

The debate became bitter: the Poles protested that the others treated their arguments with contempt; Schärf said that the Poles treated German killers and victims the same way, ignoring their own cooperation with Hitler; Lie said that Poland could not to teach about democracy and socialism to the others. The SPD was not admitted by one vote, as a result of numerous abstentions, probably because the Eastern Europeans threatened to leave. Healey was satisfied, as the votes signalled the support Schumacher enjoyed, while the intransigent opposition of the Eastern European socialists would deprive the communists of an argument against them.[74]

A German commission was formed, where Western and Eastern socialists reiterated their arguments.[75] The SPD was finally admitted at the Antwerp Conference (28 November–1 December 1947), with the bloc of Western parties voting in favour, the Eastern parties against.[76] In March 1945, Nenni alone voted against the collective guilt of the Germans, but in Zurich and Antwerp the PSI abstained as a concession to the Eastern Europeans, who supported them against the PSLI. In the socialist family too, blocs were forming.

The SPD was the only party claiming to represent German socialism, but usually there was more than one pretender asking for admission. This allowed the intervention of the International Socialist Conference, whose motivations included considerations of foreign policy and socialist idealism.

There were two competing socialist parties for Bulgaria: Nyekov's party, part of the Government bloc and allied with the communists, and Lulchev's party, which had split from the former to oppose communism. Thanks to pressure from Grumbach, Nenni and Isabelle Blume, Nyekov's party was admitted as an observer[77] and a commission was set up to investigate its claim. The commission, chaired by Isabelle Blume and including other left-wing socialists (James Crawford, Leon Boutbien, Tullio Vecchietti, Szwalbe) suggested granting full membership to Nyekov, as his was the only party able to influence the Government:

> His admission will surely strengthen him [Nyekov], making him firmer [against the communists] in some occasions and it would be unbelievable to abandon the people in Eastern Europe who have enough attachment to our ideas in order to keep alive a party [Lulchev's] that still has the name of 'Section of the International'.[78]

Crawford told the Bulgarians that even in Britain it was necessary to use coercion to force some classes to abide by the law and the general interest. Lulchev's split had damaged socialism and involuntarily helped reaction. Crawford's thoughts on Bulgaria were no different to Healey's on Poland. However, in Antwerp Schärf and Vorrink demanded the rejection of the report and for both parties to be admitted as observers, while Larock denounced Nyekov's approval of the Cominform conference.[79] The conference split exactly in half on the issue (the British Labour Party abstained) and the compromise solution was to accept Nyekov's party only as observer. In Zurich, the International Jewish Bund was admitted as an observer as a symbolic gesture, but then in Antwerp it became a full member. Uncertainty over whether the Congress Socialist Party or the Radical Democratic Party was more representative for India[80] led to the admission of both.[81]

The cohabitation of social democrats and left-wing socialists in the International Socialist Conference was partially based on the exclusion of the German social democrats, keeping the spirit of the Great Alliance alive. However, when German restoration became indispensable for the restoration of civil life in Europe, the SPD was seen as the instrument of democratisation of Germany. Paradoxically, the anti-German stance introduced the principle that the admission to the International Socialist Conference had to be regulated by stringent conditions and made the expulsion of the Eastern European socialists more traumatic.

After admission, Germany became the front line of the Cold War and the SPD won moral recognition for its leadership, especially in Berlin. However, the German social democrats became embroiled in a series of questions—which have been extensively covered by Steininger and Imlay[82]—where they found themselves isolated: the internationalisation of the Ruhr, the status of Saarland, the boycott of the Council of Europe and other forms of European integration. Van der Goes van Naters came to regard the SPD as a nationalist party and he found greater cooperation with Adenauer.[83] This reputation for nationalism was widespread among contemporaries and later commentators—though Imlay contests it. Only with the revision of the programme in the 1950s and, especially, a new attitude to foreign affairs and the European question, could the SPD regain its central position in the socialist community, eventually winning back the hegemonic leadership from the Labour Party in the 1970s.[84]

3 The Emotional Greeks

Healey's autobiography is evasive about his involvement in Greece. He brusquely set aside the issue of the Greek civil war by saying that Great Britain became involved 'willy-nilly'.[85] This reluctance to speak conceals the fact that in those years Healey swung between excusing the Labour Government complicity with the right-wing dictatorship and encouraging forceful intervention in favour of the democratic centre. In British culture the Balkans embodied backwardness, absence of rule of law and uncivilised and irrational people, where democracy could not develop. At the same time, the Balkans were the stage where Britons could act out anti-modern fantasies. Byron established the paradigm of the British saviour figure with a special mission to solve the problems of the locals— best exemplified in *The Prisoner of Zenda*.[86] Throughout the twentieth century, Greece suffered extreme internal division, the collapse of traditional political institutions and the emergence of new political groups. Competition for power invited the intervention of foreign actors to defend their entrenched position or aid their ascent—which Sfikas links to theory of imperialism of Robinson and Gallagher.[87]

At the end of 1944, Greek forces were polarised and unable to compromise: the National Liberation Front (EAM)—dominated by communists with socialists and agrarians—and its military wing (ELAS) controlled most of Greece, while the Greek Government in exile, headed by Papandreou regained control of Athens. On 3 December 1944 British troops opened fire on Greek protesters in *Syntagmata* Square, starting the Second Civil War (*Dekemvriana*). In February 1945, the *Verkiza* Agreement established a precarious peace between the communists and the government, allowing the state and right-wing paramilitary forces to persecute the former members of EAM, with tension spiralling until the Third Civil War began in 1946. During this period of transition and civil war, the British government always sided with the royalist populist rightwing governments, until the Americans took over in 1948, in line with the Truman Doctrine.

Foreign intervention is a two-way road: every action from a great power in a small country produces a reaction in the political system of the great power. Greece was probably the biggest source of embarrassment for the Labour leadership, even before coming to power. The Labour Government had to keep its commitments in Greece while preserving 'all the trappings of anti-Imperialist non-interventionist respectability'.[88] The Labour Party played its part in managing dissent, exploiting Mediterranean stereotypes.

The shootings in *Syntagmata* Square provoked the biggest protest against Labour ministers for supporting the policy of the Churchill government. On 8 December 1944, 30 MPs voted to censure the Government, including 23 Labour MPs, not just left-wingers and future critics of Bevin—like Bevan and John Mack—but also centrists like Hector McNeil. Despite little previous interest in Greece, the event was an outlet for the underling tension in the movement about other issues, such as the treatment of Germany, Spain and Italy, regulation against illegal strikes and fears about the rebirth of the extreme right and the Conservative Party. Greece served to test the commitment of the leadership to socialist goals and the degree to which it had become compromised with the Conservatives. Churchill exploited the event to drive a wedge between base and leadership. Attlee took advantage of widespread prejudices about the Greeks, telling the House of Commons not to judge Greek democracy on British terms: 'When you are dealing with people like the Greeks, who are rather temperamental perhaps, [...] you should never try to judge them exactly on your own basis'.[89]

Others exploited the stereotype of the violent and undemocratic Mediterranean to justify violent actions by the revolutionaries against a corrupt and tyrannical élite. In his first public outing at the Annual Conference in 1945, Healey warned that conditions in Greece forced the workers to adopt measures that were unthinkable in Britain, so the Labour

Party had to guard against false friends, such as the upper classes of Continental Europe.[90]

While there were expectations that the Labour victory might help Greek republicans and socialists, Bevin chose continuity and already at the Annual Conference in 1944 he secured the block vote of the main trade unions to stop the critics of the government. His only concern was preventing Greece from failing into the Soviet sphere of influence, as it was an integral part of the Middle Eastern strategy.[91] He justified this with the need to protect Britain, 'the last bastion of social democracy'.[92] The British would have preferred a centrist coalition led by Papandreou, but facing the clear-cut choice between EAM and the royalist populists, the British government chose those who would keep Greece in their sphere of influence. Cold War logic dictated that supporting democracy meant actually supporting right-wing terrorism, even if it was the reason for the civil war. The only question was how to defend this policy.

The British exploited the idea of the national character: they could admit that conditions in Greece were terrible while laying the blame on factors beyond their control—the Greek temperament. McNeil, who had criticised Churchill in 1944, complained in 1946 that it was actually Greece that created problems for Britain:

> [A] backward, extravagant and irresponsible country whose vanities are made greater and whose difficulties are therefore accentuated because for both us and the USSR Greece has strategic importance.[93]

On 27 March 1946 Richard Windle, the National Agent of the Labour Party, who also supervised the Greek elections, suggested employing the following cultural arguments to respond to criticism: the elections and their legality had to be judged on Greek standards, not British; some criticisms were legitimate but they were exaggerated; disorder and personal feuds were common in Greece and they were not politically motivated. One year later Laski discovered that Windle was trying to influence party policy on Greece and denounced him to Healey, saying that the party constitution did not authorise the National Agent to decide party policy.[94]

The trade unionist Victor Feather—sent to Greece to settle confused trade union matters—employed similar arguments. He praised the Greeks as martial and industrious people, poor but clean, with the misfortune of being led by terrible politicians. However, he described the brutal police repression idyllically: unlimited freedom of speech and press, fair trials and comfortable prisons. He conceded that the political world was fragmented, dominated by the cult of personality, political debates took too much time and the attacks were personal and libellous, but it was just the Greek temperament that gave everything a dramatic and extremist tone, even if it was just for show. They talked of terrorism, but it was just exaggeration and rhetoric. The black market came naturally to a people who were not at all afraid of the police:

> The British 'bobby' is, of course, famous throughout the world. Their British temperament is perhaps their biggest asset. The British appear to be more law abiding than most people; they are certainly not as hot-headed as people in the warmer climates. Perhaps the lack of sunshine makes us seem cold and unemotional.
> The Greeks, the Italians, the French and others, are not so behaved. They are more frank, and if they are annoyed or pleased, they show it with emphasis. We hide it.[95]

Towards the end of 1946, criticism against maintaining British troops in Greece mounted. A delegation of Labour MPs led by Leslie Solley—who would be expelled in 1948 – Norman Dodds and Stanley Tiffany visited the country and denounced the fascist transformation behind a façade of democracy.[96] McNeil organised a new delegation to visit Greece, but they too produced a critical report that shocked the party base.[97] When, on 18 November 1946, 58 Labour MPs voted for an amendment asking for a socialist alternative in foreign policy between Russia and America, Greece was a key point.

Other ministers also wanted withdrawal. The Treasury considered Greece a lost cause and a waste of money. Attlee, who had defended the Greek policy in 1945, advanced an alternative foreign policy of neutral zones and disengagement from the Middle East.[98] This time Attlee did not mention the Greek national character as the source of the problem, but misery and enormous inequality.[99] In a role reversal, Attlee had become the critical voice and repeated some of Healey's argument, while Healey had become the main apologist of Bevin. Sometimes Healey answered direct criticism from the local parties and trade union branches—he opened a whole separate folder,[100]—other times he helped the local leaders to manage dissent and to answer to the criticism from the rank and file, supplying arguments to justify the atrocities of the Greek government.

For example, the head of the Morecambe Labour Party asked for arguments to reject accusations from members of dubious loyalty and he asked to receive information through informal channels.[101] The role of the International Department was expanding: not only did it take care of the international relations of the party, but it also helped the leadership to manage dissent in foreign policy, drafting arguments to defend the Government and quelling dissenting voices.[102]

The points to make with critics were that Government policy in Greece was supported by the UNO, the TUC and the WFTU; that there was a risk of civil war; that elections had been fair by 'Balkan standards' and intimidation did not play a major role. The last argument was an obvious reference to the concurrent elections in Romania and Bulgaria, but it also meant that full democracy could not be expected from Greece. Critics of Bevin rejected the idea that the Greeks were unfit for democracy, saying they fought well and dealt with their problems in a business-like way.[103] Healey produced the most articulate defence of the government's foreign policy, *Cards on the Table*, in which he reassured the members of the party that the most unpleasant episode of British foreign policy—'Greece, Syria, Indonesia, Spain, and Palestine'[104]—had been necessary reactions to Soviet expansion.

Even other non-state organisations of the British labour movement—the TUC and the Co-operative Alliance—became involved both as apologists for the government and as government agents in Greece to improve the situation. The Churchill Government authorised the TUC to send a fact-finding mission to Greece.[105] Its leader, Citrine, was soundly anti-communist and brought back news of the atrocities committed by ELAS—he had done a similar job in the past on his visits to the Soviet Union and Finland.

The TUC intervention in Greece from 1945 to 1948 was important for the origins of the Cold War.[106] The British trade unionists, backed by the Labour Attaché at the Rome embassy, tried to build up a democratic trade union movement, failing because of communist strength and interference by the Government. The mission was a failure, but it allowed the political and trade union leadership to say that intervention in Greece had received the blessing of the WFTU, as the International Department of the Labour Party suggested telling local parties. Also, at the TUC congresses in 1947 and 1948, a trade unionist envoy to Greece said that the Greek left refused compromises because of their obstinacy, resorting once again to the Greek personality to explain a political outcome.

The project of Bevin and McNeil to expand cooperation between British and Greeks by employing the co-operatives was also a failure. They wanted to build up retail co-operatives to distribute United Nations Relief and Rehabilitation Administration (UNRAA) goods, because private distributors were inefficient and corrupt. However, the Co-operative Alliance explained that this required a long-term commitment to educate Greek co-operators in Britain and they could not ask the Greek government to cover the costs, as they would not have sent the best people but those favoured by nepotism.[107] As in many other cases, the lack of money was the main obstacle to carrying out socialist strategies abroad.

The main concern of the Labour leadership in Greece, as well as in Eastern Europe, was to avoid embarrassing the government before the electors and giving opportunity for dissent to the regular critics of the government, legitimising a pro-Soviet stance. National stereotypes proved useful: by stressing those people were different from the British, Labour leaders could justify things being done to others that the British would have never accepted being done to themselves. Also useful was direct intervention, to improve the situation or, at least, to signal the interest of the movement and to appease the demands of the rank and file.

4   The Comisco Mission to Greece

After the war, Greek socialism was squeezed between popular left-wing liberals and the Greek Communist Party (KKE), hegemonic among the small working-class. During the resistance, the Socialist Party of Greece (SKE), led by the trade unionist Dimitris Stratis, and the Union for People's Democracy (ELD), led by Ilias Tsirimokos, emerged. They were not mass parties, but rather a 'patronage-and-clientele of the party leader of the moment'.[108] Local notables provided the votes, with the same family dominating a constituency for generations like Lamia for Tsirimokos and Crete for Askoutsis, whatever the official political label—Tsirimokos started as a liberal.

In 1941, the SKE and ELD joined the communist-led EAM; they showed a degree of independence in the negotiations between the resistance and the Government in exile.[109] After the Varkiza agreement, the SKE and ELD left EAM and the revolutionary struggle, forming a new party, SK-ELD. This also included independent personalities, like Alexandros Svolos, the foremost constitutional scholar in Greece. The programme set socialist democracy as the goal, rejecting reformism but allowing freedom of discussion. In late 1945, the party dealt with the issue of government participation. On one side, the leader Kazantzakis wanted to join a coalition government and mediate between the bourgeois parties and the KKE; on the other, Tsirimokos refused to associate with the bourgeois centrist parties. Tsirimokos' line prevailed. The socialists cooperated with the communists in boycotting the 1946 elections—together with leftist liberals—and against the Government and judges, who deposed the elected executive of the trade union federation to impose yellow trade unionists.

Greek socialists did not have any traditional link with the Western parties and the Labour Party decided not to invite any Balkan party to the Clacton Conference.[110] The SFIO took up their cause, as Greece was less embarrassing for their foreign policy, Greek socialists spoke French and many Greek exiles were in France.[111] Svolos, as a scholar, was in contact with the French Institute in Athens.[112] In 1946, the Greeks hoped that the Labour Party could convince the Labour Government to stop persecution of the Greek left,[113] support Greek claims in foreign policy and help their policy of the 'Third Factor', which involved national reconciliation, amnesty and a Government including all parties. The prerequisite was an agreement between Britain and the USSR, since, employing a geographical language, Greece was both a Mediterranean and a Balkan country, lying on the fault line between the two hegemonies.[114]

The Third Civil War and the arrival of the Cold War forced the socialists to debate their role, especially after the Truman Doctrine. Tsirimokos rejected the idea of the Third Force, arguing that imperialism was the enemy and the USSR a positive example. Even if the socialists did not join the guerrilla, he justified it. Conversely, Svolos blamed the USSR for splitting the left and rejected unity of action as dangerous for socialism, which needed autonomy. However, he was disappointed by the failure of the Labour Party and the SFIO to act as the Third Force.[115]

At the Zurich Conference (June 1947), the SK-ELD condemned German atrocities and the anti-Sovietism of the SPD, but expressed satisfaction with Schumacher's commitment to denazification and nationalisation.[116] On the split of the PSLI, the Greeks shared the position with the PPS: when a communist party was bigger, socialist unity was required to achieve revolutionary goals and to keep the communists committed to democracy.[117] Tsirimokos was disappointed he could not bring the Greek question to the fore, saying that only communists spoke for Greece and they needed support against the fascist Government.[118] They did not want to embarrass the Labour Party, but the International Socialist Conference was useless if it only admitted new members and produced empty declarations.

In June 1947, the communist guerrillas announced the formation of an alternative Greek Government in the mountains. Tsirimokos gave some signs that he approved it, certainly he knew about it in advance and there is a conjecture that he had agreed to become prime minister for such Government.[119] A new wave of arrests hit the socialists hard,[120] but even worse was their political paralysis. Svolos condemned the communists as a tool of the Soviet ambition to have access to the Mediterranean. The left-wing of the SK-ELD and Tsirimokos talked about supporting the guerrillas and accepting the Soviet leadership in the world revolution. On the other side, the right-wing of the party, headed by Stratis, Grigorogiannis and Askutsis wanted to defend democracy and win autonomy from the communists. Throughout 1948 the SK-ELD was stuck waiting for developments, making no commitments to Government or guerrillas.[121] References to the Antwerp conference were made to justify appeals to national reconciliation[122] and to ask for help from the Western socialists,[123] making professions about hostility to communism and fascism, acceptance of the Marshall Plan and friendship with all powers. The ambiguity exasperated the right-wing, leading to the resignation of Stratis and many party cadres. Socialists from the Independent Socialist Group (ASO)—which had split from the SK-ELD in 1946—tried to influence the SFIO in Paris, while the leftist Archeo-Marxist Party and the independent Petsopulos appealed to Western socialists.[124]

A relatively minor issue came to dominate the attention of international socialism regarding Greece: the ban on the SK-ELD delegation travelling abroad. Far from being the harshest of persecutions, it directly involved international socialism and probably prevented the SK-ELD from being expelled like the other left-wing socialist parties. The Greek Government refused passports to the Greek delegation for the Antwerp Conference (28 November–1 December 1947). The conference voted a protest against 'an oppression incompatible with a democratic regime worthy of the name', despite resistance from some parties and demands for harsher terms from others.[125] 'The conference publishes a protest'—wrote Nenni – 'but it took two hours to decide the words to use so as not to upset Bevin and Marshal'.[126] Later, the PPS protested that the Greek socialists were kept out and the Germans allowed in.[127] Greece was among the rhetorical weapons of the Eastern socialists, as Healey witnessed in Hungary[128] and

Poland.[129] Even after their expulsion, the issue was embarrassing, so every condemnation of Cominform was balanced by a condemnation of Greece and Spain. There was a studied ambiguity in whether Greece was fascist or not, at least in the English version, while the French version equated Spain and Greece without reservation.[130] Throughout 1948, Comisco tried to have the passports issued to the Greek socialists, so that they could take part in Comisco meetings.[131] The Greek Government said that Svolos would receive his passport as soon he condemned the KKE, stating he had freedom to criticise the Government—within limits.[132] The SK-ELD answered that no foreigner would be fooled by these excuses and they understood that it was political blackmail.[133]

During this period, the Foreign Office pressured the Labour Party to cut ties with the SK-ELD, as the diplomats did not trust the Greek left, considered Svols too cautious and Tsirimokos a 'super-communist'.[134] They completely identified with the Populist and Liberal politicians and did not want to 'rock the boat', as the Greek press amplified any criticism from Britain, including the BBC.[135] 'This shows that there is not much real hope of separating the almost non-existent left non-Communist parties from KKE'.[136] The Foreign Office helped the Greek Government's strategy of isolating the socialists. In January 1948, Greek diplomats asked the Foreign Office to have Papandreou of the Social Democratic Party invited to the Socialist conference for the Marshall Plan. H.G. Gee, responsible for international affairs in the Ministry of Labour, explained that the Labour Party would not welcome this pressure—the same would be true if the TUC had been forced to invite the yellow Greek trade unions:

> I imagine that the conveners of the conference would be a little chary of switching over to a party not previously recognised as the appropriate one (e.g. for the main Antwerp conference), and would hope that the Greek Government might be prepared to let Svolos come if he is known to be generally in favour of the Marshall Plan.[137]

The British diplomats engaged in a bizarre matchmaking exercise to find a more respectable Greek party for the Labour Party to recognise. The Greek prime minister suggested Kanellopoulos and Yannios,[138] while the embassy in Athens collected information to demonstrate that Papandreou was socialist,[139] because of his programme of radical economic reforms. His party even had a socialist name![140] Gee—who as a trade unionist understood the logic of the socialists—pointed out that a few verbal commitments were not enough and the socialists would reject someone like Papandreou, close to the industrialists and the upper classes. The head of the department decided to back off from any commitment.

As expected, in February 1948 Comisco invited Svolos, who asked the Greek Prime Minister for permission to attend the Comisco meeting in March,[141] claiming he had no objections in principle to the Marshall Plan—although he had harsh words about that the month before.[142] Suspiciously, Svolos applied for vast sums of foreign currency, several thousand pounds, before his journey.[143] The American Embassy and the Greek Government wanted to reject authorisation, but, fearing a backlash from the American press, they asked the British Foreign Office to have the invitation withdrawn. McNeil was categorically opposed:

> There can be no question of the Labour Party withdrawing their invitations (which has anyway been accepted) as the object of inviting Greek Socialist Party representatives is to ascertain whether they will swallow the type of resolution to be proposed by the 'western-minded' Socialist parties and thus to place the onus on them of rejecting the anti-Soviet line.[144]

McNeil explained that the Labour Party did not want to unilaterally declare which parties were 'respectable' and it also invited Nenni to test him: a fellow-travelling party would not have subscribed to a pro-western resolution, forcing a showdown in front of the entire socialist movement:

> Thus, instead of arrogating to ourselves the right to decide on the orthodoxy of other movements we shall have achieved their condemnation united socialist opinion.[145]

Indeed, the manoeuvre worked with Nenni, and the Foreign Office wrote to the Greek Government that they had missed a chance—although the diplomats had not understood this either.[146] The Greek Government probably helped to keep the SK-ELD inside the International Socialist Conference.

After Morgan Phillips made another request for help in December 1948 and the Foreign Office rejected it,[147] the passport issue provoked rethinking within Comisco. Dutch socialist Vorrink said that the situation was embarrassing: either the Greek socialists were not democratic, therefore Comisco could not back them, or they were, and so the ban was an embarrassment for Comisco.[148] Considering the failure of the protests, the DNA proposed a mission to Greece to investigate the situation; the SFIO also wanted to check whether there were socialist parties with better credentials. Healey and Victor Larock were chosen to investigate Greek socialism.[149] The Greek press gave great publicity to this resolution.[150] The SK-ELD regretted that its isolation would lead to such suspicions, but they welcomed the exchange of views.[151]

The British Embassy in Athens was reassured that Healey knew he had to contact the Greek authorities. 'He is however anxious not to give Svolos any excuse for believing that he is being in any way influenced by the Greek Government'.[152]

> You will find Denis Healey extremely sympathetic and well-informed on the Greek issue and I am sure you will give him any help he needs. At the same time it is as well to realise that the purpose of his visit to Greece is formally to examine Svolos' Socialist Party and to determine whether its aims and programmes are suitable for the continued affiliation of his Party with the Socialist Parties of Western Europe.[153]

If he was satisfied with the Greek socialists, Healey would try to help them. Larock and Healey arrived in Greece on 28 January 1949.[154] Starting with the traditional literary comparison between Greece and Scotland,[155] their report absolved Great Britain: the elections of 1946 were fair and the Government committed fewer atrocities than the guerrillas. However, the weakness of Greek socialism was diagnosed, correctly, in the absence of ties with trade unions, since all trade unionists were communists, Government stooges or racketeers. Rehearsing a typical theme for Labour Party analysis of European socialism, the report said the inferiority complex of Greek socialists derived from them being bourgeois intellectuals who got their votes through local notables and patronage; only the KKE was a mass workers' party. The analysis did not mention the national character. Greek socialists were not communists but left-wing socialists—like Basso or Beneš—who wanted to be a bridge between Greek communists and the West. The report admitted Government persecution, deportation of leaders, censorship of the press and a ban on organising.

Prime Minister Tsaldaris hinted that the SK-ELD would be allowed to travel abroad if it showed as much anti-communism as Comisco. Healey and Larock met all the socialist groups in Athens and tried to mediate between the dominant coalition of SK-ELD, the dissenter group of Askoutsis and Stratis—the latter was particularly interesting, as one of the few good trade unionists—and the other socialist groups. They commented that the leaders of ASO, were intelligent intellectuals without much popular support, the PODN (the Pan-Hellenic organisation of democratic youth) a small student organisation, perhaps Trotskyite. Healey and Larock believed that a clarification of policy by the SK-ELD could lead to unification with ASO and PODN. Healey said to the British diplomats that the British labour attaché could have helped. Healey considered Papandreou a leader of outstanding ability and with an intellectual command of socialism, but to everyone his Greek Social Democratic Party was a right-to-centre party that had split from the liberals.

Healey and Larock convinced Svolos, despite protests from Tsirimokos, to accept anti-communism to reconcile with Askoutis and Stratis. Svolos delivered a declaration to Comisco binding the SK-ELD to democratic socialism, independence in thought and practice from communism and a Democratic Front with those opposing international capitalism and international communism.[156] The SK-ELD confirmed its support for a political solution to the civil war, the refusal to back a reactionary regime and its right to receive help from Comisco, particularly in pressuring Western Governments. The SK-ELD would divulge the declaration at a suitable time and in appropriate forms; since criticism to the Government was banned, they did not want a condemnation of communism to appear as support of the Government. However Stratis, Grigorogiannis and Askuts rejected this volte-face and, in alliance with Tsirimokos, presented a new text.[157] When the KKE removed suspected Titoists, announced urban insurrections and promised complete autonomy to Greek Macedonia in a Balkan federation—a Soviet ploy to separate Macedonia from Yugoslavia[158]— the socialists exploited the opportunity to say the communists had abandoned anti-fascism, peace and democracy to become a tool of the world communist movement.[159] This allowed a distinction between the progressive guerrilla movement and the Leninist leadership. The SK-ELD offered peace and planning as alternatives to communist dictatorship and capitalist oligarchy. They expected 'unstinted and active moral and political assistance from international socialism and from democratic public opinion throughout the world'.[160]

The Greek press and Government were not satisfied with the declaration and the British diplomats said it bore little resemblance to the binding declaration Svolos gave to Healey.[161] All the efforts of Comisco had produced almost nothing and Greek socialists were not willing to work together to suppress the fighting.[162] As McNeil said, 'It may suffice to get Svolos to Comisco: but it will also incite them to swipe at the Govt instead of getting on with the job in hand!'[163]

The Foreign Office unintentionally spotted the problem: the other parties would never view the SK-ELD as respectable.[164] Healey and Larock understood what British diplomats and the Greek politicians did not: if the Greek socialists had criticised the communists without at the same time criticising the Government, their supporters would have deserted them as having 'sold out'.[165] Respectability for the diplomats was an asset, for the socialists it was a burden. It is hardly surprising that it was the PvdA, with its obsession for respectability, that was the party most concerned with the image of SK-ELD. British diplomats identified with Populist and Liberal politicians: being 'respectable' meant being compromised with a regime that was guilty of many crimes. Indeed, Healey saw this as the biggest problem of socialists in Europe: when they did not have a majority, the socialists should have increased their popularity among the working-class outside Government, as only in opposition could they have offered a radical alternative to the bourgeois parties. The Alternative Strategy shaped his view of Greece: all European socialists had to fight on two fronts not to be squeezed between communists and reactionaries.[166] The Foreign Office considered the dissident guerrillas still communist,[167] while Healey supported a strategy of winning over the workers among the guerrillas:

> There is urgent need for a new policy aimed at disintegrating the rebel camp—a policy which distinguishes sharply between the rebel masses as victims of circumstance or propaganda, and the ruthless Cominform leadership which exploits their misery in the interests of Soviet strategy.[168]

The argument of the Foreign Office and Fleischer that the public declaration by the SK-ELD was different from the binding document delivered to Comisco is not completely correct, since the binding document was a list of points never meant for publication. The political substance was the same and Healey repeated the same arguments in his article in the *Tribune*. Anti-communism was hidden behind anti-Government rhetoric, but the party wanted anti-communist credentials without backing the Government. In this case, Labour's socialist anti-communism and the negative anti-communism of the Foreign Office did not coincide; Comisco still hoped for a socialist alternative in Greece.[169]

Healey was much bolder in his confidential document for Bevin, outlining a new radical policy of forceful intervention for Greece, which had the backing of the International Sub-Committee[170]:

> The only alternative to such a military dictatorship of the Right is a 'democratic dictatorship' of the Centre, i.e. of politicians who are not compromised by responsibility in recent Governments, who have democratic principles and some popular background, though in the 1946 'khaki' election they abstained or were swept away in the Populist landslide.[171]

Healey wanted a Third Force with SK-ELD and liberal leaders in Greece and abroad. The British Embassy could encourage this alliance by 'close friendly contacts' with the ostracised leaders of the Democratic Front, caught up in squabbles and personal ambitions. 'Constitutional scruples should have been abandoned', since doing nothing would have been a greater sin; it was necessary to elaborate a 'concrete programme' and establish a Democratic Front Government to implement it. As Greek leaders lacked the personal integrity or administrative capacity to enact social reforms, the western powers had to pressure them, provide detailed plans and supervise their enforcement. This would require diplomatic staff with technical and economic training. Ruthless communist leaders exploited misery for recruiting innocent guerrilla fighters, so eliminating misery was the only way to detach the latter from the former.

McNeil rejected the plan, saying Britain and the USA did not have unlimited powers and the people Healey wanted to lead Greece, like Svolos or Tsirimokos, were unfit; they failed to take their chance when the British Government offered it:

> They would not face up to the Communists and they did not even face up to the Right. They lack political experience certainly and I think they probably lack political fibre … All of this of course, Denis, is confidential. I regret that I am so negative but Oh! what a heartbreak Greece is.[172]

Healey did not meet Bevin.[173] The diplomats explained to him that it was not the time to rock the boat by including leftists in Government and anyway the Americans were in charge of aid, since Britain could not match their resources and experts. Healey wanted not simply social and economic reform but a long-term plan to eliminate corruption in the civil service.[174] At the time Healey attributed the endemic corruption to the economic situation and political domination of the Liberal and Populist parties, not to a natural attitude of ignoring laws, as Victor Feather did.

Comisco's intervention to Greece revealed the different strategy and culture of the socialist parties. Healey had doubts about the SK-ELD, but he admitted it was the only socialist movement with a following and some links to the trade unions. This disdain for intellectuals markedly differentiated the Labour Party from the Continental parties with an intellectual leadership—indeed, it was the reason for the low opinion the British held of them. The other parties knew it: 'when I [Healey] described [Svolos] in my report as an outstanding intellectual, Victor [Larock] asked me to strike out the phrase, on the grounds that it would prejudice the Labour Party against him'.[175] It reflected the strong links with working-class culture and the trade unions, but it also stemmed from the belief that abstruse reasoning made intellectuals unpredictable, quarrelsome and ready to betray—as MacDonald had. Healey considered the ASO to be made up of intelligent intellectuals, but without mass support.[176] The ASO had sounder anti-communist credentials than the SK-ELD, but its only possible use was to re-enter the SK-ELD to balance the left-wing tendencies—the role Healey assigned to Saragat in 1947. For the same reason, the SFIO, a party of civil servants and teacher, had nothing against ASO.

To the utter disgust of the Athens embassy and the Greek politicians, Morgan Phillips announced that the SK-ELD would keep its recognition from Comisco and the Labour Party.[177] Left liberal Tsouderos—whom the British diplomats considered a better match for the Labour Party—was disappointed because the blessing of Comisco prevented SK-ELD members defecting to his party and strengthened the hold of the dominant coalition. Indeed, the unification of SK-ELD and ASO did not take place because the former used its newfound legitimacy to increase its bargaining power. The leaders of ASO asked Comisco to remove Svolos and Tsirimokos[178] and to send a new mission to Greece, with the goal of forming a strong party backed by the Labour Party in the space between the Populists backed by the Americans and the communists backed by the Russians. However, this request had little weight since the readmission of the SK-ELD had been secured.

The SK-ELD attended the Baarn Conference (14–16 May 1949), where its status as a member was confirmed. Tsirimokos thanked the conference for their help and the resolution 'which would be valuable to his party in its domestic policy'.[179] The Conference also condemned the Greek civil war, blaming the Cominform but also blaming the reactionary regime, to a lesser degree, for the conditions of misery and violence that the communists exploited. Then the conference approved the Democratic Front led by the socialists including enemies of financial oligarchy and communist subversion. The Foreign Office was disconcerted by the resolution,[180] but Healey phoned to explain that the SK-ELD wanted to condemn the Greek Government and the communists in equal measure, but the conference approved the original resolution when Healey said that a party of Government like the Labour Party could not condemn as reactionary a Government to which its Government was bound. Healey wanted the Labour Party to be distinct from the Labour Government, but within limits.

While the status of the SK-ELD was assured, Comisco did not cease its involvement. Periodically, Western socialists and Comisco had to appeal to the Greek Prime Minister to liberate socialist political prisoners; often the same person liberated thanks to an appeal was put back in prison some months after.[181] This continued well into 1951.

In 1950, Svolos was optimistic about democratic socialism in Greece, also thanks to the assistance and money Comisco had provided.[182] Comisco kept Greek socialists out of jail as often as it could and it gave them some perspective. A more effective intervention would have required financial leverage. The Greek situation was especially desperate, not surprisingly given the poverty of the country and the persecution of the movement. The affiliation fee for the SK-ELD was not set until 1950; in 1951, it stood at £30, with the addition of £9 for the refugee fund.[183] Given a budget of £5699, 7 s., 4 p and a £1263 refugee fund in 1951, the Greek contribution was close to that of exile parties like the Bund or parties of very small territories, like Trieste and Luxembourg.

Even more revealing was the continuous request for financial help. A first appeal was made in 1947[184] and it was repeated in 1950.[185] The SFIO and SPÖ lent money for the 1950 elections, for which the Greeks were very grateful.[186] In June 1950, Comisco planned an extraordinary donation of £2000 to help the SK-ELD consolidate the foothold it had won in the 1950 election.[187] This would have been a substantial contribution, as the total budget of Comisco was just £4350. The secretary drafted a plan to share the burden among the richer parties.[188] The Germans, Norwegians, Danes and Swedes were willing to give if the other parties did the same, but France, Great Britain, Luxembourg, the Netherlands and Switzerland were not.[189]

After the 1950 general election and the 1951 local elections drained the finances of the SK-ELD, the party had to run two other electoral campaigns in 1951 and 1952 without any money—the other parties did not answer to their request for help[190]—which ended in abysmal results. Poverty and a new electoral law resulted in the disappearance of socialists from the Greek parliament.[191] The socialists joined some democrats in a new party, which accepted the principles of the Frankfurt Declaration, but was not affiliated to the Socialist International. Despite all the efforts, there was no Greek representative in the Socialist International:

> You will easily understand with what sorrow our militants felt—temporarily, we hope—remote from the Socialist International to whom, moreover, we all feel deeply grateful for the warm support it has assured us in very difficult moments.[192]

Like in Italy, resentment towards British foreign policy was a major obstacle. Greek communists appealed to nationalism against British imperialism. The standard slur against the SK-ELD was that it was 'a nest of Intelligencet Service agents', aimed particularly at Tsirimokos.[193] In April 1949, Tsirimokos announced that 'the pertinent English experiment is our ideal',[194] but he actually regretted the identification of democratic socialism with Great Britain:

> What are our hopes for the future? 'Unfortunately', it is England. […] And that is the tragedy—in particular for a Greek Socialist, who has so much to impute to the Labour Party's foreign policy—that the continental Socialism produces very nice ideas and nice words but that, as things are, the Labour [Party] represents the hope—under two preconditions: a) that it will win the election of 1950, b) that, immediately after the election, its foreign policy will be adjusted to the Socialist character of its interior policy.[195]

The SPD had the same problem. Christian Democrats regularly accused the German social democrats of being the British fifth column, with Adenauer claiming they were 'lackeys' of the British King.[196] The issue was the British Government's plans for industries of the Ruhr—meaning the SPD was accused not just of betraying its nation, but also its working-class constituency to a foreign power.

Comisco failed to help SK-ELD and, unlike in Italy, long-term personal relations were not created. Tsirimokos became an opportunist who helped weaken Greek democracy before the 1967 coup. The Foreign Office was right: it was Georgios Papandreou who offered the democratic alternative to the right in 1963 and, after the dictatorship, his son Andreas formed the Pasok, the most successful socialist party in Greek history. At the beginning, the Pasok tried to emphasise neutralism and a Third Way between communism and capitalism, refusing to join the Socialist International dominated by the pro-American SPD, despite the Greeks' model being Sweden. However, deradicalisation soon followed and in 1990 the Pasok joined the Socialist International.[197] The value of the Socialist International in Greece was to offer a reference to right-wing socialists and affiliation was a symbolic step to breaking with the revolutionary past.

There is no doubt that the International Department was used to project British influence abroad and also to defend its foreign policy at home. However, the Labour Party was not a tool of the Foreign Office and Comisco was not the British Cominform serving the interests of British imperialism. The cases analysed show that cooperation did not exclude independence of opinion and action. We have seen fruitful cooperation in Austria and Poland, but the diplomats never convinced Healey to support the respectable Papandreou or Saragat. The attempts of the diplomats to have the Labour Party start a partnership with non-socialist parties were not successful in Czechoslovakia or Poland and later attempts in Italy failed as well.[198] The frustration of career diplomats with Healey points to a complex relationship. Talks of 'the little Foreign Office of Transport House'[199] indicated the involvement of the Labour Party in the foreign policy of the Government, but also its independence from the official Foreign Office. The ambiguity and tension between the Labour Party and the Labour Government was never resolved.

Notes

1. D. Healey (1990) *The Time of My Life* (London: Penguin), 76.
2. F. Weber (1986) *Der kalte Krieg in der SPÖ: Koalitionswächter, Pragmatiker und revolutionäre Sozialisten, 1945–1950* (Wien: Verlag für Gesellschaftskritik), 28–35; 40–45.
3. K.L. Shell (1962) *The Transformation of Austrian Socialism* (New York: State University of New York), 120–122.
4. E. Scharf, Aussprache über Zeitprobleme, *Zukunft*, April 1947.
5. E. Scharf, Aussprache über Zeitprobleme, *Zukunft*, April 1947.

6. K. Czernetz, Die österreichischen Sozialisten und Sowjetrussland, *Zukunft*, June 1946.
7. Memorandum by the SPÖ, n.d [delivered on 3 February], The National Archives, Kew (TNA), FO 371/55282-C4431.
8. J. Hynd to E. Bevin, 19 April 1946; Bevin, Minute, TNA, FO 371/55282-C4654.
9. Weber, *Der kalte Krieg in die SPÖ*, 35–39.
10. W.H.B. Mack (Political adviser in Vienna) to O. Harvey, 17 April 1946, TNA, FO 371/55282-C4374.
11. W.H.B. Mack to Bevin, 18 October 1946, TNA, FO 371/55282-C12869.
12. Weber, *Der kalte Krieg in die SPÖ*, 38.
13. A. De Gasperi to P. Nenni, 22 October 1945, Fondazione Pietro Nenni (FPN), Fondo Pietro Nenni, b.23, f.1280.
14. N. Carandini to ministro, 15 October 1946, Archivio Centrale dello Stato, Roma (ACS), Fondo Nicolò Carandini (NC), b.2.
15. O. Pollak to W. Wodak, 13 January 1946; Wodak to K. Renner, 31 October 1945; Renner to Wodak, 9 November 1945, W. Wodak (1980) *Diplomatie zwischen Parteiproporz und Weltpolitik: Briefe, Dokumente und Memoranden aus dem Nachlass Walter Wodaks 1945–1950* (Salzburg: Neugebauer), 37–38; 181; 186–187.
16. A. Schärf (1955) *Österreichs Erneuerung: 1945–1955: das erste Jahrzehnt der Zweiten Republik*, (Wien: Verlag der Wiener Volksbuchhandlung), 102.
17. Wodak to A. Schärf, 10 January 1946, Wodak, *Diplomatie zwischen Parteiproporz und Weltpolitik*, 35–36.
18. Hynd to Bevin, 19 April 1946, TNA, FO 371/55282-C4654. F. Scheu (1969) *The Early Days of the Anglo-Austrian Society* (London: Anglo-Austrian Society).
19. R. Luzzatto to Nenni, 20 April 1964, FPN, Fondo Pietro Nenni, b.31, f.1535. Carlyle, Minute, 16 February 1946, TNA, FO 371/55117-C969.
20. Ivor Thomas wrote the preface for Luzzatto's book, R. Luzzatto (1946) *Unknown War in Italy* (London: New Europe Publishing).
21. P. Sebastiani (1983) *Laburisti inglesi e socialisti italiani: dalla ricostituzione del Psi(up) alla scissione di Palazzo Barberini* (Roma: Elengraf), 48–49; 90–91; 100.
22. Nenni to Bevin, 5 September 1945; Nenni to Bevin, 24 October [1945], FPN, Fondo Pietro Nenni, b.19, f.1118. Entry, 16 October 1945, P. Nenni (1982) *Diari*, Vol.1, *Tempo di Guerra Fredda: diari 1943–1956*, (Milano: SugarCo), 150–151. Also, Ross to Bevin, 20 December 1945, TNA, FO 371/50033-ZM6262.
23. Carandini to De Gasperi, 8 September 1945, ACS, NC, b.2.

24. Carandini to De Gasperi, 7, 16, 19 Januart 1946, *I documenti diplomatici italiani*, Decima Seria: 1943–1948, Vol.3, 94; 131–131; 146–149. Entry, 18–23 gennaio 1946, Nenni, *Tempo di Guerra fredda*, 173–177.
25. Hood, Minute, 6 February 1946, TNA, FO 371/57218-U1726.
26. Wodak to Schärf, 2 January 1946; Wodak to Laski, 29 January 1946, Wodak, *Diplomatie zwischen Parteiproporz und Weltpolitik*, 26–27; 62–63.
27. W. Wodak, 'Problems for discussion between British and Austrian Labour Representatives', Wodak, *Diplomatie zwischen Parteiproporz und Weltpolitik*, 64. Memorandum by the SPÖ, n.d [delivered on 3 February], TNA, FO 371/55282-C4431. Vienna to Foreign Office, 2 April 1946, TNA, FO 371/55282-C3713.
28. BBC Monitoring, 13 April 1946, TNA, FO 371/55282-C4294.
29. 'Vermerk über die Unterredung zwischen Außenminister Bevin und Vizekanzler Schärf ohne Datum, wahrscheinlich 8 April 1946', Wodak, *Diplomatie zwischen Parteiproporz und Weltpolitik*, 105. Mack to Harvey, 17 April 1946, TNA, FO 371/55282-C4374.
30. Schärf to Wodak, 31 May 1946, Wodak, *Diplomatie zwischen Parteiproporz und Weltpolitik*, 158–159.
31. Wodak to Schärf, 15 February 1946; Wodak to Schärf, 23 February 1946; Wodak to Schärf, 2 March 1946, Wodak, *Diplomatie zwischen Parteiproporz und Weltpolitik*, 82–85.
32. R. Steininger (1987) *Los von Rom?: die Südtirolfrage 1945/1946 und das Gruber-De Gasperi-Abkommen*, (Innsbruck: Haymon), 221.
33. Wodak to Schärf, 1 May 1946, Wodak, *Diplomatie zwischen Parteiproporz und Weltpolitik*, 124–128.
34. K. Gruber to L. Figl, 29 August 1946; Sitzung des österreichischen Ministerrates, 17 September 1946, quoted in Steininger, *Los von Rom*, 305–306; 329.
35. Carandini to De Gasperi, 8 September 1945 in *I documenti diplomatici italiani*, Decima Seria: 1943–1948, Vol.2, 697–701.
36. Carandini to R. Prunas, 25 settembre 1946, ACS, NC, b.2.
37. Entry, 15 May 1946, B. Pimlott (ed.) (1986) *The Political Diary of Hugh Dalton: 1918–40, 1945–60* (London: Cape), 372.
38. G.M. Jennings to Cullis, 1 July 1946, TNA, FO 371/55123-C7470.
39. O. Sargent to Bevin, 2 July 1946, TNA, FO 371/55123-C7335.
40. 'International Socialist Conference at Clacton May 17th–20th 1946', Labour History Archive and Study Centre, People's History Museum, Manchester (LHASC), Labour Party (LP), International Department (ID), Denis Healey's Papers (DH), 03, 10.
41. Gruber to Bevin, 8 September 1945, TNA, FO 371/46606-C5490. Acabrit, Vienna to War Office, 9 September 1945, TNA, FO 371/46606-C5705.

42. L. Steurer (1998) 'L'Alto Adige tra autodecisione e autonomia (1945–1946)' in A. Del Boca (ed.) *Confini contesi: la Repubblica italiana e il Trattato di pace di Parigi, 10 febbraio 1947* (Torino: Edizioni Gruppo Abele), 142–145.
43. Luzzatto, *Unknown War in Italy*, 127–128.
44. Hansard, HC Deb 25 July 1946 vol 426 cc282–335.
45. Wodak to Schärf, 17 June 1946; Wodak to Jennie Lee, 3 July 1946, Wodak, *Diplomatie zwischen Parteiproporz und Weltpolitik*, 168–169; 182–183.
46. Wodak to B. Pitterman, 22 May 1946, Wodak, *Diplomatie zwischen Parteiproporz und Weltpolitik*, 153.
47. Memorandum, 22 February 1947, ACS, NC, b.3.
48. A. Bullock (1983) *Ernest Bevin: Foreign Secretary: 1945–1951* (London: Heinenmann), 287.
49. Steurer, 'L'Alto Adige tra autodecisione e autonomia', 119–131.
50. Casardi to De Gasperi, 26 November 1945, *I documenti diplomatici italiani*, Decima Seria: 1943–1948, Vol.2, 1012–1013.
51. Vienna to Foreign Office, 8 December 1945, TNA, FO 371/46606-C9309. Vienna to Foreign Office, 3 February 1946, TNA, FO 371/55117-C1346.
52. Rome to Foreign Office, 25 January 1946; Cullis, Minute 28 January 1946, TNA, FO 371/55117-C969.
53. Deutsch to Wodak, 14 May 1946; 25 June 1946, Wodak, *Diplomatie zwischen Parteiproporz und Weltpolitik* 143; 176. Schärf, *Österreichs Erneuerung*, 137.
54. 'Austro-Italian socialist conference in Innsbruck', 30 October 1947, CIA-RDP82-00457R001000400007-3, Central Intelligence Agency, Freedom of Information Act, Electronic Reading Room, https://www.cia.gov/library/readingroom/document/cia-rdp82-00457r001000400007-3 (accessed 30 December 2017).
55. J. Lee (1981) *My Life with Nye* (Harmondsworth: Penguin books), 168–175.
56. Mack to Harvey, 17 April 1946, TNA, FO 371/55282-C4374.
57. Carandini to De Gasperi, 19 January 1946, ACS, NC, b.2.
58. K. Klotzbach (1982) *Der Weg zur Staatspartei: Programmatik, praktische Politik und Organisation der deutschen Sozialdemokratie 1945 bis 1965* (Berlin: Dietz), 78–81.
59. K. Schumacher, Brief an einen genossen in Schweden, *Sozialistische Mitteilungen*, November–December 1946. Die Internationale Sozialistenkonferenz in Bournemouth (8–10. November 1946), *Sozialistische Mitteilungen*, November–December 1946.

60. Quoted in R. Steininger (1979) 'British Labour, Deutschland und die SPD 1945/46', *Internationale wissenschaftliche Korrespondenz zur Geschichte der deutschen Arbeiterbewegung*, 15, 207.
61. Steininger, 'British Labour, Deutschland und die SPD 1945/46', 216–221.
62. 'Proceedings of International Socialist Conference, Bournemouth, 10 Nov. 1946—Discussion on Germany', International Institute of Social History (IISH), Socialist International (SI), 234. Steininger, *Deutschland und die Sozialistische Internationale nach dem Zweiten Weltkrieg*, 52.
63. T.C. Imlay (2014) '"The Policy of Social Democracy is Self-Consciously Internationalist": The German Social Democratic Party's Internationalism after 1945', *The Journal of Modern History*, 86, 1, 86–97. M. Drögemöller (2008) *Zwei Schwestern in Europa, Deutsche und niederländische Sozialdemokratie 1945–1990* (Berlim: Vorwärts Buch), 43–69. K. Misgeld. (1984) *Sozialdemokratie und Aussenpolitik in Schweden: Sozialistische Internationale, Europapolitik und die Deutschlandfrage 1945–1955* (Frankfurt: Campus Verlag), 55–93.
64. 'Proceedings of International Socialist Conference, Bournemouth, 10 Nov. 1946—Discussion on Germany', IISH, SI, 234.
65. R.B. Kirby to Healey, 28 November 1946, LHASC, LP, DH, 4, 14.
66. Schumacher to Healey, 7 April 1947; Healey to Schumacher, 23 April 1947, IISH, SI, 235.
67. Stenogramme, 7 Juin, IISH, SI, 235.
68. Entry, 9 June 1947, Nenni, *Tempo di Guerra Fredda*, 167.
69. Stenogramme, 8 Juin; 'Extract from the proceedings of the International Socialist Conference, Zurich, 6–9 June, 1947', IISH, SI, 235.
70. 'Conference Socialiste International—Zurich, 6/9 juin 1947—Seance du dimanche 8 juin 1947 (après-midi)', IISH, SI, 235.
71. Klotzbach, *Der Weg zur Staatspartei*, 54–61.
72. Drögemöller, *Zwei Schwestern in Europa*, 66–67.
73. S. Shafir (1985) 'Julius Braunthal and his Postwar Mediation Efforts between German and Israeli Socialists', *Jewish Social Studies*, 47, 3–4, 267–280.
74. D. Healey, 'Notes on the minutes of the Zurich conference', LHASC, LP, International Sub-Committee, Minutes and Documents, 1947.
75. Steininger, *Deutschland und die Sozialistische Internationale nach dem Zweiten Weltkrieg*, 83–89. PPS Executive Committee to L. De Brouckère, 30 October 1947, LPHASC, LP, DH, 9, 5.
76. Circular 88, 'Summary of proceedings, International Socialist Conference, Antwerp 28 November–2 December, 1947', IISH, SI, 47.
77. Stenogramme, 7–8 Juin, IISH, SI, 235.
78. 'Raport de la commission d'enquete envoyee par la conference de Zurich', IISH, SI, 236.

79. Circular 88, 'Summary of proceedings, International Socialist Conference, Antwerp 28 November–2 December, 1947', IISH, SI, 47.
80. Healey to A. Bottomley, 12 March 1947, IISH, SI, 235.
81. Circular 88, 'Summary of proceedings, International Socialist Conference, Antwerp 28 November–2 December, 1947', IISH, SI, 47.
82. Steininger, *Deutschland und die Sozialistische Internationale nach dem Zweiten Weltkrieg*. 98–165. Imlay, "The Policy of Social Democracy is Self-Consciously Internationalist", 81–123.
83. M. Van Der Goes van Naters (1980) *Met en tegen de tijd* (Amsterdam: Arbeiderspers), 195–208.
84. G. Devin (1993), *L'Internationale socialiste: histoire et sociologie du socialisme internationale: 1945–1990* (Paris: Presses de la Fondation national des sciences politiques), 289–300.
85. Healey, *The Time of my Life*, 76.
86. V. Goldsworthy (1998) *Inventing Ruritania: The Imperialism of the Imagination* (New Haven: Yale University Press), 42–43; 202–212. J. Black (2003) 'The Mediterranean as a Battleground of the European Powers: 1700–1900' in D. Abulafia (ed.), *The Mediterranean in History* (London: Thames & Hudson), 281.
87. H. Vlavianos (1992) *Greece, 1941–49: From Resistance to Civil War: The Strategy of the Greek Communist Party* (London: Macmillan), 248. T.D. Sfikas (1994) *The British Labour Government and the Greek Civil War, 1945–1949: The Imperialism of 'Non-Intervention'* (Keele: Ryburn Pub), 71–72.
88. Sargent to Leeper, 9 November 1945 quoted in Sfikas, *The British Labour Government and the Greek Civil War*, 62.
89. A. Thorpe (2006) '"In a Rather Emotional State"? The Labour Party and British Intervention in Greece, 1944–5', *English Historical Review*, 121, 493, 1075–1105.
90. Labour Party Annual Conference Report (LPACR) 1945, 114.
91. H. Richter (1985) *British Intervention in Greece: From Varkiza to Civil War, February 1945 to August 1946* (London: Merlin press), 187–190; 387–395.
92. Sfikas, *The British Labour Government and the Greek Civil War*, 79.
93. Sfikas, *The British Labour Government and the Greek Civil War*, 80.
94. H. Laski to Healey, 15 May 1947, LHASC, LP, ID, DH, 07, 07.
95. V. Feather, 'It happens in Greece', [December 1945], LHASC, LP, ID, DH, 03, 01.
96. N. Dodds, L. Solley, S. Tiffany (1946) *Tragedy in Greece: An Eye-Witness Report* (London: Progress Pub. Co). On Solley see D. Lilleker (2004) *Against the Cold War: The History and Political Traditions of Pro-Sovietism in the British Labour Party* (London: Tauris), 85–98.

97. Sfikas, *The British Labour Government and the Greek Civil War*, 117–122; 125–132. Twickenham Trades Council to Laski, 12 June 1946, LHASC, LP, ID, DH, 03, 01.
98. J. Saville (1993) *The Politics of Continuity: British Foreign Policy and the Labour Government, 1945–46* (London: Verso), 112–148.
99. Sfikas, *The British Labour Government and the Greek Civil War*, 130.
100. G.W. Vaughan (Sheffield Trades & Labour Council) to M. Phillips, 13 March 1947; W. Beck (Consett DLP) to M. Phillips, 19 July 1947, LHASC, LP, ID, DH, 07, 09.
101. T.E. Nixon (Morecambe Party) to the Secretary of the Labour Party, 15 November 1947, LHASC, LP, ID, DH, 07, 07.
102. F.J.C. Mennel to Braithwaite, 7 November 1947; Mennel to T.E. Nixon, 22 November 1947, LHASC, LP, ID, DH, 07, 07.
103. M. Shufeldt, Chelsea DLP in LPACR 1947, 163.
104. Labour Party (1947) *Cards on the Table* (London: Labour Party), 13.
105. Thorpe, 'In a Rather Emotional State', 1096–1102.
106. P. Weiler (1988) *British Labour and the Cold War* (Stanford: Stanford University Press), 135–164.
107. R.A. Howson to Lord Rusholme, 5 March 1946, LHASC, LP, ID, DH, 03, 01.
108. Richter, *British Intervention in Greece*, 22.
109. H. Fleischer (1987) 'The "Third Factor": The Struggle for an Independent Socialist Policy During the Greek Civil War', in L. Baerentzen, J.O. Iatrides, O.L. Smith (eds), *Studies in the History of the Greek Civil War 1945–1949* (Copenhagen: Museum Tusculanum), 189–197. Vlavianos, *Greece, 1941–49*, 39–54; 86–96.
110. Minute, 9 May 1946, TNA, FO 371/59570-R6618.
111. R. Verdier to Healey, 18 April 1946, LHASC, LP, ID, DH, 03, 01.
112. N. Manitakis (2004) 'Struggling from Abroad: Greek Communist Activities in France during the Greek Civil War', in P. Carabott and T.D. Sfikas (eds), *The Greek Civil War: Essays on a Conflict of Exceptionalism* (Aldershot: Ashgate), 102–105.
113. Examples of appeals to end persecution: SK-ELD to Labour Party, 12 June 1946; D. Paparigas to Labour Party conference, 11 June 1946; A. Svolos to Labour Party, 30 July 1946, LHASC, LP, ID, DH, 03, 01.
114. G. Georgalas to M. Phillips, 4 June 1946; Laski to Svolos, 12 June 1946; I. Tsirimokos, Svolos to NEC, 4 July 1946; Tsirimokos to Healey, 8 July 1946; Svolos to Labour Party, 30 July 1946; 'Resolution of the Central Committee of December 6, 1946', LHASC, LP, ID, DH, 03, 01.
115. 'View of the Socialist Party ELD on the Greek question. On the occasion of President Truman's message', 15 March 1947, LHASC, LP, ID, GRE, 01. Fleischer, 'The "Third Factor"', 197–210.

116. 'Conference socialiste international: Zurich, 6/9 Juin 1947—Cinquième séance: Dimanche 8 Juin à 9 heurs', IISH, SI, 235.
117. 'Conference socialiste international: Zurich, 6/9 Juin 1947—Quatrième séance: Samedi 7 Juin à 20 heurs 30', IISH, SI, 235. 'International Socialist Conference, Kongress Haus, Zurich, 6–9 June 1947—Italian Commission 7 June, 14.15. Hrs', IISH, SI, 47.
118. 'Conference socialiste international: Zurich, 6/9 Juin 1947—Première séance: Vendredi 6 Juin à 18 heurs', IISH, SI, 235.
119. Foreign Office to Moscow, 2 January 1948, TNA, FO 371/72236-R325.
120. Svolos spoke of the arrest of 15,000 people and 300 active party members he requested attention, solidarity and material help. Healey's response was no-committal (Svolos to Labour Party, 21 July 1947; Healey to Svolos, 1 August 1947, LHASC, LP, ID, DH, 07, 08).
121. Athens to Foreign Office, 6 January 1948, TNA, FO 371/72237-R270.
122. '[The Conference] formally condemns all intervention by foreign states in the affairs of Greece and considers that only a truly democratic Government free from outside pressure can restore peace and freedom in that country' ('Minutes of the International Socialist Conference, Antwep 28 November–2 December 1947—Resolution on Peace and Economic Reconstruction', IISH, SI, 47).
123. Svolos, Tsirimokos to Labour Party, 20 January 1948, LHASC, LP, ID, GRE, 01.
124. Fleischer, 'The "Third Factor"', 203–210.
125. 'Sumary of Proceedings—International Socialist Conference Antwerp 28 November–2 December 1947', IISH, SI, 47.
126. Entry, 29 November 1947, Nenni, *Tempo di Guerra Fredda*, 401.
127. Circular 80, Report of the First Meeting of COMISCO, 10 January 1948, IISH, SI, 47.
128. 'Report on Hungary by Denis Healey', February 1947, LHASC, LP, International Sub-Committee, Minutes and Documents, 1947.
129. D. Healey, 'Report on the 27th Congress of the Polish Socialist Party in Wroclaw, December 14–16, 1947', LHASC, LP, International Sub-Committee, Minutes and Documents, 1947.
130. The differences between the French, English and German versions of the resolutions were to become a recurring feature of the Socialist International, so as to make each resolution less embarrassing and more useful for every party. (Devin, *L'Internationale socialiste*, 338–342).
131. Svolos to Labour Party, 18 January 1948, LHASC, LP, ID, GRE, 01. Circular 117, 'Report by M.C.Bolle (Holland) on Activities since the Vienna Meeting of Comisco (3 June 1948)'; Circular 121, Report on Fourth Comisco meeting, 3 December 1948, IISH, SI, 47.

132. Athens to Foreign Office, 24 March 1948, TNA, FO 371/72320-R3864.
133. Published in the 'Vimaì of 28th March, 1948', TNA, FO 371/72320-R4546.
134. Athens to Foreign Office, 1 January 1948, TNA, FO 371/72237-R94. E.H. Peck, 7 January 1948, TNA, FO 371/72237-R270.
135. C. Norton to G.A. Wallinger, 7 January 1948, TNA, FO 371/72238-R953.
136. Peck, Minute, 5 January 1948, TNA, FO 371/72237-R94.
137. H.G. Gee, Minute, 14 January 1948, TNA, FO 371/72320-R795.
138. Athens to Foreign Office, 22 January 1948, TNA, FO 371/72320-R998.
139. Balfour, Minute, 30 January 1948, TNA, FO 371/72320-R998.
140. Athens to Foreign Office, 28 January 1948; Balfour, Minute, 29 January 1948; Wallinger, Minute, 29 January 1948; Gee, Minute, 3 February 1948, TNA, FO 371/72320-R1257.
141. M. Phillisps to Svolos, 4 February 1948; Svolos to the Prime Minister, the Minister for Foreign Affairs, 15 February 1948, TNA, FO 371/72320-R3759.
142. Minute, 15 January 1948, TNA, FO 371/72320-R795.
143. Athens to Foreign Office, 16 March 1948, TNA, FO 371/72320-R3487.
144. Peck, Minute, 17 March 1948, TNA, FO 371/72320-R3487.
145. F.A. Warner, Minute, 17 March 1948, TNA, FO 371/72320-R3487.
146. Foreign Office to Athens, 20 March 1948, TNA, FO 371/72320-R3487. G. Faravelli to Gelo, 20 March 1948, in P.C. Masini and S. Merli (eds) (1990) *Il socialismo al bivio: l'archivio di Giuseppe Faravelli, 1945–1950* (Milano: Fondazione Giangiacomo Feltrinelli), 296–297.
147. M. Phillips to Bevin, 5 November 1948; C. Mayhew to M. Phillips, 11 November 1948, TNA, FO 371/72320-R12874.
148. Circular 121, Report on Fourth Comisco meeting, 3 December 1948, IISH, SI, 47.
149. 'Minutes of the meetings of the Comisco Sub-committee January 6, 1949', LHASC, LP, International Sub-Committee, Minutes and Documents, 1949.
150. Athens to Foreign Office, 7 December 1948, TNA, FO 371/72320-R13774.
151. Svolos to M. Phillips, 14 December 1948, LHASC, LP, ID, GRE, 01.
152. Peck to J. Tahourdin, 21 January 1949, TNA, FO 371/78452-R516.
153. Peck to Tahourdin, 17 January 1949, TNA, FO 371/78452-R516.
154. Circular 8/49, D. Healey and V. Larock, 'Socialism in Greece', IISH, SI, 48. The ambassador reported on the visit, but was not present at the talks

(Norton to Bevin, 9 February 1949, TNA, FO 371/78403-R1612). Healey published an account in D. Healey, Mediterranean impressions-2, *Tribune*, 18 February 1949.
155. Goldsworthy, *Inventing Ruritania*, 18–20.
156. Circular 8/49, 'Declaration to Comisco by the plenum of the Central Committee of ELD, the Greek Socialist Party. 31st Jan. 1949', IISH, SI, 48.
157. Fleischer, 'The "Third Factor"', 210.
158. P.J. Stavrakis (1989) *Moscow and Greek Communism, 1944–1949* (Ithaca: Cornell University Press), 180.
159. 'ELD Resolution on the Change in KKE Policy', TNA, FO 371/78403-R1913. Circular 15/49, International Socialist Conference Newsletter, March 1949, IISH, SI, 2.
160. 'ELD Resolution on the Change in KKE Policy', TNA, FO 371/78403-R1913. However, the SK-ELD denied that the declaration was the result of pressure from Comisco (Athens to Southern Department, 23 February 1949, TNA, FO 371/78403-R2236).
161. Athens to Southern Department, 16 February 1949; Peck, Minute, 19 February 1949, TNA, FO 371/78403-R1913.
162. Wallinger, Minute, 15 February 1949, TNA, FO 371/78403-R2071.
163. McNeil, Minute, n.d. [16 February 1949], TNA, FO 371/78403-R2072.
164. Athens to Southern Department, 16 February 1949, TNA, FO 371/78403-R1913.
165. Circular 8/49, D. Healey and V. Larock, 'Socialism in Greece', IISH, SI, 48.
166. D. Healey, Mediterranean impressions-1, *Tribune*, 11 February 1949.
167. Peck, Minute, 15 February 1949, TNA, FO 371/78403-R2071.
168. D. Healey, Mediterranean impressions-2, *Tribune* 18 February 1949.
169. Comisco approved the results of the mission of Healey and Larock (Circular 9/49, 7 March 1949, IISH, SI, 48).
170. Minutes of the International Sub-Committee, 15 February 1949, LHASC, LP, ID, DH, 12.
171. 'The General Problem of Greece Today', TNA, FO 371/78403-R2071. Healey later added a more detailed plan for economic intervention (D. Healey, 'Memorandum on the Greek situation', TNA, FO 371/78452-R3463).
172. McNeil to Healey, 14 February 1949, TNA, FO 371/78403-R2071.
173. Healey to Bevin, 8 March 1949, TNA, FO 371/78452-R3463.
174. Wallinger, 'Note for the talk with labour Party delegation on Greece', 16 March 1949; Peck, 'Labour Party delegation to Greece', 22 March 1949, TNA, FO 371/78452-R3464.

175. Healey, *The Time of my life*, 92.
176. D. Healey, Mediterranean impressions-2, *Tribune*, 18 February 1949.
177. Tahourdin to Peck, 23 March 1949, TNA, FO 371/78403-R3365.
178. 'Summary of activities (18–28 January inclusive)', IISH, SI, 57.
179. Circular 34/49, 'International Socialist Conference, Baarn, Holland, 14–16 May 1949—Summarised Report of Proceedings', IISH, SI, 48.
180. Peck, "Comisco resolution on Greece", 17 May 1947, TNA, FO 371/78403-R5165.
181. 'Issued by the International Socialist Conference Committee Office on 7 January 1950'; 'Issued by the International Socialist Conference Committee Offices on 3 April 1950'; 'Report of activities 21 June—30 September 1950', IISH, SI, 57. Circular 179/50, 18 September 1950, IISH, SI, 55. Circular 55/51, Report on Comisco Meeting, 2–4 March 1951, IISH, SI, 59.
182. Circular 74/50, 'The meeting of the committee of the International Socialist Conference at Hastings, 18–19 March, 1950', IISH, SI, 52.
183. Circular 94/50, IISH, SI, 52. Circular 17/51, 'Annual Report of the Activities of the International Socialist Conference, 1 January–31 December 1950', 12 February 1951, IISH, SI, 58.
184. 'Rapport de la president Isabelle Blume de la Commission sur entr'aide', Novembre 1947, IISH, SI, 47.
185. Circular 18/50, Svolos and Tsirimokos to Comisco, 23 January 1950, IISH, SI, 50.
186. 'Letters received 1 February–6 March 1950', IISH, SI, 57.
187. Circular 139/50, 'Loan or grant to Greek Socialist Party ELD', 20 June 1950, IISH, SI, 53.
188. 'Minutes of the meeting of the International Socialist Conference Sub-Committee, 28 June 1950'; 'Loan or grant to Greek Socialist Party ELD', 26 September 1950, IISH, SI, 57.
189. Circular 186/50, Report of activities of Comisco, from June to September 1950, 30 September 1950, IISH, SI, 55. 'Minutes of the meeting of the International Socialist Conference Sub-Committee, 20 October 1950'; 'Report of activities and correspondence 7 November–11 December 1950', IISH, SI, 57.
190. Circular 102/51, 13 September 1951, IISH, SI, 61.
191. Circular B. 18/53, 'Report on activities, 15 April–30 June 1953', IISH, SI, 73.
192. Circular B. 28/53, 'The crisis in Greek socialism—Memorandum submitted by A.J. Svolos', 12 November 1953, IISH, SI, 73.
193. D.H. Close (1995) *The Greek Civil War* (London: Longman), 82.
194. Fleischer, 'The "Third Factor"', 211.
195. Fleischer, 'The "Third Factor"', 212f.

196. Steininger, 'British Labour, Deutschland und die SPD 1945/46', 189.
197. D. Sassoon (2012) *One Hundred Years of Socialism: The West European Left in the Twentieth Century* (London: Tauris, 2010), 636–642.
198. Rome to Foreign Office, 15 October 1947, TNA, FO 371/67767-Z9073. J. Ward to I. Mallet, 23 June 1949, TNA, FO 371/79300-Z4477.
199. Signor de Gasperi Surmounts Another Crisis, *Economist*, 14 April 1951.

Bibliography

I documenti diplomatici italiani, Decima Seria: 1943–1948, Vol. 2.
I documenti diplomatici italiani, Decima Seria: 1943–1948, Vol. 3.
Black, J. (2003). The Mediterranean as a battleground of the European powers: 1700–1900. In D. Abulafia (Ed.), *The Mediterranean in history* (pp. 251–282). London: Thames & Hudson.
Bullock, A. (1983). *Ernest Bevin: Foreign Secretary: 1945–1951*. London: Heinenmann.
Close, D.H. (1995). *The Greek Civil War*. London: Longman.
Devin, G. (1993). *L'Internationale socialiste: histoire et sociologie du socialisme internationale: 1945–1990*. Paris: Presses de la Fondation national des sciences politiques.
Dodds, N., Solley, L. & Tiffany, S. (1946). *Tragedy in Greece: an eye-witness report*. London: Progress Pub. Co..
Drögemöller, M. (2008). *Zwei Schwestern in Europa. Deutsche und niederländische Sozialdemokratie 1945–1990*. Berlin: Vorwärts Buch.
Fleischer, H. (1987). The "Third Factor": The Struggle for an Independent Socialist Policy During the Greek Civil War. In L. Baerentzen, J.O. Iatrides & O.L. Smith (Eds.). *Studies in the history of the Greek Civil War 1945–1949* (pp. 189–212). Copenhagen: Museum Tusculanum.
Goldsworthy, V. (1998). *Inventing Ruritania: the imperialism of the imagination*. New Haven: Yale University Press.
Healey, D. (1990). *The time of my life*. London: Penguin.
Imlay, T.C. (2014). 'The policy of social democracy is self-consciously internationalist': The German Social Democratic Party's Internationalism after 1945. *The Journal of Modern History*, 86 (1), 81–123.
Klotzbach, K. (1982). *Der Weg zur Staatspartei : Programmatik, praktische Politik und Organisation der deutschen Sozialdemokratie 1945 bis 1965*. Berlin: Dietz.
Lee, J. (1981). *My life with Nye*. Harmondsworth: Penguin Books.
Lilleker, D. (2004). *Against the Cold War: the history and political traditions of pro-Sovietism in the British Labour Party*. London: Tauris.
Luzzatto R. (1946). *Unknown War in Italy*. London: New Europe Publishing.

Manitakis, N. (2004). Struggling from abroad: Greek communist activities in France during the Greek civil war. In P. Carabott & T.D. Sfikas (Eds.). *The Greek Civil War: Essays on a Conflict of Exceptionalism* (pp. 101–113). Aldershot: Ashgate.

Masini, P.C. & Merli, S. (Eds.). (1990). *Il socialismo al bivio: l' archivio di Giuseppe Faravelli, 1945–1950*. Milano: Fondazione Giangiacomo Feltrinelli.

Misgeld, K. (1984). *Sozialdemokratie und Aussenpolitik in Schweden: Sozialistische Internationale, Europapolitik und die Deutschlandfrage 1945–1955*. Frankfurt: Campus Verlag.

Nenni, P. (1982). *Diari*, Vol. 1, *Tempo di Guerra Fredda: diari 1943–1956*. Milano: SugarCo.

Pimlott, B. (Ed.). (1986). *The political diary of Hugh Dalton: 1918–40, 1945–60*. London: Cape.

Richter, H. (1985). *British intervention in Greece: from Varkiza to civil war, February 1945 to August 1946*. London: Merlin Press.

Sassoon, D. (2010). *One hundred years of socialism: the West European Left in the twentieth century*. London: Tauris.

Saville, J. (1993). *The politics of continuity: British foreign policy and the Labour government, 1945–46*. London: Verso.

Schärf, A. (1955). *Österreichs Erneuerung: 1945–1955: das erste Jahrzehnt der Zweiten Republik*. Wien: Verlag der Wiener Volksbuchhandlung.

Scheu, F. (1969). *The Early Days of the Anglo-Austrian Society*. London: Anglo-Austrian Society.

Sebastiani, P. (1983). *Laburisti inglesi e socialisti italiani : dalla ricostituzione del Psi(up) alla scissione di Palazzo Barberini*. Roma: Elengraf.

Sfikas, T.D. (1994). *The British Labour Government and the Greek Civil War, 1945–1949: the imperialism of 'non-intervention'*. Keele: Ryburn Pub.

Shafir, S. (1985). Julius Braunthal and his postwar mediation efforts between German and Israeli socialists. *Jewish Social Studies*, 47 (3–4), 267–280.

Shell, K.L. (1962). *The Transformation of Austrian Socialism*. New York: State University of New York.

Stavrakis, P.J. (1989). *Moscow and Greek Communism, 1944–1949*. Ithaca: Cornell University Press.

Steininger, R. (1979). British Labour, Deutschland und die SPD 1945/46. *Internationale wissenschaftliche Korrespondenz zur Geschichte der deutschen Arbeiterbewegung*, 15, 188–225.

Steininger, R. (1987). *Los von Rom?: die Südtirolfrage 1945/1946 und das Gruber-De Gasperi-Abkommen*. Innsbruck: Haymon.

Steurer, L. (1998). L'Alto Adige tra autodecisione e autonomia (1945–1946). In A. Del Boca (Ed.). *Confini contesi: la Repubblica italiana e il Trattato di pace di Parigi, 10 febbraio 1947* (pp. 119–156). Torino: Edizioni Gruppo Abele.

Thorpe, A. (2006). 'In a Rather Emotional State'? The Labour Party and British Intervention in Greece, 1944–5, *English Historical Review*, 121 (493), 1075–1105.

Van Der Goes van Naters, M. (1980). *Met en tegen de tijd*. Amsterdam: Arbeiderspers.

Vlavianos, H. (1992). *Greece, 1941–49: from resistance to civil war: the strategy of the Greek Communist Party*. London: Macmillan.

Weber, F. (1986). *Der kalte Krieg in der SPÖ: Koalitionswächter, Pragmatiker und revolutionäre Sozialisten, 1945–1950*. Wien: Verlag für Gesellschaftskritik.

Weiler, P. (1988). *British Labour and the Cold War*. Stanford: Stanford University Press.

CHAPTER 8

The Rebirth of the Socialist International (1948–51)

1   Comisco's Two Roads

In 1948, the impetus to expand Comisco revealed the different projects for the Socialist International, beyond the problems with intervention in Greece and Italy. The socialists interested in national planning wanted to create an international Fabian Society and the socialists embracing federalism wanted international socialism to lead the European movement. This division would prove lasting. However, it was not enough to renounce a joint definition of democratic socialism. Indeed, the regular efforts spent trying to find a common position testify to the continuous relevance of socialist internationalism.

After the war, French and Belgian socialists insisted on rebuilding the Socialist International as an active international player and leader of the Third Force. Even during the Cold War, supranationality was a priority:

> However, the idea that Europe could become a federal entity, maybe a socialist one, survived beyond the Third Force. It would become an essential pillar of the SFIO's programmes in the 1950s.[1]

From 1948 to 1951 the federalists tried to have international socialism embrace European unification. The paradox Sassoon noted was that while the British Labour Party had no interest in European integration, the

Continental socialists wanted its involvement.[2] As a reaction to their enthusiasm, the Labour Party developed a long-lasting Euroscepticism.

In April 1948, the Selsdon Park conference of the socialist parties to discuss the Marshall Plan endorsed the Organisation for European Economic Co-operation (OEEC) and the Brussels Treaty as supranational solutions to international problems.[3] French and Belgian socialists managed to extract a vague, but real commitment to federalism and the transfer of sovereignty.[4] The Labour Party made this tactical concession to reduce the appeal of the Hague Conference of the European movement, but after the House of Commons and the Annual Conference voted against renouncing sovereignty, they had to retreat from this commitment and keep expectations low, as revealed by the pamphlet they put out in September, *Feet on the Ground*.[5] In June 1948, the SFIO put forward a proposal to create a socialist centre for documentation and propaganda for the United States of Europe, to coordinate the policies of the parties from the countries taking part in supranational institutions, such as the OEEC or the Brussels Treaty.[6] The plan was sunk by the Swedes' refusal to finance the enterprise, showing the importance of financial contributions in directing the development of international socialism.[7]

The other possible direction was to develop the Experts' Conferences, to transmit the successful experience of socialism from the centre to the periphery. In the conferences, non-political technicians could share their experience about social and economic policies. Their meetings would produce precise recommendations and plans—a toolbox all socialist parties in Government could take advantage of—while questions of high politics could be solved only through equivocal declarations. Comisco was to be 'a platform from which to publicise the British approach to problems of democratic socialism'.[8]

The idea of international meetings of experts was first developed by SPÖ, especially Karl Waldbrunner, in its contacts with the Eastern European parties, thus from the beginning it involved practical cooperation despite political divergences.[9] For Labour and the SPA, making their achievements in managing the economy exemplary also strengthened their hegemony over the movement. The experts conference could have created a 'basic Socialist theory in relation to modern conditions'.[10]

Conferences had been discussing economic reforms, nationalisation and planning since Clacton, but only abstractly, because of divergences on political means and goals. After the expulsion of the pro-communist parties, the Selsdon Park conference discussed how to enact nationalisation and planning within the framework of the Marshall Plan.[11] The Vienna Conference (4–7 June 1948) approved Waldbrunner's proposal to authorise SILO to call a conference of economic experts on planning and socialisation—as well as to gather information and experiences from the national parties, which SILO had been doing since the Selsdon Park conference.[12] After the first conference in December 1948, the second conference met in March 1949 and recommended Comisco to repeat the experiment and circulating the papers produced among the parties.[13] These conferences should not have been political: participants would not represent their party but participate as experts in their fields, and there would also be non-party members present.

The first Experts' Conference in Buscot Park (6–10 December 1948) discussed how to manage nationalised industries to benefit the community. The conference backed the British model of nationalisation, as designed by Morrison: managers needed to be competent technicians, the firms had to maintain market orientation and there was to be no interference in free collective bargaining.[14] Ultimate control and supervision belonged to Government and parliament. The report also encouraged decentralisation and workers' participation. The French objected to the latter, as in their experience communist trade unionists had pushed out socialist and Catholic trade unionists.

The Bennekom conference (14–18 March 1949), the second one, discussed international trade, employment and investments. There as well the Labour line prevailed: the problem of the European economy was a trade imbalance, which drained dollar reserves to import capital goods, food and raw materials.[15] The solution was Cripps' economic policy: expansion of exports and control of consumption with a moralist and egalitarian ethos.[16] The conference established the principle that the nation state could increase demand to fight cyclical unemployment, although this increased imports of foodstuff and raw materials and created bottlenecks in the production cycle. While capitalism would encourage luxury goods to increase profits, socialist planning would increase exports and export substitution industries, avoiding bottlenecks and protectionism. These economic arguments backed Labour's economic opposition to European unity: integration of national economies would produce competition and waste and not solve the trade imbalance with the rest of the world.[17]

The conferences suggested other forms of international cooperation, such as a monetary system to stabilise currency and a European investment bank to encourage export substitution industrialisation and productivity.

The alternative, stimulating private investments, was rejected as it would have required a rise in profits, damaging high taxation and redistributive policies. International control over energy, iron and steel was considered, probably to legitimise the plans for the internationalisation of the Ruhr. However, fundamental differences still stood: the British wanted international planning through Government cooperation, the French and Belgian wanted a supranational authority 'able to carry out the socialist measures which were not acceptable to their national Governments'.[18]

The International Socialist Conference in Baarn (14–16 May 1949) was a turning point for the evolution of the International, as it encouraged the development of the Experts' Conferences and took an ambiguous and unsatisfying position on European integration. The proposal of the Experts' Conference to become a regular occurrence was approved.[19] The French wanted to turn the report into a political resolution and use it for propaganda at the Council of Europe. 'In the present economic situation there must be planning and we should say that it must be socialist planning on a European scale'.[20] The PvdA also wanted to link the issue of international control to the Council of Europe. The SPA argued that the conclusions were contradictory and did not apply to all nations, so there could be no resolution. The Labour Party was opposed even to circulating the minutes of the plenary conference, to avoid excessive expectations.[21]

The greater role of the Experts' Conferences allowed the expansion of the Comisco Secretariat—while the French proposal to restore a political Socialist International was rejected.[22] There was confidence that the socialists could dominate culture, a typical Fabian aspiration, and that the Experts could provide the basis of discussion for the International Socialist Conference, whose role was reduced to defining the basic features of democratic socialism and communicating them to the public. Single-issue pamphlets would clarify socialist issues like class struggle, trade unions, the dictatorship of the proletariat and the role of individuals.

These new tasks required a full-time secretary with linguistic and economic skills to prepare reports, circulate documents and publicise results. Bolle's performance was harshly criticised, as secretary was only his second job.[23] It was time for Julius Braunthal to return. His work in the *International Socialist Forum* made him suspect among Labour leaders and popular on the Labour left.[24] In 1947, Gollancz closed *Left News* and could not finance Adler's project for a journal for German-speaking socialists.[25] For some time Braunthal worked on a project with Fenner Brockway[26] and considered writing a history of the LSI, with a grant from the Hillman Foundation.[27] He finally used his international contacts to help obtain the position of Secretary of Comisco.[28]

Morgan Phillips strongly opposed Braunthal and preferred Cerilio Spinelli, Altiero's brother,[29] a social observer at the Italian Embassy. The PSB and PvdA backed Bob Molenaar, first president of the International Union of Socialist Youth after the war and later secretary of the European Movement. Braunthal, whom the French supported, finally convinced the Scandinavian parties and the SPD to support him—the argument was that Spinelli would not be impartial in the ongoing conflict between PSU and PSLI. Braunthal was a very energetic secretary first of Comisco then of the Socialist International, leaving his mark particularly in the opening to the Third World.[30]

The other big issue of the Baarn Conference was European unification.[31] Larock strove for a synthesis to reconcile the opposing positions of SFIO and Labour Party. He argued that Comisco needed to set a policy or the question would become uncontrollable, diminishing the influence of socialism in the European Movement and the Council of Europe. The two institutions could not be ignored or sabotaged: 'everything which is international is ours'.[32] Larock employed a rhetoric of realism to please the Labour Party, arguing that the Council of Europe offered possibilities to exploit in economic and practical issues. Healey took to heart this suggestion and the next year used the Strasbourg assembly to make propaganda about full employment.[33]

Van der Goes van Naters assumed a stronger federalist position, saying it was deluded to wait for Europe to become socialist before starting unification. The PvdA proposed a socialist parliamentary group in Strasbourg and a federal parliament. The SPD and the Scandinavians rejected the proposal and Healey quipped, somewhat arrogantly, that not taking part in the European Movement had not reduced the influence of the Labour Party. The problems of Europe could not be solved by Europe alone, but needed the help of the Atlantic community and the Commonwealth. He said that people would refuse the sacrifices stemming from federalist commitments. For example, the British people would not make sacrifices for peoples who lacked 'the sort of social discipline accepted in Britain'.[34] He also repeated that a Labour Government would not accept binding decisions from a supranational organisation, the only cooperation was voluntary, as in the Commonwealth and OEEC.

Van der Goes van Naters' ambitious proposal was rejected and Larock's motion approved. The conference approved the Council of Europe as a step to a permanent European Union with administration under parliamentary supervision. The Labour Party was satisfied, convinced that the creation of the Council of Europe would definitely put the issue of European integration to rest—an assessment they would repeat regularly in the decades to come.[35]

In the Consultative Assembly of the Council of Europe, the British delegates opposed the Dutch proposal to form a socialist group and the French proposal to move the Council of Europe towards a federation.[36] In June 1950, the Labour Party published an uncompromising condemnation of federalism with the pamphlet *European Unity*. Soon after, Comisco held a special conference on the Schuman plan; the British hoped to bring the entire movement into opposition to the Schuman proposal, but failed.[37] At the Frankfurt Congress (30 June–3 July 1951), Van der Goes van Naters spoke once again for limiting national sovereignty and creating a strong European organisation, but the Belgians recognised that socialists lacked a common policy.[38]

While European integration was becoming the central issue of foreign policy, the Socialist International did not have a position. The starting point would have been recognising that only the parties from the Six nations of the Schuman Plan were involved, but it was the French and the Germans who were obsessed about not going forwards without the British and the Scandinavians, who were necessary to give Europe a socialist character.[39] This argument failed to impress the Scandinavian Haakon Lie and Björk, who accused the French socialists of wanting to solve their problems at international level because they could not solve them at national level.[40] A European Committee was set up in 1952, with participation from the German, the French and the Dutch parties, but it did not carry the authority of the Socialist International.[41]

Loss of sovereignty divided the socialists between those who would not sacrifice the freedom of the nation state and those who would sacrifice something they did not have.[42] The Labour Party could identify closely with its government, but the French could not. As Ernest Davies said, 'The preservation of Socialist democracy necessitates a closed economy'.[43] In 1957, Bevan said that the Treaty of Rome was a response to the malaise generated by the failure of the socialist parties to use their sovereignty to plan the economy.[44] In 1962, Gaitskell argued that the Conservatives wanted Britain to join the EEC because they did not have a policy for growth, while Labour had planning.[45] However, Labour's opposition to federalism remained consistent throughout the decades, even when state planning, nationalisation and the closed economy were no longer goals.[46]

Contingent economic arguments rested on a sound foundation of cultural explanations. The Labour Party had reworked two core ideas in British culture, the distinction of Britain from Europe and the global mission of Britain, in a socialist fashion: Labour Britain was the best example of socialism and it had to spread socialism to the world.[47] The opposition to federalism was strictly linked to the idea of unfitness of Southern and Eastern Europeans for democratic socialism; only Britain and Scandinavia had the right national character. The recent experience of the Labourites with Poland, Czechoslovakia, Italy, Greece, France and Germany had confirmed this impression.

Despite accusations of insularity, the Labour Party argued that preserving Labour's experiment from Continental corruption would allow it to serve its global mission to prove socialism possible and educate the other peoples:

> We intend to hold what we have gained here in this island and we believe that in this way we do the best service to Western Europe in showing an example which we hope will be followed in lands which have not all followed it yet.[48]

Thus, the British paid to turn Comisco into a propaganda machinery for socialism and to expand the Experts' Conference. In addition, British Labour believed that the multicultural Commonwealth would act as 'a bridge between East and West, between white and coloured',[49] thus, in the 1950s, it encouraged, and paid for, the Socialist International to extend its ties to the Third World—a new term—to avoid newer nations falling under the thrall of communism out of economic desperation.[50]

In 1951, Morgan Phillips was very satisfied with how the Experts' Conference was evolving into an international Fabian Society. He appreciated the exclusion of politics and the frankness of the debates.[51] The practice of explaining policies and circulating information encouraged clarity and technical competence. In 1952, Phillips was more restrained, since on many occasions it was impossible to find a common position, but he argued that the Experts' Conference had to strike a balance between defining a common socialist attitude to shared international problems and leaving each nation the freedom to find its own unique solution.[52] Price's vision of international socialist cooperation was fully realised. The Danes backed Morgan Phillips, even asking for the Experts' Conference to become more secretive and less political.[53]

Morgan Phillips' assessment was probably correct; Misgeld[54] and Imlay[55] agree that the Experts' Conferences were the most successful form of international cooperation in the 1950s. Still, divisions in international socialism were clear. The Dutch Nederhorst hit the nail on the head when he claimed that the recent Experts' Conference failed to produce anything useful because they lacked an agreement on the problem of European unification:

> Questions which are at present being discussed, such as the development of economic integration, European trade policy, a European bank of investments, the integration of European transport and of the supply of energy cannot be handled when a common point of view with regard to the transfer of national sovereign power is lacking [emphasis in the original].[56]

Nederhorst said that socialists did not study the European question and did not have a position. As denounced by Koos Vorrink, the desire to develop the Socialist International in Asia was an escape from the divisions in Europe—an assessment Van Kemseke shares.[57]

2 The Martyrology of Eastern European Socialists

Nothing forced the socialists to Cold War militancy more than the persecution of socialists behind the Iron Curtain.[58] Even Bevan was passionate enough about the persecution of social democrats to argue that the communists could not be trusted.[59] Assistance to Eastern European socialists was a point on which socialist unity could be found and it shaped the socialist identity. One of the reason for the expansion of Comisco in 1948 was coordinating assistance to refugees.[60] The Swiss Socialist Party directed the refugee commission, as it had experience from the Second World War,[61] and cooperated with the Swiss police to investigate individual cases. The Western European parties offered to take some refugees, but the number was small—the Swedes accepted only 15 Hungarian socialists. For the most part, refugees were assisted locally in the countries where they happened to be displaced. However, the financial commitment was not indifferent: by the end of 1948 the Labour Party gave £200 to Czechoslovak social democrats and collected £1500 through an appeal. Despite its precarious finances, even the SFIO distributed hot meals to the refugees.

The Western socialist parties were concerned about maintaining control. The ex-leader of the Hungarian social democrats, Antal Ban, requested that the refugees be allowed to continue their political activity. The commission for aid proposed that Comisco would create, finance and supervise an organisation for the Eastern European parties in exile, to carry out political and relief activities.[62] As always, the central question was who to include, because the exile parties were divided and split. Despite their intentions in 1939 and 1946 to keep exiles out, the socialists were again facing the problems of parties in exile. Before the complete communist takeover, in Eastern Europe there were 'independent' socialists who refused to cooperate with the communists. They were the right-wing elements—often the pre-war leadership—who had been purged under communist pressure or excluded when the socialist parties were re-born as pro-communist organisations. They had an international organisation, which in March 1948 took the name of *Bureau Internationale Socialiste* (BIS); it included the groups of Peyer (Hungary), Topalovitch (Yugoslavia), Zaremba and Ciolkosz (Poland) and Zissu (Romania).[63] The independent socialists argued that they were right about the communists and for this reason Comisco had to recognise them. In October 1948, the BIS demanded admission to Comisco as a regional group, the rebirth of the Socialist International, and a clear choice for humanist and democratic socialism.[64]

At first Comisco included only Eastern European parties that were already members before February 1948.[65] Straightforward was the designation of the Hungarian group led by Ban and the Czechoslovak group led by Vilim—whom the British secret services extracted from Czechoslovakia on the request of Healey. Finding an equivalent Polish or Yugoslav group was difficult. The entire PPS leadership had joined the fusion, so the only exiles were those who had never been members of the post-war party. Another problem was the overlapping: Comisco recognised Ban's group for Hungary, but BIS recognised Peyer—who had broken with the communists after the war.

At the suggestion of Comisco, the Baarn Conference (14–16 May 1949) authorised an organisation for the Eastern European socialists as a symbolic rejection of the permanent division of Europe and tyranny.[66] Comisco had already delegated the Swiss and the French to negotiate the reunification of the Hungarian and Romanian socialists, respectively.[67] The Swiss were successful,[68] but Romanian socialism was so divided that by 1951 the SFIO had not found a solution.[69] The parties representing territories of the USSR would be members of the new organisation but not recognised directly by Comisco—Mollet wanted to avoid an aggressive stance towards the USSR.[70] In July the parties in exile from Bulgaria, Czechoslovakia, Hungary, Poland and Yugoslavia formed the Socialist Union of Central-Eastern Europe (SUCEE).[71] They invited the parties from Lithuania, Estonia, Latvia and Ukraine to join. Ciolkosz and Vilem Bernard became representatives to Comisco, Bernard was also the chairman and Zaremba the general secretary.[72] This sanctioned the reconciliation of first- and eleventh-hour exiles.

While the SUCEE claimed that it was giving a signal to Eastern Europe, it was actually meant for Western Europe. Eastern European socialists were evidence of communist violence, as the Yugoslav socialists recognised: 'Our experience is the proof of the matter'.[73] Vorrink said that Western socialists had to take advantage of their experience in order to fight communism.[74] Their experience lent authenticity to the anticommunist narrative and justified the Atlantic Treaty.

After the communist takeover, the Eastern European socialists could wear three masks: the exile, the martyr and the traitor. All exiles could do was wait abroad, as ignored pretenders.[75] The traitors served as a warning against cooperation with the communists and to delegitimise dissenters. As the NEC's statement on Prague coup said:

> But Czechoslovakia teaches us something more. Communists cannot achieve their aims without support from a minority within the camp of democratic Socialism. As in Czechoslovakia so in Hungary, Rumania and Bulgaria, individual Socialists, by permitting or abetting Communist attacks on democracy, have connived at their own destruction.[76]

The martyrs fed the socialist faith as much as they had done with Christianity.[77] Socialists even had their own hagiography: *The Curtain Falls*,[78] a collection of stories about the communist takeover from the social democratic point view. Edited by Healey, it included a tale for Czechoslovakia by Majer, for Hungary by Ban, for Poland by Ciolkosz. It was a serious commitment: when Gaitskell met Khrushchev in 1956, he felt obliged to raise the question of the persecution of the social democrats, ruining the event.[79]

The role of exiles and martyrs in shaping social democratic identity emerged at the Copenhagen Conference (1–3 June 1950), whose central debate was the basis of democratic socialism.[80] The debate was prefaced by a long description of the crimes Bolshevism committed against workers and social democrats. The Germans described the continuous flow of refugees from the East and the struggle to keep the borders open and offer hospitality—a theme that was to occur regularly in post-war German history. As the flight from the East delegitimised the communist system, social democratic solidarity towards the refugees legitimised the socialist movement—particularly the SPD. Ollenhauer made the explicit comparison between Bolshevism and Nazism, as both employed concentration camps. Also, the Soviet state and people's democracy, which claimed to be the state of the free workers, needed the forced labour of millions of slaves—in the concentration camps—to survive. Jewish Bund members denounced the anti-Semitism of the Soviet system. While the condemnation was sincere, it exploited themes and information developed by the Information Research Department (IRD).[81]

3 Ideology Designed by Committee

In the twentieth century, European socialism moved from viewing bourgeois democracy with suspicion to fully embracing it. The ambiguity of the LSI was resolved with the Frankfurt Declaration: 'Without freedom there can be no Socialism. Socialism can be achieved only through democracy. Democracy can be fully realised only through Socialism'.[82] This became the feature that distinguished socialist anti-communism from negative anti-communism, although it also strengthened the Eurocentric character of the Socialist International:

> It is by invoking political freedom that the socialists sought to distinguish themselves from those they perceived as the most threatening rivals nationally and internationally. [...] In both cases, the values of political democracy were conceived as a distinctive feature but also as a set of references with universal reach that could be accepted by everyone willing to take the name of 'democratic socialist'.[83]

As soon as the pro-communist socialists were expelled, Comisco put on the agenda the problem of defining democratic socialism.[84] In March 1948, Comisco had its first comprehensive ideological resolution affirm the essential principles of socialism: social justice, peace and individual freedom from all forms of oppression. This resolution was meant to define the borders of the social democratic community by ratifying the failure of cooperation and association with communism.[85] Despite socialist goodwill in cooperation, the goal of the communists had always been to destroy the socialist parties, so the responsibility for splitting the working-class was theirs alone. While Comisco celebrated the workers' struggles against capitalist oppression, it argued that defending democracy, individual rights and the right to opposition was a priority. Socialists strove for a socialist Europe, free of internal tyranny and external aggression, built on voluntary cooperation. As McNeil explained, the purpose of the declaration was to have the pro-communist socialists reject it and enforce their self-exclusion from the socialist community.[86] The PSI responded accordingly, their representatives theatrically abandoning the room of the Comisco meeting of March 1948 to protest anti-communism and interference in Italian affairs.

The Vienna Conference (4–7 June 1948) also approved a resolution on democracy and socialism, which regretted how the hopes for democracy had been dashed by the persistence of fascism and the new dictatorships under Soviet influence.[87] People's democracies were condemned for negating civil rights and for swapping private capitalism with state capitalism, betraying democracy and socialism alike. Once again, the conference repeated that socialism was inseparable from political democracy, but political democracy needed an integration of economic democracy. A year earlier, at the Zurich Conference, Buset said that the political democracy of the West and economic democracy of the East would integrate to form socialism. The possibility of having economic democracy alone was now rejected. Political democracy—identified with the recognition of human personality—was the precondition for any socialism. In practical terms, it included freedom of conscience and opinion; access to free information; freedom of association; legal protection against arbitrary acts by individuals and society; an independent judiciary; free elections and right of opposition; equality of every citizen without distinction of class, race and sex.

Comisco produced its strongest condemnation of communism—the 'Anti-Cominform' resolution—in the December 1949 meeting. The Cominform was exposed as 'the fifth column of an imperialistic tyranny'.[88] The show trials purged any communist with delusions of national independence. The domination of Eastern Europe was compared with the Nazi domination. The workers lost their bread and their freedom, they were under bureaucratic domination; fake trade unions and fake workers' regimes were a mockery to them.

The condemnation of communism was a precondition for defining democratic socialism, but this was as far as the unanimity went. On Schärf's suggestion, the Vienna Conference created a commission to write a resolution on democracy and socialism.[89] The debate was long and some parties asked for a condemnation of Spain and Greece to balance anti-communism. The final resolution affirmed the need to integrate economic democracy into political democracy. Economic emancipation was a basic right and a means of spiritual and political emancipation. Social reforms would not be enough; a reform of the public administration was in order to have a truly democratic system—making concessions to the traditional suspicion towards the bourgeois state. The democratic system would guarantee to everyone its share of economic, spiritual and cultural riches. 'Democratic Socialism combines freedom of the individual with planned economy'.[90]

At the December 1949 Comisco meeting, the SFIO repeated its proposal to rebuild the Socialist International.[91] Failing to reach an agreement, it was decided to increase the symbolism of international cooperation as a consolation prize.[92] The planned international stamp was a failure, as few parties agreed to buy it.[93] It was decided to have a joint Mayday manifesto. While in 1950 agreement was found,[94] in 1951 the objections to Labour's draft from all parties—especially the French—proved insurmountable.[95] The most important in terms of consequences was the proposal by the Belgians, French and Dutch to have a committee define the basis of democratic socialism—according to Björk, the French exploited the exhaustion of other delegates to get their approval.[96] The committee was supposed to study doctrine and the organisation of a future International.

The ultimately contradictory strategy of the French socialists was to increase their prestige by association with the successful socialism of Britain and Scandinavia, but also to have the International confirm that Marxism was a constituent part of their identity. A few months before his death, Blum emphasised the role of Marxism while pleading with the non-Marxist socialists to join forces against communism.[97] In an open letter to Michael Foot, Blum said that what distinguished Labour from the USSR was its goal of the betterment of the human condition, which was the goal of Marxism as well.[98] Mollet, less subtly, said that the British and the Scandinavians would have suffered if the other parties had been swallowed by the communists. On this occasion Haakon Lie charged the French with being unable to win their battles nationally and Björk said that the British and the Scandinavians had made the most significant contribution to international action, always meeting French opposition. This provoked Mollet to a fury and Larock sneered derisively that the Swedes were good at writing letters and documents, but they knew nothing of real cooperation.

The debate to define the 'Basis of democratic socialism' became the central concern of Comisco in 1950 and 1951.[99] It was decided that every party would circulate a document expressing its own conception of socialism.[100] Braunthal prepared a questionnaire that shaped the debate: the parties would give their opinions on human rights, Marxism, the class struggle, socialist internationalism, political democracy and economic democracy.

Björk was the first to produce a document—despite protestations that Swedes did not care about ideological debates—which was also the most innovative, as it reflected the form socialism had taken in Sweden in the recent decades. In the 1920s, the SAP lived the contradiction of all the other socialist parties: a discrepancy between verbal radicalism, vulgarised Marxism and a commitment to full nationalisation on the one hand and a moderate Government programme based on liberal economic policies on the other.[101] The issue of nationalisation was fiercely debated at the 1932 conference, where the focus was the resolution of the LSI congress in 1931 to make nationalisation a key element of crisis policies. Georg Branting requested the integration of the motion in the party programme, while Rickard Sandler was dismissive, arguing that the LSI was as removed from Sweden as the moon from earth. The line of the LSI was rejected by only 157 against 149. While the internationalisation of domestic quarrels provided the focus for the internal debate in a key moment in the history of the SAP, in turn the successful SAP's revision became the model for foreign socialist innovators like Sturmthal or Dalton. The 1932 SAP programme made a distinction between nationalisation and control of the economy for social goals, which allowed it to back an active Government policy and a realistic programme. Björk's document said that nationalisation was not a goal, just a means to achieve full employment, economic efficiency, security and social equality—thus asserting the primacy of politics over economy.

Björk declared the liquidation of Marxism—which Tingsten had already announced in 1941—and he drew inspiration from the innovative 1944 SAP programme.[102] Björk broke with tradition, rejecting not just Marxist but also working-class tradition in the labour movement.[103] The centrality of class struggle was abandoned—as it had been in the 1944 programme—since it was no longer necessary to educate workers and trade unionists. Since industrial workers in Sweden were too few to win the elections, the SAP proposed a wide alliance of all classes of wage labourers and the self-employed. The success of the Swedish model depended on an alliance between workers and farmers, to whom the SAP had paid great consideration since the 1930s.[104] According to Albin Hansson, the SAP had to transform from a class party into a people's party.[105] He emphasised the idea of a national community—*Folkhemmet*—united by solidarity and cross-class cooperation. Also, it was time to recognise the role of small enterprises in economic prosperity. As profit margins were eroded, trade unions had a duty to increase productivity for the prosperity of the people. This would help win new votes and make coalition Governments easier.

From the manifesto of the Nordic Labour movement of 1947, Björk borrowed the core idea that democracy and freedom were not means to socialism but ends in their own right. Bourgeois democracy found a continuation in social democracy: as the former abolished political privilege, the latter would abolish economic privilege. In international affairs, ideology was no basis for diplomacy, the guiding principle was to have commercial access to all nations, regardless of their political regimes, in order to have a sound national economy. European federalism was rejected: the nation state had to control investments and plan without hindrances. At the Copenhagen Conference, Tage Erlander was more cautious and claimed that ideology was less important than practical achievements like full employment.[106] The Danish delegate Andersen said that ideological debates were as useful as theological ones.

The similarities between the strategy of the SAP and the PvdA were evident. Their cooperation gave the Frankfurt Declaration its character. The hub of the arguments which the PvdA presented in their document was opening the ranks to everyone willing to join the struggle against exploitation regardless of social condition or religion. 'Democratic socialism should form a unity in diversity'.[107] The only way to grow was to appeal to the moral sense of the masses, not their class identity. The PvdA, squeezed between the anti-Catholic Nordic parties and the anti-clerical Continental parties, valued religion as beneficial and promoted the 1953 special congress of the Socialist International, which approved the Bentveld Declaration, adopting a positive attitude towards religion.[108] The Dutch also sided unambiguously with the Atlantic Alliance and emphasised supranationality as the solution for political and economic problems.

At the Copenhagen conference, Mollet opened the debate over the basis of democratic socialism by saying there were two underlying trends: the Nordic parties emphasised moral, democratic and liberal values; the other parties asserted that the process of socialising the means of production and the disappearance of capitalism were preconditions for human happiness.[109] The second group was of many shades, from the call of the PSU to fight capitalism itself to Labour's demand to have the economic system benefiting the community. The SFIO proposed a synthesis that left room for Marxism, their model being the synthesis of Guesde and Jaurès, Marxism and morality, on which the SFIO was built.[110] Like Kautsky earlier,[111] they argued for an underlying harmony between non-Marxists and Marxists, although unbeknown to the former:

> It seems nevertheless that our British friends fear more the word than the practical application of Marxism. For it would be easy to prove that in their daily action they are continually influenced by Marxist conceptions.[112]

In response, Morgan Phillips made his famous declaration that the British labour movement owed more to Methodism than Marxism: the morals and evangelism of the former contrasted with the rejection of morality of the latter. Non-Conformist churches had spread the idea of popular education, volunteering and communal commitment. He contrasted this with the abstract ideals of the French and Russian Revolutions. Trotsky's Marxism encouraged the militarisation of the proletariat and the state, while the essence of British socialism was revolutionary transformation without physical conflict and class struggle. The insult 'reformist' was a compliment:

> Trotsky called reformist Socialism—an opprobrious phrase on his lips—as the leftward shadow of professional liberalism. If by the reformist Socialism the reference is to British Socialism, it is much more than a shadow—it is the living embodiment of an ethical inspiration and of ideas about democratic organisation and methods which contradict Marxism at almost every point.[113]

Van der Goes van Naters raised the embarrassing spectre of Henri De Man—'now held in contempt and for good reason'[114]—and other Neo-Socialist intellectuals of the inter-war period (Déat, Rosselli) to argue for a great inter-classist coalition united by an ethical undertaking. Unlike De Man, who argued that the reduction of international trade was a precondition to realise the national general plan, Van der Goes van Naters emphasised the supranational nature of politics and the application of internationalism to the real world.

In 1950, the frustration of the SFIO over the International Socialist Conference and Labour's behaviour peaked, with Mollet and Blum even considering quitting Comisco.[115] For Boutbien, the risk was limiting 'the expression of socialism to a banal democratic expression'.[116] It would be wrong to consider the ideological engagement of the SFIO as just a foible of the French. Rather, the party had to contend with the competition of the communists like no other. By increasing the Marxist content of the declaration of principles, French socialists hoped to increase the legitimacy of their leadership in the eyes of party militants, but also the legitimacy of socialism in the eyes of the communist workers.[117]

In addition, Boutbien and André Philip backed their allegation of the British and Scandinavians being 'nationalised socialists' with cogent arguments.[118] The achievement of prosperity and full employment at national level—the argument the anti-federalists used to reject limitations of the power of the nation-state—was not a socialist success if it meant exporting unemployment abroad. Björk considered the problem, only to conclude that full employment would increase international demand, benefiting poorer countries as well. Philip argued that nationalisation passed from being an instrument of the working-class to control capitalism to being an instrument of the state to build up its economic power for international competition. The level of prosperity had to be measured at international level. In addition, public or private property did not change the control of the industry by the managers. Only decentralisation and workers' participation would make public enterprises democratic. Therefore, the 'traditionalist' French made criticisms anticipating the themes of revisionism and the New Left.

The drafting committee for the document on the Basis of Democratic Socialism met in Paris in October 1950 with Grumbach as chairman. According to Björk, the absence of Mollet, the designated chairman—he was then a Government minister and did not agree with the results of the debate – made the discussions more productive. The committee decided to write a 3000-word document—Healey wanted a 'deft and short document'[119]—and assign each section to a member.[120] Healey was to write the preface, Oscar Pollak 'Socialism and political democracy,' Walther Bringholf 'Socialism and social democracy,' Björk 'Socialism and economic democracy,' Grumbach 'Socialism and international democracy'.

Ciolkosz was to produce a text on Eastern Europe to be attached to the document. Later Healey rewrote Grumbach's section, as the Swedes were unsatisfied. In the following meetings the committee set up a subcommittee of Larock, Healey and Braunthal to write the final version. Healey feared that reconciling all the interests would please nobody.[121]

'Aims and Tasks of Democratic Socialism' was the charter of principles the Socialist International approved at its first congress—therefore known as 'the Frankfurt Declaration'. It started with what all socialists—Marxists, humanists and even communists—agreed with: the myth of progress. Like the Communist Manifesto, it described how Capitalism had created immense wealth and productive forces, but it had led to the trampling of human rights and exploitation by a minority, resulting in unemployment, imperialism, war and fascism. The goal of socialism was to give economic power to all the people and create a community of equals.

The main innovation was in the agent of socialism. 'Socialism was born in Europe as a movement of protest against the diseases inherent in capitalist society'.[122] While workers were at the origin of the socialist movement, it was morality, not their social condition that united the socialists. The Declaration thus rejected historical materialism. Also rejected was the messianic vision: socialism was not the end state of history, but a responsibility to be realised. In addition, what inspired moral sentiments varied from people to people—including Marxism, religion or humanism.

Some countries were laying the foundation for a socialist society, proving democratic socialism was possible. The communist states were not a model; rather, they magnified the ills of capitalism: imperialism, dictatorship and exploitation by a minority. Fascism and communism were presented as deviations from the road of progress.

Socialism was 'democracy in its highest form'. The Declaration then described the articulations of democracy: political democracy, social democracy and cultural progress and international democracy. Political democracy included human rights and political pluralism. Economic democracy demanded the subordination of economic power to the public interest and democratic control. Full employment, social security, higher productivity and fair distribution were common goals, but the means varied according to the country. Public property was not an end in itself, but a means to have control and higher productivity. The mixed economy was defined as ideal. The liberation of the people from fear and want would allow the full development of the human personality. The Socialist International then committed itself to spreading prosperity throughout the whole world by supporting collective security and international collaboration. While the Declaration proposed transcending national sovereignty, it stated that cooperation had to be voluntary.

The Frankfurt Declaration was one of Mollet's many disappointments, who considered it a poor Declaration of Principles that would not last 25 years.[123] In his autobiography, Healey said he wrote the first draft of the preface while drinking two bottles of Dutch gin, but he was proud that the document lasted more than 30 years.[124]

4 From Frankfurt to Bad Godesberg

The greatest innovation of the post-war Socialist International was its exclusivity, leading Sassoon to call it a 'club'. While Devin and Sassoon emphasised the Cold War nature of the socialist identity, the exclusion of left-wing socialists was not tactical, but reflected the long-term evolution of the socialist movement and thought. The rebirth of the Socialist International coincided with a turning point in socialist history where the parties definitively cut their ties with their origins as a protest movement of moral revolt bent on the creation of an autonomous social order, to fully become parties fit to govern, accepting capitalism as the foundation of the economic order and representing the whole of society.[125] The Labour Party was an early example of such transformation, so it was natural for the British to guide the international socialist movement through this process.

Theory was often the weak point of reformist socialism, which, in Sabbatucci's definition, is 'a concrete praxis more than a fully developed theory. Or rather, a strong praxis based on a weak theory'.[126] 'Although the Frankfurt Declaration'—Braunthal wrote—'does not develop a theory, it nonetheless follows the spirit of the theory of evolutionary socialism'.[127] While the praxis was largely non-controversial, the ambiguity between evolutionary and revolutionary socialism was a defining feature of the labour movement.[128] Party cadres and leaders were reluctant to renege on their ideal foundation. Braunthal recognised that the re-orientation towards the principles of humanism and liberalism was already evident after 1933, so what was needed was a summary of the ideological development, – 'a socialist stocktaking on an international basis'.[129] As secretary of the Socialist International, Braunthal planned a book with contributions from every party about the 'ideological development of democratic socialism' in their nation. The chapters in English were published in the newsletter of the Socialist International and they were collected in a book in German and a pamphlet series in Italian.[130]

The 1950s saw many modernisers proposing the ideological renovation of socialism embracing revisionism—also under the name of neo-revisionism or second revisionism. If the Socialist International had simply been a signpost to mark this turning point, it would have been interesting enough. However, it had an active role. Braunthal put the Frankfurt Declaration next the Communist Manifesto and the Inaugural Address of the First International.[131] The comparison is not so outrageous. The ambition of these documents was to be a synthesis of socialist history and a prophecy of its development—while still serving the practical purpose of defining a political community. Marx's Inaugural Address was successful because it articulated new ideas in a language the people could identify with. In turn, the First International managed 'to forge and spread across Europe and the Americas a new and lasting language of social democracy'.[132] The role of the Frankfurt Declaration was the same, though the effect lesser.

According to Crosland, by taking the achievements of the Labour Government in 1951 as a model, the Frankfurt Declaration defined socialism as identical to the Welfare state—'full employment, higher production, a rising standard of life, social security and a fair distribution of property'.[133] It was the triumph of the British model of socialism, enshrined in the constitution of the Socialist International, but he considered this inadequate, as it made it impossible to differentiate socialism from the Welfare State and statism. He set his goal to give a new definition of socialism for the age of prosperity.[134] Crosland missed that the Frankfurt Declaration was not just the sum of pre-prosperity socialism, but also contained the germs of revisionism.

The Frankfurt Declaration influenced the development of socialist ideology in the national parties in ways we have become familiar with throughout this book. First, as a result of compromise and cooperation, it encouraged socialists to define their ideology and culture along the lines outlined at international level. Second, it facilitated cultural transfers from one national party to another. In addition to the British model of socialism, it helped the transmission of the emphasis of the SAP on cross-class alliances and democracy and the positive attitude of the PvdA to religion. Finally, it gave the modernising factions a rallying point and a reference with which to legitimise their requests for ideological renovation. The outcomes were unequal, yet important.

In 1951, Italian socialism considered the Frankfurt Declaration a Cold War document exemplifying what was wrong with Western social democracy—anti-communism and capitulation to capitalism. Rejection of the document was a point of pride. While returning into the fold of Western socialism, the PSI repeated in 1957 and 1961 that accepting an unrevised Frankfurt Declaration was impossible.[135] Eventually, acceptance of the Frankfurt Declaration became a condition for the respectability the PSI required to join a coalition Government, return to the Socialist International and fuse with the PSDI. What had once been scorned to mark a distance was to be accepted to achieve rapprochement.[136]

André Philip argued that the Frankfurt Declaration testified to the doctrinal crisis of the International: by substituting Marx with Keynes, it turned socialism into a bureaucratic technocracy without any revolutionary character.[137] However, the Frankfurt Declaration, in addition to contacts with British Labour, was important for Paul Vignaux and the development of the Christian Trade Union Federation (CFTC) influencing the direction of the new *Parti Socialiste*, born in 1971.[138]

At the end of the 1940s, the Labour Party fell victim of its own success: having fully implemented its programme, dissent emerged over where to go next. The left-wing close to Bevan pushed for radicalism and more nationalisation, while the right-wing proposed cultivating the middle classes and the new age of prosperity. The central role of stimulating the new revisionism was played by the Socialist Union—emerging from the ashes of the Socialist Vanguard Group—and the journal *Socialist Commentary*. They offered a sort of socialism based on equality, ethics and the development of the individual personality. Having its roots in German socialism, the group kept an eye on ideological developments on the Continent and had a network of contacts with socialists like Eichler and Silone. Their first statement of principles took the Frankfurt Declaration as an example.[139]

As mentioned, Crosland was dismissive of the Frankfurt Declaration, which he considered too vague and too committed to planning.[140] While this might be true, Crosland considered the Frankfurt Declaration a faithful reproduction of the Labour model he contested, and so he aimed at presenting his revision of socialism as innovative—one of the chapter of *The Future of Socialism* is called 'Aims of socialism'. Missing the enormous influence of Björk on the document, Crosland bypassed the Frankfurt Declaration and made direct references to Sweden.[141] Still, tactical references to the Charter of the Socialist International could be useful—especially after Gaitskell failed to scrap the commitment to nationalisation—so Crosland made one in 1962 to deny that the socialisation of all the means of production was necessary.[142] In 1989, Healey commented that the Labour Party, being 'the most conservative party in the world', adapted to changing social conditions later and worse than the other socialist parties—'much of the Labour Party now appears more wedded to a primitive sort of Marxism than any of the others'.[143] One wonders whether he unconsciously remembered that compliment by Angelica Balabanoff.

The Frankfurt Declaration had the greatest influence in West Germany, where socialist revisionism was most successful. Willi Eichler was especially responsible:

> An important role model for Eichler was the Declaration of Principles of the Socialist International of 1951 over the 'Aims and Tasks of Democratic Socialism'. He had worked on it and always came back to it.[144]

Eichler was a member of the drafting committee of the Frankfurt Declaration. In his commentary to the Bad Godesberg programme, he credited the publication of the Frankfurt Declaration with revitalising the debate over a new basic programme for the SPD.[145] Eichler praised the Frankfurt Declaration for discarding historical determinism, for giving an ethical foundation to socialism and for linking democracy and socialism.[146] Another important reference for Eichler was the Bentveld Declaration, with its positive attitude towards religion and the churches.[147] The Frankfurt Declaration influenced the Action Programme of Dortmund in 1952, which was the second step in the ideological revision of the SPD. The 1954 Congress created a committee to draft a new basic programme, with Eichler as chairman. Among the documents the committee would consider were the Frankfurt and Bentveld Declarations.

Klotzbach is more restrained in assessing the importance of the Frankfurt Declaration, especially, he argues, because Schumacher's position was very similar.[148] Misgeld argues that Eichler's role in drafting the Frankfurt Declaration was minor.[149] However, what mattered was that Eichler could legitimise his requests for ideological revision by referencing a programme the SPD was already committed to. Imlay has shown how the SPD leadership took its internationalist commitment seriously, adapting policies accordingly.[150] While Crosland dismissed the Frankfurt Declaration, as he considered it not particularly innovative for the Labour Party, it was innovative when applied to the SPD.

Erich Ollenhauer, president of the SPD at the time of the Bad Godesberg Conference in 1959, mentioned that the German social democrats were taking advantage of the ideological debates and innovations of the other European parties. The debt to the Frankfurt Declaration was explicit:

> Whoever reads the [Godesberg] draft carefully will find that in the whole outline of this draft and in the basic conceptions that we have developed, an extensive agreement with the Declaration of the International.[151]

Willy Brandt also recognised that the unbreakable connection between democracy and socialism of the Bad Godesberg programme had its foundations in the Frankfurt Declaration.[152] Herbert Wehner, the political father of the Bad Godesberg programme—as Eichler was its intellectual father—called Benedikt Kautsky on to the small committee that wrote the final draft of the programme. Benedikt, the son of Karl, was the main ideologue of the SPÖ and worked on its revisionist programme adopted in 1957.[153] Wehner's definition of socialism is almost identical to that of the Frankfurt Declaration:

> There is no socialism without freedom. Socialism can only be realised [*verwirklicht*] through democracy, democracy can only be fulfilled [*vollendet*] through socialism.[154]

> [it must be said] that democracy and socialism need each other and depend on each other and that socialism is fulfilled, realised democracy—realised for everyone [*dass Sozialismus vollendete, verwirklichte—für alle verwirklichte—Demokratie ist*].[155]

The definition of the Bad Godesberg programme is similar:

> Socialism is realised [*verwirklicht*] only by democracy, democracy is accomplished [*erfüllt*] by socialism.[156]

Imlay argues that internationalism reached a low ebb in the late 1950s.[157] Even if this is the case, the influence of the Frankfurt Declaration on the Bad Godesberg programme can be explained by a cascade effect.

The SPD still had ambitions to shape the policy of the Socialist International. In 1961, the revisionist leadership of the British, Austrian and German parties tried to enshrine their policy of revisionism and reach out to the Third World in a new declaration of principles, that would become in 1962 the Oslo Declaration, 'The World Today: The Socialist Perspective'.[158] The push to embrace full revisionism was resisted, especially by Mollet, so the new Charter dealt mostly with the development of the Third World. However, it testified to the continuous exchange of influences in socialist politics between the national and international spheres: from Frankfurt to Bad Godesberg, from Bad Godesberg to Oslo. In the decades to come, the evolution of the socialist parties continued the adjustment of declarations and resolutions by the Socialist International, which in turn legitimised the strategic and ideological changes of direction in the national parties.

5   The Frankfurt Congress and the New Foundation

In December 1950, the PBS proposed restoring the Socialist International, the same request Belgians and French had been making regularly since 1945. However, this time the Labour Party agreed. The PvdA and the Scandinavians did as well, after receiving reassurances. Different reasons can be put forward to explain why the Labour leadership finally dropped their objections. For Devin, restoring the Socialist International was a consolation prize for the federalist socialists disappointed by Labour's Euroscepticism.[159] Misgeld stresses how the Korean War restored unity in Western socialism, as the Berlin Blockade did 2 years earlier.[160] Another communist threat was the World Peace Council, which forced the socialists to offer a global response—the Peace Manifesto of the Nordic Labour Movement was produced around the same time. Also, in 1950 the Labour Party was weaker than at any time since the war: it had a slim majority after the February 1950 election, prestigious leaders like Bevin and Cripps would soon leave politics, Britain was struggling with rearmament, which then sparked the infighting between the right-wing and the Bevanite Left, afflicting the party throughout the 1950s. The restoration of the International as a formal institution put an end to the informal system dominated by the British—a dominance that irritated the Belgians and the French, but also the Swedes and the Germans.

In addition, endless rebuffs had scaled back the ambitions of the Belgians and the French. In 1947, Buset was still proposing an International making binding decisions, while Larock's proposal in 1950 was less ambitious and closer to the practice of Comisco. Mollet, then a minister, was less interested in a supranational authority.[161] The drafting process of the Frankfurt Declaration indicated that the charter of principles would be closer to the British, Scandinavians and Dutch conceptions, without embarrassing concessions to Marxism. Significantly, even the British diplomats were positive: 'It remains to be seen what difference this change in name will make to its activities'.[162]

The December 1950 congress of the PSB asked the restoration of the Socialist International in order to multiply the efforts for peace and to put forward constructive solutions.[163] The proposal was linked to a foreign policy approving the Atlantic Treaty, collective security and German rearmament in the European Defence Community. Larock turned this resolution into an open letter to Morgan Phillips, backed by SFIO and PSU. Larock used rhetorical arguments that struck a chord with the Labour Party. Like Buset, he argued that Comisco was already the International, it only needed to reclaim its name. By adopting the functionalist approach and refusing to impose decisions on the national parties—which would have irritated national electors—Comisco achieved a great deal of success in spreading information and calibrating socialist policies. The formal rebirth of the Socialist International would not be a return to the past but an extension and intensification of present activities. The reasons for changing the name were above all psychological:

> What most Socialist workers remember of the International is hardly more than its name. Yet with this name is associated a profound and powerful common aspiration.[164]

Larock repeated that the socialists were the only political family without an International, which led many to associate with organisations like the European Movement, where they mingled with conservatives. The future was uncertain, so the socialists had to stay united and act swiftly. Larock mentioned an episode the Labour leadership was very proud of: when Attlee visited Truman and urged him to be cautious about the Korean War and nuclear weapons. Larock argued that the Labour Government would have been even more effective with the world socialist movement at its back: 'Five years of experience have taught Socialists everywhere that their opinions and aims are fundamentally the same as those of the Labour Party'.[165] Larock then listed some innovations to make the International more effective: better circulation of information, more regular conferences, extraordinary meetings of socialist leaders to discuss urgent issues, moral support to the parties fighting elections, socialist coordination in the inter-parliamentary conferences, such as the Strasbourg Assembly.

Morgan Phillips was positive, appreciating Larock's statement that the International could not tell parties with Government responsibilities what to do.[166] Björk was not opposed in principle, but he argued that during an emergency the great leaders would not have had time to meet. Instead, the leaders' conferences were to become the focus of socialist cooperation at the European level by the 1970s.[167] Haakon Lie said that myths and symbols were more important on the Continent than in Scandinavia—implicitly confirming that the Northern Europeans considered Southern Europeans overly emotional.

The Comisco meeting of 2–4 March 1951 gave its unanimous approval to the Belgian and British proposal to restore the International, stating that cooperation would proceed only by consent.[168] The restoration was just 'changing the label', as Pivert said.[169] The International Socialist Conference was to become the 'Socialist International', the Comisco 'the Council of the Socialist International', the Comisco Sub-Committee 'the Bureau of the Socialist International'. Braunthal drafted a constitution based on the 'unwritten rules of Comisco', using a language similar to that of the LSI.[170] The central feature of Braunthal's proposal was the supremacy of the Bureau, vested with the power to deal with current affairs, call special conferences and supervise the organisation; the most important parties had a permanent seat in the Bureau. The ideas found in Price's works and Morgan Phillips' 1945 memorandum had been fully implemented in this constitution. Nevertheless, the Nordic parties found it excessive to even talk of coordination and asked to emphasise the freedom of the parties.

The Frankfurt Congress (30 June–3 July 1951) was a major event, with the audience allowed to witness the ratification of decisions taken earlier. One hundred and two delegates were present and 12,000–14,000 people attended a rally at the Frankfurt Fair, where Schumacher made a speech many found uncomfortable. The German stage served to show the British dominance over social democracy. Morgan Phillips, who was elected president of the International, said that the workers needed a political theory for social analysis, but there was not yet a theory that had been updated to the needs of the day.[171] Socialism had become fragmented in a range of national cases, representing complex and differing interests, achieving unequal success. The socialist answer to the threat of totalitarianism and capitalism was democratic planning. Healey was satisfied with the resolutions on foreign policy, as the neutralists did not make their dissent public—however the SAP did not publish the resolution on foreign policy in Sweden.

While André Philip's comment to the rebirth of the Socialist International was 'we are not satisfied',[172] Healey had every right to be satisfied. During his long tenure, the opinions, plans and interests of the Labour Party were always given priority and the British leadership was unanimously, sometimes begrudgingly, recognised. It was a success for the party, but also a personal one. Still a party bureaucrat without a following or even a seat in parliament, Healey had become the authority in international fraternal relations and imposed his ideas on the leaders of great socialist movements. He left his mark on the identity and workings of the Socialist International—Hanely speaks of a *'conception healeyiste'*.[173] Healey's verdict on the Frankfurt Congress can also be read as a verdict on the Socialist International and his tenure as International Secretary:

> The Labour Party can be well satisfied with the work of the Conference and its own contribution. Many of the speakers, some of whom had bitterly criticised the Labour Party's attitude in the past, paid tribute to the guidance which the British Labour Party had given to the International Socialist Movement since the war. The Declaration on the Aims and Tasks of Democratic Socialism is pervaded by the practical realism of the British and Scandinavian Parties rather than the aggressive dogmatism of the Continentals. And the resolution on Socialist World Action in the Struggle for Peace is again based mainly on a British draft.[174]

Healey's sober but satisfied assessment can well serve as the closure to this history of the rebirth of the Socialist International:

> The ultimate value of the International remains difficult to assess and easy to underestimate. It is not likely to register many dramatic successes in co-ordinating the policies of its member Parties. But its very existence creates a permanent moral obligation on its members to exploit their areas of agreement and to minimise their disagreements. For the weaker Parties in particular the existence of the International is a permanent source of strength.[175]

Notes

1. B.D. Graham (2000) 'Choix atlantique our Troisième force internationale?' in S. Bernstein (ed.) *Le Parti socialiste entre Résistance et République* (Paris: Publications de la Sorbonne), 165.
2. D. Sassoon (2010) *One Hundred Years of Socialism: The West European Left in the Twentieth Century* (London: Tauris), 237. K.O. Morgan (1985). *Labour in Power, 1945–1951* (Oxford: Oxford University Press), 390. M. Newman (1993) 'The British Labour Party', in R.T. Griffiths (ed.), *Socialist Parties and the Question of Europe in the 1950's* (Leiden: Brill), 162–164.
3. Circular 24/49, 'European Unity', May 1949, IISH, SI, 48.
4. R. Steininger (1979) *Deutschland und die Sozialistische Internationale nach dem Zweiten Weltkrieg, Darstellung und Dokumentation* (Bonn: Neue Gesellschaft), 141. Also, K. Featherstone (1988) *Socialist Parties and European Integration: A Comparative History* (Manchester: Manchester University Press), 42–47. R.T. Griffiths, 'European Utopia or capitalist trap? The Socialist International and the question of Europe', Griffiths (ed.), *Socialist Parties and the Question of Europe in the 1950's*, 13–14.
5. Labour Party (1948) *Feet on the Ground, A Study of Western Europe* (London: Labour Party).
6. Circular 115, 8 October 1948, IISH, SI, 47.
7. Circular 117, 'Report by M.C.Bolle (Holland) on activities since Vienna Meeting of Comisco (3 June 1948)'; Circular 121, 'Summarised report of the fourth meeting of the committee of International Socialist Conferences, Clacton-On-Sea, 3 December 1948', IISH, SI, 47.
8. 'Memorandum on international socialist policy', Labour History Archive and Study Centre, People History Museum, Manchester (LHASC), Labour Party (LP), International Sub-Committee, Minutes and Documents, 1948. See also Newman, 'The British Labour Party', 176.
9. J. Deutsch, Die Organisierung des Donauraumes, *Zukunft*, June 1947. K. Waldrunner, Wirtschaftsprobleme auf der Donaukonferenz in Budapest, *Zukunft*, July 1947.
10. 'Note on the Conference of Experts on nationalisation, Buscot Park, December 6–10, 1948', LHASC, LP, International Sub-Committee, Minutes and Documents, 1948.
11. Circular 96, 20 April 1948, IISH, SI, 47.
12. 'Re: International Socialist Planning—Motion by the Austrian delegates', 7 June 1948, IISH, SI, 237.
13. Circular 14/49 A, 31 March 1949; Circular 16/49, 14 April 1949, IISH, SI, 48.

14. Circular 18/49, 'Conference of Economic Experts, Buscot Park, England, 6–10 December, 1948', IISH, SI, 48. 'Note on the Conference of Experts on nationalisation, Buscot Park, December 6–10, 1948', LHASC, LP, International Sub-Committee, Minutes and Documents, 1948.
15. Circular 17/49, 'Conference of Economic Experts, Bennekom, Holland, 14–18 March 1949', IISH, SI, 48. W. Fienburgh, 'Report on the socialist conference of economic experts on international control of European basic industries, Bennekom, Holland, March 14–20, 1949', LHASC, LP, International Sub-Committee, Minutes and Documents, 1948.
16. Morgan, *Labour in power*, 363. On the role of Gaitskell and Jay see P.M. Williams (1982), *Hugh Gaitskell* (Oxford: Oxford University Press), 143–146.
17. Labour Party, *Feet on the ground*, 7–13.
18. W. Fienburgh, 'Report on the socialist conference of economic experts on international control of European basic industries, Bennekom, Holland, March 14–20, 1949', LHASC, LP, International Sub-Committee, Minutes and Documents, 1948.
19. Circular 34/49, 'International Socialist Conference, Baarn, Holland, 14–16 May 1949—Summarised Report of Proceedings', IISH, SI, 48.
20. Circular 22/ 49 A, 29 April 1949, IISH, SI, 48.
21. D. Healey, 'Report on the International Socialist Conference, Baarn, Holland, May 14–16, 1949 and COMISCO meeting, Amsterdam, Holland, May 13', LHASC, LP, International Sub-Committee, Minutes and Documents, 1949.
22. Circular 28/49; Circular 30/49, 21 June 1949, IISH, SI, 48.
23. K. Misgeld (1984) *Sozialdemokratie und Aussenpolitik in Schweden: Sozialistische Internationale, Europapolitik und die Deutschlandfrage 1945–1955* (Frankfurt: Campus Verlag), 175–188; 196–203.
24. F. Adler to J. Braunthal, 11 June 1946; Braunthal to Adler, 16 June 1946, IISH, Julius Braunthal, 23.
25. Braunthl to E. Umrath, 24 March 1947, IISH, Julius Braunthal, 88.
26. F. Brockway (1977) *Towards Tomorrow: The Autobiography of Fenner Brockway* (London: Hart-Davis MacGibbon), 147.
27. Braunthal to H. Laski, 12 July 1949, IISH, Julius, Braunthal, 119.
28. Braunthal to L. De Brouckère, 1 June 1949, IISH, Julius, Braunthal, 113.
29. W. Wodak to A. Schärf, 28 November 1949; Wodak to Adler, 28 November 1949; Wodak to Schärf, 17 December 1949, W. Wodak (1980) *Diplomatie zwischen Parteiproporz und Weltpolitik: Briefe, Dokumente und Memoranden aus dem Nachlass Walter Wodaks 1945–1950* (Salzburg: Neugebauer), 842–843; 851–852.

30. P. Van Kemseke (2006) *Towards an Era of Development, The Globalization of Socialism and Christian Democracy: 1945–1965* (Leuven: Leuven University Press), 61–64, 71–80.
31. D. Healey, 'Report on the International Socialist Conference, Baarn, Holland, May 14–16, 1949 and COMISCO meeting, Amsterdam, Holland, May 13', LHASC, LP, International Sub-Committee, Minutes and Documents, 1949.
32. Circular 34/49, 'International Socialist Conference, Baarn, Holland, 14–16 May 1949—Summarised Report of Proceedings', IISH, SI, 48.
33. D. Healey, 'The Second session of the consultative assembly of the Council of Europe, Strasbourg, August 7–28, 1950', LHASC, LP, International Sub-Committee, Minutes and Documents, 1950.
34. Circular 34/49, 'International Socialist Conference, Baarn, Holland, 14–16 May 1949—Summarised Report of Proceedings', IISH, SI, 48.
35. D. Healey, 'Report on the International Socialist Conference, Baarn, Holland, May 14–16, 1949 and COMISCO meeting, Amsterdam, Holland, May 13', LHASC, LP, International Sub-Committee, Minutes and Documents, 1949.
36. Steininger, *Deutschland und die Sozialistische Internationale nach dem Zweiten Weltkrieg*, 149–152. D. Healey, 'Report on the consultative assembly of the council of Europe, August 10th–23rd, 1949', LHASC, LP, International Sub-Committee, Minutes and Documents, 1949. D. Healey, 'The Second session of the consultative assembly of the Council of Europe, Strasbourg, August 7–28, 1950', LHASC, LP, International Sub-Committee, Minutes and Documents, 1950.
37. Steininger, *Deutschland und die Sozialistische Internationale nach dem Zweiten Weltkrieg*, 155–159. Griffiths, 'European Utopia or capitalist trap?', 14–15. D. Healey, 'Background notes for the International Socialist Conference on control of Europe's basic industries, June 16–18, 1950'; E.G. Farmer, 'Report on International Socialist Conference on Control European Basic industries, – Transport House, London, June 16th–18th, 1950', LHASC, LP, International Sub-Committee, Minutes and Documents, 1950.
38. Circular 100/51, 'Report of the First Congress of the Socialist International at Frankfort-On-Main, 30 June–3 July 1951', IISH, SI, 60.
39. T.C. Imlay (2014) '"The Policy of Social Democracy is Self-Consciously Internationalist": The German Social Democratic Party's Internationalism after 1945', *The Journal of Modern History*, 86, 1, 107.
40. Misgeld, *Sozialdemokratie und Aussenpolitik in Schweden*, 196–203.
41. Griffiths, 'European Utopia or capitalist trap?', 19. Imlay, '"The Policy of Social Democracy is Self-Consciously Internationalist"', 106–120.
42. LPACR 1948, 178.

43. Sassoon, *One Hundred Years of Socialism*, 185.
44. Newman, 'The British Labour Party', 171.
45. Newman, 'The British Labour Party', 174–177.
46. M. Broad and O. Daddow (2010) 'Half-Remembered Quotations from Mostly Forgotten Speeches: The Limits of Labour's European Policy Discourse', *The British Journal of Politics and International Relations*, 12, 2, 212.
47. E. Costa (2017) 'Labour's Euroscepticism and the Socialist International (1948–1952)' in G. Levi, A. Preda (eds) *Euroscepticism, Resistance and Opposition to the European Community/ European Union* (Bologna: Il Mulino), 337–348.
48. Labour Party Annual Conference Report (LPACR) 1950, 166.
49. Labour Party (1950) *European Unity* (London: Labour Party), 4–5.
50. Van Kemseke, *Towards an Era of Development*, 284.
51. Circular 76/51, 14 June 1951, IISH, SI, 59.
52. Circular B. 13/52, 15 May 1952, IISH, SI, 65.
53. Circular B 6/53, IISH, SI, 73.
54. Misgeld, *Sozialdemokratie und Aussenpolitik in Schweden*, 100–110.
55. Imlay, '"The policy of social democracy is self-consciously internationalist"', 106–114.
56. Circular B.17/52, 26 June 1952, IISH, SI, 65.
57. Griffiths, 'European Utopia or Capitalist Trap?', 18. Van Kemseke, *Towards an Era of Development*, 277.
58. G. Devin (1983) 'La renaissance de l'Internationale Socialiste (1945–1951)', in H. Portelli (ed.), *L'Internationale socialiste* (Paris: Les Éditions Ouvrières), 5.
59. A. Bevan (1951) 'Foreword' in D. Healey (ed.) *The Curtain falls: The Story of the Socialists in Eastern Europe* (London: Lincolns-Prager), 5–6.
60. Circular 91, 'Minutes of the Second Meeting of the Committee of International Socialist Conference, London, 19–20 March', IISH, SI, 47.
61. Circular 98, 'Summarised report of the meeting of the international refugee committee of Comisco', 19 April 1948; Circular 118, 'Summarised report of the meeting of the international refugee committee of Comisco', 30 November 1948, IISH, SI, 47.
62. Circular 7, 'Refugee relief and organisation fund', 20 February 1949, IISH, SI, 48. 'Summary of the decisions of the COMISCO meeting at Clacton, 3rd December 1948', LHASC, LP, International Sub-Committee, Minutes and Documents, 1948.
63. Bureau Internationale Socialiste (1948) *Les socialistes des pays opprimés réclament la liberté, la démocratie et l'indépendance* (Paris: Editions du Bureau internationale socialiste).

64. Bureau internationale socialiste (n.d.) *2me conférence des Partis Socialistes de l'Europe Centrale et Orientale Paris, 2–4 octobre 1948* (Paris: Bureau Internationale Socialiste du Centre-Est de l'Europe).
65. Circular 98, 'Summarised report of the meeting of the international refugee committee of Comisco', 19 April 1948; Circular 117, 'Report by M.C.Bolle (Holland) on activities since Vienna Meeting of Comisco (3 June 1948)'; Circular 121, 'Summarised report of the fourth meeting of the committee of international Socialist Conferences, Clacton-On-Sea, 3 December 1948', IISH, SI, 47. FCO Historians, 'From World War to Cold War: the records of the Foreign Office Permanent Under-Secretary's Department, 1939–51', OP 6, 77.
66. Healey to M.C. Bolle, 22 July 1949, IISH, SI, 801.
67. Circular 19/49, 10 April 1949; Circular 22/49°, 29 April 1949, IISH, SI, 48.
68. D. Healey, 'Report on the International Socialist Conference, Baarn, Holland, May 14–16, 1949 and COMISCO meeting, Amsterdam, Holland, May 13', LHASC, LP, International Sub-Committee, Minutes & Documents, 1949.
69. Circular 87/51, 'Report of the Meeting of the Committee of the International Socialist Conference at Frankfort-On-Main, 28–29 June, 1951', IISH, SI, 60.
70. G. Devin (1987) 'Guy Mollet et l'Internationale Socialiste', in B. Ménager, P.Ratte, J.-L. Thiébault, R.Vandenbussche, C.-M. Wallon-Leducq (eds), *Guy Mollet, Un camarade en république* (Lille: Presses Universitaires de Lille), 148.
71. Circular 38/49C, 'The Socialist Union of Central-Eastern Europe', IISH, SI, 49. 'Une année d'action socialiste internationale', L'Office Universitaire de Recherche Socialiste, Paris (OURS), Fond Guy Mollet, AGM 53 (Internationale Socialiste, 1949–1957), f. Comisco 1950. SUCEE narrated its history in SUCEE (n.d.) *Unity -. Prelude to Freedom. The Origin and Aims of the Socialist Union of Central-Eastern Europe*, ([London]: SUCEE).
72. A. Ciolkosz to Comisco, 5 July 1949, IISH, SI, 801.
73. Circular no. 98/50, 'The General principles of democratic socialism and the Socialist International', 14 May 1950, IISH, SI, 52.
74. Circular 155/50, 'Report of the International Socialist Conference at Copenaghen, 1–3 June 1950', IISH, SI, 54.
75. Ciolkosz spoke at the Frankfurt Congress but he had little effect (Circular 100/51, 'Report of the First congress of the Socialist International held at Frankfort-on-Main, 30 June–3 July 1951', IISH, SI, 60).
76. LPACR 1948, 23.
77. For example, Comisco spread the news of the persecution of 200 socialists (Circular 165/50, 29 August 1950, IISH, SI, 54).

78. Healey, *The curtain falls*.
79. P.M. Williams (ed.) (1983) *The Diary of Hugh Gaitskell, 1945–1956* (London: Cape), 506.
80. Circular 155/50, 'Report of the International Socialist Conference at Copenhagen, 1–3 June 1950', IISH, SI, 54.
81. A. Defty (2004) *Britain, America and Anti-Communist Propaganda, 1945–53: The Information Research Department* (London: Routledge), 151.
82. 'Aims and Tasks of Democratic Socialism', quoted in J. Braunthal (1980) *History of the International*, Vol. 3, *World Socialism 1943–1968* (London: Gollancz), 533. Also, http://www.socialistinternational.org/viewArticle.cfm?ArticleID=39 (accessed 24 January 2018).
83. G. Devin (1993) *L'Internationale socialiste: histoire et sociologie du socialisme internationale: 1945–1990* (Paris: Presses de la Fondation national des sciences politiques), 159.
84. Circular 91, 'Minutes of the Second Meeting of the Committee of International Socialist Conference, London, 19–20 March', IISH, SI, 47.
85. Devin, *L'Internationale socialiste*, 32.
86. F.A. Warner, Minute, 17 March 1948, TNA, FO 371/72320-R3487.
87. Circular 105, 'Resolution on Democracy and Socialism', IISH, SI, 47.
88. 'Report on COMISCO meeting, Paris, December 10th–11th, 1949', LHASC, LP, International Sub-Committee, Minutes and Documents, 1949.
89. 'Report to the National Executive Committee on International Socialist Conference, Vienna, June 4/7 1948', LHASC, LP, International Sub-Committee, Minutes and Documents, 1948.
90. Circular 105, 'Resolution on Democracy and Socialism', IISH, SI, 47.
91. OURS, Fond Guy Mollet, AGM 53 (Internationale Socialiste, 1949–1957), f. Comisco 1950, 'Une année d'action socialiste internationale'. 'Report on COMISCO meeting, Paris, December 10th–11th, 1949', LHASC, LP, International Sub-Committee, Minutes and Documents, 1949. Circular 61/49, 'Minutes of the meeting of the Committee of the International Socialist Conference, Paris, 10–11 December 1949', IISH, SI, 49.
92. Circular 37/49, 'Activities of the Committee of the International Socialist Conference and its London Office', 15 July 1949, IISH, SI, 49.
93. Circular 132/50, 'Orders for the international stamp', 20 June 1950, IISH, SI, 53.
94. Circular 77/50, 'May Day Manifesto', 20 April 1950, IISH, SI, 52. D. Healey, 'Report on Comisco meeting, Hastings, March 18th–19th, 1950', LHASC, LP, International Sub-Committee, Minutes and Documents, 1951.

95. D. Healey, 'Report on Meeting of Comisco, London, March 2–4, 1951', LHASC, LP, International Sub-Committee, Minutes and Documents, 1951.
96. Misgeld, *Sozialdemokratie und Aussenpolitik in Schweden*, 196–203.
97. 'Réunion du COMISCO des 10 et 11 Décembre 1949', OURS, Fond Guy Mollet, AGM 53 (Internationale Socialiste, 1949–1957), f. Comisco 1950.
98. 'Rapport de la délégation Française au COMISCO en vue d'établir les bases communes d'un socialisme démocratique', October 1950, OURS, Fond Guy Mollet, AGM 53 (Internationale Socialiste, 1949–1957), f. Comisco 1950.
99. Misgeld, *Sozialdemokratie und Aussenpolitik in Schweden*, 196–211; 283–291.
100. Circular 8/50, 9 January 1950, IISH, SI, 50.
101. V. Bergström (1992) 'Party Program and Economic Policy: The Social Democrats in Government', in K. Misgeld, K. Molin and K. Åmark (eds) *Creating Social Democracy: A Century of the Social Democratic Labor Party in Sweden* (University Park: Penn State Press), 132–144. M. Telò (1985) 'Le origini del modello svedese', in E. Collotti (ed.), *L'Internazionale Operaia e Socialista tra le due guerre* (Milano: Feltrinelli), 617–630.
102. Bergström, 'Party Program and Economic Policy', 144–152.
103. Circular No. 73/50, 'The Basis of Democratic Socialism—Prepared by the Swedish Social Democratic Party', 15 April 1950, IISH, SI, 51.
104. C.-E. Odhner (1992) 'Workers and Farmers Shape the Swedish Model: Social Democracy and Agricultural Policy' in Misgeld, Molin and Åmark (eds) *Creating social democracy*, 175–212.
105. G. Esping-Andersen (1992) 'The Making of a Social Democratic Welfare State', in Misgeld, Molin and Åmark (eds), *Creating Social Democracy*, 42. K. Molin (1992) 'Party Disputes and Party Responsibility: A Study of the Social Democratic Defense Debate' in Misgeld, Molin and Åmark (eds), *Creating Social Democracy*, 389.
106. Circular 155/50, 'Report of the International Socialist Conference at Copenaghen, 1–3 June 1950', IISH, SI, 54.
107. Circular 78/50, 'Memorandum of the 'Partij van de Arbeid', Netherlands—The Foundation of Democratic Socialism', IISH, SI, 51.
108. Braunthal, *World Socialism 1943–1968*, 208–209.
109. G. Mollet, 'Les bases du socialisme démocratique', OURS, Fond Guy Mollet, AGM 53 (Internationale Socialiste, 1949–1957), f. Comisco 1950. Circular 155/50, 'Report of the International Socialist Conference at Copenaghen, 1–3 June 1950', IISH, SI, 54.

110. 'Rapport de la délégation Française au COMISCO en vue d'établir les bases communes d'un socialisme démocratique', October 1950, OURS, Fond Guy Mollet, AGM 53 (Internationale Socialiste, 1949–1957), f. Comisco 1950.
111. S. Berger (1994) *The British Labour Party and the German Social Democrats, 1900–1931* (Oxford: Clarendon), 235–245.
112. Circular 155/50, 'Report of the International Socialist Conference at Copenhagen, 1–3 June 1950', IISH, SI, 54.
113. Circular 155/50, 'Report of the International Socialist Conference at Copenhagen, 1–3 June 1950', IISH, SI, 54.
114. Circular 155/50, 'Report of the International Socialist Conference at Copenhagen, 1–3 June 1950', IISH, SI, 54.
115. P. Buffotot (1983) 'Le Parti Socialiste SFIO et l'Internationale Socialiste (1944–1969)', in Portelli, *L'Internationale socialiste*, 92–93.
116. L. Boutbien, *Aspect International de l'Idée du Mouvement Socialiste*, [around Copenhagen Conference], OURS, Fond Guy Mollet, AGM 53 (Internationale Socialiste, 1949–1957), f. Comisco 1950.
117. In the interwar period it was the SPD that suffered this problem, see Berger, *The British Labour Party and the German Social Democrats*, 18–30.
118. A. Philip (1950) *Le socialisme et l'unité européenne: réponse a l'exécutif de Labour Party* (Paris: Mouvement socialiste pour les états-unis d'Europe), 2–8. See also Buffotot, 'Le Parti Socialiste SFIO et l'Internationale Socialiste', 92.
119. 'Drafting Commission', Handwritten notes, no date, IISH, SI, 385
120. 'Minutes of the Meeting of the Drafting Commission on the basis of Democratic Socialism', IISH, SI, 385.
121. Circular 100/51, 'Report of the First Congress of the Socialist International at Frankfort-On-Main, 30 June–3 July 1951', IISH, SI, 60.
122. Braunthal, *World Socialism 1943–1968*, 531.
123. Devin, 'Guy Mollet et l'Internationale Socialiste', 154.
124. D. Healey (1990) *The Time of My Life* (London: Penguin), 93.
125. Sassoon, *One Hundred Years of Socialism*, 113–263. I. Favretto (2002) *The Long Search for a Third Way: The British Labour Party and the Italian Left since 1945* (Basingstoke: Palgrave Macmillan).
126. G. Sabbatucci (1991) *Il riformismo impossibile: storie del socialismo italiano* (Roma-Bari: Laterza), 6.
127. J. Braunthal, Von revolutionären zum demokratischen Sozialismus, Wandlungen in der Ideologie der Sozialistischen Internationale, *Vorwärts*, 16 July 1959. Also quoted in H. Heimann (1984) 'Das Sozialimusverständnis des Godesberger Programms und seine par-

teiöffentliche sowie öffentliche Resonanz', in S. Papcke and K.T. Schuon (eds), *25 Jahre nach Godesberg: braucht die SPD ein neues Grundsatzprogramm?* (Berlin: Europäische Perspektiven), 29.
128. S. Berger (1995) 'European Labour Movements and the European Working Class in Comparative Perspective', in S. Berger, D. Broughton (eds), *The Force of Labour: The Western European Labour Movement and the Working Class in the Twentieth Century* (Oxford: Berg), 248–256.
129. Braunthal to H.F. Armstrong, 4 November 1948, IISH, Julius, Braunthal, 116.
130. J. Braunthal (ed.) (1958), *Sozialistische Weltstimmen* (Berlin: Dietz). The series 'Il socialismo contemporaneo' was published by Editoriale Opere Nuove between 1956 and 1960.
131. J. Braunthal (1958) 'Vorwort' in Braunthal, *Sozialistische Weltstimmen*, 7–10.
132. G. Stedman Jones (2016) *Karl Marx: Greatness and Illusion* (London: Allen Lane), 464.
133. C.A.R. Crosland (1952) 'The Transition from Capitalism' in R.H.S. Crossman (ed.), *New Fabian Essays* (London: Turnstile), 60.
134. L. Black (2003) *The Political Culture of the Left in Affluent Britain, 1951–1964: Old Labour, New Britain?* (Basingstoke: Palgrave Macmillan).
135. G. Scirocco (2010) *Politique d'abord: il PSI, la guerra fredda e la politica internazionale, 1948–1957* (Milano: Unicopli), 134–135; 263. P. Vittorelli, La politica dell'Internazionale, *Nuova Repubblica*, 22 July 1956. P. Vittorelli, Il VII congresso dell'Internazionale, *Mondo Operaio*, September 1961.
136. J. Perazzoli (2016) *Qualcosa di nuovo da noi s'attende: la socialdemocrazia europea e il revisionismo degli anni Cinquanta* (Milano: Biblion), 178–188.
137. M. Fulla (2016) *Les socialistes français et l'économie (1944–1981): une histoire économique du politique* (Paris: Presses de Sciences Po), 67–94.
138. Fulla, *Les socialistes français et l'économie*, 95–124.
139. Socialist Union (1952) *Socialism: A New Statement of Principles* (London: Lincolns Prager), 32.
140. A. Crosland (2013) *The Future of Socialism: New Edition with foreword by Gordon Brown* (London: Constable), 89.
141. S. Berger (2000) 'Labour in comparative perspective', in D. Tanner, P. Thane and N. Tiratsoo (eds), *Labour's First Century* (Cambridge: Cambridge University Press), 322. For a different interpretation see M. Wickham-Jones (2003) 'An exceptional comrade? The Nairn–Anderson interpretation', in J. Callaghan, S. Fielding and S. Ludlam (eds) *Interpreting the Labour Party: Approaches to Labour Politics and History* (Manchester: Manchester University Press), 94–96.

142. A. Crosland (1962) *The Conservative Enemy* (London: Cape), 117.
143. Healey, *The Time of My Life*, 93.
144. W. Euchner (2005) 'Ideengeschichte des Sozialismus in Deutschland, Teil I', in H. Grebing (ed.) *Geschichte der sozialen Ideen in Deutschland: Sozialismus-katholische Soziallehre-protestantische Sozialethik; ein Handbuch*, Vol. 2 (Wiesbaden: VS verlag für Sozialwissenschaften), 428.
145. W. Eichler (1962) 'Grundwerte und Grundforderungen—Beitrag zu einem Kommentar', in W. Eichler (1972), *Zur Einführung in den demokratischen Sozialismus* (Bonn: Verlag Neue Gesellschaft), 62–77. Also S. Lemke (1984) 'Die Rolle der Marxismus-Diskussion im Entstehungsprozess des Godesberger Programms', in Papcke and Schuon (eds), *25 Jahre nach Godesberg*, 41. K. Nemitz (1993) 'Markt und Plan—Zur Entwicklung sozialdemokratischer Konzeptionen von Wirtschaftsordnung und Wirtschaftspolitik' in H. Heimann and K. Blessing (eds), *Sozialdemokratische Traditionen und demokratischer Sozialismus 2000* (Köln: Bund-Verlag), 50–51.
146. W. Eichler (1953) 'Sozialismus als angewandte Ethik', in K. Lompe, L.F. Neumann (eds) (1979), *Willi Eichlers Beiträge zum demokratischen Sozialismus: Eine Auswahl aus d. Werk* (Berlin: Dietz), 144–145. W. Eichler (1954) 'Sozialistische Gestaltung von Staat und Gesellschaft', Rede auf dem Parteitag 1954, in Eichler, *Zur Einführung in den demokratischen Sozialismus*, 47.
147. T. Brehm (1989) *SPD und Katholizismus, 1957 bis 1966: Jahre der Annäherung* (Frankfurt: Lang), 28.
148. K. Klotzbach (1982) *Der Weg zur Staatspartei: Programmatik, praktische Politik und Organisation der deutschen Sozialdemokratie 1945 bis 1965* (Berlin: Dietz), 259–261.
149. Misgeld, *Sozialdemokratie und Aussenpolitik in Schweden*, 305f.
150. Imlay, '"The policy of social democracy is self-consciously internationalist"', 112.
151. H.K. Schellenger Jr. (1968) *The SPD in the Bonn Republic: A Socialist Party Modernizes* (The Hague: Nijhoff), 102.
152. 'Aus der Rede des Vorsitenden der SPD, Brandt, auf einer Tagung der Evangelischen Akademie Tutzing', 7 März 1976 in W. Brandt, K. Rudolph (2002) (ed.), *Berliner Ausgabe*, Vol. 5, *"Die Partei der Freiheit". Willy Brandt und die SPD 1972–1992* (Berlin: Dietz), 193.
153. C. Meyer (2006) *Herbert Wehner, Biographie* (München: Dt. Taschenbuch-Verl), 218–225.
154. 'Ziele und Aufgaben des demokratischen Sozialismus', in Braunthal (ed.), *Sozialistische Weltstimmen*, 298.
155. A.H. Leugers-Scherzberg (2002) *Die Wandlungen des Herbert Wehner* (Berlin: Propyläen), 233.

156. 'Grundsatzprogramm der Sozialdemokratischen Partei Deutschland', quoted in Eichler, *Zur Einführung in den demokratischen Sozialismus*, 138.
157. Imlay, '"The policy of social democracy is self-consciously internationalist"', 120–122.
158. Van Kemseke, *Towards an Era of Development*, 274–277.
159. Devin, *L'Internationale socialiste*, 250–271.
160. Misgeld, *Sozialdemokratie und Aussenpolitik in Schweden*, 264–275.
161. Devin, 'Guy Mollet et l'Internationale Socialiste', 152.
162. M.D. Butler, Minute, 30 January 1951, TNA, FO 371/96010-WB2191/2.
163. Circular 232/50, 'The Congress of the Belgian Socialist Party', 12 December 1950, IISH, SI, 56.
164. Steininger, *Deutschland und die Sozialistische Internationale nach dem Zweiten Weltkrieg*, 392.
165. Steininger, *Deutschland und die Sozialistische Internationale nach dem Zweiten Weltkrieg*, 393.
166. M. Phillips, 24 January 1951, TNA, FO 371/96010-WB2191/2. Misgeld, *Sozialdemokratie und Aussenpolitik in Schweden*, 264–282.
167. C. Salm (2016) *Transnational Socialist Networks in the 1970s: European Community Development Aid and Southern Enlargement* (Basingstoke: Palgrave Macmillan), 30.
168. D. Healey, 'Report on Meeting of Comisco, London, March 2–4, 1951', LHASC, LP, International Sub-Committee, Minutes and Documents, 1951.
169. Devin, 'Guy Mollet et l'Internationale Socialiste', 152.
170. Circular 34/51, 'Draft Constitution of the Socialist International', 21 March 1951, IISH, SI, 58.
171. Circular 100/51, 'Report of the First Congress of the Socialist International at Frankfort-On-Main, 30 June–3 July 1951', IISH, SI, 60.
172. Devin, 'Guy Mollet et l'Internationale Socialiste', 154.
173. D. Hanely (1983) 'Un socialisme aux couleurs de l'Angleterre: le parti travailliste et l'Internationale Socialiste depuis 1945', in Portelli, *L'Internationale socialiste*, 63.
174. D. Healey, 'Report on International Socialist Conference, Franfurt a/Main from June 30 to 3 July 1951', LHASC, LP, International Sub-Committee, Minutes and Documents, 1951.
175. D. Healey, 'Report on International Socialist Conference, Franfurt a/Main from June 30 to 3 July 1951', LHASC, LP, International Sub-Committee, Minutes and Documents, 1951.

Bibliography

Berger, S. (1994). *The British Labour Party and the German Social Democrats, 1900–1931.* Oxford: Clarendon.
Berger, S. (1995). European Labour Movements and the European Working Class in Comparative Perspective. In S. Berger, D. Broughton (Eds.). *The Force of Labour: The Western European Labour Movement and the Working Class in the Twentieth Century* (pp. 245–261). Oxford: Berg.
Berger, S. (2000). Labour in comparative perspective. In D. Tanner, P. Thane & N. Tiratsoo (Eds.). *Labour's First Century* (pp. 309–340). Cambridge: Cambridge University Press.
Bergström, V. (1992). Party program and economic policy: the social democrats in Government. In K. Misgeld, K. Molin & K. Åmark (Eds.). *Creating social democracy: a century of the Social Democratic Labor Party in Sweden* (pp. 132–173). University Park: Penn State Press.
Black, L. (2003). *The political culture of the left in affluent Britain, 1951–1964: old Labour, New Britain?*. Basingstoke: Palgrave Macmillan.
Brandt, W. & Rudolph, K. (Eds.). (2002). *Berliner Ausgabe*, Vol. 5, *"Die Partei der Freiheit". Willy Brandt und die SPD 1972–1992*. Berlin: Dietz.
Braunthal, J. (Ed.). (1958). *Sozialistische Weltstimmen*. Berlin: Dietz.
Braunthal, J. (1980). *History of the International*, Vol. 3, *World Socialism 1943–1968.* London: Gollancz.
Brehm, T. (1989). *SPD und Katholizismus, 1957 bis 1966: Jahre der Annäherung* Frankfurt: Lang.
Broad, M. & Daddow, O. (2010). Half-Remembered Quotations from Mostly Forgotten Speeches: The Limits of Labour's European Policy Discourse, *The British Journal of Politics and International Relations*, 12 (2), 205–222.
Brockway, F. (1977). *Towards tomorrow: the Autobiography of Fenner Brockway.* London: Hart-Davis MacGibbon.
Buffotot, P. (1983). Le Parti Socialiste SFIO et l'Internationale Socialiste (1944–1969). In H. Portelli (Ed.). *L'Internationale socialiste*. Paris: Les Éditions Ouvrières.
Bureau International Socialiste. (1948). *Les socialistes des pays opprimés réclament la liberté, la démocratie et l'indépendance.* Paris: Editions du Bureau International Socialiste.
Bureau International Socialiste. (n.d.). *2me conférence des Partis Socialistes de l'Europe Centrale et Orientale Paris, 2–4 octobre 1948.* Paris: Bureau International Socialiste du Centre-Est de l'Europe.
Costa, E. (2017). Labour's Euroscepticism and the Socialist International (1948–1952). In G. Levi & A. Preda (Eds.). *Euroscepticism, Resistance and Opposition to the European Community/ European Union* (pp. 337–348). Bologna: Il Mulino.

Crosland, C.A.R. (1952). The transition from capitalism. In R.H.S. Crossman (Ed.). *New Fabian Essays* (pp. 33–68). London: Turnstile.
Crosland, A. (1962). *The conservative enemy*. London: Cape.
Crosland, A. (2013). *The Future of Socialism: New Edition with foreword by Gordon Brown*. London: Constable.
Defty, A. (2004). *Britain, America and anti-communist propaganda, 1945–53: the Information Research Department*. London: Routledge.
Devin, G. (1983). La renaissance de l'Internationale Socialiste (1945–1951). In H. Portelli (Ed.). *L'Internationale socialiste* (pp. 43–56). Paris: Les Éditions Ouvrières.
Devin, G. (1987). Guy Mollet et l'Internationale Socialiste. In B. Ménager, P. Ratte, J.-L. Thiébault, R. Vandenbussche, C.-M. Wallon-Leducq (Eds.). *Guy Mollet, Un camarade en république* (pp. 143–168). Lille: Presses Universitaires de Lille.
Devin, G. (1993). *L'Internationale socialiste: histoire et sociologie du socialisme internationale: 1945–1990*. Paris: Presses de la Fondation national des sciences politiques.
Eichler, W. (1953). Sozialismus als angewandte Ethik. In K. Lompe & L.F. Neumann (Eds.). (1979) *Willi Eichlers Beiträge zum demokratischen Sozialismus: Eine Auswahl aus d. Werk* (pp. 7–34). Berlin: Dietz.
Eichler, W. (1954). Sozialistische Gestaltung von Staat und Gesellschaft', Rede auf dem Parteitag 1954. In W. Eichler (Ed.). (1972) *Zur Einführung in den demokratischen Sozialismus* (pp. 37–61). Bonn: Verlag Neue Gesellschaft.
Eichler, W. (1962). Grundwerte und Grundforderungen – Beitrag zu einem Kommentar. In W. Eichler (Ed.). (1972) *Zur Einführung in den demokratischen Sozialismus* (pp. 62–77). Bonn: Verlag Neue Gesellschaft.
Esping-Andersen, G. (1992). The making of a social democratic welfare state. In K. Misgeld, K. Molin & K. Åmark (Eds.). *Creating social democracy: a century of the Social Democratic Labor Party in Sweden* (pp. 35–66). University Park: Penn State Press.
Euchner, W. (2005). Ideengeschichte des Sozialismus in Deutschland, Teil I. In H. Grebing (Ed.). *Geschichte der sozialen Ideen in Deutschland: Sozialismus-katholische Soziallehre-protestantische Sozialethik; ein Handbuch*, Vol. 2 (pp. 15–350). Wiesbaden: VS verlag für Sozialwissenschaften.
Favretto, I. (2002). *The long search for a third way: the British Labour Party and the Italian Left since 1945*. Basingstoke: Palgrave Macmillan.
FCO Historians. (2013). 'From World War to Cold War: the records of the Foreign Office Permanent Under-Secretary's Department, 1939–51', OP 6.
Featherstone, K. (1988). *Socialist parties and European integration: a comparative history*. Manchester: Manchester University Press.
Fulla, M. (2016). *Les socialistes français et l'économie (1944–1981): une histoire économique du politique*. Paris: Presses de Sciences Po.

Graham, B.D. (2000). Choix atlantique our Troisième force internationale?. In S. Bernstein (Ed.). *Le Parti socialiste entre Résistance et République* (pp. 157–165). Paris: Publications de la Sorbonne.

Griffiths, R.T. (1993). European Utopia or capitalist trap? The Socialist International and the question of Europe. In R.T. Griffiths (Ed.), *Socialist parties and the question of Europe in the 1950's* (pp. 9–24). Leiden: Brill.

Hanely, D. (1983). Un socialisme aux couleurs de l'Angleterre: le parti travailliste et l'Internationale Socialiste depuis 1945. In H. Portelli (Ed.). *L'Internationale socialiste* (pp. 57–66). Paris: Les Éditions Ouvrières.

Healey, D. (Ed.). (1951). *The Curtain falls: the Story of the Socialists in Eastern Europe*. London: Lincolns-Prager.

Healey, D. (1990). *The time of my life*. London: Penguin.

Heimann, H. (1984). Das Sozialimusverständnis des Godesberger Programms und seine parteiöffentliche sowie öffentliche Resonanz. In S. Papcke & K.T. Schuon (Eds.). *25 Jahre nach Godesberg: braucht die SPD ein neues Grundsatzprogramm?* (pp. 18–35). Berlin: Europäische Perspektiven.

Imlay, T.C. (2014). "The policy of social democracy is self-consciously internationalist": The German Social Democratic Party's Internationalism after 1945. *The Journal of Modern History*, 86 (1), 81–123.

Klotzbach, K. (1982). *Der Weg zur Staatspartei : Programmatik, praktische Politik und Organisation der deutschen Sozialdemokratie 1945 bis 1965*. Berlin: Dietz.

Labour Party. (1948). *Feet on the ground, A study of Western Europe*. London: Labour Party.

Labour Party. (1950). *European Unity*. London: Labour Party.

Lemke, S. (1984). Die Rolle der Marxismus-Diskussion im Entstehungsprosess des Godesberger Programms. In S. Papcke & K.T. Schuon (Eds.). *25 Jahre nach Godesberg: braucht die SPD ein neues Grundsatzprogramm?* (pp. 37–52). Berlin: Europäische Perspektiven.

Leugers-Scherzberg, A.H. (2002). *Die Wandlungen des Herbert Wehner*. Berlin: Propyläen.

Meyer, C. (2006). *Herbert Wehner, Biographie*. München: Dt. Taschenbuch-Verl.

Misgeld, K. (1984). *Sozialdemokratie und Aussenpolitik in Schweden: Sozialistische Internationale, Europapolitik und die Deutschlandfrage 1945–1955*. Frankfurt: Campus Verlag.

Molin, K. (1992). Party disputes and party responsibility: A study of the social democratic defense debate. In K. Misgeld, K. Molin & K. Åmark (Eds.). *Creating social democracy: a century of the Social Democratic Labor Party in Sweden* (pp. 375–408). University Park: Penn State Press.

Morgan, K.O. (1985). *Labour in power, 1945–1951*. Oxford: Oxford University Press.

Nemitz, K. (1993). Markt und Plan – Zur Entwicklung sozialdemokratischer Konzeptionen von Wirtschaftsordnung und Wirtschaftspolitik. In H. Heimann & K. Blessing (Eds.). *Sozialdemokratische Traditionen und demokratischer Sozialismus 2000* (pp. 44–73). Köln: Bund-Verlag.

Newman, M. (1993). The British Labour Party. In R.T. Griffiths (Ed.). *Socialist parties and the question of Europe in the 1950's* (pp. 162–177). Leiden: Brill.

Odhner, C.-E. (1992). Workers and farmers shape the Swedish model: Social democracy and agricultural policy. In K. Misgeld, K. Molin & K. Åmark (Eds.). *Creating social democracy: a century of the Social Democratic Labor Party in Sweden* (pp. 175–212). University Park: Penn State Press.

Perazzoli, J. (2016). *Qualcosa di nuovo da noi s'attende: la socialdemocrazia europea e il revisionismo degli anni Cinquanta*. Milano: Biblion.

Philip, A. (1950). *Le socialisme et l'unité européenne: réponse a l'exécutif de Labour Party*. Paris: Mouvement socialiste pour les états-unis d'Europe.

Sabbatucci, G. (1991). *Il riformismo impossibile: storie del socialismo italiano*. Roma-Bari: Laterza.

Salm, C. (2016). *Transnational socialist networks in the 1970s: European Community development aid and southern enlargement*. London: Palgrave Macmillan.

Sassoon, D. (2010). *One hundred years of socialism: the West European Left in the twentieth century*. London: Tauris.

Schellenger Jr., H.K. (1968). *The SPD in the Bonn Republic: a socialist party modernizes*. The Hague: Nijhoff.

Scirocco, G. (2010). *Politique d'abord: il PSI, la guerra fredda e la politica internazionale, 1948–1957*. Milano: Unicopli.

Socialist Union. (1952). *Socialism: A new Statement of Principles*. London: Lincolns Prager.

Stedman Jones, G. (2016). *Karl Marx: greatness and illusion*. London: Allen Lane.

Steininger, R. (1979). *Deutschland und die Sozialistische Internationale nach dem Zweiten Weltkrieg, Darstellung und Dokumentation*. Bonn: Neue Gesellschaft.

SUCEE. (n.d.). *Unity – Prelude to freedom. The origin and aims of the Socialist Union of Central-Eastern Europe*. London: SUCEE.

Telò, M. (1985). Le origini del modello svedese. E. Collotti (Ed.). *L'Internazionale Operaia e Socialista tra le due guerre* (pp. 617–630). Milano: Feltrinelli.

Van Kemseke, P. (2006). *Towards an Era of Development, The Globalization of Socialism and Christian Democracy: 1945–1965*. Leuven: Leuven University Press.

Wickham-Jones, M. (2003). An exceptional comrade? The Nairn–Anderson interpretation. In J. Callaghan, S. Fielding & S. Ludlam (Eds.). *Interpreting the Labour Party: Approaches to Labour politics and history* (pp. 86–100). Manchester: Manchester University Press.

Williams, P.M. (1982). *Hugh Gaitskell*. Oxford: Oxford University Press.
Williams, P.M. (Ed.). (1983). *The diary of Hugh Gaitskell, 1945–1956*. London: Cape.
Wodak, W. (1980). *Diplomatie zwischen Parteiproporz und Weltpolitik: Briefe, Dokumente und Memoranden aus dem Nachlass Walter Wodaks 1945–1950*. Salzburg: Neugebauer.

CHAPTER 9

Conclusion

The Socialist International and the Frankfurt Declaration were not born of idealistic inspiration or pressure from social movements, they were the result of compromises laboured over in committees. Not a noble birth, but one that fitted their reformist nature and they still lived longer than their predecessors. When the Socialist International went into crisis in 2013, it was because it had wandered too far from its origins: an international association of progressive parties from the core of the liberal democratic world.[1] The original founding parties left and created the Progressive Alliance, a return to basics. As Devin argues, the Socialist International was not a failed attempt, but exactly what the national parties wanted, especially the British Labour Party. However, was it influential?

International fraternal relations were intertwined with most aspects of party life: organisation, hierarchy, discipline and factional struggle. All socialist parties had to deal with a time-consuming activity that could prove embarrassing or encourage dissent. Different contexts, organisations and traditions explain the different responses. It should be noted that the same phenomenon took place at different times in different parties. For example, in the late 1950s, Nenni would seek inspiration from the Labour Party to encourage reformism in his party, while Gaitskell, as leader of the Labour Party, would become more directly involved in international socialism. While a synchronic description is necessary to understand the events in this limited timeframe, a diachronic comparison would reveal even more similarities between parties.

Throughout the chapters, we have seen many ways through which international fraternal relations influenced the internal development of the national parties. The strict definition of democratic socialism in the Frankfurt Declaration was important: it forced the Italian Socialists to abandon their ideological ambiguities about socialism and democracy and it encouraged revisionism in German and French socialism. The 'performative' role of the Socialist International in giving democratic socialism a meaning was successful.

As an institution, the Socialist International had little power. The Socialist International is bound to disappoint the high—even utopian—expectations that come with such a glorious name. After making extensive efforts and sacrifices to be readmitted to the European socialist family, Nenni found it very frustrating that Prime Minister Harold Wilson and Foreign Minister Willy Brandt did not help him in domestic politics[2] and did not make their contribution to the fight against the dictatorship in Greece: 'the English and German comrades […] only cares about doing business with Greece'[3]:

> What has now become a congress of the Socialist International? A series of tiresome descriptions of national situations with sporadic attempts to offer a synthesis, all of this within the framework of a kind of internationalism that has exhausted its progressive force for struggle and enthusiasm.[4]

Denis Healey helped to rebuild the international socialist family, but also witnessed the destruction of social democracy behind the Iron Curtain and its impotence below the Olive Line. Symptomatically, after ending his tenure of International Secretary, he wrote an essay on the predominance of power politics in foreign affairs. The nation state was the only effective player, while ideals like internationalist solidarity did not excite the masses.[5] Others offered a different diagnosis: the power of the European nation-states was insignificant compared to the superpowers and the international economic system. They deduced the need to pool sovereignty into a federal Europe. This was the main point of disagreement in the European socialist movement for decades.

However, Healey appreciated transnational contacts, especially informal ones, as they provided 'the social tissue without which a sense of international community cannot survive the pressure of national interests'.[6] He understood track-two diplomacy:

In my experience, private international conferences such as those of Koenigswinter, and those of the Bilderberg Group have a value in world affairs far greater than the well-publicised meetings of the United Nations, NATO or the European Union. The participants are able to talk more freely and to develop lasting personal friendships which lubricate the normal diplomatic channels. Moreover, such conferences can include businessmen, bankers, trade unionists and journalists who have no other means of learning about one another's problems.[7]

Healey had learned to network while rebuilding the Socialist International. He was proud of having friends in powerful positions in every European state and they cooperated to their mutual benefit. Vittorelli, his friend in Italy, organised a meeting in 1963 between Wilson and Nenni, where the two leaders agreed to oppose the nuclear Multi-Lateral Force (MLF) proposed by NATO: Nenni would delay the MLF until Wilson's victory, who had the bargaining power to ask for it to be shelved.[8] Vittorelli became the first Italian socialist to be invited to the Bilderberg meetings, where he and Healey impressed on McGeorge Bundy how much the MLF was damaging the unity of the Atlantic Alliance. There were other examples.

According to Devin and Imlay, it was voluntary cooperation through the exchange of views that was the real strength of socialist internationalism. After the rebirth of the Socialist International, this cooperation continued. According to Van Kemseke, the Socialist International was a very effective international non-governmental organisation (NGO) because of direct access to leaders in positions of powers, influencing their ideas; it shaped policies for development in the 1950s.[9] Particularly significant was the cooperation between the Labour Party and the SPD—a return to the inter-war practice. Herbert Wehner used the 'Gaitskell plan' to legitimise his own proposal for German reunification, the *Deutschlandplan*; Healey attacked the unilateralism of the left-wingers with the argument that world socialism and the SPD backed the Labour leadership.[10] 'Disloyal MPs' were still a problem: the SPD felt that the relations of the Labour Party with the DDR were damaging, particularly left-wing MPs visiting the country. Zilliacus was once again a troublemaker.[11]

Historians have been kinder than Nenni to international socialist cooperation in the 1960s and 1970s, especially by Brandt and Wilson. Brandt would become the most dynamic President of the Socialist International. Salm describes the 1970s as the period of greatest activity for the socialist network, especially regarding international aid and the new democracies of Spain and Portugal.[12] Di Donato describes the intense contacts between European social democrats and Italian communists in the same period, which played a part in developing Brandt's *Ostpolitik*.[13] Broad and Steinnes describe how international socialist contacts influenced Wilson's European policy.[14] Ebb and flow are a natural part of socialist internationalism; reports of its death have been greatly exaggerated.

According to Salm, the Socialist International as an institution served to facilitate informal contacts. The porous border between party and government was its strength, not its weakness:

> The SI acted mainly as a platform for discussing and coordinating political matters and to form networks through informal exchange. Thus, in spite of the formalised institutions, the degree of formal integration of the SI was low when it was re-founded in the early 1950s.[15]

The greatest achievement of the Socialist International, therefore, was favouring the creation of a new breed of socialist leaders and their socialisation in an international network. Healey and Vittorelli were not isolated cases; successful careers were common for the people managing international fraternal relations. The prestige acquired in international conferences strengthened the hold of Mollet and Schärf on their parties; Larock and Ollenhauer also benefited from their international responsibilities. Other careers started from nothing. Many passed from unofficial socialist diplomacy to official diplomacy. Walter Wodak continued his diplomatic career in Paris and Belgrade, where he exploited his relations with the local socialists and communists.[16] With Kreisky as Foreign Minister, Wodak became a special envoy in the Third World and Ambassador to Moscow. Francesco Malfatti became diplomatic counsellor of Saragat, when he was the President of the Republic, and general secretary of the Minister for Foreign Affairs. Kaj Björk became Ambassador to Canada and China and had the dubious honour of being the only diplomatic representative admitted to Pol Pot's Cambodia.[17]

Others stayed in politics, like Vittorelli, who became a prominent figure in the PSI—but he also reopened relations between Rome and Beijing.[18] No one exploited his position as International Secretary more than Healey. After being given a safe seat in 1952, he became close to Gaitskell; in the 1960s and 1970s, he was a prominent member of the Labour leadership as Secretary of State for Defence and Chancellor of the Exchequer during a time of recurrent crisis for Britain. In 1980, he became deputy leader of the party and, after 1981, he acted as the focal point for the social democrats who chose not to join the Social Democratic Party's split but to stay and fight Benn's radical left. In 1981, during a brutal struggle with the extreme left, Healey received a proposal to become Secretary General of NATO, but he preferred to keep fighting for the party he loved.[19] Brandt, Kreisky and Palme were the most prominent cases. Although they were not involved with the rebuilding of the Socialist International, the contacts they developed in Stockholm during the war were important for their careers.[20] International fraternal relations gave new, ambitious politicians the opportunities to advance their career.

Another important feature was that these people belonged to the same, lucky generation. In 1956, Hugh Gaitskell said that both British parties missed the World War I generation, there were few politicians in their 50s and 60s.[21] Gaitskell's shadow cabinet was made up of people first elected in 1945, when the Labour Party had a huge influx of new MPs. The generation of the Socialist International had a different background from the veterans of the Second International and the LSI: the Great Depression and the war were its formative experiences. Around Europe, the new generation took over the socialist parties in the mid-twentieth century, a period when mass parties came to control access to positions of power. At the same time, the reach of the state expanded to cover economy, society and culture. Thus, international fraternal relations helped in nurturing a generation of leaders who played a decisive role in state and international affairs for the next 30 years.

The transnational network became an important feature of European socialism for that era. Agreement could not always be found, for example on the internationalisation of the Ruhr or European unity,[22] nonetheless the leadership could not withdraw their participation without damaging the commitment to internationalism demanded by their rank and file and their own political culture. Different from the Communist centre of world revolution, the Socialist International was a permanent negotiating table. Ideological unity was not the reason for contacts, rather the result. As the Italian Ambassador noted in 1951, the Labour Party and the Italian social democrats had a mutual friendship, despite major differences, thanks to regular personal contacts.[23] The practice of international contacts was self-perpetuating, producing an international network of leaders and secretaries based on trust and familiarity.[24]

Yet, trust and familiarity were not guaranteed outcomes. As Imlay notes, the practice of international contacts could also reinforce 'national rootedness' and 'particularist (national) identities'—indeed, he argues that the mistrust created by regular contact killed socialist internationalism.[25] Private correspondence, diaries and memoirs are full of digs and recriminations against each other. The interactions of the British Labour Party with Eastern and Southern Europe actually strengthened traditional British isolationism. In 1945, Healey hoped to see socialism develop in Southern Europe, he was still hopeful in 1949, but he was very sceptical by 1952. His many negative experiences with Italian socialists—as well as French and German—influenced the arguments against integration that he drafted in 1948 and 1950, defining Labour's European policy for decades. Familiarity or distrust varied from person to person, from period to period and the feelings were never clearly defined. Saragat and Healey exchanged insults and nurtured a respective resentment for years, but in 1975 Saragat called Healey his friend.[26]

Not every member of the socialist family was friendly to everyone else: sub-groups emerged of people sharing cultural kinship—particularly the Scandinavians—institutional allegiance—the socialists of the European Communities—ideological affinity or even personal friendship. The fact that European socialists managed to hold together makes them less like the militarised battalion of international communism and more like an actual family, though a dysfunctional one rife with incomprehension and squabbling

The challenge of a transnational approach is not just to assess the existence of transnational networks or interactions across borders, but to describe their consequences on internal development, the reasons why a transfer was a success or a failure. The same is true for culture: describing the culture of the political players is not enough if cultural traits are not used to explain political decisions. The study of culture and language is an essential part of the study of politics, but the meaning was unstable: politicians changed the meaning of words and repurposed long-term cultural constructs according to their tactical and contingent needs. Factional struggle is central not only in the study of political but also cultural history since culture and words are weapons in the struggle for power. National character was continuously repurposed and whether a stereotype was used depended on the tactical need of the faction. Thus, Healey appealed to the unity of Europe to denounce the communist domination of Eastern Europe, but he spoke of irreconcilable differences among the Europeans when he wanted to reject European unification. He talked about the Labour Party as the living example of socialism for the whole world and he talked about forms of socialism whose differences depended on national conditions. He proposed a radical policy for Greece and he absolved the British Government by speaking about a Greek character. As Hanely suggests, Healey produced his arguments—especially cultural ones—to justify his decision *a posteriori*.[27] If so, he was not the only one.

Attlee warned about the 'temperamental' Greeks in 1945, Feather contrasted law-abiding British and anarchical Mediterranean people, McNeil spoke of a 'backward, extravagant and irresponsible' country. Just as fellow-travellers employed the national character of the Eastern Europeans to justify communist domination, these Labour figures resorted to the Greek national character to deny their responsibility in the Civil war. Tsirimokos used the British example when the situation demanded it, while remaining sceptical in private. Nenni denounced the idea of cutting Europe in two to explain fascism, but he cut Europe in two to explain communism. In Italy and Greece, a faction employed the British example as a model and another faction denounced the British model for complicity with imperialism. In the case of Nenni and Andreas Papandreou, it was just the same person in a different context and at a different time.

While stressing the influence of transnational transfers, we should not exaggerate: 'But transnational-themed research should allow us to better understand the strength and limitations of the national setting, not to replace it entirely'.[28] Gramsci observed that political power was stuck at national level, while economic power was already cosmopolitan.[29] The national level was the most important for socialist politicians, even those with a cosmopolitan outlook: they competed for power inside their national parties, ran for state power at national elections, employed the power of the nation state to enact their policies. In this sense, the nationalisation of socialism is true. Yet nation states and national societies were not monolithic and homogeneous; decisions in a pluralist society are subject to the pressure of political parties, interest groups and other democratic players.[30] As the internationalisation of domestic quarrels has shown, pluralism was the reason transnational transfers could influence national outcomes; therefore, they deserve consideration. The choice of employing a national, comparative or transnational approach depends on the questions asked.[31]

The dialectic between the national and international spheres of socialism was hardly smooth, it did not always go forwards, it varied in intensity and took different forms in different eras. Nonetheless, it was a mechanism for the continuous renovation of socialism that has to be considered for a better understanding of the European labour movement in the postwar era.

Notes

1. C. Salm (2016) *Transnational Socialist Networks in the 1970s: European Community Development Aid and Southern Enlargement* (Basingstoke: Palgrave Macmillan), 173–174.
2. Entry, 1 September 1969, P. Nenni (1983) *Diari*, Vol. 3, *I conti con la storia, diari 1967–1971* (Milano: SugarCo), 374.
3. Entry, 23 May 1969, Nenni, *I conti con la storia*, 330.
4. Entry, 17 June 1969, Nenni, *I conti con la storia*, 341. Nenni said the same thing to Tony Benn (Entry, 17 September 1975, T. Benn (1990) *Against the Tide, Diaries 1973–76* (London: Arrow), 436).
5. D. Healey (1952) 'Power Politics and the Labour Party', D. Healey (1990) *When Shrimps Learn to Whistle: Signposts for the Nineties* (London: Penguin), 3–18.
6. D. Healey (1956) 'Beyond Power Politics' in Healey, *When Shrimps Learn to Whistle*, 19.
7. D. Healey (2002) *Healey's World: Travels with My Camera* (Lewes: Book Guild), 61.
8. E. Costa (2018) 'The Socialist International and Italian Social Democracy (1948–50): Cultural Differences and the "Internationalisation of Domestic Quarrels"', *Historical Research*, 90, 251, 184.
9. P. Van Kemseke (2006) *Towards an Era of Development, The Globalization of Socialism and Christian Democracy: 1945–1965* (Leuven: Leuven University Press), 11.
10. H. Wehner (1981) *Wandel und Bewährung: Ausgewählte Reden und Schriften 1930–1980* (Frankfurt/M: Ullstein), 196. E. Pearce (2002) *Denis Healey: A Life in Our Times* (London: Little Brown), 210–218.
11. S. Berger, N. LaPorte (2010) *Friendly Enemies: Britain and the GDR, 1949–1990* (New York: Berghahn Books), 94–96.
12. Salm, *Transnational Socialist Networks in the 1970s*, 20.
13. M. Di Donato (2015) *I comunisti italiani e la sinistra europea: il PCI e i rapporti con le socialdemocrazie (1964–1984)* (Roma: Carocci), 55–66.
14. M. Broad (2017) *Harold Wilson, Denmark and the Making of Labour European policy* (Liverpool: Liverpool University Press). K. Steinnes (2014) *The British Labour Party, Transnational influences and European Community membership, 1960–1973* (Stuttgart: Franz Steiner).

15. Salm, *Transnational Socialist Networks in the 1970s*, 13.
16. R. Weignleitner (1980) 'Lebensskizze Dr Walter Wodak', in W. Wodak, *Diplomatie zwischen Parteiproporz und Weltpolitik* (Graz: Styria), 5–20. B. Kuschey (2008) *Die Wodaks: Exil und Rückkehr; eine Doppelbiografie* (Wien: Braumüller).
17. N. Glover (2011) *National Relations: Public Diplomacy, National Identity and the Swedish* (Lund: Nordic Academic Press), 130. C. Cook (2012) *The Routledge Guide to European Political Archives: Sources since 1945* (London: Routledge), 21. N. Chomsky and E.S. Herman (1979) *The Political Economy of Human Rights*, Vol. 1, *After the Cataclysm: Postwar Indochina and the Reconstruction of Imperial Ideology* (Nottingham: Spokesman), 187–188.
18. E. Fardella (2017) 'A Significant Periphery of the Cold War: Italy-China Bilateral Relations, 1949–1989', *Cold War History*, 17, 2, 181–197.
19. Pearce, *Denis Healey*, 546–564.
20. G. Devin (1993) *L'Internationale socialiste: histoire et sociologie du socialisme internationale: 1945–1990* (Paris: Presses de la Fondation national des sciences politiques), 300–311.
21. H. Gaitskell to G. Fay, 11 April 1956, University College London (UCL), Gaitskell, C158.16.
22. R. Steininger (1979) *Deutschland und die Sozialistische Internationale nach dem Zweiten Weltkrieg, Darstellung und Dokumentation* (Bonn: Neue Gesellschaft), 98–123; 136–159.
23. Gallarati Scotti to C. Sforza, 6 February 1951, in *I documenti diplomatici italiani, Undicesima Serie 1948–1953*, Vol. 5, 287.
24. G. Devin (1996) 'L'internationalisme des socialistes', in M. Lazar (ed.) *La gauche en Europe depuis 1945: invariants et mutations du socialisme européen* (Paris: Presses de la Fondation national des sciences politiques), 427–428.
25. T.C. Imlay (2016). 'The Practice of Socialist Internationalism during the Twentieth Century', *Moving the Social*, 55, 21.
26. Entry, 17 September 1975, Benn, *Against the tide*, 437.
27. D. Hanely (1983) 'Un socialisme aux couleurs de l'Angleterre : le parti travailliste et l'Internationale Socialiste depuis 1945', in H. Portelli (ed.), *L'Internationale socialiste* (Paris: Les Éditions Ouvrières), 64.
28. M. Broad (2017) 'Kristian Steinnes, The British Labour Party, Transnational Influences and European Community Membership, 1960–1973', *Journal of Contemporary History*, 52, 1, 183.
29. See A. Gramsci (1975) *Quaderni del carcere*, Vol. 3 (Torino: Einaudi), 1775–1776. G. Vacca (2006) *Il riformismo italiano: dalla fine della guerra fredda alle sfide future* (Roma: Fazi), 7.
30. J. Osterhammel (2009) 'A 'Transnational' History of Society Continuity or New Departure?' in H.-G. Haupt, J. Kock (eds), *Comparative and Transnational History: Central European Approaches and New Perspectives* (New York: Berghahn Books), 45–49. W. Kaiser, B. Leucht, M. Gehler

(2010) 'Transnational Networks in Regional Integration: Historical Perspectives on an Elusive Phenomenon', in W. Kaiser, B. Leucht, M. Gehler (eds), *Transnational Networks in Regional Integration: Governing Europe 1945–83* (London: Palgrave Macmillan), 1–5.

31. S. Berger (2017). 'Labour Movements in Global Historical Perspective: Conceptual Eurocentrism and its Problems', in S. Berger, H. Nehring (eds), *The History of Social Movements in Global Perspective. A survey* (London: Palgrave Macmillan), 413–414.

BIBLIOGRAPHY

I documenti diplomatici italiani, Undicesima Serie 1948–1953, Vol. 2.

Benn, T. (1990). *Against the tide, Diaries 1973–76*. London: Arrow.

Berger, S. & LaPorte, N. (2010). *Friendly enemies: Britain and the GDR, 1949–1990*. New York: Berghahn Books.

Berger, S. (2017). Labour movements in global historical perspective: conceptual Eurocentrism and its problems. In S. Berger & H. Nehring (Eds.). *The history of social movements in global perspective. A survey* (pp. 385–418). London: Palgrave Macmillan.

Broad, M. (2017a). Kristian Steinnes, The British Labour Party, Transnational Influences and European Community Membership, 1960–1973. *Journal of Contemporary History*, 52 (1), 182–183.

Broad, M. (2017b). *Harold Wilson, Denmark and the making of Labour European policy*. Liverpool: Liverpool University Press.

Chomsky, N. & Herman, E.S. (1979). *The political economy of human rights*, Vol. 1, *After the cataclysm: postwar Indochina and the reconstruction of imperial ideology*. Nottingham: Spokesman.

Cook, C. (2012). *The Routledge Guide to European Political Archives: Sources since 1945*. London: Routledge.

Costa, E. (2018). The Socialist International and Italian social democracy (1948–50): cultural differences and the 'internationalisation of domestic quarrels'. *Historical Research*, 90 (251), 160–184.

Devin, G. (1993). *L'Internationale socialiste: histoire et sociologie du socialisme internationale: 1945–1990*. Paris: Presses de la Fondation national des sciences politiques.

Devin, G. (1996). L'internationalisme des socialistes. In M. Lazar (Ed.). *La gauche en Europe depuis 1945: invariants et mutations du socialisme européen* (pp. 413–431). Paris: Presses de la Fondation national des sciences politiques.

Di Donato, M. (2015). *I comunisti italiani e la sinistra europea: il PCI e i rapporti con le socialdemocrazie (1964–1984)*. Roma: Carocci.

Fardella, E. (2016). A significant periphery of the Cold War: Italy-China bilateral relations, 1949–1989. *Cold War History*, 17 (2), 181–197.

Glover, N. (2011). *National Relations: Public Diplomacy, National Identity and the Swedish*. Lund: Nordic Academic Press.
Gramsci, A. (1975). *Quaderni del carcere*, Vol. 3. Torino: Einaudi.
Hanely, D. (1983). Un socialisme aux couleurs de l'Angleterre: le parti travailliste et l'Internationale Socialiste depuis 1945. In H. Portelli (Ed.). *L'Internationale socialiste* (pp. 57–66). Paris: Les Éditions Ouvrières.
Healey, D. (1952). Power politics and the Labour Party. In D. Healey (1990) *When Shrimps learn to whistle: signposts for the nineties* (pp. 3–18). London: Penguin.
Healey, D. (1956). Beyond power politics. In D. Healey (1990) *When Shrimps learn to whistle: signposts for the nineties* (pp. 18–23). London: Penguin.
Healey, D. (2002). *Healey's World: travels with my camera*. Lewes: Book Guild.
Imlay, T.C. (2016). The Practice of Socialist Internationalism during the Twentieth Century. *Moving the Social*, 55, 17–38.
Kaiser, W., Leucht, B. & Gehler, M. (2010). Transnational Networks in Regional Integration: Historical Perspectives on an Elusive Phenomenon. In W. Kaiser, B. Leucht & M. Gehler (Eds.). *Transnational Networks in Regional Integration: governing Europe 1945–83* (pp. 1–17). London: Palgrave Macmillan.
Kuschey, B. (2008). *Die Wodaks: Exil und Rückkehr; eine Doppelbiografie*. Wien: Braumüller.
Nenni, P. (1983). *Diari*, Vol. 3, *I conti con la storia, diari 1967–1971*. Milano: SugarCo.
Osterhammel, J. (2009). A 'Transnational' History of Society Continuity or New Departure?. In H.-G. Haupt & J. Kock (Eds.). *Comparative and transnational history: central European approaches and new perspectivesI* (pp. 32–51). New York: Berghahn Books.
Pearce, E. (2002). *Denis Healey: a life in our times*. London: Little Brown.
Salm, C. (2016). *Transnational socialist networks in the 1970s: European Community development aid and southern enlargement*. London: Palgrave Macmillan.
Steininger, R. (1979). *Deutschland und die Sozialistische Internationale nach dem Zweiten Weltkrieg, Darstellung und Dokumentation*. Bonn: Neue Gesellschaft.
Steinnes, K. (2014). *The British Labour Party, transnational influences and European Community membership, 1960–1973*. Stuttgart: Franz Steiner.
Vacca, G. (2006). *Il riformismo italiano: dalla fine della guerra fredda alle sfide future*. Roma: Fazi.
Van Kemseke, P. (2006). *Towards an Era of Development, The Globalization of Socialism and Christian Democracy: 1945–1965*. Leuven: Leuven University Press.
Wehner, H. (1981). *Wandel und Bewährung: Ausgewählte Reden und Schriften 1930–1980*. Frankfurt/M: Ullstein.
Weignleitner, R. (1980). Lebensskizze Dr Walter Wodak. In W. Wodak (Ed.). *Diplomatie zwischen Parteiproporz und Weltpolitik* (pp. 5–20). Graz: Styria.

Index

A
Accusations of imperialism towards social democrats, 60, 105, 109–110, 116, 119, 120, 149, 159, 179, 199–200, 204, 229, 234–238, 249–250
Adler, Friedrich, 7, 24–27, 30, 31, 51, 139, 156, 268
Aims and Tasks of Democratic Socialism, *see* Frankfurt Declaration
Alternative strategy, 58, 112, 118, 143, 183, 186–189, 191, 192, 195, 196, 202, 245
American trade unions, 162, 184, 188, 189, 198–199
Anti-Catholicism, 76, 79, 95, 141, 150, 151, 177–178, 188–189, 194, 199, 279
Anti-communism
  difference between negative and socialist anti-communism, 62, 113, 119, 192, 244–246, 275
  propaganda, 62–64, 95, 113, 115, 116, 161, 178, 196, 271
  socialist anti-communism, 4, 21, 37, 103, 105, 112, 149, 160, 175, 185, 222, 275–277
Atlantic Treaty, 69, 78, 188–191, 194–196, 274, 279, 289, 311
Attlee, Clement, 52–53, 56, 59, 68, 70, 72, 103, 113, 141, 159, 234, 236, 289, 315
Austrian Socialist Party (SPÖ), 3
  internal developments, 57, 78, 186, 221–223
  international fraternal relations, 23–27, 30, 50, 55, 78–79, 149–153, 158, 163, 222–227, 266, 287–288
  South Tyrol, 200, 221, 223–228

B
Backwardness, 24–25, 105, 107, 177–178, 192, 201, 203, 233, 235

Bad Godesberg programme, *see* German Social Democratic Party (SPD), and socialist revisionism
Balabanoff, Angelica, 58, 286
Basso, Lelio, 149, 179, 188, 222, 243
Belgian Socialist Party (PSB)
  internal developments, 75–76
  international fraternal relations, 7, 8, 26, 28, 76, 144, 148, 150, 153, 158, 159, 161–163, 231, 232, 265–266, 268–270, 277–278, 288–290
Beneš, Edvard, 35, 98, 100, 113, 140, 243
Bentveld Declaration, 194, 279, 286
Bernstein, Eduard, 7
Bevan, Aneurin, 55, 59, 69, 106, 192, 228, 234, 270, 272, 285, 288
Bevin, Ernest, 29, 37, 39, 51–53, 55, 56, 61–64, 67, 68, 70, 109–111, 116–118, 142, 145, 146, 162, 180, 181, 190, 191, 194, 200, 202, 204, 222–228, 234–238, 240, 246, 288
Binding resolutions, *see* Coordination of socialist parties, centralisation
Björk, Kaj, 72, 78, 270, 277–279, 281, 285, 290, 312
Blum, Leon, 58, 73–75, 102, 121, 139, 141, 151, 159, 184, 277, 281
Blume, Isabelle, 156, 158, 232
Bolle, Martin, 157–158, 160–161, 191, 268
Boutbien, Leon, 75, 183, 184, 188, 204, 232, 281
Braine, William H., 63, 180, 237
Brandt, Willy, 3, 287, 310–313
Braunthal, Julius, 1, 30–32, 51, 140, 144, 268–269, 278, 282–284, 290
Bulgaria, 67, 113, 143, 232, 237, 274

Buset, Max, 8, 57, 76, 140, 144, 150, 151, 155–157, 182–184, 276, 289

C
Callaghan, James, 67
Carandini, Nicolò, 223–226
Cards on the Table, 70
Carthy, Albert, 64
Christian democrats, 3, 76, 79, 141, 150, 183–185, 187–189, 191, 193–195, 198–199, 222, 224, 225, 227, 249
Ciolkosz, Adam, 36, 97, 100–103, 107, 108, 112, 113, 273–274, 282
Citrine, Walter, 51, 66, 162, 237
Coalition strategy, 76, 77, 79, 184–188, 191, 194, 195, 202, 222, 239, 279
Cohabitation of social democracy and communism, 29, 96, 119–120, 139–144, 180–181, 274–276, 280, 282, 285
Cohabitation of social democracy and left-wing socialism, 96, 99, 106–107, 111–113, 144, 150–151, 153, 155, 158–160, 179, 184, 221–222, 231, 232, 242, 243
Cold War, 109, 117–121, 138, 141, 144, 147, 151, 154, 162, 180, 201, 204, 233, 235, 237, 239, 272, 283, 285
Cole, G.D.H., 29, 103, 196
Collective guilt, *see* Nazism
Cominform, *see* Communist Information Bureau
Comintern, *see* Communist International
Comisco, *see* Committee of the International Socialist Conference

INDEX 323

Committee of the International Socialist Conference (Comisco), *see* International Socialist Conference
Commonwealth of Nations, 59, 152, 269, 271
Communism
  and democracy, 100, 119, 142–144
  and nationalism, 97, 108, 226, 228
  and social democracy, 1, 6, 22, 29, 58, 60, 61, 98, 112, 119–121, 139–144, 197, 198, 203, 238–239
  and totalitarianism, 105, 139, 160, 179, 230, 231, 244, 275–276, 291
Communist Information Bureau (Cominform), 60, 119–121, 151, 159, 184, 232, 241, 245, 248, 276
Communist International (Comintern), 22, 25, 29, 58, 139
Comparative analysis, 4, 9, 49–50, 71–73, 175, 185–186, 221–222, 309–310, 315
Confidentiality, 27–28, 147, 152, 268, 271, 311
Convergence of European socialist parties to anti-communist social democracy, 4, 5, 26, 147–148, 175, 185–187, 231, 233, 283
Coordination of socialist parties
  centralisation, 24–26, 50, 145, 149, 152, 156–158, 289–290
  voluntary cooperation, 3, 5, 145–147, 150–151, 154, 157, 158, 196, 239, 266, 268, 269, 271–272, 289–291, 310–312
Cripps, Stafford, 7, 224, 267, 288
Crosland, Anthony, 57, 203, 284–287
Crossman, Richard, 6, 33, 69, 70, 196
ČSSD, *see* Czechoslovak Social Democratic Party
Cultural comparison, 8–9, 71, 104, 175–176, 192, 233, 314, 315
Cyrankiewicz, Józef, 97, 98, 101, 109, 114–118, 121
Czechoslovak Social Democratic Party (ČSSD)
  internal developments, 98–100, 113–114, 118–122
  international fraternal relations, 26, 34–35, 58, 63, 64, 100, 106, 120, 149, 158–159, 162, 180, 230, 273–275
Czernetz, Karl, 30, 105, 106, 222

D
Dallas Committee, 28–30, 32–33, 35, 38, 52, 145
Dallas, George, 28, 33, 52
Dalton, Hugh, 25, 26, 29, 33, 34, 38, 51–56, 70, 88, 100, 104, 141, 152–153, 156, 161, 192, 225, 227, 278
Danish social democrats, 26, 78, 148, 163, 248, 271, 279
Davies, Ernest, 31, 270
De Brouckère, Louis, 8, 26, 32, 75–76, 137, 139, 140, 151, 183, 188
De Gasperi, Alcide, 190–191, 195, 225
De Man, Henri, 1, 7, 26, 51, 75–76, 280
Decolonisation, 56, 195, 199–200, 233
Delegations, *see* Visits and delegations
Division of Europe, 24–25, 70, 95, 105–112, 141, 148–149, 151, 153, 157–160, 175–177, 231, 273, 315
DNA, *see* Labour Party (Norway)
Drobner, Bolesław, 98, 121

E

Earnshaw, Harry, 68, 187
Eastern European socialists, 6, 39, 62, 95–122, 144, 148–150, 152, 153, 155, 157–163, 184, 192, 221, 223, 229–232, 266, 272–275, 282
Eichler, Willi, 31, 285–287
Embarrassment, *see* International fraternal relations, and embarrassment
Erlander, Tage, 72, 78, 279
Essentialism, *see* National character, stereotypes
European integration, 2, 3, 194–195, 233, 265–272, 279, 310–312, 314
European Unity, 55, 56, 70, 270
Exchanging information and views, 5, 25–26, 38, 50–51, 55, 138, 146–147, 153, 160, 267, 271, 289–290
Exclusivity, 5, 22, 25, 71, 146, 152, 154–155, 160, 182, 228, 232, 242, 275–276, 283, 311
Exile parties, 25–31, 33–39, 51, 101, 146, 152, 181, 273–274
Experts' Conference, 152, 266–268, 271–272

F

Fabian Society, 31, 118, 162, 265, 268, 271
Familiarity, 5, 7, 73, 99–100, 153, 183, 188, 195–197, 228, 313–314
  See also Socialisation (people); Compare Mistrust
Faravelli, Giuseppe, 180, 189, 199
Fascism, 1, 23–27, 34, 40, 104, 139–140, 160, 178, 179, 182, 199–200, 226, 276, 282
  See also Nazism
Feet on the Ground, 70, 266

Fierlinger, Zdeněk, 98, 113, 119, 120
Finnish social democratic party, 27
First International, 7, 284
Foot, Michael, 67, 69, 193, 196, 277
Foreign Office (Britain)
  and anti-communism, 61, 62
  and Austria, 222–228
  and Czechoslovakia, 58, 67, 111, 113, 119
  and Eastern Europe, 62, 67, 112, 116
  and Germany, 228–229
  and Greece, 67, 233–236, 238, 241–242, 245–248
  and Italy, 56, 59, 62, 63, 67, 68, 135, 188, 190–191, 223–228
  and labour attaché, 63, 114, 180, 237, 244
  and Labour Party, 55, 56, 59–63, 67–68, 111, 113, 118, 119, 185, 190, 228–229, 241–243, 245, 250, 273
  and Poland, 63, 67, 100, 102, 109–111, 113–115, 118
  and preferential treatment of social democrats, 62, 112–115, 188, 222–223, 228–229
  See also Bevin, Ernest
Frankfurt Declaration, 5, 75, 194, 249, 275, 277–279, 282–288, 309, 310
French Socialist Party (SFIO)
  internal developments, 26, 73–75, 103, 150–151, 186, 265
  international fraternal relations, 22, 33, 38, 65, 66, 74–75, 102–104, 148, 150–153, 155–156, 158–160, 163, 183–184, 191, 195, 229, 239–240, 243, 247–248, 266–270, 273, 277–281, 289, 310
Fusion between socialists and communists, 66–67, 98, 116, 118–122, 140–141, 151, 153, 180, 181, 199, 273

G

Gaitskell, Hugh, 6, 31, 52, 56, 69–70, 270, 274, 286, 309, 311–313
Generational analysis, 8, 23, 52, 54, 73, 75–76, 96–97, 144, 150, 222, 313
Geographical determinism, *see* National character, stereotypes, and geographical determinism
German Social Democratic Party (SPD)
  internal developments, 7, 30, 66–67, 76, 77, 186, 228, 232, 233
  international fraternal relations, 7, 22, 30–34, 54, 55, 65, 72, 100, 149–152, 154, 158, 160, 162–163, 186–187, 228–233, 239, 248–250, 269, 275, 288, 311, 312
  and Nazism, 22–23, 30–31, 38, 51, 120, 228, 230
  and socialist revisionism, 7, 31, 76, 229–231, 233, 286–288
Gillies, William, 6, 7, 26–30, 32–37, 39, 41, 50–53, 55, 66, 108, 139, 156
Global agreement between social democracy and communism, 23–25, 29, 31, 36, 139–144, 146, 159, 181, 224
  See also Cohabitation of social democracy and communism; Unitary International of socialists and communists; *Compare* Communism, and social democracy
Gollancz, Victor, 31, 32, 268
Gomułka, Władysław, 101, 109, 117, 121
Gordon Walker, Patrick, 31, 106, 224
Gottwald, Klement, 120, 121, 143
Governance, 2, 221, 290

  See also State-private network; Track-two diplomacy
Greek Communist Party, 233–234, 238–241, 243–245, 247–249
Greek Socialist Party (SK-ELD)
  internal developments, 238–241, 244, 247–249
  international fraternal relations, 163, 178, 192–194, 239–245, 247–249
Grosfeld, Ludwik, 105, 109, 114, 116, 117, 229
Grumbach, Salomon, 74, 75, 121, 153, 155, 183–184, 230, 232, 281, 282
Guesde, Jules, 7, 280

H

Healey, Denis
  and Austria, 79, 221
  and British foreign policy, 56, 61–64, 68, 70, 116, 190, 221, 233, 245–248
  career, 23, 49, 50, 53–56, 72, 291, 310–313
  and Czechoslovakia, 119–121, 273
  and discipline and dissent, 65–69, 194, 236–238
  and Eastern Europe, 111–113, 274
  and Germany, 229, 231
  and Greece, 54, 110, 178, 233, 234, 236–237, 243–248
  and Italy, 54, 58, 69, 176, 178, 181–185, 187–197, 199, 202
  and national character, 103–104, 176, 201–203, 243, 314
  and Poland, 101, 116–118, 120–121, 149
  and socialist internationalism, 56, 147, 152, 155, 157, 176, 193, 204–205, 291, 310

Helping other socialist parties, 23, 62, 160–161, 163, 182, 184–190, 195–199, 202, 229, 242–245, 289, 291, 310–312
Henderson, Arthur, 50, 51, 192
Hitler, Adolf, 21, 25, 27, 77, 231
Hochfeld, Julian, 98, 102, 103, 109, 112, 113, 115, 117, 121, 159, 182, 230
Hungarian social democrats, 35, 96, 121, 155, 272–274
Huysmans, Camille, 22, 26–30, 32, 33, 36–38, 75, 140, 151
Huysmans Committee, 28–30, 33, 34, 37, 224

I
Identification of party and government, 22–23, 59–60, 145, 147–152, 155–156, 189–190, 228–229, 243, 248, 250, 270, 283, 312
Informality, 28, 137–139, 142, 221, 229, 288, 310–312
Information Research Department (IRD), 62, 64, 116, 161, 196, 275
Institutionalisation, 137–139, 288, 312
Interdependence, 118, 139, 149–150, 226, 227
Internationaler Sozialisticher Kampfbund (ISK), 30
International fraternal relations
 and bureaucratic control, 21, 27, 32, 50, 54, 55, 71–72, 137–138, 273
 and career advancement, 8, 49, 72–73, 312–313 (*see also* Healey, Denis, career)
 definition, 4
 and discipline, 51, 66, 68
 and dissent (*see* Internationalisation of domestic quarrels)
 and embarrassment, 23, 27, 33, 51, 67–68, 103, 145, 147, 148, 150, 152, 154–155, 193–194, 229, 242–243, 291
 and influence on national parties, 2, 5, 25, 146, 161, 198, 243–244, 288, 309–310, 315–316
 and the international network of leaders and secretaries, 7, 21, 51, 71–80, 311, 313
 and uncontrolled development, 3, 4, 27, 100, 138, 163
 See also Individual parties
Internationalisation of domestic quarrels
 and Austria, 221–223
 and Belgium, 7
 and Britain, 6, 7, 25, 51–52, 58–59, 66–71, 102, 110, 111, 188–192, 197, 204, 234–238, 246–247, 274, 277, 285–286, 311, 313
 and Czechoslovakia, 35, 64, 111, 112, 118–120, 180
 definition, 6, 315
 and France, 7, 74–75, 102–103, 140–141, 150–151, 183–184, 191, 195, 202, 247, 285
 and Germany, 7, 36, 66–67, 77, 203, 278, 285–288, 311
 and Greece, 237, 238, 240–247, 250
 and Italy, 6, 57, 75, 179–185, 187–188, 192, 197, 203, 277, 285, 310
 and left-wing socialism, 25, 69–70, 96, 149, 180, 182, 229–231

INDEX 327

and Poland, 67, 101, 102, 109, 110, 117, 180
and reformism, 56–60, 64, 96, 101, 109, 112, 117, 138, 140, 142, 160–161, 203, 276, 284, 288
and right of intervention, 34–36, 102, 180–185, 189, 191, 205
and Sweden, 278
and the Netherlands, 77, 191–192, 194–195
International Socialist Conference
  Antwerp (28 November- 1 December 1947), 120, 157–159, 163, 184, 231–232, 240–241
  Baarn (14-16 May 1949), 188, 247–248, 268–269, 273
  Bournemouth (8-10 November 1946), 79, 154, 229–230
  Clacton (17-19 May 1946), 2, 50, 70, 78, 101, 102, 109, 137, 141, 150, 153–154, 225, 229, 239, 266
  Comisco Sub-Committee, 157
  Committee of the International Socialist Conference (Comisco), 157
  consultative committee, 137, 154, 156
  Copenhagen (1-3 June 1950), 72, 160, 191, 202, 274, 279–280
  finances, 152, 156, 157, 162–163, 199, 204, 248–249, 266, 272
  foundation, 151–155
  observer parties, 182, 231–233
  secretary of Comisco, 32, 162, 268–269
  Socialist Information and Liaison Office (SILO), 137, 153–154
  Vienna (4-7 June 1948), 75, 160, 161, 163, 188, 267, 276, 277
  Zurich (6-9 June 1947), 8, 57, 75, 117, 144, 150, 154–155, 181–183, 230–232, 239, 276
International socialist network, *see* International fraternal relations
Intervention, *see* Helping other socialist parties; Lobbying through socialist channels; State-private network
Iron Curtain, 95, 103, 105, 153, 176, 184, 185, 201, 272
ISK, *see* Internationaler Sozialisticher Kampfbund
Italian Communist Party (PCI), 3, 61, 114, 160, 176, 179–185, 187–189, 192–200, 203, 312
Italian social democrats (PSLI, USI, Socialist Unity, PSU, PSDI)
  and finances, 183, 187, 190, 195, 198–200
  internal developments, 180, 181, 184, 187–190, 195
  international fraternal relations, 56, 60, 140, 181–184, 190–192, 202, 239, 269
Italian Socialist Party (PSI, PSIUP)
  and finances, 162, 198–199
  internal developments, 53, 57, 160–161, 175, 179–180, 187, 188, 193, 198
  international fraternal relations, 25–26, 37, 38, 53, 148, 152, 159, 179, 182, 196–197, 221–228, 276, 285, 289, 311, 312
Italy, 177–178, 199–200, 223

J
Jaurès, Jean, 7, 280
Jay, Douglas, 52

K
Kautsky, Benedikt, 7, 287
Kirby, R.B., 63, 114–116, 118
Kreisky, Bruno, 3, 224, 312–313

L
Labour and Socialist International (LSI), 5, 21–30, 50, 51, 139, 145–147, 153, 156, 162, 275, 278, 290, 313
Labour attaché, *see* Foreign Office (Britain), and labour attaché
Labour Party (Britain)
  and Austria, 186, 223–227
  and British foreign policy, 59, 62, 63, 65–71, 113, 119, 190, 228–229, 243, 250
  and communism, 37, 61–62, 140, 192, 274
  and Czechoslovakia, 100
  and embarrassment, 24, 27, 33, 37, 52–55, 57, 58, 67, 70, 100, 110, 111, 139, 154, 184, 234–238, 240
  and European integration, 3, 55–56, 68, 70, 176, 194, 265–267, 269–270, 312 (*see also Feet on the Ground; European Unity*)
  and finances, 54, 161–163, 272
  and French socialism, 33, 55, 74, 118, 121, 159, 186, 191, 193
  and intellectuals, 53, 55, 118, 181, 192–194, 243, 244, 247
  and the International Department, 50–56, 63, 65–71, 153, 161, 236–237, 250
  and the international sub-committee, 51, 52, 55, 64
  and Italy, 3, 6, 69, 180–185, 188–200
  and the Labour government, 59–65, 189–190, 243, 248, 250
  and the Labour left, 29–32, 51, 52, 59, 66–70, 110–111, 149, 158, 224, 236, 237, 268, 285 (*see also* Zilliacus, Konni)
  and leadership of the international socialist movement, 2, 4, 22, 27, 33, 37, 49–50, 56–61, 64, 137–140, 153, 154, 161, 175, 233, 270, 283, 291
  as a negative model, 59, 96, 179, 199–200, 222, 249, 281
  opposition to the Labour Party from the other parties, 26, 30, 35, 101, 113, 120, 138, 154, 157, 189–192, 222, 239, 249, 269–270, 288
  and plans for the Socialist International, 25–28, 37–38, 50, 141, 145–148, 151–152, 155–157, 161–162, 265–268, 271, 290–291
  and Poland, 100–102, 109–111
  as a positive model, 6, 56–59, 61, 77, 96, 100, 121, 146, 153, 161, 179–181, 189, 192, 197, 203–205, 222, 249–250, 266, 271, 284, 285
  and propaganda, 63–64
  and socialist internationalism, 27, 33, 38, 52, 58–59, 100, 103, 142, 146, 185, 274
  and the Soviet Union, 29, 33, 52, 61, 96, 100, 139–141, 146, 224–225
  and the working-class, 58, 110, 118, 186, 192–193

Labour Party (Netherlands) (PvdA), 3
  internal developments, 57, 77, 185–186
  international fraternal relations, 25–26, 37, 71, 77, 148, 153, 158–159, 162, 163, 185, 189, 191–195, 229, 231, 242–243, 245, 268–270, 272, 277, 279–281, 288
Labour Party (Norway) (DNA)
  internal developments, 185–186
  international fraternal relations, 37, 65, 72, 78, 148, 153, 159, 162–163, 229, 243, 248, 290
Larock, Victor, 72, 76, 157–159, 232, 243–245, 247, 269–270, 278, 282, 289–290, 312
Laski, Harold, 29–32, 36, 51–54, 61, 66, 68, 70, 73, 107, 108, 139–144, 146, 151–152, 158, 180–181, 184, 224, 235
Laušman, Bohumil, 98, 119, 120
Lee, Jennie, 54, 67, 113, 224, 226
Left-wing socialism, 5, 23–26, 64, 69, 96, 103, 120, 121, 139–141, 148, 149, 156, 179–180, 182–183, 198, 221, 232, 243, 283
Levy, Louis, 32, 41, 74, 75, 151–152, 158
Lie, Haakon, 72, 78, 160, 196, 231, 270, 277, 290
Lobbying through socialist channels, 65, 112, 114, 115, 221, 223–225, 237, 239, 243, 244
Loeb, Edith, 154
Löwenthal, Richard, 32, 57
LSI, *see* Labour and Socialist International
Luzzatto, Riccardo, 224, 227

M
MacDonald, Ramsay, 24, 50, 51, 189, 193–194, 247
Mack, John D., 67, 234
Macmillan, Harold, 56, 225–228
McNeil, Hector, 56, 68, 113, 234–236, 238, 242, 245, 246, 276, 315
Majer, Vaclav, 98, 112, 114, 119–122, 274
Malfatti, Francesco, 50, 180, 182, 223–224, 312
Marshall Plan, 117, 118, 120, 151, 158–159, 184–185, 240–242, 266–267
Marx, Karl, 21, 284–285
Marxism, 7, 26, 34, 58, 74, 76, 77, 104, 142, 179–180, 194, 203, 222, 231, 277–282, 286, 289
Matuszewski, Stefan, 98, 109
Mayday Manifesto, 27, 33, 277
Mayer, Daniel, 38, 74, 75
Mayhew, Christopher, 56, 62, 66, 67, 188, 189, 193
Mennel, Frank J.C., 64
Methodological nationalism, 2, 9–10, 315
Mikołajczyk, Stanisław, 100, 109, 112–114
Mistrust, 5, 7, 29, 36, 51, 108, 113, 189–192, 229, 241, 314
Mixed economy, 26, 51, 57, 73, 75–76, 109, 117, 282
Mollet, Guy, 59, 74, 75, 102, 103, 105, 140–141, 150–151, 155, 183, 229, 274, 277–278, 280–281, 283, 288, 289, 312
Morrison, Herbert, 37, 52, 230, 267
Mutual influence, 5, 7, 59, 61, 65, 179–180, 234, 288, 315–316

N

National character, stereotypes
  definition, 103–104
  and essentialism, 9, 29, 34, 103–108, 175–178, 198, 201–202, 234–238, 243, 271, 290, 314–315
  and geographical determinism, 24–25, 103–105, 175–176, 178, 201, 236
  and racism, 104, 204
  reaction to national character and stereotypes, 102–105, 107, 176–177, 201, 203–205
  tactical stereotypes, 176–177, 201–204, 234, 236, 314–315
Nationalisation (industry), 37, 76, 99, 109, 116, 142, 223, 266–267, 270, 278, 281, 285, 286
Nationalisation of international quarrels, *see* Internationalisation of domestic quarrels
Nationalisation of socialism, 1, 4, 21, 26, 75–76, 145–148, 150, 270, 279, 281, 310, 315
Nazism, 22, 29, 30, 34, 51, 52, 76, 105, 107, 108, 223, 226, 239, 275
Nenni, Pietro, 25, 67, 69, 70, 75, 106, 108, 110, 139–140, 151, 153, 159, 160, 179–185, 187, 188, 192, 193, 196, 198, 200, 202, 222–225, 228, 230–232, 240, 242, 309–311, 315
Neue Beginnen, 30, 31
Non-state actors, 2, 61, 221
  See also State-private network

O

Olive line, 103, 176–177
Ollenhauer, Erich, 36, 72, 76, 275, 287, 312
Oslo Declaration, 288
Osobka-Morawski, Edward, 97, 98, 113–115, 117

P

Palme, Olof, 3, 78, 313
Papandreou, Andreas, 250, 315
Papandreou, Georgios, 233, 235, 241, 242, 244, 250
PCI, *see* Italian Communist Party
Performativity, 9, 32, 34, 310
Philip, André, 1, 281, 285, 291
Phillips, Morgan, 39, 53, 54, 58, 59, 66–69, 99–101, 113, 139, 142–144, 151–152, 155–159, 161–163, 181, 185, 229, 242, 247, 269, 271–272, 280, 289–291
Planning, 23, 26, 51, 76, 78, 148, 176, 203, 244, 265, 267, 270, 285, 291
Polish Popular Party (PSL), 99, 100, 109, 112, 115
Polish Socialist Party (PPS)
  and government policies, 59, 109, 114–115
  internal developments, 96–101, 114, 117, 122
  international fraternal relations, 60, 65, 99–103, 109, 118, 122, 149, 159, 160, 180, 182, 184, 229–230, 239, 240
Polish socialists in exile, 23, 33, 96, 99–101, 108, 273
  WRN, 97, 101
Polish Workers' Party (PPR, communist), 97, 108
Political history, 1, 7–8, 315
Political language, 8–9, 32–39, 153, 201–203, 275, 282, 284, 314

Political network, 2–4, 49
Pollak, Marianne, 30, 51, 151
Pollak, Oscar, 30, 32, 51, 79, 151, 222–223, 281
Popular front, 4, 25–26, 29, 60, 98, 112, 114, 120, 121, 139–144, 148, 149, 156, 160, 179, 184–185, 198, 222, 230, 232, 238–241, 280
PPR, *see* Polish Workers' Party (communist)
PPS, *see* Polish Socialist Party
Prague Coup (21-25 February 1948), 54, 68, 71, 107, 121–122, 144, 160, 184, 274
Price, John, 49, 139, 145–148, 152, 155, 181, 271, 290
PSB, *see* Belgian Socialist Party
PSDI, *see* Italian social democrats (PSLI, USI, Socialist Unity, PSU, PSDI)
PSI, *see* Italian Socialist Party (PSI, PSIUP)
PSIUP, *see* Italian Socialist Party (PSI, PSIUP)
PSL, *see* Polish Popular Party
PSLI, *see* Italian social democrats (PSLI, USI, Socialist Unity, PSU, PSDI)
PSU, *see* Italian social democrats (PSLI, USI, Socialist Unity, PSU, PSDI)
PvdA, *see* Labour Party (Netherlands)

R
Ramadier, Paul, 183–184
Randall, Eric L., 54
Recognition, 4, 22, 34–36, 69, 101–102, 181, 184, 188–191, 228–229, 231–233, 241–242, 247, 273–274, 276

Refugees, 161, 163, 272–273, 275
Renner, Karl, 79, 223, 224, 227
Romita, Giuseppe, 188–190, 195–196, 199
Ruhr, 160, 187, 228, 233, 249, 268, 313

S
Salvemini, Gaetano, 104, 107, 195, 200–201
SAP, *see* Swedish Social Democratic Labour Party
Saragat, Giuseppe, 56, 118, 181, 183–184, 187–196, 200, 202, 247, 250, 312, 314
Saran, Mary, 31, 196
Scandinavian socialists, 25, 26, 71, 78, 144, 149, 152–153, 158, 163, 176, 186, 203, 269–270, 277, 278, 281, 288–289, 291, 314
Schärf, Adolf, 79, 222, 224–225, 227, 228, 231–232, 277, 312
Scharf, Erwin, 79, 221–223
Schumacher, Kurt, 57, 76, 187, 228–231, 239, 286, 290
Second International, 7, 21, 24, 50, 120, 313
SED, *see* Socialist Unity Party
SFIO, *see* French Socialist Party
SILO, *see* Socialist Information and Liaison Office
Silone, Ignazio, 1, 151, 180, 183, 185, 195–196, 199, 224, 285
SK-ELD, *see* Greek Socialist Party
Socialisation (industry), *see* Nationalisation (industry)
Socialisation (people), 3, 31, 195–197, 223–225, 227, 249, 250, 310–314

Socialism
  and capitalism, 23–26, 112, 140,
    149, 153, 179, 192, 203, 267,
    276, 280–283, 285, 291
  and democracy, 4, 22–25, 57,
    73–74, 104–109, 144, 146,
    153, 185–186, 192, 197, 201,
    222, 228–230, 275–277, 279,
    282, 287
  and economy, 106, 144, 276–277
  and internationalism, 1, 4, 21, 24,
    27, 77, 138, 146–148, 150,
    230, 309–314
  and nationalism, 108, 199–200,
    224–226, 229–230 (*see also*
    Nationalisation of socialism)
  and religion, 75, 77, 194–195, 279
  and revisionism, 7, 73–77,
    278–279, 284–288
  and the state, 22, 145, 277, 280
Socialist diplomacy, *see* Lobbying
  through socialist channels;
  State-private network; Track-two
  diplomacy
Socialist Information and Liaison
  Office (SILO), *see* International
  Socialist Conference
Socialist International
  and Cold War, 64
  debate over plans for the
    International, 32, 37–39,
    138–139, 145–158, 180, 277,
    289
  Frankfurt Congress (30 June - 3
    July 1951), 2, 194–195, 270,
    290–291
  and the non-European world, 3,
    152, 155, 163, 269, 272,
    311–312
  See also International Socialist
  Conference
Socialist roll-back of Eastern Europe, 6,
  60, 62, 63, 96, 101, 121, 192, 232

Socialist Union, 285
Socialist Union of Central-Eastern
  Europe (SUCEE), 273–274
Socialist Unity (Italy), *see* Italian social
  democrats (PSLI, USI, Socialist
  Unity, PSU, PSDI)
Socialist Unity Party (SED), 67, 141,
  228
Socialist Vanguard Group (SVG), 31,
  285
  See also Socialist Union
Socialist World (journal), 106, 161
Spanish socialists, 25, 30, 151, 181
SPD, *see* German Social Democratic
  Party
SPÖ, *see* Austrian Socialist Party
Stalin, Iosif, 27, 58, 69, 99, 106, 114,
  140–144, 156, 159
State-private network, 60, 61, 64, 113,
  179–180, 190, 221–225,
  237–238, 250
Statism, 4, 22–23, 25, 59, 73, 74, 76,
  78, 145, 147, 148, 153, 281,
  284, 313
Stereotypes, *see* National character,
  stereotypes
Stringent definition of socialism, 5, 9,
  22, 71, 138, 141, 146, 155, 242,
  275–276, 284, 310
Sudeten social democrats, 34–35
Supranationality, 141–142, 148, 150,
  265, 268, 269, 279, 310
Svolos, Alexandros, 238–248
Swedish Social Democratic Labour
  Party (SAP)
  internal developments, 77, 78, 185,
    186, 278–279
  international fraternal relations, 3,
    25–27, 38, 72, 77–78, 148, 152,
    158, 162–163, 185, 198, 228,
    248, 266, 272, 278, 284, 291
Swiss Socialist Party, 27, 37, 38, 54,
  151–155, 157, 228, 229, 272

T

Tactical stereotypes, *see* National character, stereotypes
Technocracy, 23, 147, 266–267, 285
Third Force, 112, 139–141, 144, 150–151, 158, 188, 195, 239, 244, 246, 250, 265
Togliatti, Palmiro, 60, 105, 197
Track-two diplomacy, 61, 64, 114, 153, 221–227, 230, 310–312
Trade Union Congress (TUC), 51, 59, 64, 66, 150, 162, 237, 239, 241
Trade unions, 23, 31, 97, 99, 110, 121, 162, 186, 188, 193–194, 198–199, 235, 237–239, 241, 243–244, 247, 267, 276, 279
Transnational approach, 2, 5, 9–10, 314–315
Transport House, *see* Labour Party (Britain)
Treves, Paolo, 32, 64, 200
Tribune, The, 32, 37, 38, 59, 66, 69, 100, 107, 109, 110, 113, 154, 190, 245
Tsirimokos, Ilias, 238–241, 244, 246–247, 249–250, 315
Turati, Filippo, 1

U

Unitary International of socialists and communists, 24, 36–38, 52, 121, 139–141, 146–147, 149, 153
United front, *see* Popular front
Unity of action, *see* Popular front
USI, *see* Italian social democrats (PSLI, USI, Socialist Unity, PSU, PSDI)

V

Van der Goes van Naters, Marinus, 53, 77, 184, 188–192, 194–196, 202, 231, 233, 269–270, 280–281
Vandervelde, Emile, 7, 24, 25, 50, 75, 139
Vansittart, Robert, *see* Nazism
Vansittartismus, *see* Nazism; *compare* National character, stereotypes, and essentialism
Vienna Union, 24, 139
Vilim, Blažej, 100, 113, 119, 122, 273
Visits and delegations, 37, 52, 54, 62, 65, 67, 68, 70–71, 79, 102–103, 110, 111, 116–118, 140, 142–144, 222, 224–226, 228, 236, 237, 311
Vittorelli, Paolo, 196, 198, 311, 312
Vogel, Hans, 30, 32, 36
Vorrink, Koos, 77, 159, 232, 242, 272, 274

W

Watson, Sam, 55, 187
Wehner, Herbert, 287, 311
WFTU, *see* World Federation of Trade Unions
Wodak, Walter, 50, 79, 143, 158, 224–226, 312
World Federation of Trade Unions (WFTU), 38, 153, 237

Z

Zilliacus, Konni, 31, 37, 38, 67, 69, 70, 107, 111, 113, 180, 193, 196, 311

CPSIA information can be obtained
at www.ICGtesting.com
Printed in the USA
LVHW02*1504220518
578095LV00003B/3/P